"This is a brilliant and insig⟨...⟩ Newfield
to write at the frontier of h⟨...⟩ of Robert
Kennedy's life. He inspired⟨...⟩."

—Governor Mario Cuomo

"A deeply moving and affectionate tribute . . . the best book on Robert
Kennedy to date."

—Christopher Lehmann-Haupt, *The New York Times*

"A masterpiece. . . . Whether this book is taken to be a biography, a political synopsis or a character analysis, it will not be taken lightly. . . . By the
end, the reader feels that he knew Robert Kennedy, not that he knew of
him. . . . Unforgettable reading."

—*Denver Post*

"Powerfully appealing. . . . Written with passion, rage, sophistication and
a clear eye . . . a sense of humor and jut-jawed determination that Kennedy
would have appreciated."

—*The Boston Globe*

"Beautiful. . . . Heartbreaking. . . . I picked up the book and simply
couldn't put it down. . . . Thank Jack Newfield for a fine, fine book."

—Robert Coles, author of the
Pulitzer Prize-winning *Children of Crisis* series

RFK

Jack Newfield is a veteran New York journalist and has written for the *Village Voice*, *New York Daily News,* and the *New York Post*. He is a fellow at the Nation Institute. Mr. Newfield is the author of many books including *Only in America: The Life and Crimes of Don King*, *Somebody's Got to Tell It: The Upbeat Memoirs of a Working-Class Journalist*, and *The Full Rudy: The Man, the Myth, the Mania.*

Also by Jack Newfield

A Prophetic Minority

A Populist Manifesto (with Jeff Greenfield)

Bread and Roses, Too

Cruel and Unusual Justice

The Permanent Government (with Paul DuBrul)

City for Sale (with Wayne Barrett)

Only in America: The Life and Crimes of Don King

*Somebody's Gotta Tell It: The Upbeat Memoirs
of a Working-Class Journalist*

The Full Rudy: The Man, the Myth, the Mania

A MEMOIR

JACK
NEWFIELD

THUNDER'S MOUTH PRESS / NATION BOOKS

NEW YORK

RFK: *A Memoir*

Copyright © 1969, 1978, 1988, 2003 by Jack Newfield
Introduction © 2003 by Jack Newfield

Originally published by Dutton, New York, 1969

Published by
Thunder's Mouth Press/Nation Books
An Imprint of Avalon Publishing Group, Inc.
161 William Street, 16th Floor
New York, NY 10038

Nation Books is a co-publishing venture of the Nation Institute
and Avalon Publishing Group Incorporated.

Library of Congress Cataloging-in-Publication Data is available.

ISBN 1-56025-531-5

9   8   7   6   5   4   3   2   1

Printed in the United States of America
Distributed by Publishers Group West

For Janie, Rebecca, and Joey
and for all those who still seek a newer world

Contents

Foreword   3
Introduction   7

Book One

Not a Myth, Only a Man   17
The Shock of Unrecognition   21
Kennedy's Character   40
Kennedy's Politics: Beyond Liberalism   60

Book Two

Bedford-Stuyvesant: Giving a Damn About Hell   87
Vietnam: Breaking with the Past   110
New York Politics: The Death of a Small Hope   142

Book Three

Lyndon Johnson:
    The Antichrist of the New Politics   169
Listening to the Voices of the Old Politics   189
The Decision to Run   209
Running Against LBJ   230
The Primaries: Indiana   252
The Last Thirty Days   266
The Day of the Locust   289

Index   305

RFK

Foreword
to the 1969 Edition

This book is a chronicle and analysis of Robert Kennedy's politics and character between the gunshots of Dallas and Los Angeles. It is not intended as a definitive or comprehensive biography of a man's life. Of necessity it is also a book about the changes and convulsions in America between 1963 and 1968—a half-decade of war, violence, racism, and social chaos—that first threatened, then educated, and finally began to change Robert Kennedy.

I began working on this volume in September of 1966 and had more than 150 conversations with Kennedy. By June of 1968, I had filled ten notebooks with quotations, observations, ideas, and anecdotes. I covered most of his last campaign and interviewed more than 100 of his friends, associates, and rivals. I also read more than 300 speeches and statements Robert Kennedy delivered after entering the Senate.

This book is not in any sense an official or authorized biography. I did not ask for access to Kennedy's private papers or correspondence, fearing that such a favor might create unnecessary entanglements. Although we became friends, I believe Kennedy, like Cromwell, would have wished to be portrayed "warts and all."

I do not pretend to offer an "objective" view of Robert Kennedy or an omniscient view of events. In that sense, this book is a memoir as well as a biography. I offer personal testament about Robert Kennedy as I saw him. When I am critical of him, for his seasons of silence on the war, for not running for President much earlier, I am critical from my own point of view rather than from the bloodless objectivity of *The*

New York Times clipping morgue. My goal here is to be fair and truthful, but not neutral.

If there is any precise purpose behind this volume, it is to rectify the mistaken public image of Robert Kennedy created by the simplified and static reporting of the mass media. It is my belief that, despite his several warts, Kennedy will eventually come to be recognized as a more prophetic and progressive figure than his brothers.

At one point, while Kennedy was still alive, I considered calling this book *Against the Grain,* since the central thrust of my views inverted the popular stereotypes of Robert Kennedy. He was not ruthless, or an excessively ambitious politician, but a conflicted, vulnerable man, impatient with the small contrivances of politics. And he was not a divisive, unpopular figure, but rather a healing force. The root of my argument is that Robert Kennedy was the one politician of his time who might have united the black and white poor into a new majority for change—and American liberalism hardly noticed.

JACK NEWFIELD
February, 1969

We lived many lives in those swirling campaigns, never sparing ourselves any good or evil; yet when we had achieved, and the new world dawned, the old men came out again, and took from us our victory, and remade it in the likeness of the former world they knew. Youth could win, but had not learned to keep, and was pitiably weak against age. We stammered that we had worked for a new heaven, and a new earth, and they thanked us kindly, and made their peace.

—T. E. Lawrence

Introduction
to the 2003 Edition

Twelve years after Robert Kennedy had been assassinated, I asked César Chavez, who loved him, what had made RFK so unique, and so permanently missed by those who knew him best.

"He crossed a line that no other American politician ever crossed," the leader of the farm workers' union told me.

When I asked César to elaborate, he spoke about Kennedy's intensity of feeling for the poor, his capacity to create hope and trust, his authenticity as a human being, despite his fame and wealth. And his ability to grow and to be changed by experience.

I witnessed this element of hope in two very personal ways in Los Angeles, two days before Kennedy was murdered, and again on the morning of his last day on earth.

On the Sunday, two days before the California primary, Kennedy invited me to ride precariously on the trunk of his open car, along with his favorite photographer, Stanley Trettick, as he campaigned through Watts and East Los Angeles. He wanted us to see what he saw in the joyful faces of blacks and Mexican-Americans, as they reached out for him, as they ran along side his car, as they raced out of bars and beauty parlors to touch him.

What I saw was hope in those shining eyes, the dawning idea that if this rich Irish Catholic became president, life at the bottom just might change for the better.

On Tuesday, June 4, 1968, I got up early and drove around Los Angeles with two friends, before the sun came up, and before the polls opened. What I witnessed was an uplifting sight. I saw poor blacks, elderly blacks, church-dressed blacks, standing on line to vote. And I saw even longer lines of Mexican-Americans waiting for their chance to participate in American democracy, as sound trucks blared in Spanish: "Today is the day César Chavez asks you to vote for Robert Kennedy."

All my life I have heard the clichés of cynicism and white superiority: blacks don't vote; Puerto Ricans don't vote; Mexicans don't vote; immigrants don't vote; the unemployed don't vote.

And on this day, I had the precious experience of seeing this elitist theory disproved.

On this day, the voter turnout in Watts and East L.A. would be higher than in affluent white Beverly Hills. Poor people voted when they had somebody to vote for. They did not vote when they thought neither candidate would better their daily living conditions. And usually they were right.

A visceral hatred of economic injustice was one of the lines that Robert Kennedy crossed that separated him from other politicians. This also allowed him to fashion his coalition between blacks and working-class whites.

Bill Clinton's coalition was between blacks and middle-class suburban whites. Partly this was because Clinton's base of contributors came from Wall Street, Hollywood, and technology entrepreneurs. Despite his working-class origins, Clinton did not have a strong sense of class injustice. During his presidency, the rich continued to get richer, while the working-class stagnated on a dead-end treadmill.

On the night before the Indiana primary in 1968, Robert Kennedy invited Jimmy Breslin, David Halberstam, myself, and a few photographers to join him for a late dinner. During the course of the evening, RFK said to us, "It's class, not color. What everyone wants is a job and some hope."

Thirty-five years later, this is still the best political platform I have heard: work and hope. It was during the Indiana primary that we saw Kennedy's astonishing chemistry with white ethnic workers from the steel mills of Gary. They supported him overwhelmingly in a three-way contest.

What made Kennedy so unique was that he felt the same empathy for white workingmen and women that he felt for blacks, Latinos, and Native

Americans. He thought of cops, waitresses, construction workers, and firefighters as his people. He respected their work ethic, and understood the limits placed on their fulfillment by the system.

And these working people trusted Kennedy. They identified with his patriotism, his toughness, his Catholicism, his sense of loss, his law-and-order background, his devotion to family.

Kennedy was able to create a coalition between the poorest people of color, and almost-poor—and very angry—whites. He was just as much at home campaigning in Indiana with the Polish former boxing champion Tony Zale, as with Warren Beatty or Saul Bellow. He had the ability of the novelist, or the poet, to imagine the world through the eyes of another person who was less fortunate. Some liberal politicians can do this with blacks and Hispanics; he was able to do this with blue-collar whites, too.

When the 1968 election was over, several studies revealed that many of those who voted for the white supremacist George Wallace that November had also voted for Robert Kennedy that spring in the primary.

Kennedy was able to make a personal and cultural connection to voters who did not agree with him. They trusted him to be fair and tell the truth. And perhaps these voters sensed that Kennedy was not really a big-government liberal like Hubert Humphrey, Lyndon Johnson, and Nelson Rockefeller.

By the start of his campaign for president, in March of 1968, Kennedy had evolved into more of a radical than a traditional liberal. But he also had a streak of conservatism in him that he never lost. He had old-fashioned values of self-sacrifice, faith, duty, stoicism, work, honor, love of country, community, and self-improvement.

He often told me how much he loathed the welfare system and how it *did* breed dependency and drain ambition. But he believed deeply that "jobs and a living wage" were the alternative.

When Bill Clinton signed his dubious welfare "reform" law of 1996, during the ceremony he quoted Robert Kennedy—or actually *misquoted* him and *distorted* Robert Kennedy by omitting his commitment to work and to day care to help mothers look for jobs.

Clinton's misappropriation angered Kennedy's children so much they wrote to the president, objecting to the misuse of Kennedy's lines and pointing out that his son (Joseph Kennedy) and his brother (Ted Kennedy) had, in fact, voted against the Clinton concept of reform.

RFK remains the lost chord of American politics: the missing unifying link between blacks and working-class whites. He was the blues note that touched all the people of no property and no power regardless of color. It was his absence that allowed the development of the so-called "Reagan Democrats," the unionized working-class whites who shifted their allegiance to the Republican Party in the 1980s.

Of course, Robert Kennedy was far from flawless. There are no perfect human beings. He was an ambitious politician, not some monk, or ivory-tower academic.

He was slow to recognize the moral imperative of the freedom riders and civil-rights community organizers in 1961 and 1962, when he was attorney general. He authorized the wiretap of Martin Luther King's home. He ran for president in 1968 only after Eugene McCarthy plunged in and demonstrated how vulnerable LBJ was and how unpopular the war was becoming. He made his human share of misjudgments and compromises. He needed majorities and coalitions to accomplish anything. And he was young—only forty-two when he was killed.

But he was still so far superior to every other political leader of the last fifty years that there should be no need to exaggerate what he did, or be defensive about his inadequacies and imperfections.

Because he changed so much while on the public stage, especially after his brother's assassination, Kennedy was often misunderstood. And since his death, with the increasing sophistication of polling and marketing, politicians have become geniuses of the fake makeover, of the cosmetic repositioning. Just look at impostors like Richard Nixon, Bill Clinton, Albert Gore, Rudy Giuliani, Joseph Lieberman, and George Pataki.

But Kennedy ignored polls and followed his instincts. He campaigned for gun control in pro-gun Oregon, knowing it would cost him votes. I saw him condemn student deferments for the Vietnam War to medical students in Indiana who had student deferments—because he didn't approve of the war being fought only by the poor of both races.

Kennedy was so protean and complex that he is now a hero to conservatives like Bill O'Reilly, Jack Kemp, and Rudy Giuliani, as well as an enduring inspiration to those on the Left, like John Lewis, Anthony Lewis, Pete Hamill, and Paul Wellstone before his death.

There was something liberating in the air during the 1960s that allowed some of its greatest avatars to keep growing in public and reinventing themselves, like Bob Dylan, Miles Davis, Muhammad Ali, the Beatles, Malcolm X, and RFK. The velocity of external change during this decade of tumult seemed to invite and validate authentic interior transformations.

Part of Kennedy's strength was that he combined thought and action in a way rare for an American political figure. This is another reason why he still matters. He understood power and used it for good. He thought deeply, but was also an activist and organizer. The glacial pace of the Senate bored him. So when he had collected his thoughts about urban decay, empowerment, decentralization, self-help, and racism, he went out and started an original community development project in Brooklyn called the Bedford Stuyvesant Restoration Corporation. He had a very different conception of the role of a United States senator. He summoned together corporate chiefs, foundation executives, and local black leaders like Judge Thomas Jones and Frank Thomas, and put something together that worked—although it wasn't part of his job description.

Kennedy seemed to believe in moral outrage as public policy. He felt that the "unacceptable"—like living conditions in Bed-Stuy—had to be changed, not just deplored in speeches.

RFK still matters as the standard for other politicians to aspire to. He still matters as the model senator, who felt compelled to step outside of senatorial conformity and constraint, to take on the risk of dirty hands. He was, perhaps, an involuntary activist. During his three years in the Senate, he felt the deprivation of others so intensely that taking direct action became his therapy and release.

The calamity of our cities was just one issue where RFK was ahead of his times. There was also his support for the rights of Native Americans and migrant farmworkers. And there was his defiance of apartheid, crystallized by his famous speech in Capetown in June of 1966 and his question to that white supremacist government: "What if God is black?"

Robert Kennedy was potentially a transforming leader because he was unafraid. He chose to challenge the darkest and most violent forces in American life: the Mafia, the KKK, and J. Edgar Hoover's FBI. He was late in joining the civil-rights movement, but when he did, with the integration of the state universities of Mississippi (1962) and Alabama (1963), and the introduction of a sweeping new civil-rights bill in June 1963, he made a difference that segregationists never forgave him for.

Part of the Greek tragedy of Robert Kennedy is that he never got the chance to test his ideas—or his values—as president. But many of us were persuaded that he would have won the nomination, and the general election in 1968, had he lived.

Shortly after Kennedy's funeral, Michael Harrington said to me late one night, at the White Horse Tavern in Greenwich Village, "Bob was the one man who could have actually changed the course of American history."

Looking back now, Kennedy's murder was a gigantic turning point in our history. The difference between Kennedy and Richard Nixon was as vast as the difference between FDR and Herbert Hoover in 1932.

From 1968 to 1992, Republicans controlled the White House for twenty of twenty-four years. From 1932 to 1968 the Democrats dominated the presidency with FDR, Truman, JFK, and LBJ. After RFK's death, five of the next seven presidents were Republicans elected with white working-class votes. The inequality of wealth in this country had been narrowed during the 1930s and 1960s. Since 1980 the gap between rich and poor has been growing.

In many ways RFK's election in 1968 would have seemed like a logical culmination of all the idealism and energy spent during that decade.

Instead, we got the lawless Nixon, and the era of Republican ascendancy. We also got soft, wavering, futile Democrats like Mondale, Dukakis, and Gore.

To this day, I feel that one of the most heartbreaking sights of my life was the view from the window of Robert Kennedy's funeral train, as we traveled through New Jersey and Maryland, to his final resting place in Arlington National Cemetery, next to his brother.

On one side of the railroad tracks, in those small New Jersey towns, were whole families of working-class whites, holding American flags, wearing hard hats, and saluting; many were clearly weeping.

On the opposite side of the railroad tracks in the larger cities of Newark, Philadelphia, and Washington, D.C., there were masses of blacks, also weeping. They were already bereft from the loss of Martin Luther King just eight weeks before. They also stood at attention and waved farewell. They had the ruined faces of the twice-wounded.

At the Baltimore station, where we arrived about five hours late, there was a crowd of about 20,000—mostly black. They were singing "The Battle Hymn of the Republic," accompanied by a mournful brass band.

When we passed Resurrection City, Reverend King's doomed shantytown of the dispossessed, the crowd sang "We Shall Overcome" through tears of rage.

Only Robert Kennedy could have united these two injured classes, trapped on the opposite sides of the tracks that still run through the middle of the American Dream of Lincoln, Walt Whitman, and Dr. King.

Oh, what might have been, if history had not slipped through our fingers.

—JACK NEWFIELD
April 2003

Book One

Not a Myth, Only a Man

He was born into a privileged world of affluence, patriotism, and power. He grew up with cardinals, movie stars, diplomats, and financiers; but he was killed reaching out for the hand of a $75 a week Mexican dishwasher, and his assassin was captured by two Negro athletes. When he died he was mourned most by America's dispossessed. His real funeral service was in the eyes of the wounded black faces that lined the poor side of the tracks, as his twenty-one-car funeral train slowly moved from New York to Washington.

Part of him was soldier, priest, radical, and football coach. But he was none of these. He was a politician.

His enemies said he was consumed with selfish ambition, a ruthless opportunist exploiting his brother's legend. But he was too passionate and too vulnerable ever to be the cool and confident operator his brother was. His ambition was not for himself, but to complete his brother's journey. Despite the frenzy he liberated in crowds, he was perhaps meant to manage, not to run. He was too tortured and too spontaneous for that artificial and carnival test. The night he finally decided to run for President, he stood shivering on his porch, at one in the morning, and asked, "Jack, you don't think I'm being ruthless for doing this, do you? You think I have a right to run like anyone else, don't you?"

He was misunderstood to the end. When he rented a jet to fly Martin Luther King's widow to Memphis, people called it a calculated ploy to win the Negro vote. When his essentially gentle nature revealed itself during the televised debate with Eugene McCarthy, a *New York Times* editorial suggested that he lost the debate because he "was less at ease because he seemed to be reining in his native aggressiveness and trying deliberately to be low-keyed." Even his watershed decision in February, 1966, to risk a piece of his career with a forthright statement against the Vietnam war was widely interpreted as an insincere bet, rather than an expression of any deep anguish.

Filled with the brooding melancholy of the Black Irish, he prized the logic of the Greeks, the courage of the Romans. He once told his friend Arthur Schlesinger, "Sometimes I wish I never was born."

He was more than a junior Senator from New York. He was a folk hero, a pop icon, a symbol of political opposition and glamorous royalty; he was his brother's brother, and his family's heir, and his party's prince.

He had an existential dimension. He defined and created himself in action, and learned almost everything from experience. His end was always unknown. He dared death repeatedly. He was preoccupied with suffering and despair. When his brother died, he passed through a night of dread, and learned about the absurd. He had the capacity to trust his instincts and become authentic. He was always in a state of becoming.

He was a contemporary man. His basic sensibility was not shaped by the Depression, World War II, or McCarthyism. It was shaped by modern traumas like the Cuban missile crisis, Dallas, Watts, and Vietnam. He quoted Bob Dylan, Erik Erikson, and Marshall McLuhan in his speeches. He spent time talking to Tom Hayden and Allen Ginsberg. He read Camus and Voznesensky. When he visited new cities, he saw the black nationalists before he saw the mayor.

He was, like very few men who seek worldly power, an alienated man. He was shy, and so were some of his closest friends, like Burke Marshall and Robert Morgenthau. He stammered and his hands trembled. He walked in a slouch like a man who did not want to be noticed. His handwriting was small and squiggly. I once asked him what he might have become if he had not been born a Kennedy, and he answered, "Perhaps a juvenile delinquent or a revolutionary."

He was "a good and decent man," as his brother eulogized him, but he allowed himself to be trapped in the venal and compromising snake pit of American politics. That was his conflict, and so he did things he must have been ashamed of. He campaigned for Abe Beame against John Lindsay for Mayor of New York. He voted for Vietnam war appropriations. He did not run for President when many of his friends urged him to. He was not a hero, only a hope; he was not a myth, only a man. But to have been a hope and a man in America during the 1960's was to be something special.

He was a changeling who matured late. He was once a theorist of counterinsurgency, and the patron of the Green Berets. While his brother was President, he participated in the decisions to enlarge America's commitment in Vietnam from 800 to 16,000 "advisers." Later, in exile, he changed his mind, spoke out against the war, fell silent for a year, then spoke out again, and finally, in the last months of his life, admitted in public, his brother was wrong in the beginning about Vietnam.

His politics fit no simple category. In his youth he was simplistic, conservative, and authoritarian. But he became a new kind of liberal, leaping over the old liberalism he thought was obsolete, dogmatic, passive, and fratricidal. He increasingly questioned the old liberal shibboleths of welfare, unions, anti-Communism, Federal paternalism, and globalism. He was more interested in the nonworking poor than in the satisfied union members, more drawn to decentralized decision-making than more Federal bureaucracy; more oriented toward the nonwhite underdeveloped world than Europe; more in tune with the new generation of urban blacks who wanted power and pride, rather than integration and sympathy. But he never lost his Puritan strain of moral conservatism that led him to urge a year's moratorium on all cigarette advertising, and refuse to permit *Playboy* to interview him "because one of my children might see that magazine." And he never lost his conservative's sense of history.

Against his nature, early in 1968, he waited for another season, hoarding his political strength, rationing his rage against injustice. When Eugene McCarthy announced his candidacy, he said he was neutral, but felt inadequate and guilty. He knew how often he had quoted from Dante to the young that the hottest places in hell were reserved for those who kept quiet in times of moral crisis. A few newspaper friends and his radical young staff urged him to run. But indecision paralyzed the activist. Then the Vietcong came into the American Embassy in Saigon. The President's popularity sagged in the polls. Eugene McCarthy's cool campaign struck fire. Powerful institutions turned out to be hollow shells. The best young stopped choosing exile and jail, and hitchhiked to

New Hampshire. And so he raced to catch up with history and his followers.

His last eighty-one-day campaign was odd. The people—especially the powerless and the victimized—came to him as if he were a faith healer. But when Lyndon Johnson quit the race, and peace talks began in Paris, he lost his cause and he lost his enemy. For the rest of the campaign he seemed lost and drifting without direction. Even as he won the primaries in Indiana and Nebraska, he seemed to be trying to find out who he was. Then he came to California, with a map of unhappy Oregon etched into his worn-out face. And at the very end he found his cause—the dispossessed—and his new target, Hubert Humphrey.

Charles Evers, whose brother, Medgar, was assassinated in Mississippi, left his job and came to California to campaign for him. "I don't want any money for this," Evers told him. "My price is that if you win, you don't forget my people."

"I won't forget," he said softly. "I want to work for all the unrepresented people. I want to be their President."

During his last hours in the Ambassador Hotel, he finally appeared liberated and serene. He had beaten Hubert Humphrey in his native state of South Dakota. He had come back from defeat to win in California, on his own, without quoting his brother or leaning on his legend. Because of him, the turnout of voters in supposedly fragmented, apathetic Watts was greater than in Beverly Hills. He finally felt he had a chance to win the nomination, and he was beginning to gain a new sense of himself.

"I'm going to chase Hubert's ass all over the country," he said. "I'll go wherever he goes."

And then Robert Kennedy was killed.

The Shock of Unrecognition

There was one obligatory paragraph that every journalist who liked Robert Kennedy felt compelled to write. It was a defensive ritual, a ransom paid to the reputation that followed Kennedy wherever he went. The shock of unrecognition when you finally got to know Kennedy was universal, and so the obligatory paragraph always managed to sound the same, no matter who wrote it.

Historian and family friend, Arthur Schlesinger, wrote in his Pulitzer Prize winning book, *A Thousand Days:*

> I do not know of any case in contemporary American politics where there seemed to me a greater discrepancy between the myth and the man. The public theory of Robert Kennedy could only appear, to those who know him, as James Wechsler later described it, a case of mistaken identity.

A few weeks before the assassination, David Halberstam wrote in a particularly perceptive piece for *Harper's Magazine:*

> His reputation was for ruthlessness, yet in 1968 there seemed no major political figure whose image so contrasted with the reality; most politicians seem attractive from a distance but under closer examination they fade; the vanities, the pettiness, the vulgarities come out. Robert Kennedy was different. Under closer inspection he was far more winning than most. . . .

Two weeks after the assassination, Jim Stevenson wrote in an unsigned reminiscence for *The New Yorker:*

We occasionally experienced a shock when we encountered the man himself. Lindsay always turned out to be Lindsay, Rockefeller turned out to be Rockefeller, McCarthy turned out to be McCarthy, but Kennedy bore little resemblance to most of what we read or heard about him.

When I began to work on this book in the autumn of 1966, my own feeling about Kennedy was suspended midway between the static reputation and the changing man. My view of his public politics was sympathetic, since he had by then voiced opposition to the Vietnam war and the military intervention in the Dominican Republic, and he was beginning to develop his identification with all of life's losers. But my sense of his private character, even though I had already met him a few times, was uncertain, influenced by what I had read about him, and by the mistakes he had made in the past. A few days before I was scheduled to spend my first full day with Kennedy, I drew up a list of the twenty adjectives most often invoked by other writers to describe him:

Intolerant, spoiled, courageous, emotional, rude, moody, cold, simplistic, tense, pragmatic, authoritarian, competitive, tough, loyal, vindictive, honest, ambitious, restless, moralistic, and ruthless.

I still vividly recalled that the first time I saw Kennedy I was picketing him. It was in June of 1963. Medgar Evers had been assassinated in ambush a few days before, and in Birmingham the fire hose was becoming history's latest symbol of oppression. About 3,000 of us, black and white—in that nostalgic season of integrated protest—were assembled outside the granite slab of the Justice Department in Washington. We were chanting and singing our demand that the Attorney General do something to protect Martin Luther King's schoolchildren, then congesting Alabama's damp jails.

After about an hour, the slight, taut brother of the President emerged in shirt-sleeves from his fifth-floor office, stood framed in the doorway, and began to talk to us. I had, by then, been jailed twice in civil rights demonstrations, and with pure fury stared at Kennedy's crew-cut face. It was, I remember, a hard, Irish face; alert, but without much character, a little like the faces that used to follow me home from Hebrew school, taunting, "Christ killer."

"We haven't seen many Negroes come out of there," an angry voice shouted out from the crowd, referring to the well-dressed white employees entering and leaving the building during the demonstration.

Kennedy tensed up even more. His skin seemed to draw even tighter around his sharp features, and the hostility radiating from his blue eyes became even more intense.

"Individuals will be hired according to their ability, not their color," Kennedy shouted back into a hand-held bullhorn that made his voice sound both squeaky and strident. It was exactly the sort of impersonal, legalistic response, blind to the larger moral implications of our protest, that we felt made Kennedy such an inadequate Attorney General.

As civil rights activists in 1963, we liked Kennedy as little as the Southern governors did. We saw him recommend Harold Cox, James Eastland's college roommate, to be a judge in the Fifth District Court, where he was to call Negro defendants "chimpanzees" from the bench. We saw him indict nine civil rights workers in Albany, Georgia, on conspiracy charges, while white men who burned down Negro churches, and shot at civil rights activists, went unpunished. We saw Negroes trying to register to vote in Greenwood, Mississippi, urinated upon by a white farmer, while lawyers from the Justice Department calmly took notes destined to be filed and forgotten. We agreed with James Baldwin, who pronounced Kennedy, after their stormy confrontation, "insensitive and unresponsive to the Negro's torment." So when he bragged about his hiring policies, while our friends languished in Southern jails, we booed him in a hoarse, throaty roar that ricocheted off the white marble walls of the Department of Justice.

I was not fully prepared for the changes in Kennedy the first day I spent traveling with him as a reporter in November of 1966. Instead of the military crew cut, his graying, ginger hair now lapped over his earlobes in the shaggy style of the alienated young. His blue eyes were now sad rather than cold, haunted rather than hostile. The freshly carved lines of sorrow in his brow, around his eyes, near his mouth, made him look ten, not five years older. The metamorphosis seemed to prove the wisdom of Albert Camus's comment that every man over forty is responsible for his own face. Robert Kennedy was two days past his thirty-eighth birthday when his brother was murdered.

Kennedy was spending the day campaigning with Frank O'Connor, the Democratic candidate for Governor of New York against Nelson Rockefeller. He had just stumped the country for friends like John

Gilligan in Ohio, Paul Douglas in Illinois, John Culver in Iowa, Teno Roncalio in Wyoming, and Pat Brown in California. And now, though tired, he was campaigning for O'Connor, who was not his kind of politician, as a duty. He felt Rockefeller would win, that O'Connor did not understand the issues, and that he would be blamed if O'Connor lost.

The first stop was in Brooklyn, where Kennedy would also campaign for Congressman Hugh Carey, who was Irish, and whom Kennedy liked, just as he liked Joe McCarthy, John Burns, and Jimmy Breslin.

Kennedy began walking down the street, smiling a fixed smile, shaking hands, and waving mechanically to the crowds. He was in a human cup, flanked by police, aides and local politicians. It was a typically impersonal campaign scene. But suddenly Kennedy's eye caught the face of a ten-year-old girl with glasses. Certain faces turned him on. He often spoke of the character in Andrei Voznesensky's face. And of the faces of Negro children before they reached the ages of thirteen or fourteen. He knelt to speak to the girl.

"You know something?" he blurted out. "My little girl has glasses just like yours. And I love my little girl very much." Then he squeezed the back of the girl's neck, because he was better expressing affection through action than words. Ten seconds later he was back, moving down the line, reaching out mechanically to press the outstretched hands, campaigning.

I got in his ordinary-looking car, and we began to ride back to Manhattan. For a few minutes Kennedy was silent. He was slouched down in the front seat, his mind someplace else, his fingers drumming nervously on the dashboard, the wind blowing his hair askew. His lips moved wordlessly as he tested some private thought.

Finally he turned and asked, "Do you still like me, Jack?" I had written a friendly article about him that June for *Cavalier* magazine, but not anything since.

"Yes," I answered, "but why do you have to campaign for a guy like Carey? He's for the war, he's against the civilian review board, and he never says anything about poverty."

"I know," Kennedy replied, still half abstracted. "But he's such a decent fellow. He works very hard and he's very bright. Whenever we meet at least he's concerned about the issues. He's not like Scheuer [James Scheuer, a reform Democrat from the Bronx] who has such a great reputation, but only asks me about patronage. It's all so complicated. Also, Carey has trouble with his district. He was telling me the Church is such a problem. I wonder why the kids who come out of parochial school are so conservative." And then he turned to look out the window, that distant look on his face, to ruminate on his own question, preventing any other.

There were three rallies for O'Connor in Manhattan. Kennedy spoke briefly at each one, playfully teasing the children who always managed to position themselves closest to the platform, closest to him. He said little about O'Connor. The crowds were small.

After the last rally on the Lower East Side, O'Connor said he was tired and cold and decided to cancel the two remaining rallies back in Brooklyn. Kennedy's face showed he felt this was a sign of softness. He was not wearing any overcoat, and it was only 5 P.M. Later, he would spend election night with the Soviet poet Yevgeny Yevtushenko, rather than with the professional politicians at O'Connor's losing headquarters. And after he would pay a brief condolence visit to O'Connor on election night, an aide would ask how O'Connor looked, and he would quip, "relieved."

As Kennedy was about to leave the last rally, he saw two girls, nurses from Albany, who left work to welcome him at the airport whenever he visited the state capitol, and who had been volunteers in his 1964 campaign. They were not very political, but they idolized the Kennedy family. They were spending their vacation together in New York, watching Kennedy campaign. He invited them up to his United Nations Plaza apartment for a drink. Blushing, they accepted.

While the record player whispered syrupy music by Andy Williams and Jack Jones, Kennedy awkwardly tried to entertain me and the two girls. He would talk to them for a few minutes about their jobs, their families, about what they thought of the day's speeches. Then he would turn to me, and talk about the St. Louis Cardinals' backfield, and about how terrible most New York Democratic politicians are. "In Massachusetts they steal, in California they feud, and in New York they lie."

Then the girls, still a little bewildered, left, and Kennedy, sitting in his shirt-sleeves and sipping bourbon, suddenly asked me with some embarrassment if I liked poetry.

I said yes, and that I especially liked William Butler Yeats and Hart Crane.

"Can I read you some poetry by a poet I like very much?"

He disappeared into the bedroom for a minute. I expected him to return with Shakespeare, whom he quoted often, or perhaps, if he was doing this just as a con job, he would march out with "Howl" by Allen Ginsberg. I recalled how his brother won Norman Mailer's vote by telling him he had read *The Deer Park,* rather than the more popular *Naked and the Dead.*

But he returned with a thin, dog-eared, jacketless volume of poetry by Ralph Waldo Emerson, the poet categorized as "minor" by the academic and literary establishments, but read by the rebel young.

Kennedy stood in the center of his own living room, silhouetted at twilight against a neon Pepsi-Cola sign in Queens, and began to read, in an unmusical monotone that was at the same time very intense in its buried feelings, a poem he must have associated with his brother:

> He pays too high a price
> For knowledge and for fame
> Who sells his sinews to be wise,
> His teeth and bones to buy a name,
> And crawls through life a paralytic
> To earn the praise of bard and critic
>
> Were it not better done,
> To dine and sleep through forty years;
> Be loved by few; be feared by none;
> Laugh life away, have wine for tears;
> And take the mortal leap undaunted,
> Content that all we asked was granted?
>
> But Fate will not permit
> The seed of gods to die,
> Nor suffer sense to win from wit
> Its guerdon in the sky,
> Nor let us hide, whate'er our pleasure,
> The world's light underneath a measure
>
> Go then, sad youth, and shine,
> Go, sacrifice to Fame;
> Put youth, joy, health upon the shrine,
> And life to fan the flame;
> Being for Seeming bravely barter,
> And die to Fame a happy martyr.

The last stanza he seemed to know from memory, and his eyes were focused on the middle distance as he recited it.

When he finished, he walked to his fourteenth floor window and looked down at the tugs and barges slicing through the East River.

"Look at that!" he exclaimed. "There's a ship called *World Justice,* and it is moving away from the United Nations."

After a silence he asked, "Do you want to hear one more?" And he began to read again, in his soft, unrhythmic voice, a poem that seemed to be a metaphor for Vietnam.

> Though loath to grieve
> The evil time's sole patriot,
> I cannot leave
> My honied thought
> For the priest's cant,
> Or the salesman's rant.
>
> If I refuse
> My study for their politique,
> Which at best is trick,
> The angry Muse
> Puts confusion in my brain.
>
> But who is he that prates
> Of the culture of mankind,
> Of better arts and life?
> Go, blindworm, go,
> Behold the famous States,
> Harrying Mexico
> With rifle and with knife!

Because rapid, superficial adjustments of image are so common in America's personality and media-centered politics, authentic interior change is doubted when it happens. The country is too skeptical. It has seen "a new Nixon" almost as often as it has seen new models from Ford. It was told there was "a new Johnson" after the President unwrapped his expansive, earthy style previously used only in Senate cloakrooms. Other political figures have claimed new incarnations after two-week visits to Vietnam, hiring new press secretaries, or after receiving professional speech lessons.

But serious men who inhabit the realm of ideas do change. Reverend William Sloan Coffin, who was convicted in June of 1968 for conspiring against the draft, once worked for the Central Intelligence Agency. André Malraux was once a Communist. Justice Hugo Black was once a member of the Ku Klux Klan. And Robert Kennedy was once a Mc-Carthyite, who often acted as if error had no rights.

Attempts by his friends to minimize Kennedy's early conservatism and aggressive, abrupt personality are not persuasive. In 1952, when he was twenty-six, and had the protection of being the candidate's kid brother, he made many enemies during John Kennedy's successful Senate campaign against Henry Cabot Lodge. When he saw union leaders or local politicians twice his age standing idly around headquarters, he would order them to lick envelopes, or get out.

In 1953, against his brother's advice, Kennedy went to work as a counsel to Senator Joseph McCarthy's investigative committee. He left after six months, mostly because of conflicts with Roy Cohn, and later went to work for the Democratic minority. In 1955 he walked out on a dinner speech by Edward R. Murrow because it was so critical of McCarthy. When McCarthy died in May of 1957, Kennedy flew to Appleton, Wisconsin, to be present for the interment.

He directed his brother's 1960 Presidential drive with a single-minded intensity. Delegates and rivals were threatened, and Kennedy seemed indifferent to substantive issues of policy. The tactics used to win the West Virginia primary were ugly and foul. At one meeting of campaign workers Kennedy said, "It doesn't matter if I hurt your feelings. It doesn't matter if you hurt mine. The important thing is to get the job done."

This seems to have been Kennedy's primitive credo, even into the early days of the New Frontier, when employees and public officials could be demoted or exiled if Kennedy doubted their loyalty or energy. There are many legends of Kennedy's rudeness and bullying during this period, and most of them are probably true.

It was during this period, from 1952 to 1961, that the classic images of Robert Kennedy were shaped, and were never to be totally erased: taunting underworld figures during the McClellan committee's investigation into labor racketeering; warning Hubert Humphrey, "We'll get you" at the 1960 Los Angeles convention, after finding out Humphrey would not support his brother; jabbing a finger into Chester Bowles' stomach, and telling him he was now in favor of the Bay of Pigs invasion, no matter what he thought privately; testifying in defense of legislation with wide provisions for wiretapping. Later he would grow and forge a new identity. Later he would become one of the Senate's most influential critics of the Vietnam war, although not its most persistent or radical critic. Later he would create and sponsor a pioneer experiment in slum regeneration in Brooklyn's black ghetto of Bedford-Stuyvesant. Later he would make the victimization of the Mexicans and Indians not just a cause, but an obsession. Later he would be one of the two Senators to receive a 100-percent rating from the Americans for Democratic Action for his 1967 Senatorial voting record. Later he would campaign against the gun lobby, against General Motors, against the oil and cigarette industries.

But his critics always insisted there was no change or growth. Or else they would say any change was opportunistic, motivated by the fact that he just had less power to abuse, or represented a new, more liberal constituency, or just anticipated coming trends. But the changes would be authentic, just as authentic as the mean little things he could always do for his brother, but rarely for himself, just as real as the narrow conservatism he believed in, until experience began to stretch him, and tragedy transform him.

It would be simplistic and melodramatic to assert that all the changes in Robert Kennedy began with the murder of his brother: grown men do not undergo total revolutions of politics and personality at the age of thirty-eight. Yet, if the assassination of John Kennedy was a traumatic experience for the entire nation, particularly for the idealistic and innocent young, who can measure its impact on his younger brother, who had no personal goal in his adult life that was not his older brother's goal first?

The assassination punctured the center of Robert Kennedy's universe. It removed the hero-brother for whom he had submerged all of his own great competitive instincts. It took away, in one instant of insanity, all of the power they had struggled together for ten years to achieve, and gave it to another, whom they both mistrusted. It thrust a man trained for the shadows, into the sunlight. It made Robert Kennedy, a man unprepared for introspection, think for the first time in his life, what *he* wanted to do, and what *he* stood for.

It took Kennedy months to begin to recover. He would slouch for hours at his desk in the Justice Department and stare out the window. He lost weight and lacked vitality. He would stroll alone, or with his dog Brumus, aimlessly around Washington's streets, or the grounds of his home in Virginia. He frequently visited his brother's grave at Arlington. Even in crowds he seemed alone. When he spoke of his brother, on St. Patrick's Day, 1964, in Scranton and at the Democratic Convention in August, he wept openly. When crowds mobbed him in Manila, and Cracow, he would mumble to aides, "It was for him, it was for him."

Kennedy was never to recover fully from the trauma of Dallas, the way his brother Edward seemed to. The President's assassination was always like an amputation that never healed. He spent each anniversary of Dallas in prayer and brooding seclusion. "All of November is a bad time for him," said one of his friends in 1967.

The tone of every conversation with him changed when his brother was mentioned. The wound would always come back into his eyes. Even in 1968 it was too painful. He walked out of a hotel room in Indiana when the conversation turned to speculation over whether there was a conspiracy in the assassination of Martin Luther King. Sitting next to him in an airplane, I would see his eyes avoid any newspaper article about the assassination. He could only speak around the event, or in euphemisms. When I asked him when he began to read poetry, he answered, "Oh, at the very end of 1963, I think."

During the months following the death of his brother, Robert Kennedy almost certainly experienced the classic identity crisis most of us go through during adolescence. For the first time he began to try to find out who he was—an exploration that was far from completed when he was shot down. The idea that he could be a voice for all the voiceless only came to him at the end of his last campaign. So did the confidence that people liked him for himself, not for his brother.

During the post-assassination period Kennedy displayed many of the same symptoms that Professor Robert Jay Lifton perceived in the survivors of Hiroshima, and reported in his book, *Death in Life*.

Like the *hibakusha*, Kennedy also suffered "survivor guilt," a feeling that if fate were fair, he should have died, and the President should have lived. He also began to feel a sense of community with other victims, like the poor and the powerless. Lifton describes several Hiroshima survivors who dedicated the rest of their lives to working among the dispossessed.

Kennedy also experienced an "immersion in death" of which Lifton wrote,

> the embrace of the identity of the dead—may, paradoxically enough, serve as the means of maintaining life. For in the face of the burden of guilt the survivor carries with him, particularly the guilt of survival priority, his obeisance before the dead is his best means of justifying and maintaining his own existence. But it remains an existence with a large shadow cast across it, a life which, in a powerful symbolic sense, the survivor does not feel to be his own.

And when Robert Kennedy finally awoke from his long night of mourning, his collar a size too large, he began to will himself into an avatar of his martyred brother. In his public speeches he quoted his brother with an almost morbid obsession. He started employing his brother's characteristic gestures—one hand thrust in his suit pocket, the other jabbing the air, crooked index finger extended. He began smoking the small cigars his brother favored. He began consulting his brother's circle of intellectual advisers. He let his hair grow longer. He filled his office with memorabilia of his brother. In a cathartic five-day effort, he climbed 14,000-foot Mount Kennedy in the Canadian Yukon. And he began to wear, or sometimes just carry, a worn-out, oversized tweed overcoat, that was once his brother's. He often misplaced the coat, leaving it behind in one town or another, but he always sent an aide back to retrieve the symbol of the past.

The assassination was also the catalyst that accelerated other changes. Softer personal qualities, long latent and repressed, came to the surface. He began to identify himself with a romanticized notion of what his brother stood for—peace, Negroes, the next generation. His deep, moralistic rage against evil did not change; it merely discovered new outlets. Violence and suffering replaced the old devils of Communism and corruption. The pragmatic man, who thought history could be manipulated through anticipation and hard work, learned the power of fate, and became a doubter and a skeptic. He would not calculate for his own future the way he did for his brother's. "I can't plan. Living every day is like Russian roulette," he would say a few months before he was killed.

In June of 1964, in a personally written speech to 3,000 students at the Free University of West Berlin, Kennedy summed up his feelings:

> There were many who felt . . . that the torchbearer for a whole generation was gone; that an era was over before its time . . . But I have come to understand that the hope President Kennedy kindled isn't dead, but alive . . . The torch still burns, and because it does, there remains for all of us a chance to light up the tomorrows and brighten the future. For me, this is the challenge that makes life worthwhile. . . .

Robert Kennedy's motto, like Andre Gide's, could have been, "Do not understand me too quickly." He was not just complex, but contradictory. His most basic characteristics were simple, intense, and in direct conflict with each other. He was constantly at war with himself.

The rational, conservative Catholic part of his nature was juxtaposed with his brooding and rebellious Irish streak. His pragmatic, goal-oriented intellect was in opposition to his emotional, romantic instincts. His political streak, with its taste for polls and safe arithmetical majorities, was in conflict with his existential streak, which hungered for action and was trained to dare.

He was an activist who thought "people should make that extra effort," and that "one person can make a difference." But at the same time he was a fatalist who knew how much of life was absurd. He radiated an animal intensity and was a sexual symbol to millions. But he was introverted and strongly Puritanical himself. The two human qualities he said he most admired were "courage and sensitivity."

"The pendulum just swings wider for him than it does for other people," Lawrence O'Brien said. Any stereotype of Robert Kennedy was bound to be inaccurate.

Hate was the third reason Kennedy was misunderstood. It was almost a fad to hate him. Often there was no reason, just a feeling. Politics didn't matter. His name was the equivalent of an epithet in seedy Southern bars, in exclusive surburban country clubs, in union offices, and in reform Democratic clubhouses of Manhattan. Logic and reason could not compete with passion and paranoia. After Lyndon Johnson announced he would not seek reelection on March 31, 1968, much of the free-lance hate in the country flowed to the magnet called Robert Kennedy.

The hatred of him on the hard Left in the last few weeks of his life was a frightening symptom of irrationality. In California, followers of the radical Peace and Freedom Party interrupted one of his campaign speeches with shouts of "Fascist pig," and then pelted him with pebbles and rotten apple cores as his motorcade drove away under an overpass.

The week he died, the *Guardian*, an Old Left weekly with pro-China politics, printed a poem by Julius Lester entitled "Not in memory of Robert Kennedy." The closing lines were:

> The martyr is not he who was killed
> but he who fired the gun

One reason people hated Kennedy was that almost all his roles and jobs had a high, built-in potential for conflict and controversy: investigator for Senator McCarthy's witch-hunting committee; chief counsel to the Senate Rackets Committee; campaign manager for his brother; Attorney General; and United States Senator. While his brother was alive it was his function to be the lightning rod that deflected hostility, and to say no to all the anxious people who wanted to hear yes.

In addition Kennedy was an active participant in some of the most emotional political events of the last fifteen years: McCarthyism; wiretapping; the 1960 Presidential campaign; the Bay of Pigs; the integration of the University of Mississippi; the opposition to the Vietnam war; the 1968 campaign. Toward the end of his life, Kennedy was an easy target to attack, since his past reputation for controversy and ruthlessness made it almost impossible for him to counterattack. Thus, Representative Joseph Resnick based most of his unsuccessful campaign for the Democratic Senate nomination from New York in 1968 on baiting the silent Kennedy. Kennedy also took some vicious barbs from Eugene McCarthy without retaliating.

John F. Kennedy was a controlled and consummate politician, cool enough to personalize his political differences rarely. Very few politicians or journalists expressed any personal dislike of John Kennedy. Lyndon Johnson and Barry Goldwater liked him. So did Joseph Alsop and James Wechsler. John Kennedy told his pre-Presidential biographer, James McGregor Burns, "When I was in the House, I used to get along with Marcantonio and with Rankin. As long as they don't get in my way, I don't want to get into any personal fights."

But Robert Kennedy was more Irish and more Boston and more volatile. Kennedy's emotionalism was one of the crucial differences between him and his brothers. It was the quality that made him so vulnerable to actual experience. For example, it was Michael Harrington's book, *The Other America,* that opened the more intellectual John Kennedy's eyes to poverty. But for Robert Kennedy, it was his walks through the ghettos, his visits to the Mississippi Delta and Latin America, that made him feel the question of poverty so personally and deeply. For Robert Kennedy, the sight of one hungry black child in Greenwood, Mississippi, had a greater impact than a million words or statistics. On December 14, 1967, he lost his temper on the floor of the Senate in a way his less emotional brothers never did. A welfare reform bill Kennedy opposed as "coercive" was quietly pushed through the Senate that morning by Majority Whip Russell Long and Robert Byrd, both of whom promised there would be open debate on the bill. But Kennedy was at a subcommittee meeting on education when Long called up the measure, and was enraged when he found out it had been passed without debate. When he reached the floor of the Senate Kennedy exploded with enough emotion to violate the Senatorial code of politeness:

"A number of us wanted to speak about the conference report prior to the vote, and asked for that elementary consideration and decency that exists among men. Then not to have received it, as we did not this morning, certainly is a reflection not only on the Senate, but also on the integrity and honesty of those who participated . . . I think what went on this morning is a reflection on all those who participated, not just as United States Senators, but as individuals and as men."

Another example of the different way people looked at John and Robert Kennedy was reflected in a report pollster Samuel Lubell released in 1961, just after the Freedom Rides:

"On the whole . . . the Freedom Rides do not seem to have hurt President Kennedy much in the South. The American voter has always made excuses for Presidents he likes, and it is 'brother Bobby' in the Attorney General's office, rather than President Jack, who has been blamed for how the Alabama bus violence was handled."

Lubell closed his report with a quote from an anonymous Birmingham fireman who said, "I don't blame Jack, but that Bobby is out for trouble."

Robert Kennedy's own considerable communications problem exacerbated what James Wechsler called his "case of mistaken identity." He was basically introverted and nonverbal. He did not come across well in artificial and impersonal settings like television studios. He was a Kennedy, and too proud to justify himself to every critic. A strong bias against interpretations of unconscious motives made him less prone to self-analysis.

When CBS announcer Roger Mudd asked Kennedy, on a network television special on June 20, 1967, to explain his ruthless reputation, Kennedy's usually mobile face became a blank mask as he tried one more time to explain himself without success:

ROGER MUDD: But, in the public prints, people are not surprised by a—they think there's always an ulterior motive in what you do. Is that—

SENATOR ROBERT KENNEDY: Is that what?

ROGER MUDD: Is that—is that accurate?

KENNEDY: No. What did you think I was going to say?

ROGER MUDD: Is this something now that's gotten started and you can't do anything to stop it, the public image that you have?

KENNEDY: I don't know.

ROGER MUDD: How did it get started?

KENNEDY: I don't know . . . I don't know . . . I don't know . . . I don't know.

ROGER MUDD: The McCarthy thing, and the Hoffa thing, and the '60 campaign.

KENNEDY: I suppose I have been in positions in which—but I don't know exactly. I don't know.

Kennedy found it painful to verbalize anything important about himself. He was not fluent, and words were too easy to manipulate. He preferred action, and wished other people judged him by what he did, rather than asking him to justify and analyze his motives.

When he became angry with a friend he would stick out his tongue. When he had to do something he didn't like, he would make a face like a child about to swallow some medicine. If he liked you, he gave you a thumbs-up sign with his fingers. Words were not necessary. But if a reporter asked why some people hated him, or thought he was ruthless, he would freeze, and mumble like a little boy. He never learned to give a glib little speech explaining it. All he could do was show it, do it, be it.

The mass media—newspapers, television, and publishing houses—were also culpable for the failure of the nation to get any accurate sense of Robert Kennedy's character. They turned him early into a one-dimensional stereotype, and never bothered to keep up with the changes. Growth, mystery, and complexity could not be simplified and packaged for wire service copy, or two minutes of film on Huntley-Brinkley. The media never had the time to probe beneath the misleading exterior.

The textbook example of the way Kennedy's motives were distorted to fit the preexisting image took place during the Indiana primary. Dozens of reporters and columnists* came to Indiana, followed the candidate for a few days, and then wrote that he was jettisoning his liberal values in order opportunistically to appeal to the provincial and conservative Hoosier electorate.

This had some validity up to a point. Kennedy did emphasize his commitment to law and order and his law-enforcement role as Attorney General more than he would have in New York or California. But his entire approach to the issue of decentralized democracy was misunderstood. To interpret this vanguard idea as conservative was not only the mistake of the wire service reporters, but also such influential opinion makers as Warren Weaver of *The New York Times*.

On April 28, 1968, Weaver wrote a lengthy analysis in the Sunday *Times* under the headline: "Kennedy: Meet the Conservative."

> It almost sounded as though Richard Goodwin and John Bartlow Martin, the Senator's speechwriters† had been put to work rewriting the old speeches of Gov. George Romney. . . . Mr. Kennedy is emphasizing criticism of the Federal Government as a bureaucracy, he is championing local autonomy, and endorsing the old Republican slogan: "The best government is a government closest to the people.
>
> "We can't have the Federal Government in here telling people what's good for them," he told a college audience at Fort Wayne. "I want to bring that control back to the localities so that people can decide for themselves what they think is best for themselves."

First, Kennedy had been urging decentralization for several years, and did not just discover the idea for the benefit of the Indiana electorate. And his decentralization was always accompanied by pleas for more

---

* See especially Kenneth Crawford in the May 20, 1968, issue of *Newsweek*.
† Most of Kennedy's speeches were written by thirty-year-old Adam Walinsky and by twenty-four-year-old Jeff Greenfield.

public spending and Federal standards. Second, much of Kennedy's thinking about democratic practice derives not from Republicans, but from radicals like Thoreau, Lewis Mumford, and Thomas Jefferson, who wrote before the Republican Party was founded, "That government is best which governs least." Also, the intellectuals closest to Kennedy, speech writers Adam Walinsky and adviser Richard Goodwin, had been vocal partisans of decentralization and participatory democracy for several years before the Indiana primary. Goodwin had written in the June, 1967, issue of *Commentary:*

> . . . the most troubling fact of our age [is] that the growth in central power has been accompanied by a swift and continual diminuation in the significance of the individual citizen. . . . More important to the growth of central power . . . is the dwindling influence of local government and private associations . . . decentralization is designed to help combat the social and spiritual ills of fragmentation; it also responds to the fact that centralized bureaucracies tend to become increasingly ineffective and coercive. . . .

Kennedy himself, in his last book, *To Seek a Newer World,* published in late 1967, wrote:

> Lewis Mumford observed recently that "democracy, in any active sense, begins and ends in communities small enough for their members to meet face to face." One may argue about the ideal size, but certainly there are strong arguments to support the decentralization of some municipal functions, and some aspects of government into smaller units. . . . We are far removed from Jefferson's time. Still, nearly a century and a half of history has also brought us new assets to help us toward his vision of participating democracy . . ."

Thus Kennedy in Indiana was testing the platform of a new liberalism, based on ideas from Mumford and Jefferson, not George Romney.

The one place where the growing margins of Kennedy's politics and personality might have been portrayed was in the books published about him. But none did, because they were mostly written from clippings, and conceived as commercial ventures to exploit his family's legend and the country's need for a royal family.

British magazine writer Margaret Laing wrote *The Next Kennedy* after following him around for a month in 1966. Dick Schaap wrote *R. F. K.* after observing his subject on and off for six weeks early in 1967.

Ralph De Toledano never interviewed Kennedy at all while writing his right-wing hatchet job called *The Man Who Would Be President*. The misleadingly titled paperback *The Bobby Kennedy Nobody Knows* was written by Nick Thimmesch and William Johnson, and published under the collective pen name of William Nicholas. It was merely an updated (from clips) version of their earlier book, *Robert Kennedy at 40*. (When he saw the paperback Kennedy asked, "Why didn't they just call it *Robert Kennedy at 40½?*")

The most perceptive pre-assassination biography of Kennedy was *The Heir Apparent* by William Shannon of the editorial board of *The New York Times*. But while discerning when analyzing Kennedy's politics, the book failed to make vivid Kennedy's contradictory character, and Kennedy claimed that Shannon had personally interviewed him "only once or twice" after his election to the Senate.

All the books written about Kennedy missed his distinctive extra dimension of myth and symbolism. Murray Kempton understood this when he exclaimed, after leaving an interview with Kennedy, "God, he's not a politician! He's a character in a novel!"

With his moralistic, gloomy nature, Kennedy might have been a character out of a novel of exile and expiation by Joseph Conrad. Conrad wrote in *Nostromo:*

> In our activity alone do we find the sustaining illusion of an independent existence, as against the whole scheme of things, of which we form a helpless part.

Any politician is much more than the computed sum of his speeches, votes, and advisers. The one authentic gesture can reveal more than a dozen carefully programmed performances on "Meet the Press." The literary imagination can often see through the mask of synthetic issues and homogenized rhetoric, when the reportorial eye cannot. Norman Mailer, for example, in his occasional articles, struck closer, I think, to the essence of John Kennedy, than did William Manchester or Theodore Sorensen in thousands of pages of intimate biography. Largely through novelistic insight and intuition, Mark Harris, in *Mark the Glove Boy,* revealed more about Richard Nixon, than did Earl Mazo and Ralph De Toledano in their square, data-filled political biographies. And the best evocation of Lyndon Johnson does not appear in any conventional biography, but in the character of Governor Arthur Fenstermaker, in William Brammer's novel, *The Gay Place.*

So much of Kennedy demanded a literary imagination to be understood. The changes in his face after Dallas. Why he became a symbol of glamour and royalty to the poor. The symbolism of his long hair, his nickname of Bobby, his trip to South Africa in 1966, his relationships with Lyndon Johnson and his brother, his compulsive confronting of death in river rapids, mountaintops, and Amazon jungles. None of this had much to do with his position on the gold crisis, or the speeches he gave, but they were a necessary guide to his interior conflicts, and to the way others perceived him.

There was, for example, a whole side of Kennedy's personality that was converted into a contemporary cultural symbol. Teenyboppers reacted to his presence as if he were a fifth member of the Beatles. Merchants in Greenwich Village sold as many personality posters of Kennedy as they did of W. C. Fields or Che Guevara. He was a pop and folk hero like Marlon Brando or Frank Sinatra, a public repository for dreams and fantasies, a myth who made people feel better than they were.

The young especially saw in him, or projected onto him, the qualities they most easily identified with—youth, dissent, authenticity, alienation, action, even inarticulateness. They saw in him the same incongruous combination of toughness, humor, and sensitivity they saw in other generational cult figures like Belmondo, Dylan, and Bogart.

The final irony may be that the existential hero Norman Mailer glimpsed was not John Kennedy, but the younger brother who so idolized the older one. In his "Superman Comes to the Supermarket," Mailer defined the existential hero as:

> . . . central to his time, a man whose personality might suggest contradictions and mysteries which could reach into the alienated circuits of the underground, because only a hero can capture the secret imagination of a people, and so be good for the vitality of a nation. . . .
> . . . a hero embodies his time and is not so very much better than his time, but he is larger than life and so is capable of giving direction to the time, able to encourage a nation to discover the deepest colors of its character . . . a man who has lived with death."

Kennedy's Character

To suggest that Robert Kennedy was an existential politician, or that his character had an existential thread, is not to call him an existentialist. It is not to suggest that he was even fully aware of this streak. It is not to suggest that this streak was any more than a small part of him, or that he could not betray it by failing to run earlier in 1968, or going through long seasons of cautious silence on the Vietnam war. But it was the quality that defined him, made him different from the other Kennedy brothers, different from other conventional politicians.

Sartre and other modern existentialist writers argue that man is not determined by any previously given human nature or essence, that each individual is what he makes of himself, that "man invents himself" in his "freedom of choice." They believe that man can be liberated from the controls of heredity and environment, and can create himself in authentic action.

Robert Kennedy said that when he was appointed Attorney General, "I didn't lose much sleep about Negroes, I didn't think about them much, I didn't know about all the injustice."

Because he had no fixed ideology, and could best comprehend himself in action, Kennedy forged his consciousness out of what he saw and felt in the rural South and the urban ghettos. The struggle to integrate the University of Mississippi, seeing dogs bite children in Birmingham, the murders of Medgar Evers and Andrew Goodman, James Chaney, and Michael Schwerner. Watching a black child in a ghetto school identity a picture of a Teddy bear as a rat. Hearing himself called a "nigger lover" by whites. Seeing police shoot at looters ten and twelve years old. His experimental project in slum regeneration in Brooklyn's Bedford-Stuyvesant. His angry debate on the Senate floor against restrictive and coercive amendments to the welfare law. The faces he looked into, touring Watts the day before he was shot. They all helped him invent himself through personal engagement.

This was possible because Kennedy leaned into the future; his emotions made him open and vulnerable to the immediate moment. Kennedy was at his best whenever he suspended his reason and trusted his instincts. When he had too much time to intellectualize about a decision, he would poll his advisers and generally take the more conventional option. But he was better—more authentic—when he followed his own passions. On several occasions during the Indiana primary, Kennedy delivered written speeches that emphasized law and order in an open bid for the backlash vote. But then a question or a comment from the audience would anger him, and he would speak spontaneously, and movingly, about the "invisible poor," or Indians, or whites in Appalachia, suddenly haranguing the parochial Indiana voters like an Abolitionist preacher.

But the existential quality was the last, unfinished element in the kaleidoscope of Robert Kennedy's character. He was first a Kennedy. Rich, Catholic, Celtic, Democratic, Boston, Harvard, and Washington. His first loyalty was always tribal, to his wife, children, parents, and brothers. He loved politics, history, and nature. He was clannish, competitive, and he matured late. He believed in God, and in no political ideology. But unlike his brothers, Robert was also something else—deeper, more unpredictable, more intuitive and more mysterious—existential. A part of him was outside the family mold, a part of him was trying to break out of the remarkably consistent genetic pattern of the Kennedys.

Robert was the seventh of the nine Kennedy children. He was the smallest, shyest, and least well coordinated of the four boys. From the beginning he was the outsider, the one who had to try hardest to keep up with the pressure of competition.

"What I remember most vividly about growing up," he once told me, "was going to a lot of different schools, always having to make new friends, and that I was very awkward. I dropped things and fell down all the time. I had to go to the hospital a few times for stitches in my head and my leg. And I was pretty quiet most of the time. And I didn't mind being alone."

As an adult he was the least poised, the least articulate, and the least extroverted of the Kennedy brothers. He was also the most physical, the most passionate, and the most politically unorthodox. "He's the Christian among the brothers, the one who is the believer," Richard Goodwin said to me in 1967. "He's the brother who has soul," Fred Dutton told a friend the night before Robert Kennedy announced his candidacy for President.

The two characteristics Kennedy inherited and had reinforced by his environment, that were at the core of his personality, were competition and religion. His central values were toughness and morality, determination and discipline, neutral enough in themselves to be put in the service of either McCarthyism or the dispossessed.

Robert's father, former Ambassador Joseph P. Kennedy, instilled an almost obsessive compulsion for self-improvement, competition, and victory in all his children. The idea was that second best was never good enough for a Kennedy. During the 1960 campaign, Ambassador Kennedy told columnist Arthur Krock, "For the Kennedys it's either the outhouse or the castle, nothing in between."

Joseph P. Kennedy felt that sports best nurtured the competitive instinct. He would not break up the wrestling matches between his two oldest sons. Even the girls had to compete. Eunice Shriver once told an interviewer, "Even when we were six and seven years old, Daddy always entered us in public swimming races, in the different age categories so we didn't have to swim against each other. And he did the same thing with us in sailing races. And if we won, he got terribly enthusiastic. Daddy was always very competitive. The thing he always kept telling us was that coming in second was just no good. The important thing was to win, don't come in second or third, that doesn't count—but win, win, win."

When Robert Kennedy was four years old, he taught himself to swim one afternoon by jumping off a boat in Nantucket Sound into water over his head. Despite his small size (five-ten, about 155 pounds) and average coordination, Kennedy drove himself to compensate for his ordinary physical assets. A ski instructor who gave Kennedy a few lessons said, "He has no style, no technique, and mediocre coordination.

All he has is determination and stamina." A contemporary on the Harvard football team said, "Bob had no right to even make the squad. He didn't have much speed and he didn't have any special moves. But he practiced harder than anybody else, and if he got knocked down he got up, and came at you harder than before."

In 1946, during his brother's primary campaign for Congress, Kennedy, then only twenty-one, insisted that he be assigned responsibility for an industrial working-class district in East Cambridge, that was the stronghold of his brother's chief opponent, Mayor Mike Neville. When the returns came in, Kennedy had run even with Neville. At Harvard he won his letter—something his bigger, older brothers never did—by playing end in the 1947 Yale game, despite the fact that his leg was badly injured. One night in 1957, Kennedy was driving Pierre Salinger home from work at 2 A.M. when he noticed the yellow light burning in James Hoffa's office in the Teamsters building. He turned right around and went back to work. The warm November night his brother was elected President in 1960, Robert Kennedy was the only person in the sprawling family house in Hyannis Port who stayed up until dawn, fighting off sleep, working the telephones, until Richard Nixon's defeat was assured when Minnesota went for Kennedy. In 1962 he hiked fifty miles in one day, even though none of his three companions was able to finish. In 1965, he climbed 14,000-foot Mount Kennedy, even though he had never climbed a mountain before in his life, and that jagged peak had never been scaled by anyone else before. During his own Presidential campaign he punished his body beyond endurance; if McCarthy worked twelve hours a day, Kennedy campaigned eighteen hours a day. After he was shot, the medical team in the Good Samaritan Hospital couldn't understand how his club fighters' heart kept beating for several hours after his shattered brain was medically dead.

Kennedy's Calvinist-like fixation with determination and self-improvement had its side effects on the rest of his personality. He tended to be intolerant of anyone he felt wasted time, was lazy, or did not make optimum use of his natural assets. One of the many reasons he did not like Eugene McCarthy was that he believed his Presidential rival was "indolent." In May of 1968 he said, "McCarthy sleeps while those marvelous kids work for him. He won't even study up on the issues his kids care about. I know they hate me, and I can respect them for it. They just work damn hard."

Kennedy's high value on moral and physical courage even affected his political judgments. He said he felt "great respect" for those draft resisters who burned their draft cards as an act of conscience and "were willing to face whatever comes." But at the same time Kennedy said he "had no sympathy" for those who exiled themselves to Canada and "took the easy way out." During his Presidential campaign his position against amnesty for students who fled to Canada hurt him on the campuses, since McCarthy advocated amnesty.

Because of his own early experiences, Kennedy was predisposed to identify with anyone who was small and had to struggle fiercely against adversity. The Mexican and Filipino agricultural workers in California, and their leader Cesar Chavez, fit into this category. So did the young, black militants he met caged up in the ghettos. So did small, young nations who had to fight for independence, like Kenya and Israel.*

There even seemed to be moments when the Vietcong seized his imagination. One night in February of 1968, Kennedy invited a strongly hawkish journalist, who was writing a national magazine piece on him, home for dinner, and began to lecture him about Vietnam.

"How can you justify a big nation virtually destroying a little one?" he asked. "And how can you not respect those little guys fighting with such fantastic guts?"

Robert was the most devout of the nine Kennedy children. He attended church regularly as a child, and served occasionally as an altar boy. When his family sent him to St. Paul's School, an Episcopal prep school in New Hampshire, he wrote his mother a letter to complain that he had to attend Protestant services in the chapel. His family quickly transferred him to Portsmouth Priory, a Catholic prep school in Rhode Island, run by Benedictine monks. There Robert Kennedy attended morning and evening prayers every day, and Mass three times a week, as part of a demanding discipline. It was during his three years in the Priory that he considered entering the priesthood.

Kennedy's strong self-image as a Catholic stayed with him the rest of his life. He went to church every Sunday and said his rosaries often. He

* Covering the Arab-Israeli war in 1948 for the now defunct *Boston Post*, Kennedy wrote of Israel, "They are a young, tough, determined nation. . . . They fight with unparalled courage."

married Ethel Skakel, who was even more religious, and had eleven children by her. In the oddest places—rural Kansas, the heart of Watts—nuns would appear in the middle of crowds, and Kennedy's face would brighten. An hour before he was shot, Kennedy was complaining to his friend, columnist Jimmy Breslin that he was convinced that *The New York Times* was anti-Catholic, "Their idea of a good story is 'More nuns leave convents than ever before.' " Kennedy also said that he felt one of the reasons that the reform-oriented, middle-class Jews on the West Side of Los Angeles, and the West Side of Manhattan, did not trust him "is because I'm a Roman Catholic with ten children."

Kennedy's Catholicism reinforced other parts of his personality. His sense of service, sacrifice, and responsibility. His loyalty to his family, with its hierarchical structure. His strong sense of Good and Evil. His tendency toward quick, moralistic judgments. Even after his politics began to change, his Boston-bred Catholicism retained enclaves of influence. Kennedy, for example, was always emotionally more sympathetic to policemen than to the American Civil Liberties Union; and to old-style Irish political leaders like Charles Buckley, Bronx party leader, and Peter Crotty, chairman of Erie County, than to middle-class reformers, who had small social vision, but just wanted to "beat the bosses."

In large part, it was Kennnedy's cultural conditioning as a Boston Catholic that made it so easy for him to make a mistake of the magnitude of working for—and admiring—Joe McCarthy. For Kennedy to drift into the atavistic subculture of McCarthyism was as logical as for a proletarian Jew at City College in the 1930's to become a Marxist.

Boston, with its large Irish Catholic working-class population, was a natural McCarthy bastion. McCarthy himself was a friend of the Kennedy family. He joined them occasionally for athletic competition, and he dated Patricia Kennedy briefly in Washington. McCarthy offered himself as a handy bludgeon against the "Yankees, Jews, and eggheads" that Massachusetts Catholics resented for so long. And Catholics, partly because of the persecution of their coreligionists in Eastern Europe, have traditionally been much more anti-Communist than Protestants or Jews.

Religion also contributed to Kennedy's Puritanism. When he turned twenty-one, his father gave him a $1,000 bonus because he had abstained from the sins of smoking or drinking until that time; his more worldly brothers had failed that test of virtue. I never heard Kennedy use the colorful profanity his brother was famous for. He agreed with his wife that it was "not right" when *Newsweek* published a nude photo of Jane Fonda on its cover. I suggested Kennedy see the Antonioni film *Blow-up*. But he found the movie, which contains scenes of murder, a seduction, marijuana smoking, and a glimpse of pubic hair, "immoral."

Kennedy, however, could still get into a public argument with a priest (named Joe DiMaggio) at Skidmore College in 1967, over his support for reform of New York's antiquated abortion law. Even more heretical was Kennedy's mood at Cardinal Spellman's funeral. The Kennedy family had long been at odds with Spellman, who favored Nixon for the Presidency in 1960. Riding to the services at St. Patrick's Cathedral, Kennedy was complaining that he would have to sit through a boring, three-hour service next to Lyndon Johnson, while keeping a solemn expression on his face. When I offered him a copy of *The Village Voice* to read, he got an even more irreverent idea, and dispatched an aide to find him a copy of the Old Testament, which he would covertly read all through the services. The next day I asked him if he had actually read the Old Testament. He answered, "All the way up to Absalom, Absalom. Test me, and I'll prove it."

Much of Kennedy's mind and personality deviated from the consistent family pattern. He did not have John Kennedy's scholarly, disinterested intelligence, and photographic memory. His mind had an impressionistic, poetic, almost mystical dimension to it. He intuited a man's character by reading his face. I once overheard a conversation between Kennedy and his friend, astronaut John Glenn. Kennedy was not asking Glenn anything technical about space travel, but rather what a sunset looked like from orbit. Kennedy had the almost literary ability to put himself inside other people, to see the world with the eyes of its casualties. A friend once said, "I think Bobby knows precisely what it feels like to be a very old woman." In November of 1965 Kennedy went down into one of the miserable coal mines of Lota, Chile, where most of the miners belong to a Communist union. When he came up, he told a reporter, "If I worked in this mine, I'd be a Communist, too."

In January of 1968 Kennedy was making no effort to disguise his private agony over whether to run for President. During this period Murray Kempton wrote one particularly angry column, taunting and mocking Kennedy over his failure to run. When asked about the column,

Kennedy said, "I can't blame him. I know just how he feels. If I was Murray I would be angry at me, too."

This ability to transcend his own ego is one quality Kennedy's older brother, for all his skeptical cool, never acquired. In *The Founding Father,* Richard Whalen quotes John Kennedy explaining his ambivalence about McCarthyism:

"I had never known the sort of people who were called before the McCarthy committee. I agree that many of them were seriously manhandled, but they represented a different world to me. What I mean is, I did not identify with them, and so I did not get as worked up as other liberals did."

Even when it came to political issues, Kennedy often intuited them before he understood them. In March of 1966 a Senate subcommittee went to California to take testimony on the conditions of migrant farm workers. Kennedy was not a member of the subcommittee. His schedule was crowded and it was a few weeks after his first, tentative criticism of the Vietnam war, and he was eager to avoid any new conflicts. But Jack Conway, of the AFL–CIO, and his own legislative aide Peter Edelman, kept urging him to go. He finally agreed, and, on the flight to California, Kennedy turned to Edelman and asked, "Why am I going?"

Kennedy sensed, before he could verbalize, that the farm workers needed recognition and a feeling of participation, and that his physical presence could give them some of that. Once in Delano, California, Kennedy was so angry with the migrants' conditions that he ended up telling the migrants' archenemy, Kern County sheriff Roy Galyen, "I suggest you read the Constitution of the United States." It took the experience of the hearings to let his head catch up to his heart.

Kennedy's mind also had a strong streak of romanticism. He loved to use quotations that were visionary and utopian. Almost every stump speech he gave during his Presidential campaign ended with George Bernard Shaw's quote that "Some men see things as they are and ask why. I dream things that never were, and ask why not." One of his favorite poetic quotations, one that provided the title for his last book. was Tennyson's "Ulysses":

> The lights begin to twinkle from the rocks:
> The long day wanes: the slow moon climbs: the deep
> Moans round with many voices. Come, my friends,
> 'Tis not too late to seek a newer world.

Push off, and sitting well in order to smite
The sounding furrows; for my purpose holds
To sail beyond the sunset, and the baths
Of all the western stars, until I die.

The objects of his romanticism were diverse: the Greeks and Romans* and rural America; the Indian; soldiers and athletes; Thoreau and Teddy Roosevelt; and almost anyone young or victimized in some way. Once during the primary in Indiana, he had tried to communicate to a hostile audience at Purdue University what it was like to be an Indian child living on a reservation, "where suicide is the most frequent form of death among adolescents." When he got back to the campaign plane, he sat alone by the window for a half hour, tears in the corner of his eyes, the familiar ravaged look on his face, unapproachable.

But at the same time, the basic cast of his mind remained practical. He was not an addict of lost but noble causes. He was not interested in abstract theory. He cared primarily about how ideas could be related to concrete action and specific programs. His mind moved instinctively to essentials, and avoided the ornamental. "What can I do?" or "What's the next step?" would always be his typical reaction to an abstract concept.

What his romanticism did was provide an emotional ballast for his pragmatism, to give it a humanist political thrust. It was what made him different from more detached and conservative friends, like Robert McNamara, Byron White, or Theodore Sorensen. Kennedy identified with people, not data, or institutions, or theories. Poverty was a specific black face for him, not a manila folder full of statistics.

Kennedy had an instinct for the contemporary. He almost seemed an addict of change. He got bored very easily, and once said that quality within himself he most disliked was "impatience." "He never looked back, only ahead," said his administrative assistant Joe Dolan. "He identifies with tomorrow," said William Haddad, a member of the New York City school board, and longtime political associate of the Kennedy family.

Part of Kennedy's contemporaneity derived from his empathy with the young. In speech after speech on college campuses, he said this was the most idealistic and generous of all generations. His staff accepted more speaking invitations from student groups than religious or civic associations. In public, children flocked to Kennedy and followed him

* Tacitus and Aeschylus were his favorites.

like a Pied Piper. He was considerably more relaxed with children than with adults. When I asked him why that was so, he replied, "It's probably because they don't take me, or themselves, seriously."

The young, in turn, treated him with special affection, and almost as an equal. One afternoon early in 1967, Kennedy and his Senate colleague Jacob Javits were visiting a tenement on the Lower East Side. The customary clot of children was waiting on the sidewalk when a late arrival asked what was happening. One of the children, about a ten- or twelve-year-old Puerto Rican, answered, "Senator Javits and Bobby are inside the house."

Even as he ran for President, there was something vaguely adolescent about Kennedy himself. It wasn't just his shaggy hair, or his enthusiastic athleticism, but something deeper. Jerome Kretchmer, a young Manhattan New York State Assemblyman, who worked for Kennedy in the Indiana primary, sensed it when he said, "Bobby was a man-child. A little bit of him was a Katzenjammer Kid."

He went out of his way to inform himself about people and ideas that were popular with young intellectuals. He read the pamphlets and books of the New Left, and stayed home one night in September of 1967 just to watch a one-hour CBS television special on the young radicals. He listened to records by Bob Dylan, Phil Ochs, and the Jefferson Airplane. He read and admired books like Jonathan Schell's *The Village of Ben Suc; Rebellion in Newark* by Tom Hayden; and *Children of Crisis* by Robert Coles. When photo-journalist Lee Lockwood returned from North Vietnam, Kennedy was the only Senator who asked to see him. When Robert Scheer of *Ramparts* came to interview him, Kennedy managed to ask half the questions. He read *The New York Review of Books* and *The Village Voice* regularly.

The circle of staff and advisers Kennedy drew around himself mirrored the divided, discontinuous layers of his biography, as well as the latent tensions between what he was, and what he was trying to become.

The first and closest layer was family. His brother Ted: conventional, an effective and popular Senator, an outgoing charmer who could sing Irish ballads in proletarian bars, and make small talk with local pols. And brother-in-law Steve Smith: contemporary, tough, with a hint of Kennedy's own interior complexity and mystery.

The second layer was New Frontier, the men who planned and then administered Camelot. Intellectuals and writers like Theodore Sorensen, Arthur Schlesinger, and Richard Goodwin. And political managers and strategists like Fred Dutton, Kenneth O'Donnell, and Pierre Salinger.

The third layer consisted of the remarkable group of men Kennedy assembled under him in the Justice Department. They were always his people, rather than his brother's. Introverted, detached Burke Marshall, who Kennedy on several occasions said "has the best judgment of anybody." Tough-minded, practical journalists like John Seigenthaler and Edwin Guthman, who met Kennedy when they were active in exposing the Teamsters in the 1950's. When there was a crisis and Kennedy needed a "tough guy" to pull his chaotic Northern California campaign together in May of 1968, he asked Seigenthaler to fly to San Francisco. Guthman and Seigenthaler were the first two people he asked to read William Manchester's manuscript. Other Justice Department veterans who received little publicity, but whom Kennedy often relied on, were John Douglas, John Nolan, and Lou Oberdorfer.

While John Kennedy made a sharp and conscious distinction between his political associates and social friends, Robert Kennedy did not. And this accounts for much of the confusion about the relative influence of Kennedy's advisers. William vanden Heuvel, for example, was a constant social companion of Kennedy's, but his political advice was infrequently taken. The same is true of Pierre Salinger. On the other hand, John Seigenthaler and Burke Marshall avoided publicity and the social whirl at Hickory Hill, but their opinions were taken more seriously by Kennedy.

The last layer was his Senate staff, who were the clearest barometer of the changes that began within Kennedy following the assassination of his brother. They were, in general, a younger, more unorthodox, more issue-oriented group than the others.*

Four of the top six men on his Senate staff were less than thirty years

---

* Robert Kennedy's Senate staff was much more radical than John Kennedy's White House staff, which, for all the talk of Camelot and glamour, was not very far out politically. Richard Rovere wrote of the JFK circle, "There is not a reformer among them . . . pragmatism—often of the grubbiest kind—was rampant." And Patrick Anderson wrote in *The President's Men*, "Kennedy's rhetoric appealed to American idealism, but he did not surround himself with idealists or reformers. O'Donnell and O'Brien were political operatives—the Irish Mafia. Sorensen started life as a crusading liberal, but in Kennedy's employ he became one of the most cautious liberals who ever lived. Bundy was a brainy opportunist. Schlesinger, the most liberal of them, was the least influential."

old when Kennedy hired them. Speech writer Adam Walinsky was twenty-eight and legislative aide Peter Edelman was twenty-seven, when Kennedy plucked them out of the lower echelons of the Justice Department in December of 1964. Jeff Greenfield was only twenty-three and fresh out of Yale Law School when he joined him in 1967. Tom Johnston was twenty-eight and a film maker when Kennedy asked him to manage his New York office after his election to the Senate. Only two of the forty-three staff members were older than the Senator himself: press secretary Frank Mankiewicz, forty-three, who quit in 1966 as Latin America regional director of the Peace Corps, and administrative assistant Joe Dolan, forty-six, a former Colorado state legislator who worked in the Justice Department for Kennedy.

All the members of the Kennedy circle agree on one fact: Kennedy influenced them more than they influenced him. Salinger had no particular feelings against the Vietnam war until Kennedy became associated with the war critics. Sorensen and his brother Edward were against his running for President until he decided to run, and then they loyally accepted major roles in the campaign. Members of his Senate staff who were exposed to Kennedy daily unconsciously picked up mannerisms and phrases from their leader.

Walinsky and Edelman made an ideal team. They were friends in the Justice Department, and volunteered together for Kennedy's Senate campaign against Republican Kenneth Keating. Stylistically they complimented each other: Walinsky is intense, abrasive, and creative. Edelman is less flamboyant, and more judicious and sensitive. Walinsky's specialty was foreign policy, Edelman's poverty and the urban crisis. Walinsky was the lyrical writer and Edelman the diligent researcher,* and intellectual synthesizer. Both were against the Vietnam war ever since they went to work for Kennedy. By the staid and Southern mores of the United States Senate, Walinsky was at least a nonconformist, and perhaps a subversive. He dressed in mod shirts, boots, and long hair—until Kennedy announced. He kept framed on his desk an old cover of *Motive* magazine with Camus's quote, "I should like to be able to love my country and still love justice." His favorite Washington journalist was I. F. Stone, and under the Senate frank, he mailed to a dozen friends reprints of the anti-LBJ speech Norman Mailer delivered at Berkeley's 1965 Vietnam Day celebration.

* Edelman wrote some speeches, but didn't like to write.

Walinsky was graduated from Cornell University in 1957, where he roomed across the hall from novelist Thomas Pynchon. He spent six months in the Marines, and was graduated from Yale Law School in 1961. After six months as a lawyer he accepted a middle-level job in the Justice Department, although he says, "I was never a John Kennedy man. Washington was just a more interesting place than Wall Street."

He got to know Robert Kennedy for the first time in June of 1964 when he spent two days briefing him on an immigration bill the Attorney General was to testify for on the Hill. While at Justice, Walinsky also drafted a long legal memorandum that helped convince the Attorney General to veto a State Department decision to prevent a peace march led by the late pacifist, A. J. Muste.

Says Walinsky, "I remember Kennedy saying, 'If an eighty-year-old man wants to march eighty miles, I don't think that's a threat to the country.' Then I knew he was my man."

Walinsky then had to "just about force myself" into the Senate campaign. He worked "about 115 hours a week" writing speeches, and, to the surprise of everyone in the campaign, was asked to go to Washington with Kennedy. One of the reasons Walinsky was hired was that Milton Gwirtzman, a rather conservative aide to Senator Edward Kennedy, drafted a memo for Robert, on how to set up his Senate office, in which he specifically recommended hiring Walinsky.

A few months before Kennedy was killed, Carter Burden, the twenty-seven-year-old press liaison in the New York Senate office, estimated that Walinsky had "as much influence on Kennedy's thinking as any other single person, certainly more than Sorensen.

"Adam is a day-to-day influence on the Senator," Burden said. "He's around all the time. He's always pushing his own ideas, especially on Vietnam. He's not afraid to fight with the Senator. He helped to write the book *To Seek a Newer World,** and he and Dick Goodwin wrote the last big Vietnam speech [February 8, 1968, in Chicago] together in one day. On the way to the airport the Senator called Sorensen to tell him as a courtesy that he was going to give the speech. That was the first he heard of it."

Edelman, a native of Minnesota, was graduated from Harvard Law School, clerked for Supreme Court Justice Arthur Goldberg, and then

* *The New York Times* book reviewer credited Goodwin with ghosting the book.

went to work as a special assistant to Deputy Attorney General John Douglas. Like Walinsky, he kept badgering Douglas until he was given a job developing and researching issues in the 1964 Senate campaign.

After the election, Edelman received a phone call from Kennedy, asking him to meet him at the White House infirmary, where he was getting a swollen knee treated.

"In the middle of this nothing conversation," Edelman recalls, "Kennedy asked me, 'You gonna work for me?' I mentioned that I had never practiced law, and he said, 'I had that problem, too.'"

Late in 1967 Edelman said, "I suppose I didn't have any real politics before I came to work here. But I've changed as the Senator has changed. Now I can see the details of how the poverty program or the welfare program are fouled up. I've met kids who have no food to eat in the Mississippi delta, while James Eastland gets Federal subsidies not to grow crops on his plantation. I've seen how the Texas Rangers beat up farm workers who are on strike. I know now how terrible the health facilities are in Bedford-Stuyvesant. So it's all been an education for me. Now I wish I was more of an activist in college, so I would have learned it all much earlier."

Jack Rosenthal, who was a press aide in the Justice Department, and worked in the 1964 Senate campaign, says, "Kennedy hired Adam and Peter on instinct. All he knew was that he wanted two young guys. I don't even think he knew Adam and Peter by name until the middle of the campaign. Hiring them, when they were both under thirty, was a sign of the kind of politician Kennedy sensed he wanted to become."

In August of 1967, Jeff Greenfield was about to start writing a book on the history of rock 'n' roll, when Kennedy asked him to join his staff. His first week in the office Greenfield was assigned to write a speech criticizing the undemocratic character of the South Vietnamese elections. Although Greenfield's draft was stronger than Kennedy wanted, he was impressed enough by the twenty-three-year-old's writing speed and feel for his own speech rhythms that Greenfield soon began writing almost as many speeches as Walinsky. Kennedy also farmed Greenfield out to his younger brother, to help ghost his book, *Decisions for a Decade*.

Greenfield's new politics and irreverent style were not quenched by the pressures of a Presidential campaign, despite his youth. Along with Walinsky and Edelman he plugged hard to keep the Vietnam issue alive in the campaign, and to rely on organizing students rather than local machines. Their style and aggressiveness occasionally locked the young triumvirate into conflict with the older and more experienced infighters in the campaign like Theodore Sorensen, William vanden Heuvel, and Larry O'Brien. The difference was that Walinsky, Edelman, and Greenfield felt their loyalty was to issues and to Kennedy personally, rather than to the Democratic Party, the Kennedy family, or to future power divorced from values.

Greenfield also liked to sit in the rear of the campaign jet with Walinsky and play civil rights and Beatles' songs on his guitar. Greenfield also did not ingratiate himself to the former New Frontiersmen in the campaign by informing a few reporters that when he was an eighteen-year-old sophomore at the University of Wisconsin in 1962, he wrote an editorial for the student newspaper, warning against the dangers of John Kennedy's Vietnam policy.

Like Walinsky and Edelman, Greenfield was, in several ways, brighter than Kennedy. But that did not trouble Kennedy, who often informed himself in esoteric areas in order to compete with his young aides.

Kennedy was also particularly turned on by Greenfield's quick wit. During the campaign, Ethel Kennedy, although she knew us both well, kept confusing me with Greenfield, calling him Jack, and me Jeff. Finally, one day, when Greenfield heard Jack once too often, he exclaimed, "Ethel, why don't you just call us both Jew?" Ethel and Robert broke up in laughter.

Dolan and Mankiewicz were closer to the traditional model of Senatorial aides. They were Kennedy's contemporaries in age, and managed to disguise their liberalism under a facade of cool professionalism. Like the men from Kennedy's Justice Department period, they were tough, terse, performed best in a crisis, worked hard, and had no patience for theory or ideology.

Dolan is as nonverbal as Kennedy was. They communicated with each other in gestures, shrugs, and sentence fragments. He administered the frenetic Washington office and often acted as Kennedy's political antennae around the Senate and in New York. When Kennedy tried secretly and unsuccessfully to install a reformer, Mrs. Ronnie Eldridge, as leader of Tammany Hall, it was Dolan who made the phone calls to the district leaders. Dolan was also responsible for keeping track of convention delegates during Kennedy's long season of indecision about running for President.

Dolan, who has some of the characteristics of a quiet Irish cop, was a state legislator in Colorado in 1959, when he and Byron "Whizzer" White began organizing, and won half the state's national convention delegation for John Kennedy. He then worked as a Deputy Assistant Attorney General in the Justice Department, responsible for screening candidates for federal judgeships. He and Nicholas Katzenbach were the two aides the Attorney General sent to Alabama to escort the first Negro students into the state university, as George Wallace kept his vow to "stand in the schoolhouse door." He worked with Steve Smith during the 1964 Senate campaign, and then Kennedy asked him to "Help me set up my office for a little while." Despite his brusque anti-intellectual exterior, Dolan, in private, kept pushing Kennedy to speak out more on Vietnam, and to run in 1968. In mid-1967, when I mentioned to Dolan that I was becoming active in the fledgling movement to oppose Lyndon Johnson for renomination, he said, "Anything that hurts him is good for America." When it appeared that Kennedy might not run in 1968, Dolan asked Kennedy for a sabbatical leave for the duration of the campaign, so that he would not have to help President Johnson.

Like Dolan, Mankiewicz was a generalist, with responsibilities broader than just a press secretary. He was an expert on Latin America, who openly opposed the Administration's Dominican intervention while still Latin-American director of the Peace Corps in April of 1965. As a former candidate for the California Assembly and Americans for Democratic Action activist, he served as Kennedy's informed guide to California politics, which Richard Nixon once aptly described as "a can of worms." He was also the best gag writer on the staff. When Kennedy declared his candidacy, the national press corps speculated that Pierre Salinger might be brought back as the press secretary because of his experience in the 1960 campaign. But just as Kennedy chose Walinsky rather than Sorensen as his first-string speech writer, he kept Mankiewicz in the top press job.

In 1967 Mankiewicz said, "Kennedy works against the grain of the obvious. He would have made a great Hollywood director because he casts against type. Who could have predicted that he would hire two young, inexperienced guys like Peter and Adam? I hadn't worked for a paper in more than fifteen years when he hired me in 1966. He hired me after just one conversation. He hardly knew me except for a briefing I had given him on Latin America. I didn't have any experience on the Hill either. What struck me was that he was willing to take a risk with me.

After Dallas, the awareness of death, I think, conditioned every minute of Kennedy's life. He understood his own existence was contingent, and this made him increasingly melancholy. He once said to me, "I guess I'm very gloomy about things. I don't expect much anymore. But you have to make yourself keep trying anyway. Whenever I see a Cesar Chavez, or a Marian Wright, or a VISTA volunteer, then I get reconvinced that maybe one person can actually make some difference. But mostly I expect the worst."

His death awareness also made Kennedy fatalistic. Reporters would constantly ask him about his political plans for 1972, and he would say again and again, "I can't plan, I don't even know if I'll be alive in 1972. Fate is so fickle."

There were two particular moments during the final months of his life, each spontaneous, each triggered by his preoccupation with death and suffering,* that seemed to me to define his authentic dimensions.

The first was on November 26, 1967, on the CBS television interview show, "Face the Nation." Kennedy had seen a picture in the *Washington Post* a few days before of an American paratrooper pointing a rifle at the bloodied head of a South Vietnamese woman, and it had been haunting him ever since. He came to the studio in one of his withdrawn and depressed moods.

Early in the program Tom Wicker pressed Kennedy about whether he would challenge the President for renomination. Kennedy replied in a soft, weary voice, "No matter what I do, I am in difficulty . . . I don't know what I can do except perhaps try to get off the earth in some way."

Wicker and Martin Agronsky continued to hector Kennedy on the contradiction between his opposition to the war and his refusal to oppose the President's renomination. Suddenly Kennedy's face filled with feeling, and he began to say everything he had so cautiously cut out of his speeches:

> We're going in there and we're killing South Vietnamese, we're killing children, we're killing women, we're killing innocent people because we don't want to have the war fought on American soil, or because they're 12,000 miles away, and they might get to be 11,000 miles away.
>
> Do we have the right, here in the United States, to say that we're going

* Frank Mankiewicz told me that Kennedy had difficulty remembering "remedial statistics," but that he never forgot "victim statistics," like the number of casualties for a given week in Vietnam, or the unemployment percentage in Northeast Brazil, or the suicide rate on Indian reservations.

to kill tens of thousands, make millions of people, as we have, millions of people refugees, killing women and children, as we have?

Those of us who stay here in the United States, we must feel it when we use napalm, when a village is destroyed and civilians are killed. This is also our responsibility. This is a moral obligation and a moral responsibility for us here in the United States. And I think we have forgotten that. . . . I think we're going to have a difficult time explaining that to ourselves. . . .

I think that the picture in the paper of a child drowning should trouble us more than it does, or the picture last week of a paratrooper holding a rifle to a woman's head—it must trouble us more than it does. . . .

When we say we love our country, we say it for what it can be, and for the justice it stands for, and what we're going to mean for the next generation. It is not just the land, it is not just the mountains, it is for what the country stands for. And that is what I think is being seriously undermined in Vietnam, and the effect of it has to be felt by our people.

The second existential moment came on the April night that Martin Luther King was assassinated. Kennedy was told that King was killed as his campaign jet landed in Indianapolis. Journalist David Murray, who was sitting opposite Kennedy when he found out, said later, "He just broke down. It was unbearable to watch him, to know that he was thinking about his brother getting it the same way. I don't want to go through that again."

But Kennedy composed himself and went directly to the Indianapolis ghetto, and spoke without a text, holding back tears, to a crowd of about 600 Negroes on a street corner. He informed them that King was dead, and heard the gasps and moans rise up from the crowd. Then he spoke.

. . . we must make an effort, as Martin Luther King did, to understand with compassion and love. . . . I had a member of my family killed, but he was killed by a white man. But we have to make an effort in the United States, we have to make an effort to understand . . . What we need is not division . . . what we need is not hatred—what we need is not violence, but love and wisdom, and compassion towards one another, and a feeling of justice towards those who still suffer within our country, whether they be white or they be black.

Robert Kennedy then quoted from Aeschylus to the crowd of ghetto Negroes, some of whom were weeping:

In our sleep, pain which cannot forget falls drop by drop upon the heart until, in our own despair, against our will, comes wisdom through the awful grace of God.

The most poignant example of Kennedy's preoccupation with death came one morning early in 1967. Frank Mankiewicz noticed in the morning papers that a California political figure had been nominated for a judgeship. He went into Kennedy's office and asked him if he had heard about so-and-so? Kennedy, deep in thought, looked up and replied abstractedly, "Why, did he die?"

Another motif was his sense of the absurd. The senseless, purposeless murder of his brother showed him how ten years of the most careful planning can be undone in one violent instant, that traumatic events can be meaningless.

Kennedy, for all his mania for competition, could also see his own comic aspects, his own contingency, the dependence of his own fate on the transient fluctuation of polls and events beyond his power to influence.

One evening of the Indiana primary, Kennedy was in the shower when there was an urgent phone call for him. He stumbled out of the shower, his hair askew, soap in his eyes, a towel around his waist. As he groped toward the phone, he announced to the three people in the room, "Make way for the future leader of the free world."

Early in 1967 Kennedy flew to Albany for a series of meetings with county leaders. About 11 A.M. the "Caroline" landed at the Albany airport, which was windblown, deserted, and blanketed with freshly fallen snow. As Kennedy was getting off the plane, he suddenly waved to the empty airport, and clasped his hands over his head in the boxer's salute, as if there were actually thousands there to greet him. Then he winced, and laughed at me and the one reporter who witnessed his little charade.

After the Indiana primary I asked him why he thought the supposedly anti-Negro, ethnic working-class vote in Lake County, went for him, rather than his two opponents, who were much less identified with the black movement. He replied, "I think part of it is that Gene comes across as Lace Curtain Irish to those people. They can tell I'm pure Shanty Irish."

And he sent a copy of his book, *To Seek a Newer World,* to Senator Eastland, with the scrawled inscription, "It is still not too late. Repent now!"

The most concrete expression of Kennedy's existential quality was his involvement with the writing of Albert Camus. He discovered Camus when he was thirty-eight, in the months of solitude and grief after his brother's death. By 1968 he had read, and reread, all of Camus's essays, dramas, and novels. But he more than just read Camus. He memorized him, meditated about him, quoted him, and was changed by him.

He read *Resistance, Rebellion and Death* several times. His worn copy had a sentence or paragraph underlined on almost every page. He told me the essay in that volume, "Reflections on the Guillotine," convinced him to change his mind and oppose capital punishment.

He quoted Camus on the Johnny Carson Show, in stump speeches and hamlets in Nebraska, in his televised debate with Eugene McCarthy. By the end of his campaign in California, his supporters waved signs at airports that read "Kennedy and Camus in '68."

Like Camus, Kennedy was a nature sensualist. Clouds and rain depressed him; sun, wind, and the sea elated him. Mountains, rapids, and animals exhilarated him.

By the end, Camus's themes had merged with his own themes. Man must neither be a victim nor an executioner. A man must rebel, but with a sense of limits and moderation. Men are not happy and they must die. Action and courage are everything. And from Camus's notebooks, a paragraph Kennedy read and underlined:

> Living with one's passions amounts to living with one's sufferings, which are the counterpoise, the corrective, the balance and the price. When a man has learned—and not on paper—how to remain alone with his suffering, how to overcome his longing to flee, the illusion that others may share, then he has little left to learn.

About a month before Kennedy was killed, the British television personality and author, David Frost, taped an interview with him. Toward the end of the interview, Frost asked him, "How would you like to be remembered? What would you like the first line of your obituary to say?"

Kennedy's reply was:

> Something about the fact that I made some contribution to either my country, or those who were less well off. I think again back to what Camus wrote about the fact that perhaps this world is a world in which children suffer, but we can lessen the number of suffering children, and if you do not do this, then who will do this? I'd like to feel that I'd done something to lessen that suffering.

Kennedy's Politics:
Beyond Liberalism

Robert Kennedy's three years in the back benches of the United States Senate between 1965 and 1968 coincided with the period of the most concentrated and violent change in American life since the 1930's.

Politics became fragmented, polarized and mass. Millions of people became instantaneously and intensely politicized. Hundreds of thousands joined in marches against the Vietnam war. According to the National Student Association (NSA), more than 35,000 college students participated in demonstrations on campuses during the 1967–1968 academic year.

Lyndon Johnson, re-elected by a "consensus" landslide in 1964, four years later became the first incumbent President since 1884 to be forced politically not to seek reelection. Opposition to the Vietnam war, the lonely cause of a few students and professors in 1965, became the cause of a majority of voters in the 1968 Presidential primaries. The black revolt unraveled swiftly, from pleading for integration at Atlantic City in 1964, to rioting in Watts in 1965, to insurrection in Detroit in 1967, to guerrilla warfare and shoot-outs in Cleveland and San Francisco in 1968, to control separate black studies programs at universities from Brandeis to Berkeley in 1969.

Television, mass education, and widespread affluence combined to speed up the dissolution of the thirty-five-year-old New Deal electoral coalition. The brokers, the old organizations that interpreted politics to the voters, were becoming obsolete. Television began to do the job of the union leader, the ward politician, and the newspaper publisher in opinion formation and candidate selection. Television, and the media in general, are now more powerful in determining politics than heredity is. The issue of race split the Northern and Southern wings of the New Deal alliance. The issue of Vietnam divided the union leaders from the intellectuals. Blue-collar union members began to enter the middle class and become more contented, and more resistant to the Negro thrust for economic equality. The big city Democratic political organizations were threatened by middle-class reformers like John Lindsay in New York, and Negro insurgents like Carl Stokes in Cleveland. The new generation of ghetto blacks, weaned on the photographs of Birmingham and the therapeutic rhetoric of Malcolm X, began to outrecruit the old-line leaders of the NAACP and the Democratic Party politicians. In the elite universities, a new generation of middle-class whites, rejecting both cobwebbed Marxism, and Vietnam and CIA-tainted liberalism, began to forge an anarchic and activist New Left. They defined a new politics, a new life style, and a new adversary culture against the middle class and against liberalism.

America institutionalized violence. A generation grew up watching, each night on television, American soldiers burn down Vietnamese huts with cigarette lighters, and torture Vietcong prisoners. The Vietnam war legitimated the use of violence. And the summers of ghetto riots brought it all home. There were Speck and Whitman and other mass murderers. James Bond and Bonnie and Clyde became culture heroes. Assassinations became part of the political reality. Medgar Evers. John Kennedy. Malcolm X. The near miss on James Meredith. Martin Luther King. And finally Robert Kennedy himself.

More than any other conventional politician—and that's all he was—Robert Kennedy was attuned to these convulsive changes. He did not approve of them all, he did not understand them all; but he knew they were happening, he was groping for their meaning, and he was open to their potential.

During the years of change in Robert Kennedy, organized liberalism remained static, and began to show symptoms of historical exhaustion. Liberalism became "pragmatic" and "realistic." It was less visionary, less politically combative, less intellectually flexible. Liberalism became suburbanized during the 1960's. It no longer spoke of redistributing the wealth, but of improving the quality of life. It fretted about the stability of the system, and about the rage and paranoia at the edges of the black movement. Like two ships in the night, Robert Kennedy and orthodox liberalism passed each other without noticing it.

The history of liberalism informs us that it has suffered similar seasons of sluggishness and inertia in the past, and that these slumps have often coincided with periods of war and nationalism. The War of 1812 stemmed the reform tide unleashed by Jefferson. The Mexican War of 1845 signaled the end of the Jacksonian expansion of democracy. Woodrow Wilson's New Freedom vanished with the August guns of World War I. The innovations of the New Deal ended with the war clouds of 1938. And the New Frontier's spirit of service and reform was aborted with the Americanization of the Vietnam war in February of 1965.

The Vietnam war was, of course, the major reason for liberalism's internal crisis. Vietnam was, as William Pfaff wrote, "liberalism's war," the war expanded and explained by John Kennedy, Hubert Humphrey, Adlai Stevenson, Arthur Goldberg, John Roche, Robert McNamara, McGeorge Bundy, Averell Harriman, and Lyndon Johnson.

In addition to Vietnam, Establishment liberalism suffered from other maladies. The whole Federal complex of welfare, antipoverty, public housing, and manpower programs was being proved inadequate by four summers of riot and revolt in the urban slums of the North. The New Deal's proud public housing projects were just barricades to the children of Malcolm X.

The 1966 off-year Congressional elections saw the defeat of New Deal Democrats like Pat Brown in California, G. Mennen Williams in Michigan, and Paul Douglas in Illinois.

The generation that passed through American universities during the 1960's developed their politics with liberals in power, as Presidents, as Governors, as university presidents. And they saw those liberals execute Caryl Chessman; invade Cuba and then try to lie about it; dispatch 24,000 Marines to the Dominican Republic; begin bombing North Vietnam; accept covert funds from the CIA; and order police onto campuses from Columbia to Berkeley to eject students from university property. Between 1965 and 1968, Peace Corps recruiting on campuses dropped by more than 40 percent. To a new generation, the old liberalism became symbolized by Lyndon Johnson embracing General Ky, and Hubert Humphrey embracing Mayor Daley.

The ADA, founded by anti-Communist liberals in 1948 who wanted to support Harry Truman rather than Henry Wallace, was the best barometer of the liberal condition during the 1960's. In September of 1967, more than a hundred of ADA's national board members—mostly over forty and affluent—assembled in Washington for their semiannual meeting. They first voted down, by a lopsided margin, a "dump Johnson" resolution. And then they gave a standing ovation to a luncheon speech by Professor Daniel Moynihan, who urged liberal alliances with moderates and conservatives to "save and protect the social fabric of the nation" against campus radicals and ghetto militants. The speech was later read into the *Congressional Record* by Republican Congressman Melvin Laird, and praised in a syndicated column by William F. Buckley, Jr.

A few days after the ADA meeting, Kennedy remarked to me, "I think the ADA should just fold up and go out of business. They're so out of touch with things. Most of those people are only interested in making money and having influence. . . . Your generation should go out and start a new ADA that isn't dependent on the unions for money, and is engaged in direct action, instead of just voting on resolutions."

Kennedy could say that because he was never an ADA member, and never thought of himself as a New Dealer. They were not his people. He didn't think like them, nor have any shared experiences with them. They were fighting McCarthy when he was working for McCarthy. They were supporting Adlai Stevenson and Hubert Humphrey for President when he was managing his brother's Presidential campaign against them. When Kennedy used the phrase "my people," he meant Negroes, or Catholics, or children, and not liberals or intellectuals.

Kennedy's politics were too dependent on mood and impulse to fit neatly into the ADA's urban Jewish style. He was too Catholic, too physical, too combative. He cared too much about unfashionable moral issues like gun control, conservation, and cigarette advertising. He was too emotionally involved with the Indians and the poor whites. His umbrella of Good and Evil was too unpredictable. Tom Hayden was Good because he worked hard with the poor in Newark. The hippies were Evil because they were selfish, promiscuous, and apolitical. Cesar Chavez was Good because he preached love, was humble, and religious. Stokely Carmichael was Evil because he preached violence, was egotistical, and hated America. George McGovern was Good because he was tough and incorruptible. Russell Long was Evil because he didn't keep his word, and was mixed up with special interests.

Kennedy's moral conservatism was also out of joint with the ADA's modern sophisticated style. Kennedy stood in the tradition of Benjamin Franklin and Louis Brandeis. He believed in Spartan virtue, self-reliance, and that spiritual values were more important than material values. One of the clearest statements of Kennedy's politics of the spirit came in a speech he gave in Detroit on May 5, 1967:

> Let us be clear at the outset that we will find neither national purpose nor personal satisfaction in a mere continuation of economic progress, in an endless amassing of worldly goods. We cannot measure national spirit by the Dow-Jones Average, nor national achievement by the gross national product.
>
> For the gross national product includes air pollution and advertising for cigarettes, and ambulances to clear our highways of carnage. It counts special locks for our doors, and jails for the people who break them. The gross national product includes the destruction of the red-woods, and the death of Lake Superior. It grows with the production of napalm and missiles and nuclear warheads, and it even includes research on the improved dissemination of bubonic plague. The gross national product swells with equipment for the police to put down riots in our cities; and though it is not diminished by the damage these riots do, still it goes up as slums are rebuilt on their ashes. It includes Whitman's rifle and Speck's knife, and the broadcasting of television programs which glorify violence to sell goods to our children.
>
> And if the gross national product includes all this, there is much that it does not comprehend. It does not allow for the health of our families, the quality of their education or the joy of their play. It is indifferent to the decency of our factories and the safety of our streets alike. It does not include the beauty of our poetry or the strength of our marriages, the intelligence of our public debate or the integrity of our public officials. It allows neither for the justice in our courts, nor for the justness of our dealings with each other. The gross national product measures neither our wit nor our courage, neither our wisdom nor our learning, neither our compassion nor our devotion to country. It measures everything, in short, except that which makes life worthwhile; and it can tell us everything about America—except whether we are proud to be Americans.

Although the poor and the powerless gave Robert Kennedy almost all their votes, organized, white, middle-class liberalism never trusted him. When he ran for the Senate in 1964, the New York chapter of ADA refused to endorse him against Republican Kenneth Keating, and men like I. F. Stone, Gore Vidal, and Nat Hentoff vigorously opposed him. When he sought the Presidential nomination in 1968, liberal publications like the *New York Post,** *The Nation, Progressive,* and the *New Republic,* all endorsed Eugene McCarthy. And so did Alfred Kazin, David Riesman, and George Kennan. (Stone, Vidal, Hentoff, and the ADA also opposed him again.)

Because he began his public life as a political, economic, and moral conservative, Kennedy was uniquely qualified to perceive many of orthodox liberalism's rigidities and contradictions. He saw liberalism's doctrinaire faith in New Deal solutions, its preference for theory to action, and its petty factionalism, all as critical flaws.

So when Kennedy began to grow and change, he seemed to leap over most of the New Deal and Cold War episodes of liberal history, to emerge as a fully contemporary liberal, a step beyond the ideas of the Roosevelt and Stevenson generations. But Kennedy never developed a systematic liberal ideology. Almost all of his actions and ideas flowed out of concrete experience. It was all intuited rather than intellectualized. One could never predict in advance what position Kennedy would take on a given issue. One could never anticipate what new vessels his passion would discover. "He was strictly a counterpuncher," said his friend, writer Peter Maas.

The one other mainstream political figure who has been able to transcend the enshrined wisdom of the New Deal has been New York Mayor John Lindsay. Lindsay has done it because, like Kennedy, his starting point was outside the liberal tradition. Lindsay is a Republican WASP, who began in politics skeptical of the Federal bureaucracy, labor union leaders, and big city Democratic machines.

If Kennedy's thinking was pushing beyond liberalism, his actions were circumscribed by his drive for power within the existing system. In the end he was a transitional figure, caught midway between ambition and outrage, midway between Robert McNamara and Adam Walinsky, midway between the decaying old politics and the embryonic new politics. He was trying to test a revisionist liberalism before there was a party or a coalition to sustain it. He seemed to grasp exactly how desperate the crisis of the old order was, but he was also a Senator, and the oldest surviving Kennedy son, and he felt that limited his freedom of action.

* Reading the *New York Post* a few days before he announced for President, Kennedy said to me, "You know, I've done something Eleanor Roosevelt couldn't do. I've managed to unite Kempton and Weschler."

He praised Lyndon Johnson more often than he had to, and he ran for President later than he should have. His speeches against the Vietnam war were separated by months of self-imposed silence. He went to South Africa to address an integrated student group, but on his return to America, he still refused to endorse an economic boycott of South Africa, or criticize Democratic Party imperialists like Charles Englehardt, who had large investments there. And like FDR, he made no sustained effort to democratize or reform the Democratic Party from below. But these are also examples of the inherent limits of electoral politics in America. No other elected, major party politician was any more visionary and daring about the same issues.* Robert Kennedy was, at bottom, a reform politician, not a social critic, and not a revolutionary. He was, from the time he woke up from his trance of grief in 1964, a candidate for President of the United States.

The final shape of Robert Kennedy's politics was an iconoclastic mix of fundamentalist Puritan moralism, Jeffersonian individualism, and a marginally radical, new liberalism. And although their beginnings took quite a different form, many of the underlying assumptions remained surprisingly constant. The best way to trace the trajectory of Kennedy's political development is through three of the books he published, in 1960, 1964, and 1967.

The Enemy Within, Kennedy's first book, was written quickly during the summer of 1959. Kennedy was then thirty-three years old, and was neither a liberal, nor much concerned with the world of ideas, books, or culture. His self-image was that of hard-nosed political manager, and an effective investigator. He was still working sixteen hours a day as chief counsel to the (McClellan) Senate Rackets subcommittee, trying to put Teamsters president James Hoffa in jail, and he did not waste any time thinking about blacks or foreign policy. People who knew Kennedy during the late 1950's say his most memorable qualities were energy, loyalty to his brother, and his obsession with Hoffa. They do not remember him as either especially complicated or brilliant. One news-

* Senator Eugene McCarthy was more progressive than Kennedy on issues like control of the CIA and amnesty for draft resisters. And Mayor John Lindsay of New York is no less committed to the black poor than was Kennedy. But I think no other political figure combined a total vision—domestic and international —as avant-garde as Kennedy's.

paperman, who covered him regularly during this period, says Kennedy reminded him of a bird dog because of his narrow, repetitive intensity. Kennedy's martial, well-mannered, athletic personality made him particularly popular with Southerners during this time, and his first assignment in his brother's 1960 campaign was to work with Southern delegates and political leaders. At the end of 1959, his father, Herbert Hoover, Arkansas Senator John McClellan, and the late Joseph McCarthy were still the men Robert Kennedy looked up to as his models and patrons.

The Enemy Within was a remarkably parochial and primitive volume. The prose was wooden, and colloquial. (". . . Dio and other racketeers has (*sic*) muscled into the labor movement. . . . He couldn't stomach having the International Brotherhood of Teamsters turned over to the underworld . . ."). And the book opened with generous acknowledgments to J. Edgar Hoover; Henry Anslinger, the former head of the Bureau of Narcotics; and the late Los Angeles police chief, William Parker.

The Enemy Within is essentially a straightforward narrative of Kennedy's investigative work on the Select Committee on Improper Activities in the Labor or Management Field. The bulk of it is an overemotional account of Kennedy's crusade to "clean up" the Teamsters union, which was a "conspiracy of evil." Kennedy's basic thesis, a bit overdrawn, was that "a man with Hoffa's power and position, and so corrupt, cannot survive in a democratic society, if democracy itself is going to survive."

The book is wholly grounded in the experience of the Select Committee, which was an unusually conservative group, since most liberal Senators refused to serve on a committee organized expressly to probe labor unions. The committee included its chairman John McClellan, Joseph McCarthy until his death, Barry Goldwater, Homer Capehart, Carl Curtis, Karl Mundt, and Sam Irvin. The only moderates on the panel were John Kennedy, Charles Ives (until 1958), and Frank Church (after 1958). Thus the book's scope and subject matter excluded even the possibility of liberal sympathies. Kennedy's own conduct while working as chief counsel for the committee was probably best summarized by Yale law professor, Alexander Bickel, who wrote, "With Mr. Kennedy in the lead . . . [The committee] embarked on a number of purely punitive expeditions [involving] relentless, vindictive battering [of witnesses]. . . . Mr. Kennedy appears to find congenial the role of prosecutor, judge and jury, all consolidated into his one efficient person."*

Kennedy's basic sensibility when he wrote *The Enemy Within* was clearly that of a puritanical prosecutor. He wrote of witnesses who invoked the Fifth Amendment, that

> it is less than human not to reach some conclusion [about them] . . . I can think of very few witnesses who availed themselves of it, who, in my estimation, were free of wrongdoing. . . . I know of none whom I should like to work for, or have work for me—or have anything to do with.

And in a generalized defense of Congressional investigative committees, he wrote:

> The stock exchange and investment banking, Teapot Dome, the five percenters, Alger Hiss, conflict of interests and hundreds of more worthwhile investigations have been conducted with dignity and honor. More than this, much of our most important legislation has grown out of the factual basis laid by Congressional investigations.

Kennedy ended the book with an inspirational peroration in favor of "toughness."

> . . . that corruption, dishonesty and softness, physical and moral, have become widespread in this country there can be no doubt.
> The great events of our nation's past were forged by men of toughness, men who risked their security and their futures for freedom and for an ideal. The foot soldiers at Valley Forge, the men who marched up Cemetery Hill, and those who stood by their guns at the summit, the men who conquered the West, the Marines who fought at Belleau Wood and at Tarawa did not measure their sacrifices in terms of self-reward. . . .
> It seems to me imperative that we reinstill in ourselves the toughness and idealism that guided the nation in the past. The paramount interest in self, in material wealth, in security must be replaced by an actual, not just a vocal, interest in our country, by a spirit of adventure, a will to fight what is evil, and a desire to serve.

The same values and emotions fueling those sentiments can be seen eight years later, in the service of quite different politics, in the personal postscript Kennedy drafted for his last book, *To Seek a Newer World.*

* In 1968 Professor Bickel campaigned for Kennedy in California.

There is discrimination in New York; Apartheid in South Africa; serfdom in the mountains of Peru. People starve in the streets of India; intellectuals go to jail in Russia; thousands are slaughtered in Indonesia; wealth is lavished on armaments everywhere. These are differing evils, but they are the common works of man. They reflect the imperfection of human justice, the inadequacy of human compassions; the defectiveness of our sensibility towards the sufferings of our fellows. . . .

It is not realistic or hardheaded to solve problems and take action unguided by ultimate moral aims and values. It is thoughtless folly. For it ignores the realities of human faith and passion and belief, forces ultimately more powerful than all the calculations of economists or generals. . . . Moral courage is a rarer commodity than bravery in battle or great intelligence.

What the two quotations reveal, I think, is the consistent moralistic and emotional root of Kennedy's politics. Kennedy always hated Evil with a certain and principled passion. In 1959 Hoffa equaled Evil. So Kennedy fought him with the same single-minded intensity, and confidence in his own rightness, that he would later display in his fight against poverty and racism. Both were simple and polarized issues to Kennedy. The ends justified the means. It was immoral and hypocritical to see Evil and not act against it. *The Enemy Within* began with an epigraph from Jefferson: "I have sworn upon the altar of God, eternal hostility against every form of tyranny over the mind of man." Kennedy always was, as his friend Richard Goodwin said, a Christian and a believer.

The Pursuit of Justice was published in 1964, and consists of twelve updated speeches Kennedy delivered while he was Attorney General. The book freezes Kennedy at midpassage in his political pilgrimage. He is still a virtuous Puritan, a wiretapper, and a committed cold warrior. But his Christian conception of Evil has been stretched by time and events to include segregation, restrictive immigration laws, juvenile delinquency, and legal procedures that deny constitutional rights to defendants.

Kennedy was always prone to obsessions, and he developed a few while serving as Attorney General. Juvenile delinquency was one, and he spent considerable time working on a special committee in this area. He visited street gangs and reformatories. He read all the existing literature. And then he persuaded Congress to appropriate $618,000 for a pilot project that led directly to the Mobilization for Youth project in New York, and indirectly to the poverty program.

But mostly, it was concrete emotional experience that began Robert Kennedy's second education. He discovered poverty—unfed children, idle men—for the first time in his life during the Presidential primary in impoverished West Virginia. He learned at the Bay of Pigs that what the CIA, and the generals, and the secret cables called facts were not necessarily facts. Slowly, the nonviolent struggle of the Southern Negro educated and sensitized him, first as the Freedom Riders were brutally beaten in Montgomery; later as James Meredith sought to integrate the University of Mississippi; and then as the fire hoses of Birmingham pinned little children against trees, and Medgar Evers was murdered the night President Kennedy went on television to announce the introduction of new civil rights legislation. Robert Kennedy learned that white children go to bed hungry, and black men are denied the right to vote in America. Discovering such facts in his middle thirties, and as Attorney General, shocked him much more than if he had learned them at fifteen or twenty-five. All these events set into motion changes inside of Robert Kennedy. Some, like his growing sympathy for the black movement, or his growing skepticism of Federal programs that were not controlled by ordinary people in their communities, or his special sensitivity to children as the most poignant victims of injustice, became visible by the time he finished *The Pursuit of Justice*. Other changes would not be completed until later, like his partial liberation from the demonology of the Cold War. Or his opposition to the Vietnam war. Or his total identification wtih the dispossessed as his children, his parents, his brothers.

Kennedy's notions of Communism and Communists in *The Pursuit of Justice* are still primitive.

> The Communist Party is dominated, financed and controlled by a foreign power. In this respect it poses a danger at all times, because it takes instructions and orders from an outside government. . . . The Communist Party here in the United States has had the vigilant attention of the Federal Bureau of Investigation. That is necessary and that will continue.

Two years later, in 1966, Kennedy publicly criticized his protege, and successor as Attorney General, Nicholas Katzenbach, for refusing to permit the burial of former Communist Party leader and World War II hero Robert Thompson in Arlington National Cemetery. On January 27, 1966, he told the ADA's Roosevelt Day banquet in New York, "We have spoken out against inhuman slaughters perpetrated by the Nazis and the Communists. But will we speak out also against the inhuman slaughter in Indonesia, where over 100,000 alleged Communists have been not perpetrators, but victims?" And in 1967, Kennedy was one of two Senators to vote against extending the life of the Subversive Activities Control Board.

Kennedy's 1963 views of "international Communism" are reflected in the final chapter of the book entitled, "Counter-insurgency, Counterintelligence and Counter-offensive." He wrote:

> The Communist purpose, now as in 1917, is to remake the world in the Communist image. . . . The Communist conviction is that any means is justified to undermine and capture free governments. . . . If the free world is to survive, it must above all resist aggression . . . the surest gurantee of peace at present is the power to wage war. . . ."

In 1963 Kennedy assumed America's global role to be interventionist. He could not distinguish anticolonial nationalism and civil war from "Communist terrorism." He seemed to believe in the domino theory of Asian nations toppling one after another. And he seemed to believe the Communist bloc to be monolithic rather than polycentric.

But he changed. On April 24, 1968, in the midst of the Indiana Presidential primary, he spoke at the state university at Bloomington, and delivered what he later called, "my no more Vietnams speech." He said:

> It is sometimes asserted that Vietnam is "the battlefield . . . where we must make the decision which may well determine the future shape of Asia." But it is unlikley that whatever the outcome of the war in Vietnam, the dominoes will fall in either direction. . . .
>
> Is there a threat of Vietnam-styled insurgency beyond Asia—in Africa or Latin America? In Africa, the active anticolonial movements, in Angola and Mozambique, are led by native nationalists. . . . In Latin America the case is more complex. Latin America threw off colonialism shortly after we gained our own independence, and guards its nationalism fiercely. The one Communist government in this hemisphere achieved power by overthrowing a government which was not only corrupt and repressive; it was a regime heavily identified with and protected by the United States. . . .

We cannot continue, as we too often have done in the past, to automatically identify the United States with the preservation of a particular internal order within those [underdeveloped] countries or confuse our own national interests with the rule of a particular faction within them . . . the danger [is] that in seeking universal peace, needlessly fearful of change and disorder, we will in fact embroil ourselves and the world in a whole series of Vietnams.

The Pursuit of Justice also provided a passing but crucial insight into Kennedy's attitude toward the concept of change itself. He wrote:

Change means that someone's professional feathers will be ruffled, that a glass-topped desk might be moved to another office or abandoned, that pet programs might die.

Progress is a nice word. But change is its motivator. And change has its enemies.

The willingness to confront that change will determine how much we really do for our youth . . ."

The last two threads of Robert Kennedy's politics—his decentralized, participatory democracy, and his post–New Deal liberalism—flourished only during the last few years of his life. Again it was direct, personal experience that generated the raw material for his growth. His constant visits to the other America, where he actually came to listen to what people said, about existing programs not working, about the feeling of powerlessness, of not belonging to the rest of the society. He went to campuses—at least once a month—and again asked questions and listened to the inarticulate voices of alienation talk to him about the war in Vietnam, about remote, impersonal administrations, and about soulless affluence. He argued with his avante-garde staffers, Adam Walinsky and Peter Edelman. He went to South Africa and Latin America and learned to see America from the outside. And all this time, he felt himself more and more estranged from the centers of power in Washington. Between March of 1967, and April of 1968, Kennedy spoke to President Johnson only once—about a piece of housing legislation. But even his exile after a while became the raw material for growth and change. "Now I know how Negroes who riot feel," he said in September of 1967. "No influence in the government that makes decisions that affect my life."

Mistrust of power, empathy with the little guy, underdogism. These were characteristics of Robert Kennedy even during the conservative

1950's. When he attacked Hoffa, it was from the point of view of the ordinary, dues-paying Teamster, who was being exploited. When he wrote an article for *The New York Times Magazine* in 1955, criticizing the Soviet Union, it was from the point of view of Ivan, the faceless citizen, whose freedoms were being violated. So it was not surprising that the final content of Kennedy's politics should be strongly Jeffersonian in its insistence on individualism and local control.

The New Deal and the ADA were committed to collectivization; to the concept that a centralized Federal bureaucracy in Washington was necessary to plan and administer national social programs. But Kennedy's passion ran to individual participation. To a sense of community, and to grass-roots control—the values of Jefferson rather than Roosevelt. Kennedy preferred the small town to the big city, the factory worker to the agency under secretary. In *To Seek a Newer World*, which was completed in November of 1967, Kennedy wrote:

> Today's young people appear to have chosen for their concern the dignity of the individual human being. They demand a limitation on excessive power. They demand a political system that preserves the sense of community among men. . . . Too often in the past we have been enmeshed in the traditional debate between liberals and conservatives over whether we should or should not spend more government funds on programs. What we have failed to examine with any thoroughness is the impact of those programs on those we have sought to assist, indeed whether they have had any impact at all. . . . To rely exclusively, even primarily, on governmental efforts is to ignore the shaping traditions of American life and politics . . . the development of new institutions could place some responsibility for the control of many new services—not just education—but also welfare and recreation, health and sanitation—back in the hands of the people they are supposed to serve. . . .

Since his decentralist position was so badly misunderstood, it must be emphasized again that Kennedy's ideas in this area had nothing in common with either the states' rights notions of George Wallace, or Barry Goldwater's fiscal conservatism. Kennedy favored more—not less—Federal activity against social injustice. He favored Federal minimum wage laws, Federal guidelines for desegregation, vigorous Federal intervention to prevent price-fixing, and Federal tax incentives and tax credits to help rebuild the slums. He did not want power passing onto local elites and local bureaucracies, which he knew were even more conservative than the Federal bureaucracies. Kennedy was speaking *for the creation of new institutions* that ensured greater participation for those trapped at the bottom of the society. He wanted to create "self-sufficiency and self-determination within the communities of poverty. . . . What we must seek is not just greater programs, but greater participation," he often said.

There were three basic components to the new liberalism that Kennedy was in the midst of developing when he was killed.

The first was his receptivity to the ideas, leaders, and organizations on the growing margins of the black movement. As Attorney General, Kennedy was not a partisan of the civil rights movement during its early Southern and integrationist phase. And, in part, this permitted him to respond with more intellectual openness and emotional fervor to the urban and separatist movement that developed after the riots of the summer of 1964.

Kennedy regarded the NAACP and the Urban League as inadequately militant and without any base in the urban ghettos. He also felt that Martin Luther King's Southern Christian Leadership Conference (SCLC) was too Southern, too religious, and too middle class to develop a mass following in the slums. On the other hand, he told me he thought "CORE and Floyd McKissick were on the right track. . . . They at least can talk to the kids between fifteen and twenty who hang around the streets." On at least one occasion in 1967, when CORE was at the edge of bankruptcy, Kennedy was instrumental in raising emergency funds to save the organization. Five days before he was shot, Kennedy took time out from his grueling California campaign for a secret and stormy meeting in an Oakland church with one hundred black militants, including three leaders of the Black Panther organization. Although their hatred of him shocked and hurt Kennedy, he still admired the parts of the Panther program that stressed racial pride, community control, and political organization. And Colin Carew, a black nationalist, ran and was elected as a Kennedy delegate to the national convention from the District of Columbia.

Kennedy had a special relationship with the urban black masses. According to a survey published in the July 29, 1968, issue of *New York* magazine, 92 percent of the residents of Harlem said the assassination of Robert Kennedy affected them as much, or more, than the assassination of John Kennedy; only 28 percent of the middle-class,

Upper East Side whites interviewed shared that reaction. In addition, 52 percent of the blacks interviewed said they visited his coffin in St. Patrick's Cathedral, compared to 8 percent of the middle-class whites polled. In the California primary, there were dozens of Negro districts where the voter turnout exceeded 90 percent and with Kennedy getting more than 90 percent of the actual vote.

Emotionally, Kennedy's sympathies, with their bias in the direction of the young, the activist, and the powerless, were with the more militant sections of the black community. And intellectually, he was not only more original and radical than most mainstream politicians, his thinking on race and the cities was also ahead of many academics and sociologists.

He wrote in *To Seek a Newer World,* that blackness "must be made a badge of pride and honor." He understood that the racial and urban crisis was "getting worse, not better. . . . It is the most terrible and urgent domestic crisis to face this nation since the Civil War." He understood that the existing welfare system is "restrictive and bureaucratic . . . demeaning and dehumanizing . . . the price is too often a broken home and illegitimacy." He understood that "it will be necessary to create new community institutions that local residents control," and that school decentralization "can and should occur, regardless of the economic status of the neighborhood involved."

Kennedy's programmatic response to the ghetto was embodied in his community development project in Bedford-Stuyvesant, which will be examined fully in the next chapter. The project had two innovating ideas built into it. Regenerate and rebuild the ghetto immediately, without waiting for an integrationist impulse to seize the suburbs. And use capital investment and tax incentives to create private sector jobs and community self-sufficiency. Both these ideas clash with the conventional liberal wisdom about integration as a moral imperative, and business being less progressive than labor. But here Kennedy's departures from New Deal liberalism happened to coincide with the black militant demands for community control, racial pride, and jobs rather than welfare.

Kennedy was no less firm against rioters in *To Seek a Newer World* than he was when he spoke in the smallest and whitest Indiana hamlet. He wrote:

The riots . . . are an intolerable threat to every American, black or white: to the mind's peace, the body's safety, and the community's order. To all that makes life worthwhile. A violent few cannot be permitted to threaten the well-being of the many. . . . Those who lead others to burn and loot must feel the full force of the law. The full force of the law means just that: the swift apprehension and punishment of law breakers.

But although Dallas had made guns and violence Robert Kennedy's natural enemy, he was still able to hear the message behind the rioter's choked rage, and to reject the easy reflex of repression. On August 4, 1967, Kennedy addressed a political dinner in San Francisco, just two weeks after the bloody rioting in Detroit and Newark, and when the backlash slogan of not "rewarding the rioters" was at a crescendo.

It must be for us a cruel and humbling fact—but it is a fact nonetheless—that our efforts have not even maintained the problem as it was: economic and social conditions in these areas, says the Department of Labor, "economic and social conditions are growing worse, not better."

But this is not all that the young man of the ghetto—the Negro, the Puerto Rican, the Mexican-American—this is not all he sees. Every day, as the years pass, and he becomes aware that there is nothing at the end of the road, he watches the rest of us go from peak to new peak of comfort.

A few blocks away or on his television set, the young Negro of the slums sees the multiplying marvels of white America: more new cars and more summer vacations, more air-conditioned homes and neatly-kept lawns. Every day he is told, by the television commercials we broadcast, that life is impossible without the latest products of our consumer society. But he cannot buy them.

He is told that Negroes are making progress. But what can that mean to him? He cannot experience the progress of others, or should we seriously expect him to feel grateful because he is no longer a slave, or because he can vote, or eat at some lunch counters. He sees only the misery of his present and the darkening years ahead.

Others tell him to work his way up as other minorities have done; and so he must. For he knows, and we know, that only by his own efforts and his own labor will the Negro come to full equality. But how is he to work? The jobs have fled to the suburbs, or been replaced by machines, or have flown beyond the reach of those with limited education and skills. He is powerless to change his place, or to make a better one for his children.

Thus he is denied the most fundamental of human needs; the need for identity; for recognition as a citizen and as a man. . . .

When the entire nation was sunk in Depression, Franklin Roosevelt assured us we had nothing to fear but fear itself. Today, when there are islands of depression in the midst of affluence, there is even more to fear. We must be afraid of the leadership of fear,* the cries of those who find repression more congenial than justice; and anger more popular than compassion. Let them go their way. It is not ours.

The second element in Kennedy's revisionist liberalism was his partial liberation from the rhetoric of anti-Communism and the Cold War. The most obvious omen of this was his opposition to the escalation of the Vietnam war.† Other signs were his criticism of the military intervention in the Dominican Republic; his opposition to a rigid containment policy toward China; his repeated speeches in favor of arms control and a nuclear nonproliferation treaty; and his deepening commitment to civil liberties domestically.

Again, one of the ironic reasons for this was Kennedy's early conservatism. He was not a participant in the permanently scarring factionalism that split the Left during the 1940's and 1950's over the issue of Stalinism. Unlike Hubert Humphrey, he did not help to expel the Communists and their allies from the Minnesota Farmer Labor Party. Unlike Walter Reuther, he did not contest a Stalinist faction for the soul of a labor union. Unlike John Roche or Irving Kristol, he did not exchange personal polemics with pro-Soviet intellectuals. His distance from this ugly period of left-wing factionalism gave Kennedy an emotional and psychic freedom that other politicians, unionists, and intellectuals could never achieve. Kennedy did not have to spend the McCarthy era convincing critics that liberals were just as anti-Communist as anyone else by sponsoring the Communist Control Act. Thus he could write in *To Seek a Newer World*:

> This is a war [Vietnam] surrounded by rhetoric they [the young] do not understand or accept; these are the children not of the Cold War, but of the Thaw. Their memories of Communism are not of Stalin's purges and death camps, not even of the terrible revelations of the Twentieth Party Congress, or the streets of Hungary. They see the world

* The phrase, "leadership of fear," was meant as a direct reference to President Johnson. The day before Kennedy delivered this speech he told me, "The big problem with Johnson is that he is personally a coward. That's why he had to have half the Cabinet stand behind him when he went on television during the Detroit riot, that's why he doesn't go out and meet the people, and that's why he had to sneak into Vietnam."

† The chapter, "Vietnam, Breaking with the Past," will trace Kennedy's relationship with the Vietnam war.

as one in which Communist states can be each other's deadliest enemies, or even close to the West, in which Communism is certainly no better, but perhaps no worse, than many other evil and repressive dictatorships with which we conclude alliances when that is felt to be in our interest.

Even as the declared foreign policy of our government is to "build bridges" to this new Communist world, they see us, in the name of anti-Communism, devastating the land of those we call our friends . . ."

But Kennedy did have at least one blind spot—the Central Intelligence Agency. After the fiasco at the Bay of Pigs in April, 1961, President Kennedy appointed his brother Robert chairman of a special committee (Interdepartmental Committee in Charge of Central Intelligence) to investigate what went wrong. Other members of the committee were General Maxwell Taylor, Admiral Arleigh Burke, and Allen Dulles.

It was in the course of the panel's three-month investigation that Kennedy became intimately involved* in the operations of the intelligence agency, and developed his passion for the techniques of counterinsurgency. One of the few times that Kennedy sided with the conservative bloc within his brother's Administration was when he supported the recommendation that John McCone replace Allen Dulles as director of the CIA. In February of 1967, when the CIA's clandestine financing of student groups, unions, and publications was revealed, Kennedy defended the agency. "We must not forget that we are not dealing with a dream world, but with a very tough adversary," he told reporters at the time.

A few days after he made that remark, I engaged Kennedy in an off-the-record argument about the CIA. I suggested that there was inadequate Congressional or public supervision of the agency. That it made policy on its own. That it was secretly involved in the right-wing coup in Guatemala in 1954, and was responsible for the death of Diem in Saigon in 1963. I also argued that it had a right-wing bias, so that "liberal" Cuban exiles like Manuel Ray were excluded from the Bay of Pigs landing. I also said it was "deceitful and immoral" for the CIA to have secretly subsidized organizations like the National Student Association and publications like *Encounter*. I said that if I had been active in NSA, or contributed to *Encounter,* I would now feel "cheated and used,"

---

* Arthur Schlesinger wrote in *A Thousand Days* that Kennedy "took a personal interest in the CIA, and became an informal presidential watchdog over covert operations."

and that for years older liberals had been preaching to my generation about being deceived by Communists, but now we found out we had been deceived by those same older liberals.

Kennedy listened to my somewhat emotional monologue, and then tried to respond randomly to a few points. He conceded that "At the time, I was not informed of what the CIA did to Manuel Ray, and in retrospect, I think it was a mistake. . . . What you say about Diem is complicated. What happened to him was decided in Saigon, not in Washington."

Then Kennedy began to justify the CIA in a more general way.

"What you're not aware of," he said, "is what role the CIA plays within the government. During the 1950's, for example, many of the liberals who were forced out of other departments found a sanctuary, an enclave, in the CIA. So some of the best people in Washington, and around the country, began to collect there. One result of that was the CIA developed a very healthy view of Communism, especially compared to State and some other departments. They were very sympathetic, for example, to nationalist, and even Socialist governments and movements. And I think now the CIA is becoming much more realistic, and critical, about the war, than other departments, or even the people in the White House. So it is not so black and white as you make it."

Also, most of the intellectual advisers who worked inside John Kennedy's Administration, and had direct experience with the CIA, shared, and probably reinforced, Robert Kennedy's beliefs. Arthur Schlesinger wrote in *A Thousand Days*:

> In my experience its [the CIA's] leadership was politically enlightened and sophisticated. Not seldom CIA representatives took a more liberal line in White House meetings than their counterparts from State. A great deal of CIA energy went to the support of the anti-Communist left around the world—political parties, trade unions and other undertakings. . . .

Three years later, Richard Goodwin expressed the morality of counterinsurgency when he wrote in *The New Yorker* of May 25, 1968, at the end of a personal reminiscence of Che Guevara:

> In the note that accompanied the cigars, Guevara referred to me as an enemy. He was right. Had I been in office, I would have joined in recommending that we assist the Bolivian government to subdue the guerrillas.

The final element of Kennedy's new liberalism was his recognition

...at most labor unions had become middle class and satisfied, and that the underclass must be reached in new ways.

Unlike most liberals of the New Deal–Fair Deal era (Johnson, Humphrey, etc.), Kennedy had no illusions about the AFL-CIO as a vanguard agent of social reform. Here Kennedy's formative experiences were not the crusade to pass the Wagner Act, or the UAW sit-down strikes in Michigan. Rather they were his investigations into corruption and criminal influence in international unions like the Carpenters and Teamsters. Once again it was his early conservative role as prosecutor and investigator that prepared Kennedy to see through a generation's liberal clichés about progressive unionism. To Kennedy's eyes, the AFL-CIO leadership was committed politically to Lyndon Johnson, committed emotionally to the Vietnam war, and not committed at all to organizing the new, invisible poor. In *To Seek a Newer World,* he wrote:

> Nor painful as it may be for liberals to acknowledge, are these young people enchanted with liberal institutions. . . . They think labor has grown sleek and bureaucratic with power, sometimes frankly discriminatory, occasionally even corrupt and exploitive, a force not for change, but for the status quo, unwilling or unable to organize new members, indifferent to the men who once worked the coal mines of Appalachia, a latecomer to the struggles of the grape pickers of California, or the farm laborers of the Mississippi delta. . . .

It is not good politics to attack union leaders, but Kennedy was not a tidy politician when his emotions got in the way. On April 18, 1967, during Senator Abraham Ribicoff's subcommittee hearings on urban poverty, Kennedy ignored the code of Democratic Party politics, and publicly rebuked leaders of the Building Trades unions.

At one point, C. J. Haggerty, president of the Building and Construction Trades Department of the AFL-CIO, testified that a four-year program to abolish discrimination in eighteen building trades unions was "99 percent successful."

Kennedy winced, put on his glasses, consulted with Peter Edelman, and interrupted to quote from official Labor Department statistics that showed that of 8,164 journeymen in 11 Houston construction unions, only 60 were Negroes, and all but one of the 60 were cement masons.

Peter T. Schoemann, president of the Plumbers and Pipefitters Union testified later the same day that there were few Negroes in his union because Negroes lacked motivation and skills. "We can't take a boy," he said, "that can't read, and a boy that is a school dropout. We have certain minimum requirements. . . ."

"Well," Kennedy interrupted again in an icy voice, "I would think that there are more than twenty-one Negro boys in all of Cincinnati who can read."

Because of comments like that, George Meany would barely speak to Kennedy, and in 1968 not one of the AFL–CIO's twenty-nine international vice presidents endorsed the candidate who received the overwhelming majority of the votes of the black and white poor in the Presidential primaries.

(In the Indiana primary of 1968 Kennedy got 86 percent of the Negro vote statewide, and swept the seven largest counties where George Wallace ran strongest in 1964. He also carried white backlash bastions like Hammond, Gary, South Bend, East Chicago.)

Although he never verbalized it, and almost certainly never thought about it in conceptual terms, Kennedy's response to the bureaucratization of the labor movement was to work with new institutions that represented the underclass, and find new sources of insurgent energy. As Fred Dutton put it, "Kennedy wasn't antiunion. He was just un-union. He thought the middle-class labor leaders didn't have any of the answers, and the poor were someplace else. So he went where he could find them."

He went to Delano, California, and found Cesar Chavez and the grape strikers and became their best publicist and fund raiser. He went to the Mississippi delta and upstate New York, and found migrant farm laborers who average $1,200 a year income, and sponsored legislation to extend to them the right of collective bargaining. He went to the sprawling slum called Bedford-Stuyvesant and decided to initiate a community development corporation there, with the support of corporation chairmen and bankers, rather than union leaders. He visited Indian reservations, and had the Senate create a special subcommittee on Indian Education with him as chairman. He traveled to Wolfe County in Appalachia, where 5,000 of the county's 6,500 inhabitants exist below the Federal poverty line, and attacked his brother-in-law's poverty program as an "unacceptable failure," and again endorsed Senator Joseph Clark's Federal job program.

None of this was part of any worked-out theory or program Kennedy had for building alternative institutions to labor unions. He did not have that sort of abstract mind, nor so grand a dream, nor so much actual power as a junior Senator at odds with the Administration of his own party. It was rather improvised, impressionistic politics by the man who Senator Javits said in a eulogy, "endured personal torture . . . literally shook with indignation at the sight of starving children."

The incident Senator Javits had in mind might have been the early morning he and Kennedy visited a migrant farm worker camp just outside of Rochester, New York, in September of 1967. As the two Senators, a few union officials, and about a half-dozen reporters reached the campsite, they were welcomed by a sign that read, "Anyone entering or trespassing without my permission will be shot if caught." Most of the people in the entourage stopped, except for Kennedy: he kept on walking, head down, into an abandoned bus that was converted into living quarters for three migrant families. Inside the stench-filled bus, Kennedy saw six children, all less than ten years old. Their bodies were covered with unhealed scabs, and flies, and most of them had running noses. They were all black. Kennedy's face suddenly recaptured the terrible look it had in the months after his brother's assassination. Compassion, anger, and pain mingled and flattened his features. An old, bent woman wandered into the bus, and Kennedy asked her how much money she earned. She said, as she looked at her feet, that she earned $1 an hour picking celery. Kennedy made a face, and shook his head.

He went out and looked into the next dilapidated bus. It was empty except for one child playing on a filthy mattress. The windows were filled with torn cardboard. There was no running water and no stove. As Kennedy looked down at the child, his hand and his head trembled in rage. He seemed like a man going through an exorcism, or a religious experience.

He walked out and confronted the camp's owner, Jay DeBadts.

"You had no right to go in there," DeBadts shouted at Kennedy, gesturing to his sign. "You're just a do-gooder trying to make some headlines."

Kennedy looked at him, still struggling to control his emotions, and almost whispered, "You are something out of the nineteenth century. I wouldn't put an animal in those buses."

"It's like camping out," replied DeBadts.

Kennedy turned and left. But the memory was burned into his imagination. He talked about it again and again in other places. He wrote letters to Governor Nelson Rockefeller asking for an investigation of health conditions at the migrant camps. He wrote letters to labor leaders urging them to organize the migrants, and lobby to gain for them the right of collective bargaining. And he thought about what it might feel like to live in a bus and pick celery for $1 an hour.

Robert Kennedy did not have a monopoly on the insights about elimating poverty. He knew no more than Saul Alinsky, CORE, Michael Harrington, the New Left, and Daniel Moynihan. But Kennedy may have been the only national political leader to have at least a piece because he knew where to look for it. He knew, on instinct, that he had to experience—see, smell, hear, touch—places like the DeBadts' migrant camp, just as he sensed that he had to experience physically Delano, and Wolfe County, and Bedford-Stuyvesant, and all those Indian reservations. It was sensual politics.

Robert Kennedy was quite likely the last mainstream politician of his generation who might have served as a bridge between the black and white faces that lined the opposite sides of the railroad tracks to wave farewell to his funeral train.

The militant young blacks, who wore "Free Huey Newton" buttons as they cheered Kennedy in San Francisco the day before he was shot, and the low-income whites who signed George Wallace petitions in July, would have both voted for Kennedy in November.* He was able to talk to the two polarities of powerlessness at the same time.

Kennedy was able to do that partly because he was a Kennedy and a Catholic, but also because no matter how cold and unconvincing he seemed on television, in person, he was able to communicate his rage against poverty, violence, and indifference to the unemployed, to the housewife, and to the factory worker. Somehow, the ordinary people sensed, as Fred Dutton said, that he was the Kennedy with soul. They understood that if he won, he would try to be the "President of the poor people."

---

* In a penetrating piece on the Wallace campaign in *The Village Voice* of July 18, 1968, Paul Cowan wrote, "I realized for the first time how important Robert Kennedy's candidacy had been. He was the last liberal politician who could communicate with the white working-class America." Cowan then went on to report that many of the poor, white Catholics who signed the Wallace petitions would have voted for Kennedy. He quoted one ardent Wallace backer as saying of Kennedy, "He wasn't like the other politicians. I had the feeling that he really cared about people like us."

Book Two

Bedford-Stuyvesant:
Giving a Damn About Hell

Diseased debris rotting under a halo of mosquitoes in a vacant lot. Teen-age girls feinting and punching with the fluent fury of grown men. Burned-out houses with families still living behind the boarded-up windows. Roaches so bold they no longer flee from the light. A shabby record store loudspeaker blaring Aretha Franklin singing, "I can't get no satisfaction," while a junkie shoots up with heroin in the doorway. Bedford-Stuyvesant's everyday reality is filled with the surreal imagery of a bad LSD trip.

There is the sour stench of urine that pollutes the Myrtle-Willoughby IND subway station. The bittersweet monologue of the red-wigged prostitute after she has been shaken down by a white cop. The visor of suffocated hatred that comes down across the taut face of every black youth before his thirteenth birthday. And the counterfeit escapes wherever you look. Neon signs promising credit. Bars. Pimps. Churches. Pushers. TV sets on sale. Liquor stores. Pawnshops. More storefront churches. Numbers runners.

Then, the statistics. Eighty percent of the teen-agers are high school dropouts. Thirty-six percent of the families headed by women. Twenty-eight percent with annual incomes of less than $3,000. The highest infant mortality rate in the nation. The highest incidence of lead poisoning in the country.

More than 90 percent of the housing was built before 1920. Almost half of it officially classified as "dilapidated and insufficient." A fifth with hall toilets.

And no one has ever counted all the rats.

Harlem has always been viewed as the universal symbol for the Negro ghetto. It is the place that suffers and swings. It is the place James Baldwin writes about and Billie Holiday sang about. It is where the Federal antipoverty funds go first. It is home for Sugar Ray and Adam Powell. Harlem has its own newspaper, its own mayor, its own identity. It is a community. It had a black Congressman more than twenty-five years before Bedford-Stuyvesant did.

But the unromantically baptized ghetto of Bedford-Stuyvesant (named for the Duke of Bedford and Peter Stuyvesant) is much poorer than Harlem. It is the place where people land when they fall out of Harlem; it is where the Wagner Administration used to dump black people after they were uprooted by the urban renewal bulldozer.

Bedford-Stuyvesant is larger and more diffuse than Harlem. Harlem is compact, limited on three sides by rivers, and on the south by Central Park. But Bedford-Stuyvesant's borders keep growing like an amoeba's. Its exact geographical definition keeps changing, pushing into Crown Heights, East New York, and Brownsville. "Bedford-Stuyvesant is wherever Negroes live," says a local politician. While Harlem lost 50,000 in population between 1950 and 1960, Bedford-Stuyvesant gained about 50,000. It now consists of about 450,000 people jammed into 500 square blocks, or about the same population as Kansas City or Cincinnati. According to a 1967 study compiled by the New York University Graduate School of Social Work:

> Bedford Stuyvesant is more depressed and impaired than Harlem —i.e., fewer unified families, more unemployment, lower incomes, less job history. . . . Furthermore, the Bedford-Stuyvesant youth have (*sic*) a vastly lower degree of self-esteem than does Harlem youth, with much less hope for his future. . . .

At the turn of the century Bedford-Stuyvesant was an elite, white, middle-class community. Sturdy brownstones, numerous churches, and tranquil, tree-lined streets gave the section its character. Employment was plentiful and the crime rate low. In 1907, after the completion of the Williamsburg Bridge, a few working-class Jews and Italians emigrated from the Lower East Side of Manhattan.

During the 1930's, the first wave of black migration from the West

Indies and the rural South deposited thousands of Negroes into Brooklyn. Farm mechanization—especially the cotton picker—and the Depression drove millions of jobless Negroes into the spreading black slums of the North. At the same time, the A train—immortalized by Duke Ellington—began to operate, and transport thousands of Negroes from 125th Street in Harlem, to Fulton Street in Brooklyn.

The second wave broke over Bedford-Stuyvesant during World War II. The Brooklyn Navy Yard, only a few minutes away, offered employment, and war economy prosperity was enabling many of the area's older Jewish and Italian residents to move to Queens or Long Island. In 1930 the black population of Bedford-Stuyvesant was 30,000; by 1950 it was 155,000, or about 55 percent. By 1960 it was about 85 percent, and now it is more than 90 percent.*

Bedford-Stuyvesant became a ghetto because real-estate speculators and professional blockbusters, abetted by banks and mortgage companies, were there to exploit it, and pocket millions in panic profits. During the 1950's, many Negro families paid as much as $20,000 for brownstones that speculators had acquired for $12,000 the week before. The remaining white families, mostly elderly, became the targets of wild rumors, staged street brawls between Negroes, and almost daily mimeographed postcards claiming, "We have a buyer for your house."

I was growing up in Bedford-Stuyvesant during the early fifties, and remember white real-estate brokers offering my Negro friends fifty cents an hour to slip circulars under the doors of white-owned houses, saying there was a buyer available. Real-estate speculators easily obtained loans from banks, but the stable, hardworking Negro family next door to my house could not get a bank loan to rehabilitate their dirty, peeling frame house. I remember how one frightened white family two blocks away from me—on Hart Street—became a neighborhood legend by simply walking out of their home one day, leaving all their furniture behind, and never returning. Quite rapidly the community became segregated. Garbage collection grew less frequent. Bopping youth gangs were organized. Newspapers began to write about the "crime wave" in Bedford-Stuyvesant. Unemployment increased. The hospitals, high schools, and libraries in the community continued to decay, and the city

* The same pattern created other urban ghettos. Between 1940 and 1960, the black population of Philadelphia doubled, the black populations of Chicago and Detroit tripled, and that of Los Angeles multiplied five times.

would not build any new ones to replace them. Boys High School was sixty-four years old by the time I was graduated in 1956. The senior class was 90 percent Negro, but 80 percent of those of us who went on to college were white.* And several of the Negroes who went to college were able to do so only because of athletic scholarships. By 1956, the old, white, middle-class Bedford-Stuyvesant was dead, a "For Sale" sign its venal epitaph.

Although few recognized it at the time, the history of race relations in America changed on July 16, 1964. On that day a fifteen-year-old Negro boy named James Powell was shot to death on a Manhattan street by a white, off-duty police lieutenant named Thomas Gilligan. That gunshot signaled the end of the civil rights movement and the beginning of the long, hot summers.

James Powell had been an almost-too-perfect symbol of the new generation of the black youth. The summer before he died, when he was fourteen, he went to Washington to join the biggest civil rights march in history. He was shot while attending a summer school for remedial reading, subsidized by the then new and hopeful war on poverty. Two days after his death, on July 18, a hot, restless Saturday night, rioting broke out in Harlem. Two nights later, as if the trouble itself had taken the A train, violence, looting, and vandalism exploded at the intersection of Fulton Street and Nostrand Avenue, the Times Square of Bedford-Stuyvesant.

Compared with what was to come in following summers, the three nights of rioting in Brooklyn were an abortive skirmish. There were no deaths. No sniping. Almost no fire bombing. The violence was limited to an eight-square-block area. When it was over, the accounting came to 276 arrests, 22 injuries, and 556 incidents of property damage, estimated to total $350,000. The rioters were almost all young Negroes—that revolutionary class between fourteen and twenty-one—that roams the limbo between school, work, and the Army. They were the vanguard of the lost black generation that has grown up in the North—not the South—watching the sit-ins and Freedom Rides on television, and listening to black nationalist orators on the street corners.

* Kennedy once said to me, "I'm jealous of the fact you grew up in a ghetto. I wish I did. I wish I had that experience."

On the third night of the riot I was sent to cover it by the *New York Post*. Early in the evening the familiar fugue of the police siren and the burglar alarm began to play along Fulton Street. At about 9 P.M. a sound truck manned by officials of the NAACP parked at the corner of Fulton and Nostrand, its loudspeaker shouting:

"Ladies and gentlemen, will you please return to your homes. Help our community. Help save our community. Help us make Bedford-Stuyvesant a safe place again. Please do not destroy our community anymore. *Please get off the streets.*"

A group of teen-agers, with that remarkable *élan* and energy of the streets, began to taunt and jeer the middle-aged ministers inside the truck. Suddenly, a large, buxom black woman of about fifty, with a back bent from washing too many white people's floors, shouted at the truck from the doorway of a looted store. "Sheet, man. *These are our streets.* You fools, *you go home.*"

The dream deferred had dried up and become desperation. And Bedford-Stuyvesant, in July of 1964, was a portent of the next four summers, whose history would be written in the geography of violence: Watts, Newark, Cleveland, Detroit, Chicago, Washington, D.C.

The riot gave Bedford-Stuyvesant national visibility, and there was considerable press release jargon about "crash programs," "task forces" and "target areas." But the sense of urgency quickly passed, and nothing was done. There was no new job program, or new school construction, or rat extermination program. Six months after the violence the only change was that one vacant lot had been blacktopped. The shopkeepers along Fulton Street did not even bother to replace their broken windows; they kept them boarded up with plywood, expecting another outbreak any day.

In November of 1964 Lyndon Johnson was reelected President, Robert Kennedy was elected the new Senator from New York, the first Democrat to win a statewide election for Governor or Senator in ten years, and the well-publicized "unconditional war against poverty" was beginning to build up hopes inside the other America. On November 21, the Central Brooklyn Coordinating Council, a loose federation of over ninety local organizations, sponsored an all-day conference at Pratt Institute, in the heart of Bedford-Stuyvesant. The meeting was called in response to the summer's violence, and 600 civic, religious, and political leaders came to tell each other how desperate the situation was, and how urgently the area needed a coordinated and comprehensive rehabilitation program. The one concrete result of the conference was the decision to commission Pratt's Planning Department to make a six-month survey of the community's problems, as well as its potential for becoming more attractive to the middle class.

The study, directed by Planning Department chairman George Raymond, concentrated on a twelve-block area, more than 95-percent Negro, that contained 2,900 dwelling units occupied by 8,600 persons. The survey found the area at the point of decay. Only 10.5 percent of the buildings were "in a dilapidated condition," but 28.5 percent were "seriously deteriorating," and in need of "immediate attention."

The Pratt study also suggested that the chances of rehabilitation of the area were "greatly enhanced" by the fact that 22.5 percent of the buildings were owner occupied, another 9.7 percent owned by individuals who lived in close proximity, and that homeowners had lived in the area on an average of fifteen years. All this indicated the presence of a stable, middle-class base in the community, able to provide leadership for reform. The report concluded with a plea that the city "mobilize all necessary antipoverty and other social welfare and educational programs" to save the community from imminent violence and deterioration.

But less than a month after the study was released, Bedford-Stuyvesant's city antipoverty agency, Youth-in-Action, reported its budget slashed. Dorothy Orr, the executive director of YIA, had originally requested $5.5 million for summer programs in 1965. Later, she reduced that to $2.6 million. But in the end, YIA was allocated only $440,000. The project had to abandon many of its programs, like prekindergarten classes and college-preparatory courses. YIA received 1,000 more requests for summer jobs than it could fill in 1965.

Late in 1965 Robert Kennedy decided he wanted to make a major address on the themes of race and poverty, and sent Adam Walinsky to work collecting data and talking to experts. Kennedy had been shaken by the Watts riot and felt that the racial crisis had now shifted its focus from the rural South to the urban North. He also felt that support for

Negro demands within the white community was declining, and that race relations had reached a historical turning point—that if something were not done quickly to stem the white backlash, then violence and separation would increase.

It developed, however, that Kennedy had so much he wanted to say, the single speech grew into three separate speeches, which were delivered consecutively in Manhattan on January 20, 21, and 22 of 1966. The speeches were not revolutionary in content. For the most part, they were a rehash of New Frontier programs—job training, rent subsidies, student loans for the poor, housing desegregation. But they were well crafted and documented, and they did offer an impressive synthesis of the practical, fueled by Kennedy's insatiable drive for immediate, concrete action.

They also provided the first glimpse of Kennedy's own insights into the problem. Going against the grain of liberal optimism and Great Society rhetoric, he asserted that the plight of the Negro was getting worse, not better, and that some of the accepted liberal formulas like welfare and stricter code enforcement were not working. He placed new emphasis on the need for a sense of community inside the ghettos, on the need for ghetto residents to participate in governmental decision-making, and the need for private industry to enlist in the war on poverty.

The three speeches also dramatized Kennedy's emotional urgency and feelings of frustration. "We are now at the crossroads," he said. "The present pace is unsatisfactory . . . at such a pace we can expect continuing explosions like Watts. . . . We must break down the ghettos . . . we must begin to do so immediately."

A few days after giving the last of the three speeches, Kennedy decided to create his own antislum project. In his typically vague, offhand manner, he told Adam Walinsky, "I want to do something about all this. Some kind of project that goes after some of these problems. Why don't you and Tom [Johnston] see what you can put together."

In mid-February, Kennedy spent a cold, cloudy afternoon touring Bedford-Stuyvesant. He saw what visiting Senators and celebrities have always seen. Unemployed men lounging on street corners, or in bars. Pyramids of uncollected garbage. Children playing in the street without coats in temperatures of thirty degrees. After the tour, Kennedy went to a meeting with community activists arranged for the Bedford-Stuyvesant

YMCA. At that point Bedford-Stuyvesant was unable to receive a single urban renewal grant from the Federal Government despite ten years of trying. The community also received almost no antipoverty money; most of it went to Harlem.

The meeting turned out to be reminiscent of the famous confrontation Kennedy had as Attorney General in 1963, with James Baldwin, Harry Belafonte, and other Negro cultural and civil rights leaders. The Brooklyn Negroes, bitter over Federal indifference to the area, despite the 1964 riot, took out their frustrations on the surprised Senator. They insulted and lectured him, insisting he explain the failures of Washington, Albany, and City Hall. At one point, Civil Court Judge Thomas Jones, the highest ranking black politician in the community, who had pointedly refused to accompany Kennedy on his tour, told the Senator: "I'm weary of study, Senator. Weary of speeches, weary of promises that aren't kept. . . . The Negro people are angry, Senator, and judge that I am, I'm angry, too. No one is helping us."

1966 was the year the country began moving to the Right, and Robert Kennedy began moving to the Left. And both these trends contributed to the project in Brooklyn continually expanding in concept during the nine months Kennedy and his staff worked on it. They did, however, start out with two negative premises. One was that because of the Vietnam war the Federal Government was unlikely to appropriate any new funds for antipoverty legislation. Therefore, the private sector—corporations, foundations, universities, banks—must be convinced to pick up the slack. Second, the existing Office of Economic Opportunity programs had suffered from three flaws: an insufficient emphasis on jobs as the critical factor in poverty; not enough community participation in the creation and control of programs; and a piecemeal approach that was inadequately coordinated.

Back in February of 1966 Kennedy declared his independence from the Johnson Administration by directly challenging its Vietnam policy. In May, Kennedy broke with Tammany Hall by actively campaigning in the Democratic primary for a reform candidate for surrogate against the regular organization's choice. In August he badgered Cabinet level officers of the Johnson Administration during committee hearings on the poverty program. In October he went to the Berkeley campus, mecca of student radicalism, to make a speech on "the duty to dissent."

Meanwhile, the Vietnam war continued to escalate and absorb the money and energy of the government. The poverty program began to falter, as some of its best staff quit the agency; an effort by Kennedy and Senator Joseph Clark to increase its budget failed, and its community action program was curtailed. In the November election, forty-seven Democrats—almost all of them supporters of OEO—lost their seats. The civilian review board, despite the backing of Kennedy, Senator Javits, and Mayor Lindsay, was turned down by the voters of New York City in a referendum. And Ronald Reagan, Claude Kirk, and Lester Maddox were elected governors.

Through the violent summer of 1966 Walinsky and Johnston spent almost half their time working on the project. They traveled across the country several times, picking the brains of black militants, university urbanists, Federal administrators, journalists, mayors, foundation executives, millionaires from the banking and business communities. Johnston spent many of his evenings in Bedford-Stuyvesant, talking to the hostile street radicals, and trying to sort out the Byzantine feuds that split the middle-class leadership. Kennedy, meanwhile, realizing that both the Johnson Administration in Washington and the local white Democrats in Brooklyn felt threatened by his experiment, lined up crucial bipartisan support from Republicans Mayor Lindsay and Senator Javits. Then he went to his personal friends in the corporate world like Thomas Watson of IBM; William Paley of CBS; investment banker André Meyer; and Douglas Dillon, the Republican Secretary of the Treasury of his brother's Cabinet. After some sharp jabs to their conscience, they agreed to help. André Meyer, however, had one half-serious condition to his participation—that Kennedy give another speech against the Vietnam war. The only person who rejected Kennedy's invitation to join the corporation board was David Rockefeller. Daniel Moynihan, then a professor at MIT, privately urged Kennedy not to attempt the project at all.

By October, Kennedy, his staff, and the community leaders agreed not to try to rehabilitate a single block, or attack one problem area like health or housing, but attempt a community development project for almost the entire ghetto of Bedford-Stuyvesant.

"We must grab the web whole," Kennedy said in a 1966 speech, and that idea of a holistic, systematic attack on the ghetto itself was at the heart of the Bedford-Stuyvesant project.

The initial plan included coordinated programs for the creation of jobs, housing renovation and rehabilitation, improved health, sanitation and recreation facilities, the construction of two "super blocks," the conversion of an abandoned bottling plant into a town hall and community center, a mortgage consortium to provide low-cost loans for homeowners, the starting of a private work-study community university geared toward dropouts, and a campaign to convince industry to relocate in the community.

"An effort in one problem area," Kennedy said when the project started, "is almost worthless. A program for housing, without simultaneous programs for jobs, education, welfare reform, health, and economic development cannot succeed. The whole community must be involved as a whole."

The October decision to go was made even though the dry bones of failed projects littered many of the nation's urban slums. Martin Luther King had failed in his campaign to "end slums" in Chicago. The Student Nonviolent Coordinating Committee (SNCC) project had folded up in Atlanta. The SDS-initiated Newark Community Union Project (NCUP) was barely surviving. Despite grandiose plans, Walter Reuther's Citizens Crusade Against Poverty (CCAP) had never gotten off the ground. In Bedford-Stuyvesant itself, CORE had failed to grow beyond 60 or 70 dedicated activists. The Mobilization for Youth pilot project on Manhattan's Lower East Side had lost its momentum after a series of red-baiting articles published by the *Daily News*. HARYOU in Harlem had been demoralized by scandals and factionalism. The Saul Alinsky approach to urban organizing had not scored a success since the formation of The Woodlawn Organization (TWO) in Chicago in the early sixties.

A few days before the Bedford-Stuyvesant project was publicly unveiled, Kennedy was saying, "I'm not at all sure this is going to work. But it's going to test some new ideas, some new ways of doing this, that are different from the government's. Even if we fail, we'll have learned something. But more important than that, something has to be done. People like myself just can't go around making nice speeches all the time. We can't just keep raising expectations. We have to do some damn hard work, too."

On December 9, 1966, before almost 1,000 people, mostly over thirty and black, in the auditorium of Public School 305, on tenement-lined Monroe Street, and with Mayor Lindsay and Senator Javits on the platform, Kennedy announced his plan for Bedford-Stuyvesant. He revealed the formation of two private, nonprofit corporations. One, the Bedford-Stuyvesant Renewal and Rehabilitation Corp. (later reconstituted as the Bedford-Stuyvesant Restoration Corp.) was made up of twenty established civic and religious community leaders, headed by Civil Court Judge Thomas Jones. Its purpose was to draft programs for "the physical, social and economic development of the community." It would retain basic decision-making authority. A second businessman's corporation named D & S (for distribution and services) was set up to provide the community corporation with "access to funds and managerial expertise." Its all-white board of directors included Kennedy's social friends Dillon, Watson, Meyer, and Paley, as well as David Lilienthal and J. M. Kaplan. Later, Roswell Gilpatric, James Oates, and Benno Schmidt were added, and became three of its most active members.

At the same time, Kennedy also announced the receipt of foundation grants from the Stern and Kaplan Funds, and the Ford and Astor Foundations. Seven months later the Department of Labor funded the project with a grant of 7 million dollars, under an amendment to the 1966 Economic Opportunity Act, drafted by Kennedy and Javits to provide incentive payments to private industry for helping to develop special impact areas like Bedford-Stuyvesant.

The response to the project was both mixed and predictable. *The New York Times* and *Post* praised it immediately in editorials. James Ridgeway, in the January 7, 1967, *New Republic,* compared Kennedy's plan with the OEO approach and with Senator Charles Percy's home ownership program, and concluded:

> Kennedy's New York plan is the most interesting, and over the long run, holds out the best hope for real change of any of these proposals. . . . Kennedy is moving in the right direction by seeking to employ people in planning and building their own communities. His program allows for, and encourages local diversity; it is meant to place control with the people. . . . Work, not just income, is what determines one's sense of self-importance in the country. The Kennedy plan aims to put people to work.

But the more ideological intellectuals of the Old and New Left did not approve of Kennedy's unorthodox mixing self-help and capitalism with black power. Robert Scheer wrote in the February, 1967, issue of *Ramparts:*

. . . the solutions which he [Kennedy] has begun to propose would not be likely to shock even the more conservative members of the Senate. . . . The Kennedy plan, then, involves a return to the market economy, and he has described the Bedford-Stuyvesant project in terms more reminiscent of Ronald Reagan than Herbert Lehman.

Michael Harrington, meanwhile, in several speeches and articles, criticized the Kennedy plan for "putting too much trust in private business, which remains motivated by profit, rather than by social and esthetic goals."

Ironically, the churl of conservatism, William F. Buckley, was impressed by Kennedy's approach,* and in July, wrote in his syndicated column:

> Senator Robert Kennedy was distributing a statement on the poverty program so sensible that it made recommendations I made three years ago. . . . It is widely known what the senator went on to recommend. A series of tax inducements to private enterprise to (a) give jobs to poor and unskilled workers; (b) build and operate plants in ghetto areas; and (c) replenish the capital machinery of those plants by generous tax depreciation schedules. . . . The stock market went up on the day Mr. Kennedy made his poverty proposals. Appropriately.

Despite speeches to Chambers of Commerce and real-estate boards, private dinner parties, and support from Republicans like Douglas Dillon, Henry Ford II, and Mayor Lindsay, Kennedy met only modest success in energizing the private sector.

A few corporations like IBM, Xerox, and U.S. Gypsum quickly responded to Kennedy's invitation into the ghetto, but most did not. The corporation executives and bankers Kennedy spoke to complained there was no profit in community development for them, that the unions would not cooperate; that they couldn't deal directly with black militants; and that they feared the climate of violence within the ghetto would deter most white employees from working there.

One company president told Kennedy, "Senator, the afternoon I walk into my board of directors and tell them that Bobby Kennedy was here today, and he thinks we should put a plant in Bedford-Stuyvesant, that is the afternoon they'll have me committed."

On September 29, 1967, Kennedy addressed 1,000 businessmen at

* Mr. Buckley's column was written in response to two bills in the areas of employment and housing that Kennedy introduced to implement legislatively the thinking behind the Brooklyn project.

the World Trade Conference of the Atlanta Chamber of Commerce. He told them, "there is a global revolution which we must understand and which we must join." "We cannot denounce extremists who reject our social system if we do not prove that system is capable of helping people lead a better life." "This is the challenge that I have come to offer you—whether you are willing to apply the flexibility of our fiscal and economic tools to the great task of rebuilding our nation's shame—and providing promise to the next generation of the poor, now dying slow, quiet deaths in our ghettos." Not once during the forty-five-minute speech in Atlanta's ultramodern Regency Hyatt House Hotel was anything Kennedy said applauded by his affluent audience.

An article in the March, 1968, issue of *Fortune* magazine described Kennedy as the least popular Presidential politician among businessmen since FDR. The article, based on a national survey of business leaders, reported that "at each meeting with businessmen, mention of the name Bobby Kennedy produced an almost unanimous chorus of condemnation."

But some corporations, and some of the most powerful corporate leaders, did rise to meet Kennedy's challenge. The D & S board of directors was assembled, and began to function as a tenuous link between the worlds of Fulton Street and Wall Street.

Lou Winnick, the Ford Foundation's director of urban programs, who worked with Walinsky and Johnston in devising the project, explained to the bimonthly magazine, *City,* the potential impact of the D & S directors:

It's no Mickey Mouse game when these big Wall Street guys come in. Companies represented on the D & S board, including ones in which members are trustees, plus others in which they have close relationships, are so big that they can set up a 200-man plant without the slightest risk that even a total loss would significantly affect the profit line of their balance sheet. . . .

With no more investment than a phone call these men can put a Negro in business, open a line of credit at a bank, or give him an order which in itself takes care of his credit and insurance problems—and these are what a black man trying to start just can't get. At the level where the D & S men are, it's almost a feudal system. All they have to do is move the smallest amount of muscle, and the city bounces.

Benno Schmidt is the managing partner of J. H. Whitney Co. He is reputed to have multiplied the original capital of the firm by at least sixteen times in twenty years. He is a Republican, who voted for Richard Nixon in 1960, and for Kenneth Keating rather than Robert Kennedy in 1964. I visited him in his office on the thirty-second floor of a Rockefeller Center tower early in 1968, and asked him how he got involved in the Brooklyn project. He replied in a voice both Southern and measured:

"One day six months ago Bob Kennedy walked into this office. I had never met him before in my life. Some mutual friends had to arrange the meeting. He told me the situation in the slums was dynamite, and asked me what I personally was willing to do about it. And what private enterprise was willing to do about it. It sounded like a dare. . . . We talked a little and found out we agreed that this was a problem that had to be attacked locally. And it had to be above politics. I told him I didn't care for his views about Vietnam and public power, but that we agreed on this question. I talked to Lindsay and Javits about it, and they both urged me to get involved. So here I am, spending 25 percent of all my time working on the renewal of a slum in Brooklyn."

Schmidt, a confident, strong man, accustomed to giving orders, said he had no problems following the lead of the all-black community corporation.

"It was clear from the start that our job was not to tell the community what to do, but to help implement what they wanted. I have no desire to impose my judgment on Judge Jones or Frank Thomas [executive director of the Restorations Corps]. They are very competent men. I'm here to help, not lead. I've been saying for twenty-five years that the Federal Government can't solve all these problems, that the localities themselves have to do it. And that's what this project is trying to do. It sure took those New Dealers a long time to wise up."

William Paley is a sixty-seven-year-old Republican. He is board chairman of CBS, which boasts a net annual sales of over $900 million. His son-in-law, Carter Burden, was a member of Kennedy's New York staff. And it was Kennedy, he says, who "opened my eyes to just how desperate things were in Bedford-Stuyvesant." Like Schmidt, he saw no problem in having one all-black board and another all-white board.

"I'm not defensive about it," he said. "It's a division of labor. Our job is to raise capital and give advice, when we're asked, on technical business matters. I suppose it would be better if we had a black businessman on our board, but, frankly, I didn't know any who were interested. I'm just here to do something about a problem. We all agree the community makes the decisions. And what is really important, is that Kennedy's office acts on that principle, too. There is real control in the community corporation."

Paley, despite his other commitments, also allocates about 25 percent of all his time to the project. "Whenever I called him," Frank Thomas said of Paley, "he called me back the same day." And although he didn't receive any of the credit in the press, it was Paley who played a crucial role in helping persuade the City University to build a branch in Bedford-Stuyvesant.

The bruised inhabitants of Bedford-Stuyvesant did not welcome the Restoration Corp. with enthusiasm. They were too cynical, too disillusioned, and too passive for that. They had seen publicized projects come and go, and white politicians tour at election time, make extravagant promises, and then vanish. The people at first didn't understand what the project was; they thought it was just another urban renewal plan that would ultimately tear down their homes.

Modesto Bravo was the president of the Halsey Street Block Association. He had lived in the community for more than twenty years. Shortly after the project started, the Restoration staff contacted Bravo, and told him his block had been chosen as one of the first to receive exterior renovation. Bravo's job was to collect $25 from each homeowner as a token payment for work valued at $325, to be performed by unemployed youths from Bedford-Stuyvesant, who were being paid $1.75 an hour by the community corporation.

"I just couldn't believe it," Bravo said. "I started going around, telling my friends on the block about the renovation. But they weren't interested. They didn't want to cooperate. They thought it was some trick, some hustle. They couldn't believe it was something good, almost for nothing. I went to every house, but no one would sign up. I tried to explain how these kids would fix their stoops, railings, and sidewalks. That they would sod their backyards, paint their garbage cans, put in moldings, prune trees, do everything. But these people, they were just apathetic.

"Finally, I got the police to send over barricades, and we had a meeting right out on the street, to get people to pay attention. People walking on the street stopped out of curiosity, and asked questions. In a few days we got 98 percent of the block signed up. But it was hard work. The residents, they were so skeptical."

Other symptoms of ghetto pathology afflicted the job trainees. Frank

Thomas says, "Our staff literally had to walk the streets recruiting people for the job training program. A lot of kids were afraid to sign up because they had criminal records, or contact with narcotics. We had to explain again and again that it didn't matter to us. . . . We expected to attract only teen-agers, but we ended up with a group averaging about twenty-four, including some over forty, who had never held full-time jobs before in their lives."

"After we placed some of the trainees," Thomas' assistant, Jim Lowery says, "there was still the problem of confidence. Some of them didn't know how to travel to the Bronx. Their heads were too messed up by the ghetto. They didn't think they could learn how to rig a scaffold, or cement a sidewalk. In many cases, too much had already happened to them by the time we reached them. At ten a kid realizes a man is sleeping with his mother. At seventeen he's so hung up he can't make it anymore."

Like most ghettos, Bedford-Stuyvesant was fragmented by factions within a leadership historically embittered by defeat, and suddenly sensing money and power. The infighting in Bedford-Stuyvesant during 1967 was exacerbated further by the fact that all the competing leaders knew the community would elect its first Negro Congressman the following year. So from the outset the project was threatened by the political cannibalism that has always flourished among the upward-striving poor.

The original community corporation, set up in December of 1966, was almost exclusively middle class, and about one-third female. Kennedy and Judge Jones recognized their mistake, and in March of 1967, they tried to expand the corporation from twenty to fifty members, adding unaffiliated street leaders, militant clergymen, officials of Brooklyn CORE, and Puerto Ricans. The original board of directors refused, and the dispute broke into the open. Old wounds were opened, and Kennedy found himself caught refereeing a rumble between competing factions of blacks.

A coalition of local organizations formed against Kennedy and Jones. One was a group of militant middle-aged women, long active in fighting for good causes in the community. They had a long-standing personal grudge against Judge Jones, who, in turn, exploited the sensitive ghetto issue of matriarchy against them. A second group was Youth-in-Action, the city funded antipoverty agency in the community, whose leadership felt threatened by the newer and bigger project being planned by Kennedy. A third group was the middle-age, middle-class leaders associated with the Central Brooklyn Coordinating Council, whose initiative was primarily responsible for the project itself.

For a few days it seemed the whole effort might be aborted. Kennedy dropped all his other activities, went to work trying to save his experiment by forming a new community corporation. He won the necessary support from Mayor Lindsay and Senator Javits for this move, arguing that unless the corporation was made more representative it would have difficulty securing Federal and foundation funds. On April 1, Judge Jones announced the formation of a new corporation that would "include the young and the militant."

A few days later 1,000 angry people returned to the auditorium of PS 305 for a public meeting called by the old corporation. The evening's script could have been written by either Genet or Daniel Moynihan. The representatives of the matriarchy and YIA spoke with deep emotion against "the outsider" Kennedy and Jones. But the proud, goateed, very masculine members of CORE took over the meeting. They shouted, sometimes incoherently, against the "black bourgeoisie" trying "to make it uptown on the backs of the brothers." They called Kennedy a "colonialist," and Jones a "Tom," but also said their new corporation was better. They attacked the women for "emasculating the community, denying us our models of black manhood."

When emotions subsided, Jones announced the membership of the new community corporation. It included Sonny Carson, the chairman of Brooklyn CORE, who was to quit the national organization in 1968 because it wasn't revolutionary enough; Albert Vann, president of the radical Afro-American teachers; the former warlord of one of Bedford-Stuyvesant's more notorious fighting gangs; a local judo teacher with a large following among the young black nationalists; Puerto Rican lawyer Frank Ortiz; and two union organizers.

"These are the people we have to reach," Kennedy said of the new directors of the community corporation. "Some people may not like it, but they are in the street, and that is where the ball game is being played. You can't just talk to the middle class."

The most exhaustive pieces of legislation ever drafted in the Senate office of Robert Kennedy were the companion bills that incorporated the concepts behind the Bedford-Stuyvesant project in the areas of employment and housing. Legislative-fellow Michael Curzan began working on the legislation in January of 1967, and did not finish until six months later. In the interim, almost one hundred economists, lawyers, industrialists, and Federal officials were consulted on the drafting of the complex legislation.

According to Jeff Greenfield, "The two bills were incredibly intricate. They involved almost a total rewriting of the tax codes, and, at the same time, safeguards ensuring real community control."

The bills reflected one significant change in Kennedy's thinking since his first sequence of urban speeches in January of 1966. This was the inclusion of tax incentives and low cost loans to make slum regeneration economically realistic to private industry. "I've learned you can't rely on altruism or morality," Kennedy remarked at the time. "People just aren't built that way." Although neither bill got out of committee because of opposition from the White House, Kennedy and his staff, despite the pressures of the campaign, were preparing to reintroduce the two measures when he was assassinated.

Kennedy made more than twenty speeches during 1967 to groups of businessmen and bankers, trying to explain his notion of community development, and the need for equivalents of the Bedford-Stuyvesant project in other ghettos across the country.

He was again going against the grain, reminding people of things they wanted to forget, goading them to do things they didn't want to do. As so often in the past, Kennedy was being abrasive and pushy, rather than diplomatic and charming. He was making speeches telling people things were getting worse, that they had to do more, that the present was unacceptable. He was telling bankers and politicians that an apocalypse was coming, and they had better pay attention to the ghettos, or else share responsibility for whatever comes. He was a strident Jeremiah at a time when white America longed to hear a soothing Pollyanna.

Kennedy introduced the employment bill on July 12, 1967. He defined its objective as "the creation of new jobs in poverty areas, to be filled by the residents of those areas." As incentives to private industry to open job-producing plants in a poverty area the legislation provided:

Tax credits against the original investment in the plant and machinery; accelerated depreciation schedules for that investment; extra deductions for wages paid to previously unemployed individuals; liberal carry-forward and carry-back allowances; and assistance in training new workers.

The following day Kennedy introduced the housing measure that would do the following:

Construct or rehabilitate 300,000 to 400,000 low-cost housing units in the slums over a seven-year period, at an eventual cost to the Federal Government of $3.3 billion;

Establish through long-term, low-interest loans, rents for these housing units of between $73 and $100 per month;

Provide, at the same time, a net return on industrial investment of between 13 and 15 percent, for those entrepreneurs wishing to build low-rent housing.

As inducements to investors, the bill provided mortgage money from the Housing and Urban Development Department; a reduction of local real-estate taxes; project insurance so that a builder would not suffer any cash loss on the constructed housing; and tax credits and depreciation benefits. The bill also included a provision guaranteeing the initial cost to the Federal Government would not be more than $50 million.

The paranoia of Presidential politics doomed the two bills from the start. The Johnson Administration, after the worst summer yet of urban rioting, was not about to let Robert Kennedy get the credit for coming up with an original plan for the cities. According to both *The Wall Street Journal* and the *New Republic,* the President organized a task force with the specific responsibility of "discrediting" the Kennedy proposals. So when the Finance Committee began three days of public hearings on the housing bill in mid-September, Robert Semple began his front-page dispatch in *The New York Times:*

> The Johnson Administration mounted a concerted attack today on a proposal by Senator Robert F. Kennedy to build more and better low cost housing in the slums through private enterprise.

Robert Weaver, Secretary for Housing and Urban Development, called Kennedy's plan "superfluous," and Joseph Barr, Under Secretary of the Treasury, termed it "a threat to the tax code," and argued that the tax system should not be used to solve what he called "narrow social problems."

Kennedy countered on the next day of hearings with testimony in favor of his legislation by former Treasury Secretary Douglas Dillon; former Commissioner of the Internal Revenue Service Mortimer Caplin;

and Urban League executive director Whitney Young. Dillon, a Republican, directly challenged Barr's phrase "narrow social problems," saying, "The crisis in our cities has created a problem of the highest priority which, so far, has defied solution. Under such circumstances we cannot turn our backs on the use of tax policy, or any other policy, that might help us reach a successful solution."

Three weeks later, the Johnson Administration suddenly announced its own program for involving the private sector in ghetto rehabilitation. Although similar in concept to Kennedy's, it was considerably less ambitious and innovative. Much of the press also felt it was politically motivated, in order to blunt the appeal of Kennedy's program, and Senator Percy's homeownership legislation. The day after the Administration program was announced, Kennedy said to me, "How can they be so petty? I worked on my plan for six months, and we talked to everyone in the Administration in all the relevant agencies. We accepted many of their ideas and put them in our bill. Now they came out with this thing, and the first I hear about it is on television. They didn't even try to work something out together. To them it's all just politics."

In January the White House did call Kennedy and offer to work out a compromise bill. There were several meetings between Johnson's assistant Joseph Califano, Curzan, and tax lawyer Steve Ziegler, a Kennedy adviser. But the Presidential campaign was beginning, mutual trust was absent, and the talks quickly broke down.

By the time of his death, Kennedy's ideas about private enterprise and community development, which sounded so avant-garde in 1966, were becoming the new conventional wisdom among urban reformers and black militants.

The Urban Coalition was organized in August of 1967 on the premise that big business had to join the effort to combat urban poverty. The Ford Foundation began to subsidize experiments in community control, and projects like the New Detroit Committee, Cleveland CORE, and the Restoration Corp. The Kerner Commission Report explicitly endorsed the concept that private enterprise had a unique role to play in renewing slums. In October of 1967, Governor Rockefeller announced that he would ask the state legislature to pass a tax incentive program to attract business and jobs into the ghettos. President Johnson, in his State of the

Union Message of January 17, 1968, called for "a new partnership between government and private industry to train and to hire hard core unemployed persons."

Negro psychologist and educator Kenneth Clark told the Kerner Commission:

"Business and industry are our last hope. They are the most realistic elements of our society. Other areas in our society—government, education, churches, labor—have defaulted in dealing with Negro problems."

Reverend Albert Cleague, the Black Power leader with the largest base in Detroit, has said:*

"We should teach the white establishment to invest in the ghetto just as he would in any other foreign nation. . . . Neo-colonialism is all right; it's the old colonialism, still practiced in Rhodesia and South Africa, that was wrong. The neo-colonialist realizes that the nation in which he invests has to have . . . a just return of the profits, and full ownership over a reasonable length of time."

The 1968 national convention of CORE adopted a platform calling for white capital investment and black-controlled community corporations in the ghettos. CORE also helped draft a 172-page bill that would provide Federal financing for neighborhood controlled corporations in the ghetto. The bill, introduced in July of 1968 by Congressman, now Senator, Charles Goodell, also included a provision for tax credits to private firms willing to set up a business in the ghetto, the ownership of which would eventually be turned over to residents of the ghetto.

But it is much easier for a new approach to become popular with reformers and activists than it is actually to change the pathology of the ghetto itself. It is easier to create an intellectual fashion than it is to create jobs. Or cure disease and narcotics addiction. Or cut through bureaucratic rules and red tape. Or just find a way to guarantee daily garbage collection in the ghetto. The connection between goodwill and healing action is never easy to make. And there are no panaceas for the urban crisis.

* As quoted in *The Second Civil War,* by Garry Willis. New American library, 1968.

Each forward step taken in Bedford-Stuyvesant has required maximum effort. To advance an inch, every available resource had to be concentrated on that one spot. Progress has been slow, slower than the two corporations had expected, slower still since Kennedy's death.

Nevertheless, six months after Kennedy's assassination, two years after the experiment was launched, concrete achievements were finally becoming visible to the ghetto's justly suspicious residents.

Fourteen new, black-owned businesses had opened, creating 570 new jobs. The exteriors of 400 brownstones and tenements had been restored. The work was done by 272 local residents, 250 of whom were later placed in full-time construction jobs. Renovation of the abandoned Sheffield bottling plant was more than half completed. Two Neighborhood Restoration Centers were opened, and providing free advice and legal assistance to the community. Twelve hundred area residents had received vocational training through a manpower program subcontracted to the Opportunities Industrialization Center.

Also, the mortgage pool of $65 million, established by a consortium of 65 banks, had loaned 115 residents $1.7 million in the first four months of operation. IBM located a computer cable plant in the center of Bedford-Stuyvesant, creating 300 new jobs. The City University of New York agreed to build a new community college for 5,000 students in Bedford-Stuyvesant, with control of the planning in the hands of local residents. Three businesses were sponsoring a twice-weekly, citywide television program, on WNEW–TV, called "Inside Bedford-Stuyvesant," viewed by about 500,000 people each week. Construction on the two "super blocks" had begun, after more than 3,000 residents had participated in approving and altering the blueprints. The super blocks include rehabilitated housing, parks, new street lighting, and benches. The plans were drawn up by I. M. Pei, architect of the John F. Kennedy Memorial Library at Harvard.

The theme of many of the eulogies delivered immediately after Robert Kennedy's murder was that the Bedford-Stuyvesant project would be his greatest monument. Whether or not this prophecy is true, it is still too early to tell. The project is so unique, there seems to be no agreed-upon yardstick for measuring its success or failure.

What can be said now is only that the accomplishments of this private, voluntary experiment appear more substantial than any equivalent governmental antislum effort. Thousands of brutalized individuals have been helped and healed. A mood of community and possibility has begun to infuse portions of the ghetto. New eruptions of large-scale violence have been averted.

But the project's impact is still limited. The ghetto is too big, and the project has directly touched the lives of perhaps only 25,000 of Bedford-Stuyvesant's 450,000 inhabitants. The corporate community and the Congress have not responded adequately. If Robert Kennedy were still alive, he would probably walk through the dark ghetto and mutter, This is still *unacceptable. We can do better.*

Robert Kennedy gave a damn, but Bedford-Stuyvesant is still hell.

Vietnam:
Breaking with the Past

Like the transcendent issues of slavery, free silver, and Prohibition in other times, the Vietnam war came to dominate American life during the 1960's. It aborted the hopeful war on poverty, contributed to the climate of domestic violence, and helped to generate the gold crisis. It alienated the generation that was being asked to fight the war. And it created and ruined careers in Washington.

Words like hawk, dove, escalation, and credibility gap leaped into the language. The war began to permeate the entire culture. A library of books was published: history by Fall and Lacouture; polemics by Howard Zinn and Mary McCarthy; analysis by Theodore Draper and David Schoenbrun. Norman Mailer even wrote a novel about an allegorical bear hunt in Alaska, and called it, *Why Are We in Vietnam?*

The nation became two countries. On one day in New York City, several hundred thousand people participated in competing pro- and antiwar demonstrations. The tradition of bipartisan foreign policy ended, and the two political parties split into antagonistic hawk and dove factions. And caught in the eye of the storm was Robert Kennedy, who began the decade helping to fashion the policy of counterinsurgence, and ended it running for President on a platform that pledged "no more Vietnams."

The bloody roots of America's policy of intervention and escalation must be traced back into the bureaucratic bowels of the New Frontier. Vietnam was, according to McGeorge Bundy, the most divisive issue in the Administration of John Kennedy. It was also, I think, even more than the Bay of Pigs, John Kennedy's gravest failure as President.

All the standard histories and memoirs of the Kennedy Administration claim that it was dramatically split into two distinct factions over Vietnam. The "military" group included, at various times, Secretaries Rusk and McNamara; Vice President Johnson; White House Assistants Walt Rostow and McGeorge Bundy; General Paul Harkins, the American military commander in Saigon; Ambassador to South Vietnam Frederick Nolting; John McCone of the CIA; and the Joint Chiefs of Staff, led by General Maxwell Taylor. From the beginning they favored the sending of American combat troops to Vietnam, and since 1961, Taylor and Rostow advocated bombing North Vietnam.

The second group consisted of Roger Hilsman, Averell Harriman, White House aid Michael Forrestal, John Kenneth Galbraith, and Robert Kennedy. They preferred a "political" solution to the war, meaning political and social reforms in South Vietnam, plus the limited and flexible military strategies of counterinsurgency.

President Kennedy is generally painted as leaning toward the political faction, but, at decisive moments, yielding to the demands of the military. As Theodore Sorensen put it in his book, *Kennedy:*

> Formally, Kennedy never made a final negative decision on troops. In typical Kennedy fashion, he made it difficult for any of the pro-intervention advocates to charge him privately with weakness. He ordered the departments to be prepared for the introduction of combat troops, should they prove to be necessary. He steadily expanded the size of the military assistance mission [2,000 at the end of 1961; 15,500 at the end of 1963] by sending in combat support units, air combat and helicopter teams, still more military advisers and instructors, and 600 of the green-hatted Special Forces to train and lead the South Vietnamese in anti-guerrilla tactics.

Arthur Schlesinger, in his book, *A Thousand Days,* also admits that President Kennedy's decision at the start of 1962 "was to place the main emphasis on the military effort. When the social and economic program developed in Washington in 1961 encountered the usual resistance in Saigon, it was soon dropped." But Schlesinger, with extreme charity, also observed that Kennedy "had no choice now but to work within the situation he had inherited," an alibi he never made for Lyndon Johnson, who inherited a more difficult situation.

What most of the histories of the Kennedy Administration tend to neglect, however, was that there was always a third possible alternative—negotiation with the National Liberation Front and North Vietnam for a settlement because the war could not be won. This point of view was advocated within the government by Chester Bowles and George Ball, both of whom feared America being drawn into an escalating land war in Asia. This view received implicit, or indirect support, by the reporting of several young, independent American correspondents in Saigon, including David Halberstam, who later was awarded the Pulitzer Prize for his dispatches.

In the spring of 1962, Bowles, then, in effect, Ambassador-at-large, proposed to Kennedy and Rusk that the Administration make a strenuous effort at a negotiated settlement of the war, and, at the same time, seek the neutralization of all of Southeast Asia, including Burma, Thailand, and South Vietnam. Roger Hilsman, in his revealing memoir, *To Move a Nation,* described the President's reaction to Bowles' formula:

> He accepted the concept as a far-seeing expression of the ultimate goal for Southeast Asia toward which we should work, but . . . its time had not yet come.

But Bowles, instead of being rewarded for his foresight, was instead later demoted, and exiled as Ambassador to India. Bowles, who like Stevenson did not belong to the so-called "realistic" or "tough-minded" school of liberals, had, in fact, been out of favor with the Kennedys ever since his private reservations about the Bay of Pigs adventure found their way into public print.

By late 1962, Halberstam, and his colleagues, Peter Arnett, Malcolm Browne, and Neil Sheehan, were coming to the conclusion that the Diem government was irrational, hopelessly corrupt, and the war could not be won as long as Diem remained in power. This view, however, was being aggressively rebutted by the older group of Saigon correspondents and visitors like Kenneth Crawford, Marguerite Higgins, Frank Coniff, and Bob Considine.* This was largely a generational split, later to be repeated in Washington, in the liberal community, and finally in the nation at large. Its immediate significance was that it provided President

---

* Halberstam says that a major reason for the division along generational lines was that the younger, more ambitious reporters simply got out of Saigon more and into the countryside.

Kennedy with an independent source of facts and opinions about the war. Unfortunately, he rejected it, since it conflicted with what his own advisers were telling him.

But he did take the Saigon dissenters seriously. Hilsman reports that before his December, 1962, visit to Vietnam, President Kennedy asked him to go and see the critical correspondents privately "to see what we in Washington might do to help improve their difficult situation and also, he had made a point of saying, 'Find out how they think the war is going.'"

But the conflicted Kennedy also tried to talk *The New York Times* into pulling Halberstam out of Saigon. And Edward Weintal and Charles Bartlett, in their book, *Facing the Brink,* quote the President as saying of Halberstam, "I'll be damned if I intend to let my foreign policy be run by a twenty-seven-year-old reporter." (Despite the President's anger, Halberstam kept receiving encouraging missives in Saigon from White House assistant Fred Dutton, who later became one of Robert Kennedy's more influential confidants.)

During 1961 and 1962 Robert Kennedy was a true believer in the vanguard theories of counterinsurgency. He read, and often quoted, Mao and Che Guevera. Like the President, he was deeply influenced by the writings of British guerrilla fighter and diplomat, Sir Robert Thompson. And he was partially responsible for the expansion and upgrading of the Special Forces (Green Berets) over the strong opposition of the old-line generals and strategists of the Pentagon, and the Joint Chiefs.

It is necessary to recall now that, back in 1961, counterinsurgency was regarded by men like the Kennedys and the bright young men in the State Department to be an original, flexible, and even humanistic concept to remedy the Dulles nostrums of massive retaliation and nuclear capability. And that social and political reform was an integral part of the concept. Counterinsurgency was in harmony with the ethos and style of the New Frontier: fresh, tough, and practical. Its charter could be found in John Kennedy's celebrated Inaugural Address:

> Let every nation know, whether it wishes us well or ill, that we shall pay any price, bear any burden, meet any hardship, support any friend, oppose any foe to assure the survival and success of liberty.

In February of 1962 Robert Kennedy visited Southeast Asia, and wherever he went, he was quoted in enthusiastic support of the American military role in Vietnam. At a press conference in Hong Kong, Kennedy asserted bluntly, "The solution there [Vietnam] lies in our winning it. This is what the President intends to do." He gave similar militaristic and cocky comments to the press corps in Saigon.

But at the same time, he was told by the younger members of the embassy and military staff that the pacification program was not working, that the war was being won by the Vietcong, that Diem was despised by the people, and that the senior American military personnel did not understand the nature of a guerrilla war. These were the seeds of the first doubts in Kennedy's mind. Their flowering would be years away. But they were the beginning of his skepticism about official memos, statistics, and White Papers about Vietnam. The contest for Robert Kennedy's mind on the question of Vietnam began here.

By the summer of 1963 the political and military situation within South Vietnam began to deteriorate badly, and it was becoming obvious that the President could not keep up his juggling act between the military and political factions inside his own Administration.

The Buddhist majority in South Vietnam began to demonstrate against Diem's dictatorial regime, and against his increasing religious persecution. In retaliation, Diem's troops broke up several peaceful Buddhist rallies, killing eight people in Hue. The U.S.–trained South Vietnamese Special Forces also raided the sacred Buddhist pagodas. When several Buddhist monks immolated themselves in sacrificial protest against Diem's repression, Madame Nhu, Diem's powerful sister-in-law, ridiculed the immolations as "barbecue shows," and proposed that David Halberstam follow their example. She even offered to provide the matches and gasoline. At the same time, the Vietcong, more clearly than ever before, began to score military victories, and win the backing of the disaffected peasants in the countryside.

These events began to push President Kennedy, haltingly and uncomfortably, away from further support of the Diem government. On June 27 he named the Republican Henry Cabot Lodge to be the new American Ambassador to South Vietnam, replacing Frederick Nolting, who had become a crony of Diem's. On Saturday, August 24, George Ball, Hilsman, Harriman, and Forrestal sent Lodge a secret and subsequently controversial cable, recommending that he should not try to block any spontaneous attempt to overthrow Diem. ("Do not abort.") The draft of the cable, however, had not been read by Taylor, Mc-

Namara, Rusk, or John McCone of the CIA. The President was in Hyannis Port, and Forrestal read him the text over the telephone.

By Monday, the Administration, in Kennedy's phrase, had "fallen apart." There was an acrimonious National Security Council meeting that morning at the White House. Hilsman reported the President as being "annoyed both at the possibility the government might have moved too fast, and at the signs of disagreement among his advisers." Schlesinger wrote that the President "felt rather angrily that he had been pressed too hard and fast." The reliable Weintal and Bartlett book describes the NSC meeting more colorfully:

> McNamara, McCone and Taylor were furious . . . Nolting, who had weekended in Virginia after his return from Honolulu, was on hand and he bluntly denounced the Harriman-Hilsman-Forrestal cable as an improvident act. Harriman yelled at him to shut up. Kennedy sternly interjected that he wanted to hear what the ambassador had to say. The agitation at the meeting was compounded with surprise that nothing had happened in Saigon. The fuse had been lit—why hadn't the bomb exploded?

Schlesinger's summary of the meeting is similar, and he concludes it with the observation that the President "began a process of pulling away from the cable of August 24th."

What is significant, I think, is that in none of the accounts of this meeting, or of any of the subsequent NSC meetings, is there any evidence that anyone at the highest levels of the Kennedy Administration was suggesting direct negotiations with the Vietcong, or less military involvement. There appears to have been no serious reevaluation of the theoretical assumptions of our Vietnam commitment: interventionism, anti-Communism, and limited war. Even the most sensible, antiescalation spokesmen in these meetings, like Hilsman, appear to have been primarily interested in proving counterinsurgency worked as an alternative to limited, conventional, or nuclear war. And as a historic refutation of Mao's theory of wars of national liberation.

The NSC convened again in a crisis atmosphere on August 31, with Rusk chairing the meeting, since the President was again at Hyannis Port. According to Hilsman's description of the session in his book, *To Move a Nation:*

> The Secretary of State said in his opinion the disaffection had not yet spilled over from the cities to affect the war effort. . . . McNamara,

Taylor and the Joint Chiefs of Staff were not so convinced as we [The Hilsman-Harriman faction] that guerilla warfare was fundamentally political. They were less worried about the consequences of a continuation of Diem's and Nhu's policies of repression, and they were more sympathetic to the argument that Vietnam really needed a certain amount of authoritarianism if it was to beat the Vietcong. But it was the question of how the war was going that stirred up the most emotion. McNamara and Taylor, especially, had made so many public statements that we were winning, that they interpreted any suggestion that we were not, as a criticism of their judgment, and of the whole Pentagon effort. . . .

So, with his advisers divided and indecisive, Kennedy suddenly appeared on Walter Cronkite's network newscast on September 2, and settled most of the diplomatic and bureaucratic disputes:

I don't think that unless a greater effort is made to win popular support that the war can be won out there. In the final analysis, it is their war. They are the ones who have to win it or lose it. We can help them, we can give them equipment, we can send our men out there as advisers, but they have to win it, the people of Vietnam, against the Communists. . . . We are prepared to assist them, but I don't think the war can be won unless the people support the effort, and, in my opinion, in the last two months, the government has gotten out of touch with the people.

Four days later the NSC met again, and Robert Kennedy, for the first time, raised within the government the possibility of American withdrawal from Vietnam. He raised it more as an option to be considered, rather than as a policy preferable to others.

Kennedy's suggestion probably did not reflect any fundamental shift in his thinking about Vietnam, since his first cautious, public reservations about the war did not come till 1965, and he did not pronounce the war as immoral until 1967. Kennedy's NSC comments were probably more an index of his temperament and intelligence, than his politics. He was appalled by the corruption and military weakness of the Diem regime. The courage and determination of the Buddhist movement, with its self-immolations, must have appealed to Kennedy. And his detached, pragmatic judgment probably saved him from the self-deceptions about imminent military victory that plagued most of the other NSC members. It is also possible that Kennedy's remarks reflected a change in the President's thinking in the days following the September 2 telecast. According to Hilsman's account of the September 6 meeting:

During the Cuban missile crisis, it had been the Attorney General who had asked some of the more fundamental and wiser questions, and he did so again at this meeting. The first and fundamental question, he felt, was what we were doing in Vietnam. As he understood it, we were there to help the people resisting a Communist take-over.* The first question was whether a Communist take-over could be successfully resisted with any government. If it could not, now was the time to get out of Vietnam entirely, rather than waiting.

At the end of September, Secretary McNamara and General Taylor made another frenetic "fact-finding" mission to Vietnam. In Saigon, Ambassador Lodge and General Harkins gave conflicting testimony about the state of the war, but their differences were more tactical than philosophical. Both felt the war was still being won, but Lodge favored more political pressure on Diem for reform.

On October 2 McNamara briefed a NSC meeting at the White House, and the following statement was released to the press at its conclusion:

"The military program in South Vietnam has made progress and is sound in principle. . . . Secretary McNamara and General Taylor reported that in their judgment 'the major part of the United States military task can be completed by the end of 1965 . . .' They reported that by the end of this year [1963] the U.S. program for training Vietnamese should have progressed to the point that one thousand U.S. military personnel assigned to South Vietnam can be withdrawn. . . ."

On November 1 Diem and Nhu were overthrown and murdered in a coup plotted by South Vietnamese generals.

What role, if any, the CIA or the American Embassy played in the coup remains a matter of historical dispute. Schlesinger has written that, "It is important to state clearly that the coup of November 1st, 1963, was entirely planned and carried out by the Vietnamese. Neither the American Embassy nor the CIA was involved in the instigation or execution." Ambassador Nolting, however, has alleged that the plotters were "encouraged by the United States government." When I asked Robert Kennedy whether "the American government had anything to do

---

* Hilsman's paraphrase of Kennedy again betrays the limits of even the "good-guys" faction within the government. Communist is always capitalized. Were all the anti-Diem guerrillas committed Communists? And an emotionally charged word like "take-over" is used, rather than civil war or revolution.

with the overthrow of Diem," he replied enigmatically, after a pregnant silence, "Not in Washington."

"I saw the President soon after he heard that Diem and Nhu were dead," Schlesinger wrote in his book. "He was somber and shaken. I had not seen him so depressed since the Bay of Pigs. No doubt he realized that Vietnam was his great failure in foreign policy, and that he had never really given it his full attention."

Three weeks later Kennedy himself was dead, and Lyndon Johnson was sworn in as President.

Mystery still shrouds the precise point in time when the fateful decision to begin bombing North Vietnam was actually made. The official government version is that the bombings were a direct retaliation for the Vietcong mortar attack on the Special Forces camp at Pleiku, which killed eight Americans on February 7, 1965.* Richard Goodwin and Bill Moyers, the two most dovish White House staff members at the time, also maintain that, despite considerable contingency planning, the hard, final decision to bomb was not made until after the assault on Pleiku, and largely as a result of the pro-bombing position of McGeorge Bundy, who was in Saigon at the time.

But there is evidence that the decision was actually made much earlier, perhaps even while Johnson was still promising the country "no wider war" during the 1964 Presidential campaign.

Tom Wicker, in his book, *JFK & LBJ: A Study of the Influence of Personality on Politics,* wrote:

> In the fall of 1964, Lyndon Johnson may or may not have known that he was not going to deliver on his promises that he would not "go North." He told Charles Roberts of *Newsweek* that he had decided to bomb North Vietnam as early as October, 1964. He told me in 1965 that as early as October, 1964, the targets had been chosen for attack . . . as early as 1961, Walt W. Rostow had been an ardent advocate of bombing, and his proposals and justifications had been brought to Johnson's attention. General Taylor, who had succeeded Lodge as Ambassador to Saigon in 1965, advocated bombing strikes in October, 1964, after earlier opposition.

* This brought the total of American fatalities up to 294. As of February, 1969, it was 31,000.

And Weintal and Bartlett wrote in *Facing the Brink:*

> It was not publicly known at the time that, since March of 1964, the government had a plan for "measured pressure" against North Vietnam. The plan had been thrashed out by an inter-agency task force and was to become the blueprint for escalation."

During 1964 and early 1965 there was a modulating chorus of prophetic warnings against expanding the war. In October of 1964 George Ball was apparently sufficiently aware of escalation planning to write a hundred-page memo to the President urging withdrawal from the "gluepot" of Southeast Asia, or at least not to expand the war, via air power, to the North. On March 10, 1964, Senator Ernest Gruening urged on the floor of the Senate, "Let us get out of Vietnam on as good terms as possible—but let us get out." And on May 28, 1964, Walter Lippmann wrote in his *Washington Post* column:

> It is not easy for any country to repair its mistakes, especially those in which it has invested lives, money and moral judgments. But the original mistake in Southeast Asia has to be repaired. The way to do this is to go to a conference. . . . The military outlook in South Vietnam is dismal beyond words.

Kennedy's views on Vietnam during this period seemed to have been drifting slowly from support of the war toward an unsettled transition. At one point in mid-1964 he asked President Johnson to appoint him Ambassador to South Vietnam, something that is now titillating to consider in retrospect.

Vietnam was not an issue in Kennedy's New York Senatorial campaign against Kenneth Keating. However, on a radio interview show two weeks before the election, he was asked about Vietnam and gave a rather muddled and ambiguous response:

> Well, I've given advice before as to what I think needs to be done. I think that . . . [there] has to be the support of the [Vietnamese] people for the military effort that is being made, [and there] has to be support of the people for the government. . . . I think the people have to feel that there is political progress being made and that they can be protected in their communities, protected in their villages, and I think once there is that confidence, then I think the war will be won.

On February 17, 1965, ten days after the first air raids against North Vietnam, and while Washington was rife with rumors of a major new escalation, four Senators—Frank Church, Gaylord Nelson, George Mc-Govern, and Stephen Young of Ohio—rose to speak against escalation, in support of immediate negotiations to settle the war, and for the neutralization of Southeast Asia, which Bowles had urged in 1962. Kennedy, a freshman Senator of one month, did not speak, and on February 28, Johnson declared a policy of continuous air strikes against military targets in North Vietnam. And on July 28, the President announced he was sending 50,000 men to Vietnam.

The bombing missions created the first stirrings of an antiwar movement in America. The teach-ins against the war began in mid-March at the University of Michigan, and quickly spread in a chain reaction to several hundred other campuses. On April 17, about 25,000 people, mostly students, marched on Washington in a peace protest sponsored by Students for a Democratic Society (SDS). Among those who addressed the rally in the late-afternoon shadow of the Washington Monument were Senator Gruening, Professor Staughton Lynd, SNCC's Bob Parris Moses, maverick journalist I. F. Stone, and Paul Potter of SDS.

These spiraling events apparently made some impact on Kennedy. On May 6, he spoke about the war for the first time as a member of the Senate. His remarks were made during the debate on a new appropriation for the war, and came after his colleagues Wayne Morse, Ernest Gruening, and Gaylord Nelson declared their intention of voting against the subsidy. Kennedy said he intended to vote for it, but added that he felt the Administration should work harder for "honorable negotiations" between the Vietcong and the South Vietnam government. He also said, "I believe that we have erred for some time in regarding Vietnam as purely a military problem, when in its essential aspects it is also a political and diplomatic problem. I would wish, for example, that the request for appropriations today had made provisions for programs to better the lives of the people of South Vietnam."

Speaking at the commencement ceremonies of Queens College, New York, on June 15, 1965, Kennedy stated:

> It is not helpful, it is not honest, to protest the war in Vietnam as if it were a simple and easy question. . . . But the complexity and difficulty of any situation should not keep you from speech or action.

By making the right to dissent an issue, Kennedy was able to postpone taking a position on the heart of the matter, the bombings of North

Vietnam, and the disinclination of the American government to negotiate with the Vietcong. A similar ploy was used by Senator Edward Kennedy during 1967, when he placed the plight of the two million Vietnamese refugees at the center of his concerns, rather than the bombing, escalation, negotiations, a coalition government in Saigon, or the undemocratic nature of the South Vietnam elections.

But Kennedy did feel a visceral sympathy with the campus dissenters against the war, and it finally got him into a damaging controversy. On November 5, at a news conference at the University of Southern California, he was asked whether he approved of radical student groups sending blood to North Vietnamese victims of American bombing.

"I'm willing to give blood to anyone who needs it," Kennedy replied. Within hours Barry Goldwater denounced Kennedy's answer as "close to treason."

By the start of 1966 Kennedy was deeply troubled by the larger dimensions of the war, and the price it was exacting on domestic antipoverty programs. But he still had no alternative policy to offer. He felt an attack by him on the Administration's policy would give encouragement to the enemy, split the Democratic Party, and hurt his own career, since the war, according to the polls, had the support of a majority of the country. Privately, Kennedy was becoming devastatingly critical of Johnson and Rusk, but publicly he kept mute.

During the 1965–1966 period of quietude, the private struggle for Kennedy's thinking on Vietnam, that had begun in Saigon in 1962, grew sharper. Kennedy interpreted the departure from the State Department of Roger Hilsman early in 1964 as an omen of military ascendancy. This was confirmed for him by the diminished influence of Harriman and Forrestal, and the corresponding elevation of Rostow and Rusk. The decision early in 1965 of the Senate colleague whose judgment he most respected, George McGovern, to break with the Administration's policy also made an impact on him. But the strongest pressure on Kennedy came from the events in Vietnam, the constantly expanding scope of the war, and its violence. Finally, Kennedy's new role as New York Senator, and potential rival of the President's, played its unconscious role in his thinking.

At the same time there were powerful countervailing pressures on him in favor of keeping the Vietnam commitment. It was his brother's originally. Some of his closest friends were still fully in favor of it: Douglas Dillon; Lord Harlech; Joseph Alsop; General Taylor; Robert McNamara; and his brother Ted.

According to columnist Joseph Kraft, who was especially close to Kennedy during this period, "The controlling thing that kept him silent all through 1965, I think, was his genuine desire to avoid a public fight with Johnson."

There had been one episode, in July of 1965, that demonstrated Kennedy's almost neurotic ambivalence about risking a public break with the President's Vietnam policy. Adam Walinsky had worked for several days on a speech about guerrilla warfare, scheduled to be delivered by Kennedy on July 9 at the International Police Academy. The final draft contained several direct criticisms of the Administration's Vietnam policy, including the passage:

> Victory in a revolutionary war is not won by escalation, but by de-escalation. . . . Air attacks by a government of its own villages are likely to be far more dangerous and costly to the people than is the individual and selective terrorism of an insurgent movement. . . .

Kennedy approved of the text, his office mimeographed copies, and they were delivered by messenger to newspaper and wire service offices in Washington. But before the speech was actually given, Kennedy personally deleted the critical passages and did not deliver them. The wire services, however, had already written and moved on their tickers lengthy dispatches about the speech, leading with the "break" with the Administration over Vietnam.

By January 10, 1966, when the second session of the 89th Congress opened, it was apparent to the doves that after eleven months, the bombing had not achieved any of its stated objectives—stopping infiltration into South Vietnam, forcing Hanoi to the negotiating table, and shoring up morale in South Vietnam. On the contrary, it was making new enemies for the Administration at home and around the globe. Congress reconvened in the middle of a bombing pause of indefinite duration, announced by the President on Christmas Eve, and followed by a flurry of mysterious diplomatic activity, and rumors of an impending peace.

The Senatorial opposition to the war, originally only Gruening and Morse, had meanwhile grown to about twenty, including three of the

Senate's most respected foreign policy specialists, Mike Mansfield, George Aiken, and J. W. Fulbright, chairman of the Foreign Relations Committee. On January 26, Senator Vance Hartke of Indiana drafted a letter asking the President to consult the Senate before he resumed the bombings. Fourteen other Senators affixed their names to the letter, and late in the afternoon it was sent to the White House by messenger. Neither Mansfield, Fulbright, Aiken, or Kennedy would sign the letter, although the text quoted Fulbright and Aiken against a resumption of the air raids. Instead of signing the Hartke letter, Kennedy released his own statement, which was ambiguous on whether the bombings should be resumed, but warned, "If we regard bombing as the answer to Vietnam, we are headed straight for disaster."

Johnson, infuriated that Hartke, a former friend and protégé, was assuming leadership of the divided and timorous rebels in the Senate, curtly responded to the letter two days later with a calculated snub of the Senate as an institution. In a two paragraph note, the President thanked the fifteen Senators for "this expression of opinion," and asked them to read a longer statement sent to a group of seventy-seven House members, who had respectfully asked for negotiations the week before.

On the same day that Johnson answered the Hartke letter, the Foreign Relations Committee began public hearings on Vietnam on the fourth floor of the new Senate Office Building. The technical justification for the hearings was the request for another $272-million appropriation for Vietnam. But in reality, the hearings were intended by the committee chairman, Senator Fulbright, as a seminar for the nation on the war. Dean Rusk and General Maxwell Taylor came to testify in support of the Administration's policy, and George Kennan and General James Gavin came to testify against it. The television networks carried large chunks of the hearings live into millions of homes, opening up the war to legitimate debate across the country for the first time. (In the first three weeks after the hearings concluded, the committee received 20,000 letters.)

Two days after the hearings opened, the President summoned the Congressional leadership to the White House to inform them that he was resuming the bombing of North Vietnam. He asked if there were any objections. Majority Leader Mansfield dissented first, and Johnson listened impatiently. When Fulbright began to speak, Johnson turned his back and began a conversation with Secretary McNamara.

The hearings, however, with their inherent drama of conflicting personalities, began to transfix the nation. The hunger for reasons and explanations for Vietnam was finally being satisfied.

The President counterattacked in typical overkill fashion. On Friday, February 4, he announced at an impromptu press conference, which knocked the committee hearings off the air, that he was flying to Honolulu the next day for a conference with General Nguyen Cao Ky, the new thirty-three-year-old boss of Saigon's military government. When the press openly speculated that the Honolulu conference was scheduled just to push Fulbright's hearings off the front pages, Vice President Humphrey responded by asserting, "This is one of the most important meetings of modern times, a blueprint of hope."

The final day of the Vietnam hearings was Friday, February 18, and Dean Rusk was the witness. The national television audience was treated to a skillful debate between two Southerners, two Rhodes Scholars, the man John Kennedy appointed Secretary of State, and the man he almost appointed to that position. For a while Robert Kennedy, absorbed, occasionally muttering at Rusk's unflappable image, watched the civilized diplomatic duel between the two men on the portable television set in his office. Kennedy felt that Fulbright, McCarthy, Morse, and the other doves on the committee were too vague and intellectual, and failed to ask the most vital concrete questions. What was the future role of the NLF going to be? And what was the United States prepared to give up in order to get a negotiated peace in Vietnam?

For the afternoon session, Kennedy walked over to the crowded hearing room, and sat slouched in the last row, shaking his head, and making a few notes. At 5:20 P.M. the hearings adjourned, and Robert Kennedy, lost in reverie, wandered into his office to tell Adam Walinsky that he had decided to put out a statement on Vietnam the next morning. This elated the ebullient Walinsky, who had been preparing an antiwar statement for several weeks, and was pressing hard for his boss to release it.

Recognizing that Johnson as President had infinitely more political power than he did, Kennedy had no desire to get into a public quarrel with the Chief Executive. Naïvely Kennedy concluded that he could make a statement about Vietnam that would be judged on the issues, and not be personalized, and dragged into the jungle of Presidential politics.

On Saturday morning, February 19, Robert Kennedy called a press conference. There was no sense of tension in Kennedy's office before he read his statement. His mood, and his staff's mood, was relaxed. After all, he was only going to say what twenty other Senators had been saying, what Eugene McCarthy had said the week before without generating a single headline. Kennedy was so calm about the press conference that he had sent his wife up to Stowe, Vermont, a skiing resort, the night before, and planned to join her right after giving his statement.

Sitting in the front row was I. F. Stone, resembling a professor watching his unruly but favorite pupil reading his prize-winning essay. Kennedy's careful, moderate statement was seven pages long. He proposed that a reasonable compromise in Vietnam would have to involve "a share of power and responsibility" for the Vietcong in the future political life of South Vietnam. At the same time Kennedy rejected withdrawal as "impossible for this country," but emphasized, "We must reveal enough of our intentions to Hanoi to eliminate any reasonable fear that we ask them to talk only to demand surrender."

After reading the statement Kennedy left Washington to join his wife in Vermont, convinced there would be few headlines the next morning. This, however, turned out to be one of his less astute judgments. The Johnson Administration, already edgy over the impact of the Fulbright hearings, and preoccupied by the fact that Kennedy was the only war critic in the country with legions to match his rhetoric, gave way to its instinct for overkill.

Vice President Humphrey called a press conference in Wellington, New Zealand, to brand Kennedy's formula for a coalition government, "Like putting a fox in a chicken coop," or "an arsonist in a fire department." The influence of politics and personality on policy was revealed when George Ball, an original skeptic about escalation, but loyal to Johnson, said that a coalition government that included the Vietcong was bound to disintegrate rapidly into a Communist government. But at the same time, Maxwell Taylor, a hawk, but a close personal friend of Kennedy's, released several statements designed to protect Kennedy's exposed flank. He told the *New York Herald Tribune* that "Senator Kennedy's position is very, very close to what I consider my position." And he told several Washington reporters that he favored "unconditional negotiations, followed by free elections."

The attack which most deeply wounded Kennedy came from Presidential special assistant McGeorge Bundy, who quoted his own brother against Kennedy. Bundy quoted John Kennedy's abstract axiom about popular front governments in Europe—"I do not believe that any democrat can successfully ride that tiger"—to discredit Robert's Vietnam proposal. This was a distortion of the record since John Kennedy had spoken frequently in 1962 in favor of a coalition government in Laos, a much more relevent precedent. Kennedy later told me he could "not forgive" Bundy for such a "cheap trick."

The three days following Kennedy's statement were filled with a torrent of confusing press conferences, backgrounders, and clarifying statements. Kennedy rushed back from his skiing vacation to try and defend himself against the cross fire of his critics. He called dozens of newspapers and magazines, and appeared on the "Today" television show to explain his complex position. The general impression was that Kennedy got the worst of the political exchange because of the subtleties of his own position, and the potency of the simplistic anti-Communist rhetoric of his opponents.

On Tuesday, February 22, White House press secretary Bill Moyers, a foe of escalation and a friend of Kennedy, injected himself into the dispute as a peacemaker. At his regular afternoon press briefing he told reporters that he saw "no real disagreement" between Kennedy and the President, "if Senator Kennedy did not propose a coalition government with Communist participation before elections are held."

Kennedy quickly telephoned Moyers, said he agreed with that point, and then summoned his own press conference to announce, "I find no disagreement between what Mr. Moyers said and what I have said." A few months later, reflecting on his first guerrilla skirmish with the Administration over the way, Kennedy said:

"I think now that whole episode hurt me politically. What I said wasn't popular with most people in the country. Also, I wasn't ready for the blowup it caused. Maybe I hadn't worded my statement as clearly as I should have. And I was shocked that the press gave equal weight to what I said, and to what White House staff members like Bundy and Moyers said. That way Johnson was able to keep above the battle and not get involved while I was debating with his staff."

For the rest of 1966 Kennedy avoided talking about Vietnam. He made no formal speeches about the war. When questioners, and sometimes hecklers, asked him about Vietnam, he gave vague and evasive answers like "I have some reservations about the government's policy," or "These are all complicated matters." In the fall he campaigned extensively across the country for Congressional candidates, and the October 17 *Wall Street Journal* observed, "Actually, Mr. Kennedy has been careful of late to avoid sharp attacks on the President. When he expressed doubts about Vietnam policy he always stresses that 'these are very complex problems, with no simple solutions.' "

But on through 1966 the war continued to escalate: 150,000 more American troops were committed to Vietnam, bringing the total by the end of the year to over 350,000. The air war was expanded, and new targets added, many of them population centers. And the first cutbacks in the Great Society's domestic programs were announced in the fall.

On December 16 I had about an hour's conversation with Kennedy about Vietnam. I was by then deeply involved in the antiwar movement. I had joined the April, 1965, march against the war, and had made the decision to withhold part of my 1966 income tax in protest against the continuing escalation. I had written and spoken against the war, and felt that Kennedy, more than any other liberal politician, had it within his power to take a fifth of the nation with him into political opposition to the war.

I began the conversation, mistakenly now I think, by making several abstract arguments against the premises of the war. I suggested that counterinsurgency never worked because it could not generate serious economic and political reforms, that interventionism was bad in principle, and that the domino theory was a product of anti-Communist paranoia. These arguments clearly bored Kennedy, and he did not try to conceal his impatience.

But as soon as I began to make concrete, precise points against the war, he began to nod enthusiastically, and even try to take away the conversation. He agreed that the South Vietnamese army was ineffectual, and that we were probably losing rather than winning the war. He agreed that any further escalation created the danger of greater participation by the Soviets or Chinese. And he agreed that the war was causing severe erosion of domestic antipoverty programs.

On the decisive question of the bombings of North Vietnam, Kennedy was still conflicted. "I said in Berkeley recently that the bombings were not immoral. They were just counterproductive," Kennedy said. "Now I just don't know. They certainly haven't diminished our casualties. I have to have another talk with McNamara and Taylor, and get some figures I can trust on infiltration rates into the South."

Finally, at the close of our talk, I made a very clumsy emotional statement to the effect that he was carrying, whether or not he liked it, or realized it, a burden of trust from people like myself, who felt the war could be stopped only when people like him stood up against Johnson. And that the bombing was a separate and particular horror.

"You haven't said anything for a year. When will you talk again?" I asked. He replied:

"If I become convinced that by making another speech that I could do some good, I would make it tomorrow. But the last time I spoke I didn't have any influence on policy, and I was hurt politically. I'm afraid that by speaking out I just make Lyndon do the opposite, out of spite. He hates me so much that if I asked for snow, he would make rain, just because it was me. But, maybe I will have to say something. The bombing is getting worse all the time now."

As I left him that day, my essential ambivalence about Kennedy was at its height. His personal qualities of decency, anguish, and intelligence remained immensely appealing. But his reluctance to speak was unforgivable. I regarded the bombing as criminal, and its sponsors no less guilty, morally, than the Germans sentenced at Nuremberg. Kennedy, although he wasn't verbalizing it, was placing his own political future above the dead, burned, and homeless of Vietnam. He was still a good and decent man, but trapped by the conventional ambitions of conventional politics. How harshly to judge him for his compromises about the war remained a dilemma that troubled me the rest of his life. Should he be measured against my absolute and abstract standards, or only against other flawed liberal politicians? Man's character is his fate, Saul Bellow wrote in *The Adventures of Augie March*. But Kennedy's character and fate were in conflict.

I was also of two minds about Kennedy's remark that he would consult with McNamara and Taylor. I was astonished that after four years of unfounded optimism and faulty judgments, Kennedy still prized their counsel. But I also felt sympathy for how difficult it must have been for Kennedy to break with intimate friends like McNamara, Taylor, Harriman, and Katzenbach over the issue of Vietnam. And deeper than that, break with a policy that, although grown distorted and deformed, was still conceived by his brother's Administration, and was still being executed by his brother's appointees. To risk the future, Robert Kennedy first had to repudiate the past.

At the start of 1967, the full torment and tumult that the war brought home to America was being felt. Draft cards had been burned and people had immolated themselves in America. Blood had been spilled on American streets and campuses, as demonstrators fought with police and supporters of the war. A third of the Harvard graduating class indicated they wouldn't fight this war. Several thousands had gone into exile, and many more thousands had flooded Kennedy's office with desperate and despairing letters.

By the time Kennedy left on January 28, 1967, for a ten-day tour of European capitals, his mind was almost made up to give an antiwar address that would finally burn all his bridges to the Administration. The events of the next three weeks would convince him that he actually should have broken with Johnson's policy of escalation much earlier.

On January 28, Wilfred Burchett, the Australian Communist journalist, published an interview with Nguyen Duy Trinh, North Vietnam's foreign minister. In the interview Trinh told Burchett, "If the United States really wants talks, it must first halt unconditionally the bombing raids, and all other acts of war, against the Democratic Republic of Vietnam . . . if the bombings cease completely, good and favorable conditions will be created for talks. . . ."

Because of Burchett's close relationship with the government of North Vietnam, the interview was read by almost all diplomats and journalists; it marked for the first time a change in North Vietnam's negotiating position.

On February 1, Robert Kennedy was in Paris, where he had a meeting with Etienne Manac'h, the director of Far East Affairs of the French Foreign Office, and with John Dean, the first secretary and resident Vietnam scholar of the American Embassy. The fullest and most accurate account of that now famous meeting was published by David Kraslow and Stuart Loory in their book, *The Secret Search for Peace in Vietnam.* For that reason I take the liberty of quoting from it at some length.

Despite the uncomfortable turbulence in the upper echelons of their respective governments, Dean and Manac'h found their relationship salutary. This was to become apparent on February 1 when Dean accompanied Kennedy to the Manac'h meeting. Manac'h had an important communication for the United States government from the North Vietnamese government. He had received it within the previous two or three days from Mai Van Bo, the chief of North Vietnam's diplomatic mission in Paris. The message was this:

The Hanoi government wanted the Johnson Administration to realize that the interview Nguyen Duy Trinh had given Wilfred Burchett was important. Trinh had been sincere in saying talks "could" follow an unconditional cessation of the bombing. The interview did indeed represent a shift in the bargaining position of the Hanoi government.

Manac'h had held this information to himself for a short time rather than relay it immediately to Dean so that it could be delivered in Kennedy's presence. He might have felt that transmitting the message with Kennedy's knowledge would assure that it received the greatest possible consideration in Washington.

Ironically, though Kennedy had been saying that a "critical" period for negotiations was at hand, he very nearly missed the point of his meeting with Manac'h, as one source recalled later. The senator, of course, was unfamiliar with the intricate details of Vietnam diplomacy and he had difficulty following the conversation in French which Dean was translating for his benefit. But Dean grasped the possible significance immediately. In fact, he interrupted Manac'h to make sure he had not misunderstood.

Was Manac'h saying that Bo had said the statement was "important"? Dean asked.

Precise, Manac'h replied.

That point settled, Manac'h went on to discuss ideas for a three-stage peace negotiation. Some confusion developed over whether this was a North Vietnamese proposal, but American officials later said they understood from the beginning that these were simply Manac'h's own ideas of what might be acceptable to Hanoi for a long-range solution in Vietnam.

The meeting over, Dean left Kennedy and hurried back to the embassy to draft a memorandum on the conversation. He returned to Manac'h's office later in the day, showed him the memorandum and told him it would be transmitted to Washington. He asked Manac'h to read it carefully. Manac'h verified the account and then reiterated that Bo had attached great importance to the Trinh interview. That night Dean cabled a two-page memorandum on the meeting to the State Department.*

Kennedy returned to the United States on February 4, amidst growing

* This was the cable that was leaked to *Newsweek*.

speculation that he had received a "peace feeler" from Hanoi. The next evening advance copies of *Newsweek* were distributed to newspaper offices, containing the story of Kennedy's meeting in Paris with Dean and Manac'h, and Monday morning's *The New York Times* made that story its right-hand lead under the headline:

> Hanoi Said to Give
> Kennedy a Signal
> It's Ready to Talk

President Johnson immediately jumped to the conclusion that Kennedy had intentionally leaked the story in order to embarrass him politically. This, however, was not true. A middle-level State Department official, with no political motives, had leaked John Dean's cable to Washington to Edward Weintal, *Newsweek*'s industrious diplomatic correspondent.

Kennedy, fearful his Vietnam policy dissent would be tainted by Democratic Party politics, phoned the White House early in the morning of February 6, offering to see the President and clarify the *Newsweek* story. Kennedy had an "unsatisfactory" conversation with White House aide Marvin Watson, who kept insisting that Kennedy state formally that he was "requesting" an audience with the President.

About an hour later, Kennedy received a call from his friend and former deputy in the Justice Department, Nicholas Katzenbach, who was now Johnson's Under Secretary of State. They agreed to have lunch in Kennedy's office. Later, in an interview with me, Kennedy described the lunch with Katzenbach as "perfectly nice and casual. I explained to him what happened in Paris, and that I didn't leak anything to *Newsweek*. He seemed to believe me."

At about 3 P.M., with Katzenbach still in his office, Kennedy received a phone call from Watson, saying the President would see both of them at 4 P.M. in the oval office.

Kennedy went to the White House without any members of his staff, and saw the President in the presence of Katzenbach, and Walt Rostow. The forty-five-minute meeting later became the subject of considerable speculation and gossip. *Time* magazine reported that the confrontation was so bitter that Kennedy called the President a "sonofabitch" at one point. Kennedy insisted this was untrue, and a few weeks after the meeting, gave me this account:

"It wasn't very pleasant. Johnson was mean. He didn't believe me about *Newsweek,* and said I was lying. He was very abusive. . . . He was shouting and seemed very unstable. I kept thinking that if he exploded like that with me, how could he ever negotiate with Hanoi or De Gaulle or Mao. . . . He said a lot of unpleasant things, like I was responsible for prolonging the war and American soldiers dying in Vietnam, and that the doves like me didn't have much of a political future. I didn't say much, except to inform him that I planned to make a speech on the war soon that would propose a halt in the bombing. At the end of the meeting he told me he never wanted to hear my views about Vietnam again. . . . What I learned from the meeting was that the government felt the war was going so well in the battlefield, they didn't really want to negotiate now."

On February 8, two days after the Johnson-Kennedy confrontation, the four-day Tet (lunar New Year) truce went into effect in Vietnam. On the same day Soviet Premier Aleksei Kosygin arrived in London for talks with British Prime Minister Harold Wilson. On Thursday afternoon, February 9, Kosygin agreed to hold an internationally televised press conference, which was telecast live to the United States, via satellite. Kosygin used the opportunity to draw attention again to Trinh's peace formula.

"That proposal," the Soviet leader said, "was highly constructive, and we think the United States should take advantage of it." He added that it offered "a way out" of the stalemate over negotiations.

Robert Kennedy watched the press conference in his home in Virginia, and later said, "I almost fell over when I heard what Kosygin was saying. It seemed to be a direct invitation to extend the Tet bombing pause, and enter negotiations."

On February 13, President Johnson announced the resumption of "full-scale hostilities," including the bombings of North Vietnam. Johnson blamed his decision on the fact Hanoi had used the truce period for "major resupply efforts of their troops in South Vietnam."

This excuse, however, has been contradicted by many sources, including *Le Monde,* American Air Force statistics, *I. F. Stone's Weekly,* and Theodore Draper's book, *The Abuse of Power,* which Robert Kennedy told me "was one of the very best about Vietnam, even though it isn't too kind to me and my friends."

On February 16, Kennedy asked Adam Walinsky to start working on a major speech on Vietnam. That same afternoon he told columnist

Mary McGrory, who had been needling him for several weeks to speak out, "I'm going to escalate this matter. I'm going to give that speech."

Kennedy was now persuaded, mostly as a result of his ugly scene with Johnson, that the Administration was deluded by the military's sanguine statistics, and didn't really want to negotiate a compromise settlement of the war. Kennedy was also persuaded that the war was exacting an intolerable toll on domestic programs, and on the government's prestige around the world. He was haunted by the films and photos of napalmed or homeless Vietnamese children. And his last excuse for keeping silent was now gone. His meeting with Johnson made it clear he could have no influence on policy, whether he spoke, or stayed silent. So he was finally prepared, to admit to himself, that strange prophets like Chester Bowles, I. F. Stone, and those angry, panicked kids in SDS had been right all along, and that he, his brother, and their friends had been tragically wrong.

Even as he began a last round of conversations with Vietnam experts, and reading the first drafts of speeches submitted by Walinsky, Schlesinger, and Goodwin, Kennedy was still being subjected to enormous pressures to pull back and not give the speech.

Averell Harriman, his old friend, after whom he named one of his children, came to see him and plead "in the national interest" not to provoke needlessly another fight with the overburdened President. Some of his closest friends and advisers also offered the counsel of silence: Theodore Sorensen, William vanden Heuvel, Robert McNamara, and his brother Ted.

His friend, newspaper columnist Joseph Alsop, wrote a melancholy column warning Kennedy that if he gave the antibombing speech he would never become President, and would end his career as the hero of a small, fringe cult. Former Postmaster General James Farley gave a vicious speech in Hartford, Connecticut, accusing Kennedy of "undermining" the President, and "imperiling the safety of the nation." The Gallup Poll revealed only 24 percent of the country favored a suspension of the bombing of North Vietnam.

But there were also forces pulling Kennedy in the other direction. His Washington office staff, especially Walinsky and Edelman, were lobbying for the strongest speech possible. To balance McNamara's data, there was antiwar leader Allard Lowenstein feeding him ideas and scenarios. To balance Sorensen's caution, there was Schlesinger's boldness. To balance Alsop's pragmatism, there was Murray Kempton's romanticism:

> And yet, he [Kennedy] might really speak out, and there is the chance, speaking, that he might destroy this war. There is a larger chance, of course, that he might destroy himself as a Presidential candidate. All that would remain to him then is that there might be young men born after his children's children are born, who will read about him and say that this had been a man.

But Kennedy's mind was made up. He felt that his brother had made mistakes, and that he had made mistakes, and now, with 410,000 American troops on Vietnamese soil, he must cross the Rubicon, and risk something to rally the nation against the war.

During the three weeks prior to his speech, Kennedy read and studied two books on Vietnam—*The United States in Vietnam* by Cornell Professors George McT. Kahin and John Lewis, and *The Vietcong* by former United States Information Agency (USIA) official Douglas Pike. He also consulted with a variety of war critics among his friends— Bill Moyers, Allard Lowenstein, Burke Marshall, Fred Dutton, John Kenneth Galbraith, UN Ambassador Arthur Goldberg, and Norman Cousins. One of the purposes of these conversations was probably educational, since Kennedy felt he was intellectually unprepared to debate and defend fully his February, 1966, proposal for a coalition government.

Two of the people he saw in February of 1967 were Tom Hayden and Staughton Lynd, coauthors of *The Other Side,* a report on their illegal trip to Hanoi in December of 1965. Since this meeting has subsequently become the object of some historical interest, particularly among student radicals, I will describe the encounter in some detail.

In early January of 1967, I had suggested to Kennedy that he meet Hayden, a friend of mine, not as an expert on Vietnam, but in connection with Hayden's efforts at organizing a black community union in Newark. I gave him Hayden's small book on the Newark riot, *Rebellion in Newark* to read. (Independently, Walinsky had also urged Kennedy to meet Hayden and read the book.)

A few weeks later Kennedy told me he had read the book, and was impressed by its "feeling and honesty," although he didn't "care for the parts that seemed sympathetic to violence."

Kennedy had an instinct for excellence, for recognizing talented people before anybody else. The same instinct told him Hayden was the most serious and most original of the young radicals. Kennedy knew they would never agree on most issues, but he wanted to open a line of communication to the student Left, and he was curious to meet someone with a college degree who had voluntarily spent the last four years working with the wretched of Newark.

On the morning of February 13, Tom Johnston called me and asked if I could find Hayden and Lynd and bring them up to Kennedy's apartment at 5 P.M. He requested also that I keep quiet about the meeting, because if word of it leaked out, conservatives might use it to smear Kennedy as a dupe of the New Left. I called Hayden in Newark and told him that Kennedy wanted to see him and Lynd that afternoon. Hayden's reaction seemed to be a mixture of suspicion and curiosity, but he agreed to come and track down Lynd, who was in Philadelphia, taking his son to a doctor.

The actual meeting, which lasted a little more than an hour, was quite uneventful. Both Kennedy and Lynd were fundamentally shy, and Hayden, at that point, still deferred to Lynd as older and more experienced. The initial awkwardness did not break up until Staughton's son, Lee, accidentally spilled some Coke on the rug, and Kennedy picked him up and said, "Don't worry about that. It makes the rug grow better." At another point, early in the meeting, Kennedy was pacing his living room, noticed thick smog rolling up the East River, and called Con Edison himself to protest the air pollution caused by the company's 14th Street power plant.

For a few minutes Kennedy questioned Hayden about the project in Newark. What was the mayor like? How was the poverty program being run? How did white students like working in the slums? Was there anything he could do to help?

Finally, the talk turned to Vietnam. Since neither Lynd nor Hayden made the case for unilateral withdrawal, the discussion was cordial and largely an exchange of information. Lynd emphasized the political differences between the NLF and Hanoi, and the need for a unilateral cessation of the bombings without demanding any reciprocal act by

Hanoi. Kennedy agreed, and said that he would ultimately "settle" for a "Laos-type" solution in Vietnam. But he added that "there has to be some guarantees by the other side that the border to Thailand would be sealed to infiltrators. I am concerned that we just don't end up by moving the whole damn thing over one country."

At about 6:15 Kennedy said he was already late for a dinner appointment with Schlesinger and Galbraith, and invited us along. Lynd and Hayden declined, explaining that they each had to speak at antiwar rallies that night.

Going down in the elevator I asked the two radicals what they thought of Kennedy.

Lynd said, "He seems very fair-minded. Sort of detached, and not authoritarian at all. But still very much a liberal." Hayden thought he was "kind of European. He reminds me more of Mendes-France than of any American liberal. He's not at all like Reuther or Rauh or any of those guys in the way he thinks."

A few days later I asked Kennedy what he thought of them, and he replied, "They're very nice, decent, bright fellows. But I didn't think they told me everything they felt about immediate withdrawal."

The psychological and political buildup for Kennedy's speech continued all through February, until it seemed the speech itself would be an anticlimax. There were almost daily news stories anticipating the speech, and the final break with Johnson. On February 17, the *New York Post* ran a five-column headline that read: "RFK Sets Major Speech on Bombing." On February 28, the *Post*'s four-column headline read: "Senate Awaits Kennedy's Viet Speech." On February 28, press secretary Frank Mankiewicz received fifty-five calls about the speech, including twenty-five from reporters representing foreign papers.

While this dramatic buildup was going on, a dozen other Senators, virtually unnoticed by either the press or the President, endorsed a halt in the bombing as a prelude to negotiations. Republicans like Brooke, Javits, Aiken, Hatfield, and John Sherman Cooper. And Democrats like Morse, Gruening, Pell, McCarthy, McGovern, Church, and Nelson. But it was Kennedy who now seized the dramatic imagination. For, in fact, only he could, in Malraux's phrase, "put a scar upon the map," rally the Senate, and split party and the country. The news wasn't the substance of the position Kennedy was taking, but rather the fact that he was moving to take that position.

And all this time, the war inexorably kept on escalating. On February

22, American artillery for the first time began shelling across the De-militarized Zone (DMZ) into North Vietnam. On February 26, Ameri-can warships for the first time began firing on supply routes on a round-the-clock basis. On February 27, American airplanes started mining North Vietnam's rivers. Also, on February 27, President Johnson, with uncharacteristic understatement, declined to describe the new escala-tions as escalations. They are, he insisted, only a "step up," and "more far-reaching."

The speech Robert Kennedy read in a quiet, tense voice from his desk at the rear of the Senate chamber on March 2, was 6,000 words long, 104 pages of large-sized type in his loose-leaf speech notebook.

Kennedy had been up till 3:30 A.M. the night before, finishing the carpentry on the speech with Goodwin, Walinsky, and Mankiewicz. In the morning he had called Senators Mansfield, Fulbright, and Mc-Govern, the Senate doves he most respected, and alerted them to his speech. Before he left his house, he received an emotional phone call from his friend, Maxwell Taylor, who told him, "No matter what you say, I'm with you." Although the temperature was less than thirty de-grees, Kennedy drove to work himself that day, with the top down on his convertible, at eighty miles an hour, through several red lights, his mind 10,000 miles from the road. When he arrived at his office he asked Peter Edelman, "Well, am I a big enough dove for you now?"

"No, not quite," Edelman replied.

"Well, that makes me feel a little better," smiled Kennedy.

He began the speech by accepting, for himself and his brother, part of the blame for the past. "Three Presidents," he said, "have taken action in Vietnam. As one who was involved in those decisions, I can testify that if fault is to be found or responsibility assessed, there is enough to go round for all—including myself."

Then Kennedy turned to his own existential preoccupations—the "pain," the "anguish," the "horror," and the "responsibility."

> Let us reflect for a moment . . . on the horror . . . All we say and do must be informed by our awareness that this horror is partly our re-sponsibility. . . . It is our chemicals that scorch the children and our bombs that level the villages. We are all participants . . . we must also feel as men the anguish of what it is we are doing.

Next there were defensive passages, the careful attempt to prevent the speech from being personalized and politicized away from the issues.

"For years," Kennedy said, "President Johnson had dedicated his energies in an effort to achieve an honorable peace." He also praised the President for his "restraint."

Finally he came to the heart of his speech.

> I propose that we test the sincerity of the statements by Premier Kosygin and others asserting that if the bombardment of the North is halted, negotiations would begin, by halting the bombardment and saying we are ready to negotiate within the week. . . . An international group should be asked to inspect the borders and ports of the country to report any further escalation. And under the direction of the United Nations, and with an international presence gradually replacing American forces, we should move towards a final settlement which allows all major political elements in South Vietnam to participate in the choice of leadership and shape their future direction as a people.

The President responded to Kennedy's moderate speech with a flurry of activity, reminiscent of his transparent journey to Honolulu in an effort to push the Fulbright hearings off the front pages. Within a few hours on March 2, Johnson called an impromptu news conference to announce that the Soviet Union had agreed to a proposal made weeks before to discuss methods of limiting the arms race. ("I wonder how long that was lying at the bottom of his desk?" Kennedy mused.) Johnson also made unscheduled visits to Howard University for a civil rights speech, and to the Office of Education for another spontaneous speech. He invited all fifty Governors to the White House for a meeting later in the month. Johnson also released a letter defending his Vietnam policy (dated March 1) and gave it to Senator Henry Jackson, who read it into the record at the conclusion of Kennedy's address. Finally, Dean Rusk announced in the evening that Kennedy's approach had already been tried without success, and General William Westmoreland declared in Saigon that it was too dangerous to try at all. On March 9 President Johnson said, in rejecting Kennedy's suggestion for a unilateral halt in the bombings, "We would be glad to halt our bombing if they would halt their aggression and their infiltration." And finally, on March 10, the Administration had the last word when the air war was escalated another notch, as American bombers for the first time hit a major industrial complex in North Vietnam, at Thainguyen, thirty-eight miles north of Hanoi.

In the days immediately following his antibombing speech, Kennedy suffered a severe battering in the press from political supporters of the President, who chose to interpret his speech almost exclusively in the context of domestic politics. Kenneth Crawford, in the March 20 edition of *Newsweek,* in a column entitled, "Henry A. Kennedy," sought to equate Kennedy with Henry Wallace, who led a Communist-dominated splinter party campaign for President in 1948. In the March 23 issue of the now defunct *Reporter* magazine, Dr. Max Ascoli wrote in an editorial:

> The speech on the floor of the Senate on March 2nd has made it brutally clear: there are two U.S.A.'s . . . I am proud to belong to that America which has its leader in Lyndon Johnson.

The editorial went on to accuse the "Kennedy family" of plotting to impose on the nation "its own Bonapartism that aims at permanent power."

Within a few days Kennedy was admitting to friends that his Senate speech had come too late to capitalize on North Vietnam's February peace signals. He also understood that the speech had hurt him politically. But the March 2 speech also was a watershed; it emancipated Kennedy psychologically and intellectually about Vietnam. Having confessed guilt for the past, and having heard not the cautious counsel of his friends but the promptings of his passions, he was a freer man.

For the remaining 15 months of his life, Robert Kennedy spoke and wrote against the war with growing frequency and certainty. His written texts still tended to be defensive and cautious, but more and more there were public moments when his warm passions drowned his cool reason.

On August 11, with more than 12,000 Americans already dead in Vietnam, Kennedy spoke in the Senate against the undemocratic procedures of the South Vietnamese elections. It was a very prudent speech, much less combative and inclusive than a speech given by Senator Javits earlier the same day. As Kennedy read his speech, which seemed squeezed out of a tube and edited with a slide rule, I brooded in the press gallery. I recalled how he cut the antiwar passages out of his 1965 speech at the last minute, and how he still went back to McNamara and Taylor for advice on Vietnam. His speech did not mention the possibility of withdrawal, or future Senate votes against war appropriations, the way Javits' speech had. It seemed that political ambition, bad advice, intellectual ambivalence had reappeared to gut the speech.

But after Kennedy had finished reading the text, he got into a spontaneous colloquy with several colleagues, loyal to Johnson, and loyal to the war. And suddenly, all the bold ideas and deep emotions that had been so carefully kept out of the speech, spilled out in a torrent.

"These elections are a hoax," Kennedy said with animal intensity in his voice and eyes. "It has become a white man's war against the Asians. . . . Our strongest argument was that America wanted free elections, and North Vietnam didn't. That argument is gone now. . . . Where is our whole moral position in that part of the world now? I don't believe it is there any longer. And I believe that, under those circumstances, obviously a reassessment of the entire situation is required. If they [the South Vietnam military government] are not going to cooperate so that the people can decide things for themselves, what is our moral position in Vietnam? I think it is destroyed."

On "Meet the Press" in November, and before several hundred students at Marymount College at Tarrytown, New York, in December, Kennedy, speaking without benefit of any written material, again condemned the war in apocalyptic and moralistic language. At Marymount he polled the students and discovered that the majority of girls favored greater, not less, bombings of North Vietnam.

"Do you understand what that means, when you ask for more bombing?" he asked. "It means you are voting to send people, Americans and Vietnamese, to die. . . . Don't you understand that what we are doing to the Vietnamese is not very different than what Hitler did to the Jews?"

The last time Kennedy spoke on the floor of the United States Senate was on March 7, 1968. He had already decided to run for President on an antiwar platform. All his inhibitions were gone as he rose to speak spontaneously on Vietnam, confessionally, in moral terms, and still obsessed by the suffering of innocents.

> Every time we have had difficulties over the last seven years, over the period during which I was in the Executive Branch, and since I left . . . the answer has always been to escalate the conflict. . . . The fact is that victory is not ahead of us. It was not ahead of us in 1961 and 1962 when I was one of those who predicted there was light at the end of the tunnel. There was no light in 1963 or 1964 or 1965 or 1966 or 1967. And there is not now.
>
> Moreover there is question of our moral responsibility. Are we like

the God of the Old Testament that we can decide in Washington, D.C., what cities, what towns, what hamlets in Vietnam are going to be destroyed? . . .

Do we have that authority [to kill] tens and tens of thousands of people because we say we have a commitment to the South Vietnamese people? But have they been consulted—in Hue, in Ben Tre, in other towns that have been destroyed? Do we have that authority?

As to our own interests in Vietnam, could not the Germans have argued the same thing before the beginning of World War II—that they had the right to go into Poland, into Estonia, into Latvia, into Lithuania, because they needed them as a buffer. I question whether we have that right in this country . . . What we have been doing is not the answer, it is not suitable, and it is immoral, and intolerable to continue it.

Ninety days later, the last surviving Kennedy brother stood in the pulpit of St. Patrick's Cathedral, and said of Robert Kennedy, "He saw suffering and tried to heal it, he saw war and tried to stop it."

New York Politics:
The Death of a Small Hope

Robert Kennedy was not a good practicing politician. And that was the reason he fitfully tried, but finally failed, to revitalize the cannibalistic Democratic Party of New York State. Although at times a skillful politician, he could not tolerate the cant, the pointless, time-wasting meetings, the vacant rituals of status and ego. He had no talent for small intrigues. He was too fatalistic and impulsive to plot ahead for himself. He would rather fly two hours to talk to a college audience in Michigan than go to Queens to sit on a dais and make small talk with local politicos. Politicians generally made him up-tight and bored him. He once told me, "You know, there aren't ten politicians in the whole state I like and trust." And on another occasion he said, "They all want me to become the boss of the state until the time comes to make the first decision. Then they go at each other's throat. And meanwhile they can't even carry their own districts."

The fact was that Kennedy's violent emotions were sometimes too much for him to handle. His hatred of President Johnson, or Roy Cohn, made the normal faked cordiality among warring politicians impossible for him. The professionals, of course, sensed this attitude and at most New York political functions he was greeted with far less warmth than either Carmine DeSapio or James Farley.

His reputation for ruthlessness made him gun shy, and he frequently tried to overcompensate for it, like a baseball pitcher who cannot throw tight after he has beaned a batter. If anything, Kennedy could be criticized for not being forceful and decisive enough in New York. He remained ambivalent till the end about whether it was actually necessary for him to control the party in New York, and how he wanted to exercise that control if he ever got it. Except for the small cadre of Manhattan reformers who often exasperated him with their gabby, backbiting style, he had no allies for a sustained effort at party reform. In addition, there were few top-caliber candidates available to the state party.

Kennedy's fundamental loyalties were to his family and to a few friends, rather than to the Democratic Party as an institution. Like his brothers in Massachusetts, he ran his 1964 campaign with volunteers, independent of the party tribes. His shrewd brother-in-law, Steve Smith, was his chief operative and adviser in New York, rather than the state chairman. As someone who only came into the state in 1964, he was never able to comprehend fully the interlocking maze of factions based on ideology, ancient feuds, geography, ambition, and ethnic blocs. As a freshman Senator in conflict with the White House, he had very little actual power and patronage to use as an instrument of reform.

During his three years as New York's junior Senator, Robert Kennedy lost every factional fight he engaged in, except one. And he won that one because it was the only opportunity he had to go above the heads of the party leaders, directly to the voter, in a primary.

In March of 1968, looking back on the ruins of the Democratic Party in New York, Kennedy said, "The only problem is that the party has no attractive candidates, no money, and no new ideas. Otherwise it's every bit as healthy as the party in Massachusetts."

The New York Democracy, according to legend, was founded jointly by Thomas Jefferson and Aaron Burr during a nature walk together along the banks of the Hudson River, in 1792. And for more than a century and a half, New York, with its powerful bloc of convention and electoral votes, was the progressive anchor of the national Democratic Party.

But by the summer of 1964, New York State's Democratic Party was running to rot. The golden era of FDR, Herbert Lehman, Al Smith, and the Wagners was coming to a close. The Democrats had not elected a Senate candidate in New York since 1950, and had not elected a Governor since 1954. Despite a statewide Democratic margin of 500,000 in registration, both houses of the state legislature and a majority of the Congressional delegation were Republican.

Robert Kennedy did not have a driving urge to run for the Senate from New York. In May and June of 1964 he still acted like a wounded animal. He still wore a black mourning tie for his brother, and he still had to shake off fits of black melancholy. Stephen Smith, John English, the Nassau County leader, and Peter Crotty, chairman of Erie County, kept suggesting he run in New York. On June 22, three days after his brother Ted was nearly killed in a plane crash in Massachusetts, Kennedy issued a statement saying, "I will not be a candidate for United States Senator from New York."

Kennedy still nurtured a vagrant and undeveloped hope that Lyndon Johnson would ask him to run with him for Vice President. But once the Republicans nominated Barry Goldwater, it became apparent that Johnson would not need a Kennedy. On July 29, Johnson invited Kennedy into his office, and, reading nervously from a prepared sheet of paper, informed the Attorney General that he had been eliminated from consideration for the national ticket.* A week later, driving through the twilight drizzle of Washington, toward Arlington Cemetery, a depressed Kennedy told a friend, "I don't think there is much future for me in this city now."

His mind again turned reluctantly toward the Senate race in New York. Smith, English, and Crotty were still for it. So were most of the victory-starved, old-line political leaders in the state, like crusty Bronx boss Charles Buckley, Representative Adam Powell, and Brooklyn leader Stanley Steingut, all of whom were feuding with the leader of the party, Mayor Robert Wagner. The only other candidate for the nomination was upstate Congressman Sam Stratton. Neither the unhappy and exhausted United Nations Ambassador Adlai Stevenson, nor Mayor Robert Wagner, whose wife had recently died, wanted the nomination. Finally, without enthusiasm, still healing from the wound of Dallas, Kennedy agreed to run, out of a sense of duty to continue his brother's mission, and perhaps as therapy for a broken life.

There was, however, strong opposition to Kennedy's candidacy among liberals and reform Democrats. They viewed him as a carpet-bagger without credentials, entering the state under the sponsorship of the most backward elements in the party. *The New York Times,* a reliable Kennedy foe, published a series of hard-hitting editorials against his running. On August 12, *The Times* commented:

* Kennedy believed that the President secretly taped this tense conversation.

Why he [Kennedy] has any special claim on New York to rescue him from non-office is a mystery. . . . The cold fact is that Mr. Kennedy appears to have decided that his ambitions will best and most immediately be served by finding a political launching pad in New York State. If his brother were not already representing Massachusetts in the Senate, Mr. Kennedy would have undoubtedly run in that state. But to run now would mean that he would have to elbow out another Kennedy. Thus Mr. Kennedy apparently needs New York. But does New York really need Bobby Kennedy?

The *New York Herald Tribune* described Kennedy in their cascade of editorials as "an adventurer determined to remain in public office as a personal necessity," and termed his candidacy as "bossism gone mad in the obeisant welcome of a carpetbagger. . . ."

Kennedy's patrons tried hard to find liberal and Jewish support. The best names they could find, after Mrs. Herbert Lehman refused to endorse him, were former Governor Averell Harriman, and radio station executive R. Peter Straus. The majority of pro-Wagner, pro-Humphrey reform Democrats supported the hopeless candidacy of Congressman Stratton, although a group of anti-Wagner West Side reformers in Manhattan did rally to Kennedy's side. The three principal leaders of this faction within a faction were Assemblymen Albert Blumenthal and Jerome Kretchmer, and district leader Mrs. Ronnie Eldridge.

Kennedy was easily nominated on September 1, but his campaign was unimpressive. He reminisced about, and quoted, his brother excessively. He tended to avoid issues, and ran primarily as a glamorous personality. As a stump speaker he was tentative and awkward, clearly still a man better suited to managing than running. On the day the *Warren Report* was published, he was unable to campaign.

He won with 55 percent of the vote although he ran almost two million votes behind Lyndon Johnson. He fashioned his victory over Kenneth Keating in New York City, taking 90 percent of the black votes, about 70 percent of the Catholic votes, and 70 percent of the votes in Brooklyn. He ran poorest in rural, upstate sections, and ran 10 percent behind Frank Hogan, the 1958 Democratic candidate for the Senate, in Jewish areas. He received a record low of only 272,000 votes on the Liberal Party line.

On the day Kennedy was sworn in as a United States Senator, reporters noticed he was in one of his dreamy, almost drugged moods, and one of them asked what he was thinking about.

"I was remembering and regretting the situation that gave rise to my being here," he answered.

Politics is patronage, plus ambition. And those were the two forces behind the intense struggle for control of the New York State legislature at the start of 1965.

The Republican rout in November had been so complete that the Democrats, in spite of gerrymandering that favored the Republicans, had won control of both houses of the state legislature for the first time in thirty years. With the new legislative majorities went the job of Speaker of the Assembly, which includes authority over $4 million worth of patronage jobs.

The Democratic minority leaders in Albany had been incarnations of the party's bankruptcy. Penguin-like Joseph Zaretzki led the Democrats in the Senate, and in William Shannon's fine phrase, "To call Zaretzki a hack, would be undue praise." Anthony Travia was minority leader in the Assembly. Brighter than Zaretzki, he was equally conservative and subservient to the wishes of Mayor Wagner. For several years Travia had enjoyed a cozy relationship with Governor Rockefeller, similar to Everett Dirksen's symbiotic arrangement with Lyndon Johnson.

Just before the legislature convened, an uneven coalition came together in an attempt to deny Travia and Zaretzki their logical promotions. Reform Democrats, anti-Wagner Democrats (including Charley Buckley) and upstate Democrats united behind two other candidates— Senator Jack Bronston, a liberal from Queens, and Stanley Steingut, the issue-oriented boss of Brooklyn. Secretly brokering and backing this alliance, but publicly claiming neutrality, were Robert Kennedy and Steve Smith. Their motives were an inexact compound of power and virtue. They wanted a rich source of patronage to reward their allies in the tribalized party. And they genuinely wanted new, more progressive and independent leaders in Albany, who would make a respectable legislative record, and oppose Rockefeller rather than quietly dealing with him.

The attempted coup by Kennedy and Smith was so complicated and covert, that even Assemblyman Kretchmer, a leading strategist for the Steingut-Bronston forces, never knew for sure that Kennedy was behind it.

"Kennedy never said a word to me about it," recalls Kretchmer, "even though I saw him several times during the fight. As far as I was concerned, I was for Steingut because he was more liberal. And it was a social thing. We were both Jewish, and I felt more comfortable with him. And Zaretzki was such a neanderthal, he walked around with raw knuckles, because they kept scraping the ground. But Robert Kennedy wasn't in the picture at all for me."

Coaching the Travia-Zaretzki team were two astute politicians—Mayor Wagner and Tammany leader J. Raymond Jones. Wagner, only a middling mayor, had been a genius at maintaining a vacuum at the top of the state party, so that no potential rival could accumulate more power than he. In 1953, for example, he chose as his citywide running mates ciphers like Lawrence Gerosa and Abe Stark. In 1959 he pushed the elderly and ailing Thomas Murray for the Senate nomination. In 1962 he backed an obviously weak candidate—Robert Morgenthau—for the nomination for Governor. Jones, meanwhile, had been a traditional enemy of the Kennedy's, even going so far as to vote as a delegate to the 1960 Los Angeles convention for Lyndon Johnson.

Although a majority of Democrats supported both Steingut and Bronston for leadership, Travia and Zaretzki refused to accept the verdict of the party caucus and took their case before the entire legislature even though twenty-one of the thirty-three Senate Democrats voted for Bronston, and Steingut, at times, outpolled Travia by as much as 52 to 35. With the Republicans voting for their own candidates, no one approached a majority. Unable to introduce or enact legislation, the lawmakers spent five weeks day after day vainly voting for leaders.

Midway through the marathon struggle (more than twenty-five ballots were ultimately taken), Mayor Wagner called a news conference at Gracie Mansion, and accused the pro-Kennedy state chairman William McKeon of making an offer "tantamount to a bribe" to Jones in an Albany hotel room. Most of the alleged witnesses denied it, and there was an incomprehensible volley of denials and name-calling. The State Investigation Commission held a few headlined days of inconclusive hearings.

Finally, on February 3, Mayor Wagner played his ace. He reached an arrangement with his old friend Governor Rockefeller, whereby Rockefeller provided Republican votes to elect Travia and Zaretzki, and in return, the Democrats agreed to vote for the Governor's unpopular 2-percent sales tax. Kennedy had been outmaneuvered, and lost his first bid to lead and renovate the crumbling New York Democratic Party. In the future, he would be less bold.

On June 10, 1965, Robert Wagner, faced with a strong challenge from Congressman John Lindsay, and a divided Democratic Party, unexpectedly announced his decision not to seek a fourth term as Mayor of New York City. This set the stage for the feuding tribes to fragment among four rivals in the anarchic Democratic primary.

The anti-Wagner Bronx and Brooklyn baronies lined up behind the unimaginative Comptroller, Abraham Beame. The pro-Wagner Manhattan, Queens, and Staten Island forces and the more opportunistic elements among the reform Democrats sided with the martinet-like City Council President, Paul Screvane. The purist Manhattan reformers supported liberal but colorless Congressman William F. Ryan. And a few Irish trade unions and old radicals backed the badly financed campaign of Councilman Paul O'Dwyer, the rebellious brother of former Mayor William O'Dwyer.

None of the contenders appealed to Kennedy, and he spent almost a month trying to find his own candidate. Labor mediator Theodore Kheel and Manhattan District Attorney Frank Hogan informed Kennedy they would only accept the nomination if it was offered to them without a primary fight. Tom Johnston recalls:

"The Senator, Steve, and a few of us kept drawing up lists of possible candidates. We had names like Tom Watson and James Hester. But after a few days of checking, we always found out that half the people on our lists didn't live in the city, and the other half were Republicans."

The tragedy of the situation was that 1965 should have been the year the reform Democrats nominated a candidate for mayor. But after eight years in business, the reform movement was faltering badly. Within the last few years they had lost their patron saints—Herbert Lehman and Mrs. Roosevelt—as well as their unifying enemy—Carmine DeSapio, former Manhattan County leader. They had spent themselves in bargaining for patronage, and trying to win control of the traditional party machinery, while neglecting the bread-and-butter issues of poverty, housing, and education. As a result, they had colonized the Jewish, middle-class sections of Manhattan and the Bronx, but failed to make any headway in the ghettos, or in Brooklyn and Queens. Their beachhead secured, they quickly turned to killing each other off in intramural struggles for parochial offices. They never came close to building an issue-oriented, statewide movement, as had equivalent insurgencies in California and Minnesota. And they never developed any leaders with broad appeal.

The reformers split three ways in the primary. Establishment, pro-Wagner clubs on the East Side went to Screvane, as did the insurgent clubs in the Bronx, who felt Screvane would win, and help them in their local contests against the Buckley barons. The two freshman reform Congressmen—James Scheuer and Jonathan Bingham—also backed Screvane, rather than their reformist colleague from the House, William Ryan. The West Side reformers, a ghetto of militants, worked hard for Ryan. A few scattered reformers and small clubs endorsed O'Dwyer.

A distressed Robert Kennedy sat by in impotence through the summer. And John Lindsay organized a citywide network of grass-roots storefronts, independent of the Republican Party, as the city's Democratic tribes practiced their cannibalism. Even though Mayor Wagner eventually gave Screvane a lukewarm endorsement, Kennedy remained authentically neutral.

Although most observers thought that Screvane would win the primary, and inherit Wagner's meld of unions, Jews, Negroes, the Liberal Party, industry, reformers, and the Catholic Church, political coalitions tend not to be transferable. Lower-class Jews were switching to Beame because he had a chance of becoming the first Jewish mayor in the history of the city. The Liberal Party and its affiliated unions jumped to Lindsay, making him a fusion candidate. When the votes were counted on September 14, Beame had beaten Screvane by 59,000 votes out of 737,000 cast, and Ryan had run a fast-closing third, with 114,000 votes.

Robert Kennedy, who was supposed to be the second most powerful Democrat in the nation, spent an unhappy and grouchy autumn, trapped between the tawdry, old-fashioned Beame campaign, and the exciting, threatening candidacy of John Lindsay.

As the Democratic Senator, Kennedy had no choice but to campaign for Beame. But it was painful. He knew that his ancient nemesis Roy Cohn was secretly active as a fund raiser and strategist in the Beame campaign. He knew that other shadowy figures with underworld connections were prowling the corridors in Beame's Summit Hotel headquarters. His brother-in-law Steve Smith spent a few days at the Summit, quarreled bitterly with Beame's machine managers, Bert Podell and Edward Costikyan and walked out. Kennedy personally felt that Beame was an embarrassing, losing candidate, who did not have any grasp of the larger issues. At the same time, Kennedy was being attacked by his liberal friends for campaigning too hard for Beame. James Wechsler, who backed Lindsay, wrote in the *New York Post* that Kennedy has "engaged in excesses of stimulated enthusiasms that diminished his own stature, especially among dedicated young voters. . . ."

I watched Kennedy campaign the final weekend of the campaign and he was not displaying much enthusiasm. To a small street corner crowd in Washington Heights, that was dominated by schoolchildren, he shouted playfully, "I urge you to vote for Abe Beame, a great Democrat in the great tradition of Al Smith, Herbert Lehman, and Huey Long."

At a Bronx rally near a parochial school, Kennedy encountered a group of teen-age hecklers supporting the Conservative Party candidate, William F. Buckley.

"Buckley is going to have school on weekends," he said. "He's going to have the nuns hit you with a ruler, very hard. Let's go everybody. Let's hear a very loud boo for Bill Buckley." The crowd of children obliged with a raucus chorus of booing.

On Election Day Kennedy visited with Justin Feldman, a knowledge-able reformer, who had been in charge of scheduling during his 1964 Senate campaign.

"Do you think Beame can run the city if he wins?" asked Kennedy.

"This is a heck of a time to ask at this point in the game. I suppose it depends on who he listens to," replied Feldman.

"Who does he listen to?" said Kennedy.

"I thought you would have made sure of that before you agreed to campaign for him."

"You think I'm ruthless, too," smiled Kennedy.

The Democrats enjoyed a better than three-to-one ratio in registration and they had occupied City Hall for twenty years, but in November, John Lindsay, a potential national rival to Kennedy, was elected Mayor of New York, and Kennedy suffered another setback. He was identified with a loser. He annoyed the issue-oriented liberals who felt he had worked too closely with Beame, and the old-liners, who felt he was too aloof. And he had lost another chance to gain a base of political power and patronage—City Hall.

In April of 1966 a routine deal was made for a routine judgeship in Manhattan.

There is an unwritten code in New York City, whereby the Democratic and Republican county leaders quietly cooperate on judicial nominations, to avoid the expense of campaigning, and to foster the myth that the courts are not dominated by one political party.

In this tradition, J. Raymond Jones reached a gentleman's agreement with the Manhattan Republican county leader (and a former Democrat) Vincent Albano. Under the arrangement, Arthur Klein, an old-line Democrat, would get bipartisan endorsement for Manhattan surrogate, in exchange for William Shea, a Republican protégé of Albano, getting bipartisan backing for Justice in the First District of the State Supreme Court (Manhattan and the Bronx). The Surrogate's Court, in addition to its other functions, appoints guardians to manage the affairs of widows, orphans, minors, and mental incompetents and with about $800 million annually constitutes one of the richest patronage troughs in politics.

With Lindsay's reform Administration in office, the Tammany organization and its clubhouse lawyers were particularly dependent on this form of patronage for survival.

Manhattan's weak and fratricidal reform district leaders, ignorant of the deal, were opposed to Klein simply because they felt he had been a poor Congressman, and a poor Supreme Court Justice, and did not merit promotion. They supported Judge Owen McGivern in the May 6 county executive committee meeting, but were narrowly outvoted by the pro-Klein regulars. They then accepted Jones's motion that the nomination be made unanimous. A week later, at a farcical five-minute meeting, the Republican county executive committee gave its unanimous consent to the deal.

The good-government watchdogs in the city, however, immediately rebelled. *The Times* commented in an editorial:

> A veteran of the Tammany machine, Mr. Klein owes his public career to his party regularity, and his personal affability. . . . Nothing in his record recommends him for this significant promotion. . . . It is imperative that the Republican and Liberal parties unite in choosing a truly impressive lawyer.

Even more upset than *The Times* editorial board was Alex Rose, the cagey leader of the Liberal Party, then at the peak of his influence as a result of the Liberal Party's role in Lindsay's election as mayor. Rose went to Lindsay and asked him to denounce the deal, and help find a suitable good-government candidate. Lindsay was opposed to the deal, but felt there wasn't anything he could do about it, since it had been hatched by his friend Albano, with the apparent acquiescence of his own deputy mayor, Robert Price. Although he would not fight, Lindsay confessed to the press, "I certainly do not feel happy about it."

On Thursday, May 19, James Wechsler wrote an explosive column in the *Post*, attacking the Klein deal. In his column Wechsler published part of a wiretapped conversation, recorded in 1943, involving underworld powerhouse, Frank Costello. The transcript of the conversation revealed that Klein had helped a friend of Costello's secure a judicial nomination.

On the same day Wechsler's column appeared, Kennedy met Alex Rose for a few drinks in a hotel bar around the corner from Rose's Hatters' union headquarters on 28th Street. The purpose of the meeting was for Kennedy to firm up his ties to the Liberal Party, which had become frayed during the mayoralty campaign. Since political conversations with Kennedy are often silence-filled and monosyllabic, and punctuated with long silences, Rose began by showing Kennedy the Wechsler column. Kennedy's holy hatred of the Mafia and gangsters began during his investigation of the Teamsters in the 1950's. As Attorney General, he waged the most systematic attack on the Mafia's power in history. As he read the column, Rose later recalled that he could see Kennedy's face change dramatically. Rose then asked him to consider backing a primary fight against the Klein nomination. As bait for the competitive Kennedy, Rose casually remarked that Lindsay had felt the situation was hopeless. As soon as Kennedy left the meeting, he deputized Steve Smith and William vanden Heuvel to explore the possibility of finding a candidate to challenge Klein in the June 28 Democratic primary. Once again Kennedy was listening to his instincts, rather than his practical intelligence.

An attempt to persuade Columbia law professor, Herbert Wechsler, the brother of the *Post* columnist, to enter the primary, proved futile. Other lower court judges also turned aside suggestions they run against Judge Klein. With time running out, and the election only five weeks away, Justin Feldman, the pro-Kennedy reformer, hit on the idea of State Supreme Court Justice Samuel Silverman as an alternate candidate in the primary. After a phone conversation with Senator Kennedy, Silverman seemed willing, if not anxious, to make the challenge.

On Sunday afternoon, May 22, Mrs. Ronnie Eldridge and reform leader Russell Hemenway began phoning reform leaders and inviting them to attend a meeting with Kennedy that evening in a rented room at the Commodore Hotel, to decide on whether to make the primary race with Silverman. At about 9 P.M., the middle-class reform leaders, some still wearing slacks and sunglasses, began returning from the country and gathering at the Commodore. One female district leader even carried a sleeping baby to the meeting.

The meeting showed Kennedy at his evangelical best, and the reformers at their nit-picking worst. To Kennedy's surprise, several of the more influential East Side reform leaders were unwilling to support a primary campaign against Klein on a good-government platform. Mrs. Joan Carroll argued that there was not enough time to conduct an effective campaign. Mrs. Edith Wagner said she supported Klein, and regarded the press attacks on his record as "McCarthyism of the worst sort." Harry Sedgewick rose to ask Kennedy if this meant that he was "now formally working with the reform wing of the party." Kennedy, his anger mounting by this time, told Sedgewick that he hoped everyone was there for the cause of judicial integrity, not to help a particular faction of the party. Some of the reform leaders also balked at uniting behind Justice Silverman, and urged a campaign for "our own" Civil Court Judge Arnold Fein. Mrs. Marjorie Cox, the reform movement's only Negro district leader, drew a few laughs when she said, "The average Negro on the streets of Harlem never heard of Sam Silverman. But he has heard of Arnold Fein."

Finally, Kennedy asked for a show of hands by all those willing to make the fight for Silverman. About ten of the sixty reform leaders still dissented. By now it was midnight.

Kennedy then got up in disappointment and began to leave, saying, "I've always been told that reform Democrats were committed to reform of the judiciary. But I do not see much evidence of that here tonight. I no longer know what my feelings are about this matter, in light of your lack of total commitment. Thank you."

Panicked by Kennedy's blunt farewell, the reform leaders asked Kennedy to postpone his exit a few minutes, caucused, and quickly agreed to join Kennedy and the Liberal Party in a primary against Tammany and the Republicans.

The normally routine and obscure election of a Manhattan surrogate swiftly became a nationally significant test of strength between the only

Negro county leader in the nation—Jones—and a potential President—
Kennedy. The two soft-spoken judges, whose names were on the ballot,
were ignored, and embarrassed by the political storms.

The election was obviously important to Kennedy. It offered a chance
to cement his lines to the reformers and the Liberal Party. A victory
would void a sordid deal that smelled of the underworld, and would help
expunge the stain of Kennedy's appointment of racist judges in the
South while Attorney General, and his Senatorial support of an un-
qualified family crony Francis Morrissey for a Federal judgeship. A
victory would crack Jones's base of power and patronage, and would
help Kennedy consolidate his influence in the state. And a victory would,
incidentally, in Kennedy's words, "stick it to John Lindsay."

Jones also had much at stake: his authority as county leader, his
freedom to deal with other politicians, his control over a critical source
of patronage, and his ability to nominate his old friend and ally, Robert
Wagner, for Governor that September. At age sixty, this was perhaps
Jones's last great ambition.

Jones devised a typically adroit strategy for the one-month campaign.
He tried to depict Kennedy as anti-Negro in Harlem for opposing his
choice, and depict him as a ruthless tyrant among Jewish liberals, for
trying to take over the party apparatus. Almost all the politicians and
civic leaders within Harlem signed statements supporting Klein, including Roy Wilkins and the respected author and psychologist, Dr. Kenneth
Clark. One such statement, issued by eighteen Harlem legislators and
district leaders said that Kennedy's intervention was "aimed solely at
J. Raymond Jones, because he is a Negro." Kennedy could only respond
with Silverman endorsements from two old friends who had little political clout in Harlem—James Meredith and James Farmer.

Downtown, Francis Adams, one of the founders of the reform
faction, called a press conference to characterize the Silverman candidacy as "merely a political power grab by Kennedy." Former Mayor
Vincent Impellitteri also invoked the same phrase to strike at Kennedy.

Kennedy returned from a tour of South Africa ten days before the
election. In his absence, the Silverman insurgency had lacked fire. None
of the voters recognized Silverman's name or face. Show business
celebrities kept telling Steve Smith, Silverman's campaign manager, they
would only appear at Silverman rallies if Kennedy was present, too. The
press was more interested in the dramaturgy of a Jones-Kennedy

confrontation than the details of the deal, or the issue of court reform. The day before Kennedy's return, a reform leader confessed to me, "Only Bobby can save this campaign. We've run out of gas, and since Silverman can't campaign for himself, we need Kennedy to get our message across, to give it some pizazz and sex."

On Sunday, June 19, Kennedy bounced off a plane, and his first whimsical words at an airport press conference were, "Would you believe that just everyone in Africa is for Sam Silverman?"

For the last week of the campaign Kennedy kept up a brutal pace, working the dull Senate by day in Washington, and working the hot streets of Manhattan by night. It was like a quarter-mile sprint run at top speed right out of the blocks. One night after campaigning on corners for three hours, Kennedy returned to the campaign headquarters at the soon-to-be demolished Sheraton East Hotel, and noticed most of the city's reform leaders sitting around a room, discussing the possible candidates for Governor.

"You know, my old man was right about you people after all," Kennedy said, smiling, but meaning to hurt. "You talk, but don't work."

Mostly as a result of Kennedy's work, Silverman won the primary— 70,771 to 47,625. Silverman almost held his own in Harlem, and swept reform-minded Greenwich Village, 8,100 to 3,800.

Kennedy's improvised victory statement was witty, and self-deprecatory; similar in spirit to the one he would give the last night of his life, two years later in Los Angeles.

"I would like to make a few personal remarks," he began, a just-ate-the-canary grin on his face. "I remember well that Sunday when I called him [Judge Silverman] to see if he would run. And he said in a ruthless kind of way, 'Just you remember, Mr. Kennedy, Silvermans don't finish second!' "

Kennedy continued, "I would like to introduce a relative, a beloved figure, who is replacing me on the American horizon, ruthless, mean, Stephen Smith. . . ."

On that sweltering June night, Robert Kennedy stood at the zenith of his power, above the jungle of New York politics. He could do anything now: topple Jones, dictate the gubernatorial candidate; organize a new, liberal coalition in the state. But instead, inexplicably, he let the golden moment pass, with nothing more than a few revealing, self-conscious jokes about his reputation for ruthlessness. His hesitation and introspection during the following days were a poignant symptom of his misunderstood character, but also a political blunder of the first magnitude.

An important part of politics is momentum. Robert Kennedy had the momentum in early July of 1966 to pick the Democratic Party candidate for Governor. He would never have that momentum again.

He even had a private preference among the aspirants—Nassau County Executive Eugene Nickerson, a protégé of Jack English, who proved he could win an important suburban county that was once Republican. Kennedy liked him, and thought he would make a good Governor. But yet he didn't act. He wasn't absolutely sure he could get Nickerson the nomination, since the reform Democrats, as usual, were split almost equally among four candidates. He wasn't certain Nickerson could unseat Governor Rockefeller; of all the clichés about the Kennedys, the truest one is they don't like to lose. And last, Kennedy wasn't convinced it was really in his best interest to control New York politics and make the enemies necessary in forcing Nickerson's nomination.

Few Senators, Kennedy rationalized, actually control the politics of their home state. That is generally done by Governors and county chairmen. John Kennedy never interfered decisively in Massachusetts politics, and he still became President. So, Robert Kennedy procrastinated, while 57-year-old City Council President Frank O'Connor methodically rounded up the delegates he needed to be nominated. And O'Connor was hostile to Kennedy's leadership; in part because O'Connor understandably nursed a grudge over the fact that the Kennedys intervened against him during the 1962 struggle for the gubernatorial nomination. (The Kennedys had foolishly forced Robert Morgenthau's nomination from Washington.)

Kennedy liked millionaire manufacturer Howard Samuels even less than he liked O'Connor. His dislike of Samuels was personal. It was essentially bad chemistry between two public men. Kennedy said after running into Samuels on a plane: "You know, that fellow talks to me just as if he's on 'Meet the Press,' and I'm Larry Spivak. He was talking in slogans about Federal-state relations, and I'm just waiting for the shuttle to take off. And I didn't understand any of it, it was so vague."

Supporting his old enemies, Congressman Otis Pike, who nominated Samuel Stratton in 1964, or Robert Wagner (backed by Jones and Travia) was unthinkable for Kennedy. Franklin D. Roosevelt, Jr., was an old family friend, but Robert Kennedy, the Puritan, no longer respected him because of his playboy habits, and his unfortunate association with Dominican dictator Trujillo.

But instead of taking a small risk with Nickerson, an able, serious, and liberal candidate, Kennedy shopped around for an alternative. He talked to John Gardner, who turned out to be a registered Republican. He sent William vanden Heuvel to feel out Xerox executive Sol Linowitz, but Linowitz wanted the nomination handed to him without a messy fight, and no one could guarantee that in New York. Cornell University President James Perkins wasn't interested. In desperation, a few associates proposed that Kennedy support the aging and bland State Controller Arthur Levitt. But Kennedy roared only half in jest, "He's constipated! He's an accountant! He puts me to sleep! Is that what the New Frontier means to you? Arthur Levitt?"

By then it was nearly August, and O'Connor had the votes to be nominated.

In late July, FDR, Jr., charged that O'Connor had obtained secret pledges of gubernatorial support from Stanley Steingut and Charley Buckley (meaning 250 of the necessary 573 votes) in July of 1965, in return for accepting second place on the Beame mayoralty ticket. According to Roosevelt, the deal was made in Buckley's Bronx home, and in the presence of millionaire party contributor, Martin Tannenbaum, president of Yonkers Raceway. Tannenbaum had raised $100,000 for Beame, and seemed to have magical lobbying powers over the state legislature; the New York State Thruway was built right past Tannenbaum's track, which was also used to provide hundreds of jobs for Buckley's faithful clubhouse workers.

Roosevelt's allegation—which almost all independent observers tended to believe—backfired. Instead of causing the upstate political leaders to recoil back from the specter of a backroom deal between two big city bosses, it instead convinced them that O'Connor really did have all the votes he needed for a first ballot nomination, and they had better jump aboard the bandwagon.

Backroom deals and bossism are incendiary issues in primaries open to the voters, but meaningless in a convention contest, where everyone is a boss trying to make the best deal.

On August 10, Alex Rose announced that the Liberal Party "under no circumstance" would endorse O'Connor; the Liberal line in a statewide race is worth between 400,000 and 500,000 votes. Privately, Rose hinted he still favored Wagner for the nomination.

On August 12, the Suffolk County delegates caucused, and broke heavily for O'Connor, even though Nickerson was the executive of the adjacent suburban county.

Kennedy was once again boxed in without room for maneuver. The bosses had beaten him. He had no candidate. Nickerson's campaign had, in fact, been hurt by Kennedy's failure to endorse him, after the weeks of rumors that he would. Kennedy's brief alliance with the Liberal Party was ended. And he would have to spend another dismal autumn campaigning for a dull candidate he did not believe in. On August 15, Nickerson withdrew, and the next morning, after a staged unity breakfast with O'Connor, Kennedy declared his neutrality and willingness to accept the choice of the convention.

Buffalo, a dying provincial city, seemed an appropriate place for the party barons to nominate their pretender. Buffalo is a city that is losing population and jobs. Local journalists joke openly about the Mafia's influence in municipal government. The week before the convention opened, a grand jury had summoned several local political figures. Naturally, the Democrats crowned their meeting by putting the Mayor of Buffalo on the statewide ticket.

At 6 P.M. on Wednesday, September 7, the delegates assembled to nominate their candidate for Governor. Even more than in national conventions, the delegates to state conventions are ordinary political hacks, with no independence and often holding patronage jobs provided by the party. They are court clerks, the wives of Assemblymen, and clubhouse hangers-on, people whose careers are mortgaged to the machine.

The nominating speeches were rasped into a microphone that had gone dead; but no one cared. The roll call began with the most original ploy of the season. The roll of the sixty-two counties was read backward, starting from Z, the reason being that the convention managers wanted O'Connor to be nominated without the 154 votes of Stanley Steingut's Brooklyn delegation. If the roll had been read in the traditional alphabetical manner, O'Connor would have been nominated on the votes of Steingut and Buckley. By avoiding the recording of Brooklyn's 154 votes, the Democrats felt that they were disproving Roosevelt's charges of a deal between Steingut and Buckley.

At 9:55 P.M.—just in time for prime television viewing—the votes of Staten Island put O'Connor over the top, and Samuels, with only 137 votes, rushed to the podium, on cue, to concede.

It was Robert Kennedy's burden to introduce O'Connor. He did it coolly and correctly. While O'Connor read his overlong acceptance speech, Kennedy tried very hard to look serious, somewhat like a six-year-old attending his first funeral.

On Thursday afternoon the party leaders met in an air-conditioned room at the Statler Hilton Hotel to pick the rest of the ticket. An "Italian caucus," led by New York City Controller Mario Procaccino, threatened a walkout unless Buffalo Mayor Frank Sedita was put on the ticket. The militant West Side reformers urged that State Senator Manfred Ohrenstein be nominated for Attorney General. But the Establishment wing of the reform faction (Manhattan's East Side and the Bronx) pushed for twice-beaten (for Congress and Council President) Orin Lehman, whose only visible assets were his name and his money. The upstate leaders demanded that Samuels, an upstater, be given a place on the ticket. Kennedy, assuming the ticket would lose, despite its wide margin in the early polls, made only one suggestion—that Columbia law professor Jack Weinstein,* a vigorous fresh face, be nominated for Attorney General.

For several hours the barons bargained in the hotel room: O'Connor and his friends, National Committeeman Edward Weisel, representing the President, businessman ADAer Marvin Rosenberg, looking after the Vice President's interests; State Chairman John Burns protecting Kennedy's fortunes, and the county leaders speaking for themselves— Crangle of Erie, English of Nassau, Steingut of Brooklyn, with Henry McDonough acting as the ailing Charley Buckley's agent.

The convention was scheduled to reconvene at 3 P.M., but the barons kept quarreling. Finally, at 5 P.M., they agreed on Mayor Sedita and Orin Lehman. By then Kennedy had shrewdly left town in the "Caroline," and the delegates were restless, smelling indecision at the top.

A revolt was brewing on the floor of the convention. Steingut ran into Justin Feldman and began bragging about the brilliant stroke of putting the revered name of Lehman on the ticket.

"Smart," shouted Steingut, pointing to his head.

"No. Mechanical," countered Feldman.

* Now a Federal judge.

"We want Howard. We want Howard," the delegates chanted. Signs and placards sprang up, remnants of Wednesday's demonstration. They thought, mistakenly, that Lehman was Kennedy's choice, and now they were going to stick it to Bobby Kennedy. They knew Bobby disliked Samuels, and now they would make Robert Kennedy swallow him.

The first big county leader on the floor of the convention to break for Samuels was J. Raymond Jones. He would get his revenge now for the humiliation of the Silverman campaign. Besides, Lehman came from Manhattan and no one had consulted Jones. A dozen, small upstate counties jumped to Samuels as soon as word of Jones's defection spread. Even Jack English, bitter over the defeat of Nickerson, more bitter still over the rejection of Jack Weinstein, a Nassau activist, joined the Samuels' revolt. The clerks were killing the barons.

O'Connor had no choice but to abdicate leadership and throw the choice open to the delegates. Lehman arrived at the convention hall with his acceptance speech already written. By the time the roll call was over, he was drafting a graceful concession statement.

"Poor Orin," said one reformer, "he can't even win a fixed fight."

That night I saw delegate Hulan Jack, who was removed as Manhattan Borough President in a kickback scandal several years before, at the bar of a restaurant, jubilantly telling a cluster of pols, "This year we've got a great ticket."

Flying out of Buffalo that evening, Robert Kennedy told an aide that the Democratic Party in New York was "a zoo!"

The O'Connor campaign was a trial for Robert Kennedy. He didn't want to be identified with a loser, but he also did not want to be blamed by the regulars for defeat. The compromise he arrived at was to campaign around the country for his friends and allies during most of October, and then give O'Connor a solid week in the stretch run.

By the end of October it was becoming clear that O'Connor had dissipated his early lead. Rockefeller was outspending him ten to one. When Kennedy returned to the state, one of the county leaders responsible for O'Connor's nomination told him, "I should have listened to you about that guy. He's a loser. He's running like he doesn't want to win." An O'Connor speech writer told me, "Frank is a hell of a nice man, but he thinks he's running for monsignor, and not Governor." Another campaign aide remarked perceptively, "Frank wanted to be nominated for Governor, he doesn't want to be Governor."

Kennedy lent Steve Smith, Peter Edelman, and Milton Gwirtzman to the O'Connor effort, and cajoled Assemblymen Kretchmer and Blumenthal into helping.* They worked hard, but never got along with O'Connor's old-fashioned Queens cronies who were making the decisions. "Are you learning what not to do?" Kennedy teased Edelman near the end.

Kennedy spent election night at Steve Smith's apartment with the poet Yevgeny Yevtushenko and John Steinbeck, instead of at O'Connor's headquarters. It wasn't until after 1 A.M. that he briefly visited the defeated candidate to offer his condolences, an attitude the pols resented and remembered. Rockefeller's victory margin was more than 399,000 votes; FDR, Jr., attracted 507,000 votes as the Liberal Party candidate.

Newspapers and columnists during the next few days predicted that Kennedy would now pick up the pieces and establish himself as the top Democrat in the state. But the inner dynamics of politics just don't work that way. The more pieces there are, the more they tend toward dispersal, and the harder it is for any central figure to unite them. The reputations of political bosses seem to continue unharmed by past error. Just as those most responsible for the Vietnam war continue to enjoy favorable reputations, the political leaders in New York responsible for the Beame and O'Connor failures continue to be thought of as crafty and cunning men. Stanley Steingut, who played an important role in both losing campaigns, did not lose any influence because the voters repudiated his judgment. The bosses who backed O'Connor for the nomination were just as entrenched after his defeat as before it. Meanwhile, the bosses no longer trusted Kennedy: they only resented his popularity.

Kennedy had managed his brother's 1960 primary and election campaigns the old way, in cooperation with the machine politicians: Representative Charles Buckley in the Bronx; Representative William Green in Philadelphia; Governor Michael DiSalle in Ohio; Speaker Jesse Unruh in California. He did not waste time with reformers or independents. He went to power.

In 1964 he had come into New York under the sponsorship of Buckley, Steingut, Peter Crotty, and Adam Powell. But his unorthodox break with the Democratic President over Vietnam made the bosses suspicious. And his support of the Silverman campaign convinced them

---

* "If only all the reformers were like Kretchmer and Blumenthal," Kennedy once said to Peter Maas.

that no county leader and no deal was safe with Kennedy around. They regarded him as someone with radical tendencies, who was emotionally erratic, and who spent too much time with those self-righteous reformers who didn't even respect party loyalty.

Kennedy's last effort at party reform was his attempt to influence the election of a new leader of Tammany Hall. Like his first try it was clandestine, because he feared that he would be associated with failure if his choice lost.

On March 10, 1967, Jones resigned as county leader, citing as a major reason Kennedy's opposition to him. He said, "Kennedy has let it be known in every way a politician could that he does not support me."

Kennedy's first choice to replace Jones was Maurice O'Rourke, an Irishman of the old school, who was then Elections Commissioner. However, it would require a change in the party rules to make O'Rourke eligible to become county leader since he was not a district leader. Frustrated by this procedural barrier, Kennedy eventually gave up on O'Rourke, who was not anxious to give up his well-paying job for the privilege of refereeing the party's civil wars.

The reform bloc, meanwhile, began to meet and two candidates emerged: Shanley Egeth, who had the backing of the pro-Humphrey East Side clubs; and Ronnie Eldridge, who was backed by the antiwar, pro-Kennedy West Side district leaders. The old-line faction united quickly behind acting county leader, sixty-year-old Assemblyman Frank Rossetti, once a boxing manager, later a friend and ally of former Tammany boss Carmine DeSapio. For Kennedy, Rossetti was not the reincarnation of Camelot.

On June 29, ten days before a new leader was to be elected, Kennedy gave Mrs. Eldridge a private commitment that if she got six votes from the reform leaders he would round up two more votes to elect her as the first woman, and the first reformer, ever to head Tammany. (The county chairman is elected by majority vote of the seventy-eight male and female district leaders in the county, some with half-votes others with even a smaller fraction.)

On July 5, with the vote three days away, the reform leaders met in a closed caucus, in an attempt to unite on a single candidate to oppose Rossetti. Despite their traditional concern for majority rule, the reformers voted that it would require a two-thirds vote to unite the caucus.

Through seven ballots Mrs. Eldridge led Egeth by margins fluctuating between four and eight votes. Egeth, however, declined suggestions that he withdraw and the caucus broke up at 3 A.M. without a decision. This is what doomed the Eldridge candidacy. The next afternoon Rossetti secured a majority by locking up the votes of several wavering Negro district leaders.

The next night, July 6, the reformers met again and continued their futile deadlock. Just before midnight, Kennedy's assistant, Joseph Dolan, phoned the caucus to tell a few doubtful leaders that the Senator did in fact favor Mrs. Eldridge, and urged them to accept a simple majority rule to bind the caucus. This suggestion was voted down and the meeting dragged on. At 1 A.M., reform leader Charles Kinsolving declared his support for Rossetti. After a shocked recess, the reformers agreed to support Mrs. Eldridge if Kennedy personally asked them to. But by this time it was already too late.

The next morning Kennedy flew back from a holiday in Montreal and started making phone calls for Mrs. Eldridge. One old-line leader, Joseph Walsh, agreed to switch from Rossetti but Senate Majority leader Zaretzki refused and Manhattan Borough President Percy Sutton would not accept five separate phone calls. Mrs. Eldridge was one vote short. As usual the reformers had been too divided and Kennedy had been too indecisive and had moved too late. Mrs. Eldridge withdrew as a candidate and Rossetti defeated Egeth—he even received the votes of four reform district leaders as part of a deal for a Civic Court Judgeship.

When it was over, everyone, including Kennedy, denied he had tried to intervene. After his election, Rossetti's first words to the press were, "Our first goal is the reelection of our great leader, Lyndon Johnson."

Kennedy told Mrs. Eldridge, "If I had forty-eight hours we could have put it together. But two hours just wasn't enough time. I didn't even connect on half my phone calls. I have no clout with politicians. My only chance comes in primaries. . . . But your reform friends are sick. They hate each other so much. They really could have put me on the spot, if they had just gotten together."

The last day Robert Kennedy ever spent in New York passed like a black-humor parody of all his previous efforts in his adopted state. He had seen a candidate knocked off the state ticket because the delegates had mistaken him for a Kennedy man. He had campaigned for candidates that privately repelled him. He couldn't even get a Borough President to come to the phone when he needed a favor.

And on May 8, 1968, in the middle of his last campaign, Kennedy had to return to New York to plead with the shabby clubhouse operators, who were delegates from Brooklyn and Queens, to support him for President at the national convention.

It was a painful day for Kennedy. He had won the grueling Indiana primary the night before, but the next morning's news stories and columns in *The New York Times* had interpreted his triumph as a defeat in disguise. He was very tired and ornery.

With one hundred delegates, six rabbis, and some of his staff crowded into the living room of his apartment, Kennedy typically spent a half hour with Norman Mailer in another room. On the flight back from Indiana, Kennedy had told me that he looked forward to meeting Mailer, and that he considered him, "some sort of crazy genius." He greeted Mailer with, "Mr. Mailer, you're a mean man with a word." The two men then spent twenty-five minutes arguing over Kennedy's late entry into the race, shifting precariously back and forth between rancor and respect. Mailer departed as he had arrived, one of the few New York intellectuals supporting Kennedy rather than McCarthy.

Kennedy then saw the six rabbis. He had no patience with them. He had gone on his knees to the rabbis for his brother, but now he was more liberal than they and he would not make ritualistic attacks on the Arabs to pander for their support. Someone suggested Kennedy hire a public relations man to handle his contacts with the "Jewish Community," but Kennedy lost his temper at the suggestion.

Then the Brooklyn and Queens delegates trooped into his bedroom: and these men, the lowest common denominators in politics, told Robert Kennedy they would not support him for President, that they were neutral. While they had waited to see him, they had talked openly in his living room, in front of his staff, of going for Humphrey if the deal was sweet enough in Chicago. Late that afternoon Kennedy once again described the New York Democracy as a "zoo."

Today the New York Democracy is deservedly in ashes. There are a Republican Governor, two Republican Senators, and a Republican

Mayor in New York City. The Republicans even won back the State Assembly in the 1968 election, thus saving the Democrats from another embarrassing civil war over the Speakership. The reform faction continues its bitchy decline. Those few, young politicians who had looked to Kennedy for leadership are now lost. What Robert Kennedy did in New York, just by his presence, was personalize an alternative to the barons.

Although he came into the state as a master manager of the old politics and under the patronage of the biggest barons, his own instincts soon took him in the direction of more democratic procedures, more liberal candidates, and toward the unrepresented blacks. He did not fight the barons when to fight would conflict with his own self-interest. His involvement in New York was sporadic: Vietnam, poverty, and Presidential politics remained his abiding concerns. And in the end the barons endured to humiliate him. But no one before him had toppled the barons—not even Herbert Lehman, Averell Harriman, or Robert Wagner. In no state in the union has a Senator taken responsibility for reform.

As in so many realms, Robert Kennedy remained only a potential in New York politics. He kept getting better, but he had not yet taken his stand. So his loss was felt most keenly after his assassination because his death was also the death of a small hope.

Book Three

Lyndon Johnson:
The Antichrist of the New Politics

Robert Kennedy reached the pinnacle of his popularity during the autumn of 1966. Never again would he hear such cheering—except perhaps for the fifteen days he was running directly against Lyndon Johnson in March of 1968.

Robert Kennedy traveled across the tense landscape of America that election season, campaigning for his friends and for those who had helped his brother in 1960. Hugh Carey in Brooklyn, John Gilligan in Cleveland, John Culver in Iowa, Teno Roncalio in Wyoming, Jeffery Cohelan in Oakland. He was forty years old, a freshman Senator who was not running for any political office. Most of his brief stump speeches were barren of substance, but Robert Kennedy was filling a need that had no name.

Time, Life, and *Newsweek* published cover stories on him. Seventy reporters from ten countries followed him. The Harris and Gallup polls showed him to be more popular, both with Democrats and voters at large, than the incumbent President. In the capital of Lyndon Johnson's home state, 10,000 farm workers held a rally and chanted, "Viva Kennedy." Robert Kennedy in 1966 was a happening that was happening too soon.

The response Kennedy evoked across the country in September and October was without precedent. He came to most places only to be seen at the side of local candidates. Yet the crowds were so large that he seemed to be running for President. Their enthusiasm for him was

boundless. In a small Iowa hamlet 2,000 people waited at an airport till
1 A.M. to see him. In the larger cities they broke through police barricades to touch him and snatch mementos like his PT-109 tie clasp, his
cuff links, or even a lock of his hair. Young people especially screamed
at him to run for President. At most stops there were crayoned signs:
RFK IN '68, '72, OR ANYTIME. RFK SI, LBJ NO. RETURN TOUCH
FOOTBALL TO THE WHITE HOUSE. KEEP ON HARASSING LBJ. A woman
in Marion, Iowa, said, "I can't hear a word he's saying, but I agree with
him." A Michigan Congressman remarked, "It's magic; people like him
because they like him."

Except for one eloquent speech at Berkeley against racism, most of
what Kennedy said on tour was as perishable as cotton candy. He
tended to avoid Vietnam, except when asked about it. He spoke more
about the accomplishments of John Kennedy than of Lyndon Johnson.
He stressed that things were getting worse, that there was no reason for
satisfaction, and everyone could do more—an indirect challenge to the
President's you-never-had-it-so-good theme. But mostly he just came
and bantered. In Los Angeles, when he was given a key to the city
governed by his enemy Sam Yorty, he quipped, "Does this mean you've
just changed all the locks?" In Lakewood, California, he noticed a
Reagan supporter in a tree and cracked, "If that man falls out of that
tree, and he's over sixty-five, he won't get Medicare if Ronald Reagan
gets elected Governor." One day in Brooklyn he saw the inevitable
group of nuns in the crowd and said, "The sisters always come out for
the Democrats, but the monsignors and bishops always stay home and
pray for the Republicans."

All of Kennedy's appearances were professionally advanced for maximum exposure and smoothness. But the explosion of adulation was
spontaneous. He was a politician, for that brief season, in perfect
harmony with his time. The nation wanted him. They did not like
Lyndon Johnson, and they did not like the wooden boxes coming home
from Vietnam. But everybody said that tradition and reason dictated
that Kennedy must wait, at least till 1972. They said he should develop
a "low silhouette," and try to stay out of the headlines. They said he was
peaking too soon.

But one person disagreed. On the morning after the 1966 elections,
Adam Walinsky handed Robert Kennedy a memo urging him to run for
President in 1968. Walinsky perceived the urgency and intensity of

feeling in the crowds that came out for Kennedy. He read the returns that cost the Democrats forty-seven House seats, as a rejection of President Johnson's leadership. Walinsky understood that the movement for Kennedy was a fragile and transient passion; that the young and the intellectuals might find another hero if the moment was not seized; that the hatred of the war bubbling up would not wait for a leader paced by a calendar. Walinsky was thinking of John Lindsay or Charles Percy, but McCarthy proved his fear generally correct. So Walinsky began his memo by writing on November 8, 1966, "Lyndon Johnson is a lame duck . . ."

From December, 1963, to the spring of 1965, Lyndon Johnson seemed invincible and likely to be judged by detached historians as a superior President. In November of 1964 he achieved the greatest triumph in the history of Presidential elections, defeating Barry Goldwater by a margin of 16,951,220 votes. He received 61 percent of the popular vote and carried forty-five of the fifty states. In the landslide victory the Democrats gained two seats in the Senate and thirty-seven in the House. The debacle was so complete that journalists and political scientists speculated about the future viability of the Republican Party.

Johnson had held a dazed nation together in the weeks following Dallas. He pushed and finessed civil rights, antipoverty, Medicare, and other programs begun by his predecessor through the Congress.* For a while the polls showed 75 and 80 percent of the nation approving of his leadership. His popularity during this period equaled that of Franklin Roosevelt during his first term.

On August 21, 1964, Johnson, in an expansive mood, spoke to two Washington journalists about his success at the polls, his popularity, and his imminent renomination for President by acclamation.

"You see," the President said, "right here's the reason I'm going to win this thing so big. You ask a voter who classifies himself as a liberal what he thinks I am, and he says, 'a liberal.' You ask a voter who calls himself a conservative what I am and he says, 'a conservative.' You ask a voter who calls himself a middle-of-the-roader, and that's what he calls me. They all think I'm on their side."

By the autumn of 1966, the disintegration of the President's super-coalition of 1964 was well under way. And so was his own dramatic

---

* Sixty-nine percent of all the bills President Johnson submitted to Congress in 1965 were passed, a record accomplishment.

decline in popularity. The President who was so skillful at acquiring power was proving to be less skilled in exercising power.

It wasn't that certain groups had turned against Johnson, while others had rallied to his side. But that everyone, for different reasons, was becoming slowly disillusioned with him at the same time. His trouble was that no group, and few individuals, felt any deep personal loyalty to the President. Even such relatively unpopular Presidents as Herbert Hoover and Harry Truman had a protective cocoon of loyalists. A Glassboro summit conference, or a burst of global traveling could always boost his stock at the polls for a while, but the percentages would eventually come tumbling down again because Johnson never had that hard core of followers who liked him for himself.

There were, I think, at least six general reasons to explain Johnson's dramatic decline in popularity and power between 1964 and 1966.

First, of course, was the steady, open-ended escalation of the war in Vietnam. In the beginning this only caused the young and the intellectuals to bolt out of Johnson's consensus. But gradually the war came to alienate the ordinary voter, who saw it pragmatically, not in the moral and geopolitical terms of the dissenters, but merely as a failure in American terms. There were no mass protests across the nation against the Dominican intervention because it seemed to work. Johnson's sin in Vietnam was failure: mounting bloodshed, national impatience with stalemate, and the growing sense that a guerrilla war in Asia could not be won.

The second reason was Johnson's own defects of character and personality. The tip of this iceberg became known as the credibility gap, as the Washington press kept catching the President telling unnecessary lies on even the smallest matters. A typical experience was Hugh Sidey's, who covers the White House for *Life* magazine. Richard Goodwin was a friend of his, and in 1964 Sidey saw Goodwin in an office ghosting speeches for the President. When Sidey directly asked the President about this harmless development, Johnson flatly declared that Goodwin "has not written a single speech for me." The President then proceeded to draw a White House organization chart for Sidey to prove his point, and at the bottom of the chart sketched in the name of "Goodman," as if the misspelling would convince Sidey that what he saw with his own eyes was not true.

The submerged part of the character iceberg was more serious.

Johnson had run on the campaign promise in 1964 of "no wider war," and had enlarged the war two months after his 1965 inaugural. He had promised that American bombing missions were not causing civilian casualties, but television and newspaper reports showed this to be untrue.

Johnson's political and personal idiosyncrasies gradually drove most of his more worldly and intellectual aides like Bill Moyers, Eric Goldman, and Goodwin out of the White House. And by the end, the White House came to resemble the Alamo, with the President surrounded by a brigade of loyal Texan assistants and friends like George Christian, Harry McPherson, Marvin Watson, William S. White, and Abe Fortas. By early 1967, the temperate Richard Rovere could write in *The New Yorker* that "what may well be a majority of American people are persuaded that the President is a dishonest and dishonorable man."

If the war alienated the young, and the credibility gap estranged the press, it was Johnson's own political style that cost him the allegiance of many of the professional politicians. Johnson, in his mania for control, frugality, and secrecy, dismantled the independent staff, financing, and power of the Democratic National Committee, and transferred these responsibilities into the White House, under Marvin Watson. Fund raising, patronage dispensing, campaign financing, all the minutiae of daily politicking, became centralized under Watson's charter. "I'm damned if I can see why one guy and a couple of secretaries can't run that thing," Johnson once said of the DNC.

John Kennedy had done the same thing, by placing Kenneth O'Donnell, Larry O'Brien, and Steve Smith in control of patronage, his own campaign plans, and keeping up political contacts. But that was a troika of considerable sophistication and subtlety. The general consensus among Washington columnists was that Watson was conservative and conspiratorial. Joseph Kraft once quoted an anonymous Administration official as calling Watson the "crudest" man he ever saw in the White House. Roland Evans and Robert Novak converted Watson into a regular villain in their columns, generally identifying him as a former "union-buster from Texas." Under Watson's rule, voter registration projects stopped, political leaders with liberal views were cut off from the President, local feuds festered, and patronage was employed in an increasingly vindictive manner.

The fourth reason for Johnson's fall was the emerging pattern of increasing summer violence in the black ghettos. As with Vietnam, there was no upsurge of enlightened liberal opinion, but rather a spreading sense that the President did not have the leadership capability to deal with the problem.

A fifth reason was the growing myth, formed by the country's guilt and nostalgia, around the memory of John Kennedy. Johnson became haunted by a ghost. The President's style, personality, intelligence all suffered when measured against the memory of his martyred predecessor. A Harris Poll, released on the third anniversary of John Kennedy's murder, showed that 70 percent of the country felt that the dead President was "greater" than the living one. Only 15 percent felt that Johnson was superior.

And the last reason was that Johnson became a victim of his own exaggerated rhetoric. Constant talk of a Great Society built up expectations too fast and too far. Johnson, perhaps because he felt so haunted by the memory of John Kennedy, kept trying to prove that his record was really better, and this trapped him in the quicksand of his own oversell. In the fall of 1966 he said in Nashville, "We've passed more bills, spent more money, reached more people, provided more comprehensive efforts in three years than in the rest of history." In a strict statistical sense that might have been near the truth, but the reality of the war, the riots, the social chaos, and malaise was what people felt and saw.

Yet, not one political leader or commentator of stature believed that the President could be denied renomination, or that there was any possibility Robert Kennedy would try to challenge him for the Democratic nomination. The canons of politics dictated that an incumbent President was impregnable from insurrection from below. It said that a sitting President derived too much legitimacy from the history of his office; that he could control the media, the convention ground rules, the state chairmen, and the delegates themselves through the use of patronage and funds for Federal projects. That a sitting President of Johnson's power and political guile would destroy the career of anyone who dared to challenge him from inside the Democratic Party. And besides, the mathematics of rebellion were hopeless since only fourteen of the fifty states had primaries.

Joseph Alsop, who was fond of Kennedy, and who was more mindful than most of the President's vulnerabilities, wrote late in 1966 that "No imaginable number of pleas from state chairmen and others is going to tempt Senator Kennedy to bid for the Democratic nomination against President Johnson. He will never do it, simply because he is, above all, no fool."

But Lyndon Johnson was to become the first victim of the new politics in America.

The new politics is diverse, contradictory, and has already passed through several incarnations. Its gestation began deep within affluent America in 1960 and 1961, with the sit-ins and Freedom Rides. It set down roots on elite and urban campuses in 1963 and 1964 in *ad hoc* movements against poverty, racism, and bureaucracy. With the expansion of the Vietnam war in 1965, the middle class and the intellectuals adjusted the new politics to fit their foreign policy and peace concerns. By 1967 the new politics was beginning to define itself against Lyndon Johnson.

Lyndon Johnson's style was bureaucratic and manipulative, and the new politics was rooted in activism and participatory decision-making. Johnson perfected his politics of consensus and intrigue in one-party Texas, and wheeling-dealing Senate cloakrooms. The new politics took its ethic from the spontaneity and anarchy of the campuses, and the civilized, college-educated reformism of the suburbs.

Johnson liked to deal personally with leaders in closed rooms, and depend on men like George Meany, Everett Dirksen, Roy Wilkins, and Henry Ford to control or deliver their constituencies. But the new politics was antiorganization and antideal. And it was made up largely of younger people, whose few leaders belonged to a generation very different from Johnson's.

Johnson was the father of the war in Vietnam. And the soul of the new politics was moral horror at the war in Vietnam. Johnson's Presidency was one of the most personal—and personality-centered—of this century. And the new politics prided itself on its elevation of issues and movements above personality and party.

And almost as vital as the war was Johnson's own character. The New Class in the suburbs, shaped by television, Freud, and college educations, simply did not trust or like the President. They abhorred his deceitfulness, his corniness, his crudity.

At the start of Johnson's second term, the new politics was still embryonic and subterranean. It had few allies and no leader. At that point it seemed likely that the new politics would not enter the national political bloodstream until 1972. But from the start, it was destined that Lyndon Johnson be its antichrist.

It is difficult now to rummage from memory the frustrated messianic mood some of us were in early in 1967. By April I came to believe that Johnson had to be defeated for reelection. But we had no candidate, nor any hope of getting one. My friends spoke vaguely of a Martin Luther King–Benjamin Spock protest ticket in 1968, but I was not excited by the idea of symbolic dissent.

I spoke at a few campuses in the spring and watched the violence and fury against the war mount, turning English majors into guerrilla fantasists. Several thousand white, middle-class college students, with successful careers already tracked inside the system, burned their draft cards, risking five years in jail. Other thousands became men without countries by exiling themselves to Canada to avoid the rising draft calls. Despairing of changing the world, more and more students were turning to new chemicals to shut out the world, and change the universe inside their heads. And within the deepest coils of the New Left, kids talked of sabotage and assassination—"like in France during the Algerian war."

I was in a funk much of the time. Sometimes the footage of the war on the seven o'clock news shows would depress me for the rest of the evening. The Administration was reviving its insinuations that the antiwar movement was Communist manipulated. The House Un-American Activities Committee had released a report in early April red-baiting the movement. On April 16 Dean Rusk was asked on television whether he thought the war protests were Communist inspired, and he replied with a knowing grin, "I am giving you my responsible personal view that the Communist apparatus is working very hard on it."

Meanwhile, whatever we did to protest the war seemed impotent. Writing essays had as much influence on policy as going to jail, or tripping with LSD. The war kept escalating as if we didn't exist, and the President's renomination seemed inevitable. In April, mostly as a result of my gloomy mood, I refused to pay 20 percent of my Federal income tax as a futile gesture of defiance. On April 6, I published a piece in *The Village Voice* that was faithful to my feelings of the time:

> I voted for him [Johnson] in 1964, and now I don't believe a word he says. . . . I am a Democrat, so the thing to do is defeat him next year.

The conventional wisdom among politicians these days is that LBJ's political strength has been underestimated. They feel he is now gaining in popularity, much the way Nelson Rockefeller did before he was re-elected Governor in 1966, and that he will defeat any Republican candidate next year.

I disagree. My perception of LBJ is that, like Sonny Liston, he is a bully with a quitter's heart, that he will not run if he thinks he cannot win. . . .

I am too old to defy the draft, too content to volunteer as a hostage in North Vietnam . . . so I will withhold twenty per cent of my taxes this year.

At Auschwitz a child who knew he was about to die screamed at a German guard, "You won't be forgiven anything."

This is my saying the same thing to Lyndon Johnson. He is not my President. This is not my war.

A few days later I saw a familiar acquaintance at a party who remarked that he liked the article. Then Allard Lowenstein said, "I'm going to be spending the rest of the year organizing a movement to dump Johnson. Do you want to help?"

Allard Lowenstein is a protean man of virtuoso talents. He is a glib orator and debater with a brand of charisma most appreciated on college campuses. He has a sure instinct for the next liberal step. He is brilliant at maneuver and manipulation. And he has relentless energy and optimism. This grab bag of qualities happened to be ideally mated to his dream of dumping the President of the United States.

In 1966 Lowenstein had tried to win the reform movement's designation for Congress in Manhattan's 19th Congressional District. But his rivals claimed he was more interested in Southwest Africa than in his district, since he seemed to spend more time there. At one point in the campaign I proposed to Lowenstein that his slogan be "Yesterday the World. Today the 19th C.D." In the end he was narrowly defeated. So by April of 1967 very few people took Lowenstein seriously anymore. His older friends like Norman Thomas and Irving Howe gave him Polonius-like lectures about getting a steady job, starting to wear a suit and tie, and stop hanging around with twenty-year-old students. When he tried to explain that he had this new project to deny the President renomination, they smiled and wished him good luck.

So Lowenstein began his movement without money, without an office, without an organization, without the support of one labor union or a single liberal leader of national reputation. And without a candidate. All he had was the technological equivalents of Fidel Castro's twenty-six guerrillas in the Sierra Maestre, his cluttered Manhattan apartment, his phone, his address book of thousands of names, and his credit card.

Lowenstein, by nature, is a reformer and not a radical. He feels more competitive with the New Left than allied with it. He threw himself into the antiwar movement in late 1966 because he wanted to rally "moderate, reasonable student opinion" against the war, to create the political pressure for Johnson to alter his policy. Lowenstein was the guiding force behind the series of letters and ads of student editors, Peace Corps returnees, and Rhodes scholars against the war. In connection with these letters he had audiences with Walt Rostow and Dean Rusk in early January of 1967.

"Rostow was unbelievable and Rusk was worse," recalls Lowenstein. "I began to think that maybe they really wouldn't change on the war. Then I saw Humphrey and had this feeling reinforced. Then Kennedy told me about his February 6 meeting with Johnson, and I became convinced that the Administration was hopeless, that it didn't really even want to negotiate. So, sort of by lurches, I came to the position by March of 1967 that the only hope of ending the war was to directly oppose Johnson within the political system for renomination."

But by the spring of 1967, Lowenstein, at the age of thirty-eight, was in danger of being dismissed as an eccentric, as the oldest student leader in the country. He did not seem to have a profession, or an office, or a political base. He bounced around the globe and was almost impossible to reach on short notice. There is a legend claiming that the information operators in New Haven, Raleigh, Palo Alto, and Manhattan all knew Lowenstein's number by heart. Being his friend was also somewhat like being stranded on a telephone hold button. Once Lowenstein, after six weeks of silence, called me up at 5 P.M. and invited me to have dinner with him and Mrs. Juan Bosch at 6 P.M. at his family's restaurant. When I got there, seventeen of his friends—many of them famous— were seated around the table, and I never got to say a word to Mrs. Bosch, who was at the other end of the table. On another occasion, Lowenstein and I flew to Mississippi together to participate in the last leg of James Meredith's voter registration march to Jackson. An hour after we arrived, Lowenstein was closeted with Martin Luther King, Floyd McKissick, Charles Evers, and Stokely Carmichael, trying to mediate their bickering, since they were all his friends.

Many people with small pockets of influence like myself were ready, at no personal risk or sacrifice, to join as spear carriers in a safari against the President. New York psychiatrist, Dr. Martin Shepard, had already started an amateurish chain of clubs to draft Robert Kennedy. A few reform Democrats in New York, and several of the leaders of the 33,000-member California Democratic Council (CDC) movement in California were also ready to sign up for such a rebellion. But only Lowenstein had a vision of the whole of it, and the leadership instincts to conceive the movement, plan it, start it, and lead it. In April of 1967, out of his apartment on West 82nd Street, and his family's restaurant on East 49th Street, he began to hold the first implausible meetings, make the first exploratory phone calls, and chart those first lonely visits to Wisconsin, New Hampshire, and Minnesota, to find the one county chairman, the one marginal politician who might spark a grass-roots movement.

History does not move in a straight line or on a single level. During the spring, summer and early fall of 1967, changes were taking place within the country whose meaning would not become clear until after the Tet offensive.

First, the middle-class opposition to the war grew, and grew, and grew, although the opinion polls did not seem to reflect it. More than 100,000 people marched to United Nations Plaza in New York on April 27, for an antiwar rally addressed by Martin Luther King. During the summer, several thousand college students joined the Vietnam Summer Project (sponsored by King and Spock) as volunteers visiting door to door, talking about the war to people in seven hundred communities in forty-eight states. In October, another 100,000 people, many of them middle-class professionals, marched across the Potomac River to the Pentagon under the sponsorship of the most militant of the antiwar organizations. This was all part of one cord of events, that began to unravel with the teach-ins and SDS march in April of 1965, and would end with thousands of college students quitting for a semester, and going to New Hampshire in February of 1968.

In the short run these unpopular demonstrations antagonized many people, and appeared actually to hurt the cause of the antiwar movement. But in the long run, I think, they were vital to the political miracle of 1968. They were unpleasant evidence of exactly how deeply people felt against the war. At the Pentagon, I saw middle-aged men, in conservative business suits, swing back at Federal marshals who pushed them. These unruly demonstrations showed that the fabric of the culture, a very thin membrane, was in danger of being shattered; that America was becoming ungovernable under Lyndon Johnson; that there could be no law and order in the country as long as Johnson remained President and followed his policy of escalation. After a while, people associated the tumult not with the activists, but with the President.

Second, the President's political position continued to worsen. It wasn't just that American casualties in Vietnam continued to mount, and that a tax increase seemed necessary to pay for the expanded war, and that 1967 was the most violent summer yet of urban rioting. It was that the combination of these three trends together undermined confidence in Johnson's leadership, and in his choice of national priorities. The riots persuaded many people that the money being spent in Vietnam could be more wisely spent in the cities, and the proposed income tax surcharge to subsidize the war was an example of this misplaced emphasis. And all the while, the Democratic Party machinery continued to atrophy, as relations between the state chairmen and the White House became more difficult under Watson. Also, the professional politicians began to fear serious local defeats in 1968 with Johnson at the top of the ticket.

And third, there was finally some small motion within the liberal Establishment. Lowenstein's dream still seemed quixotic and irresponsible, but Joe Rauh, of the ADA, while calling Lowenstein a mad revolutionary, began circulating a memo calling for a fight at the 1968 convention for a peace plank in the party platform. Much of the ADA leadership, which still felt residual ties to Hubert Humphrey, quickly lined up behind this position, and counterposed it to Lowenstein's. Longtime ADA leader Leon Shull and Michigan Congressman Wes Vivian were especially forceful proponents of what became known as the "Rauh position."

By the end of the summer, however, ADA's chairman, John Kenneth Galbraith, was not only quietly converted to Lowenstein's bolder strategy, but even offered to run himself against Johnson in the New Hampshire primary if no one else was available. It was also Galbraith, at around this time, who got off the best political epigram of the year— "This is the year when the people are right, and the politicians are wrong."

Meanwhile, Lowenstein beavered across the country like a postindustrial Lone Ranger, jetting into a city, setting up a local dump Johnson group, firing up a crowd of two hundred or four hundred students, and then flying off alone after midnight, to the next outpost on his lengthening itinerary. On August 15, at the National Student Association Congress in College Park, Maryland, he formally unveiled the movement, and six hundred students signed up on the spot, even though SDS was boycotting the Congress in favor of a rival meeting nearby, to protest NSA's covert complicity with the CIA.

Speaking every day to a civic luncheon in Nebraska, or a synagogue in Minnesota, or to a small agricultural college in Texas, Lowenstein could feel the hunger in the land for an alternative to Johnson. He felt it was there to be put together, this miracle of his. He would find the party dissidents and the activist students, and together they would work *inside* the political process. From this would come a movement so powerful that it would pull Robert Kennedy into the race. For from the beginning, Lowenstein's candidate was Robert Kennedy, and even during the agonized months of 1968 when he would be publicly for Eugene McCarthy, Lowenstein would remain, in the privacy of his divided heart, partial to Kennedy.

All these forces, pressures, and events fed Robert Kennedy's existing ambivalence: the President's decline in popularity, and his own rise; his sharpening opposition to the war, and the apparent public support for the war in the opinion polls; Lowenstein's reports of stunning grassroots successes, and the fact no organization, no newspaper, no union, no Senator, had yet defected to the guerrillas; his own sense of duty, history, and national crisis, and the seeming futility of a struggle against the President. And just below the surface, Shakespearean in its symmetry, was the twisted past relationship between Kennedy and the President. Probably not since Theodore Roosevelt and William Howard Taft had two national leaders of the same party disagreed so politically, and clashed so personally. In the summer of 1967 national leadership, for the third time in eight years, was balanced between them.

Starting in 1959, Robert Kennedy and Lyndon Johnson began competing for the power of the Presidency: Johnson for himself, Kennedy for his brother. It was dirty and personal on both sides. The Kennedys certainly fouled and savaged Hubert Humphrey in West Virginia. On the eve of the Los Angeles convention, the Johnson forces tried to smear both Robert Kennedy's brother and father. John Connally, chairman of the Citizens for Johnson Committee, charged at a press conference that John Kennedy was secretly suffering from Addison's disease and was not healthy enough to serve or survive as President. Other backers of Johnson revived the old charge that Joseph P. Kennedy was anti-Semitic, and had been pro-Hitler in the late 1930's. On July 14 Johnson himself told several caucuses, in a clear reference to Kennedy's father, "I wasn't any Chamberlain umbrella man. I never thought Hitler was right."

John Kennedy, detached and professional, could easily forgive such tactics once nominated. But the more tribal and moralistic Robert Kennedy could not. And according to most accounts, he opposed his brother offering the Vice Presidential nomination to Johnson. And even if he didn't, Johnson and his friends left Los Angeles feeling that Kennedy had tried to thwart his nomination. From that moment on, trust between the two men was impossible, and suspicion natural.

Elected to the office of Vice President, Johnson watched helplessly as Robert Kennedy acted like the Vice President. Johnson was rarely consulted on patronage matters. He was often absent from important meetings when Robert Kennedy was invited. And he certainly had much less access to the President than did the Attorney General.

Johnson sulked and suffered periodic rumors that he would be dropped from the ticket in 1964. On the morning of November 22, 1963, the *Boston Globe,* in the lead news story of its first edition, claimed that Johnson would definitely be dumped.

Then the gunshots. Robert Kennedy's brother was assassinated in Texas, where he went to settle a Texas political feud, and now he was being replaced by a Texan. Overnight everything was inverted. Johnson had the power, sat at his brother's desk, and now Kennedy was powerless. Now it was Kennedy who half desired the Vice Presidency, and Lyndon Johnson who had the authority to give it, or deny it.

After months of tension, Johnson not only denied it, but afterward called in several friendly reporters and told them in cruel and profane language, laced with mimicry, how badly Kennedy had accepted the news. And how much pleasure he got in delivering it.

Johnson and Kennedy seemed strapped onto opposite ends of the same seesaw, separated by generation, geography, politics, temperament, and ambition. One of them could not rise in popularity without the other falling. The nation could only perceive them as the alternative masks of the Democratic Party.

But Kennedy carried an extra burden that distorted his reactions to the President. Kennedy was plagued by the memory that Lyndon Johnson was President because of the decision of his own dead brother. To run against Johnson would be to run against his brother, too. It was part of the same attitude that held Kennedy back from criticizing the war because he felt part of the responsibility was his brother's and his brother's appointees'. This block cut Kennedy off from his greatest asset—his instincts. And this is why he violated his own nature each time he pulled away from a confrontation with Johnson.

The first clear symptom that Kennedy was not himself when forced to face the problem of challenging Johnson for the nomination came in June of 1967.

Kennedy by then disagreed with Johnson's conduct of the war, regarded his leadership to be disastrous for the country, and viewed him personally as "a monster." Yet he agreed to introduce the President at a gala Democratic Party fund-raising dinner on June 3 at the Americana Hotel in Manhattan.

Several of the Manhattan reformers Kennedy felt closest to, including Assemblymen Blumenthal and Kretchmer, had announced in advance they were boycotting the $100-a-plate affair. The night of the dinner about 1,500 pickets—as many dissenting Democrats as student radicals—marched in an antiwar, anti-Johnson protest.

But Kennedy, instead of giving his typical wry, self-deflating speech, introduced the President in language more like Hubert Humphrey than his own. Kennedy began by quoting Webster's definition of "greatness" and then went on to say of his rival:

> He has poured out his own strength to renew the strength of the country . . . he has sought consensus but he has never shrunk from controversy . . . he has gained huge popularity, but never hesitated to spend it on what he thought important. . . . He has led us to build schools, to clean water, to reclaim the beauty of the countryside, to educate children, to comfort the oppressed on a scale unmatched in history. . . .

I was in Stratford-on-Avon when Kennedy gave this speech, and after reading his quotes, I sent him a tourist's postcard that only said, "To thine own self be true."

When I returned, I asked Kennedy's office for a copy of his remarks introducing Johnson, and Frank Mankiewicz reported there were none available. Adam Walinsky tried to convince me (unsuccessfully) that if the text could be analyzed closely, it became clear that it was all a subtle exercise in irony. The first time I saw Kennedy after my return from England he quipped, "I was going to send you back a card that said, 'Out, damned spot.'" But when I asked him what possessed him to introduce the President that way, he looked angry and said, "I don't know. I don't want to get into that. It's in the past."

By the end of August, however, Kennedy clearly regretted his effusive language, and had reopened, in the solitude of his own mind, the possibility of running in 1968. It was about this time that he had his first private conversation with Lowenstein.

Kennedy and Lowenstein had first met in May of 1966, when Lowenstein came to brief him on South Africa before his visit there, and ended up rewriting most of Kennedy's major addresses scheduled for Johannesburg. Quickly Kennedy came to respect Lowenstein's blend of political guile, energy, and toughness, not qualities he normally expected in a disciple of Eleanor Roosevelt and Norman Thomas.

Kennedy and Lowenstein talked for about an hour in a commercial plane flying from New York to San Francisco. As Lowenstein recalls the conversation:

"I was traveling tourist class and he was traveling first class, so I had to trade seats with Mankiewicz in order to talk to him. . . . I did not make any attempt to ask him to run. I was aware that I was a flea and he was an elephant, and that we had a lot more organizing to do before I could ask him that. I just explained to him what the dump Johnson movement was really all about. I explained to him very carefully that we were not kooks, or the New Left, or just the same old peace people. I explained we were recruiting thousands of students and many regular Democrats who were against Johnson. I tried to convince him that his stereotype of these people was wrong, and that we were committed to working inside the electoral system. Then I talked about how deep the feeling across the country was for him to run against Johnson. Finally I said we would have a candidate entered in the New Hampshire primary, and I mentioned I would soon be talking to General Gavin about doing this. His reaction was, 'If you get Gavin, you've got a new ball game.'"

Lowenstein and I saw Kennedy together at his home in McLean,

Virginia, on Saturday night, September 23. The dump Johnson movement had grown rapidly in the provinces in the intervening month. Lowenstein now led a newly created national organization—the Conference of Concerned Democrats. He had found local leaders in the first two primary states, David Hoeh in New Hampshire, and Donald Peterson in Wisconsin. And he was beginning to raise money.

Lowenstein and I arrived about 10:30 P.M. and were greeted by a relaxed Kennedy, dressed in bright green slacks and a green sweater. Arthur Schlesinger and James Loeb, the publisher and former Ambassador to Peru, were with him, and we adjourned to the living room. Adam Walinsky was also in the house finishing work on Kennedy's book, *To Seek a Newer World*.

With Kennedy sitting there, a bemused smile on his face, listening intently, and making only occasional comments, Lowenstein and I debated with Schlesinger and Loeb for an hour and a half about whether Kennedy should try for the Presidency in 1968.

Lowenstein kicked his shoes off and sat cross-legged on a thick chair, college-bull-session style. He argued first against the Rauh position, which Schlesinger then held. Schlesinger said it was "impossible" to dump Johnson, that 1968 would be "a Republican year," and that Kennedy should wait till 1972. Lowenstein made Vietnam the centerpiece of his remarks rather than Presidential politics, and emphasized the moral imperative of stopping the war by dislodging Johnson. He then raised the possibility that Johnson might not run if the insurgents won the early primaries.

It was at that point that Kennedy entered the colloquy for the first time, saying, "I think Al may be right. I think Johnson might quit the night before the convention opens. I think he is a coward."

"Do you think his people will ask him not to run if he loses some early primaries?" Loeb asked.

"I'd like to see who the first person is who goes in there alone and says, please, Mister President, don't run," Kennedy answered.

Schlesinger and I then debated the merits of the Rauh position. Schlesinger thought it was the only practical out since there was not going to be another candidate in the field against Johnson. I argued that a campaign for a peace plank was "absurd," and recalled that the 1964 platform had a strong—but irrelevant—peace plank on Vietnam.

At this point Kennedy intervened again with a needling, "How do you run on a plank, Arthur? . . . When was the last time millions of people rallied behind a plank? . . . If I was Lyndon Johnson, I would be much angrier at Jack and Al, than at you, Arthur."

After some more jousting between Lowenstein and Loeb, who seemed to be pro-LBJ, Kennedy said in a slow, serious voice, "I would have a problem if I ran first against Johnson. People would say that I was splitting the party out of ambition and envy. No one would believe that I was doing it because of how I felt about Vietnam and poor people. I think Al is doing the right thing, but I think that someone else will have to be the first one to run. It can't be me because of my relationship with Johnson. And his feeling toward me has more to do with my brother than me."

"Everything Kennedy says about other people," Andrew Kopkind once wrote, "has an autobiographical ring."

In the next few weeks events began to move quickly toward trapping Kennedy in a situation without solutions.

Feeling that Kennedy was "sympathetic, but very skeptical," and with time becoming critical, Lowenstein began to sound out other men on the possibility of entering the New Hampshire primary against the President.

Most published reports of Lowenstein's quest for a candidate have been simplified into a clear-cut sequence of offer and rejection. But rather, there was an ongoing, fluid interaction between Lowenstein and those he asked to run. None of them gave him a flat negative. The response was more like, "I don't think I'm the one you want, but if no one else is willing to do it, then come back and see me."

One of those who had this reaction was the first Senator Lowenstein approached after Kennedy—George McGovern. McGovern's problem was that he was up for reelection in 1968, but he was interested enough to ask Lowenstein to make a trip to his home state of South Dakota and try to evaluate the impact a primary race against the President would have on his hawkish South Dakota constituency. Lowenstein spent three days in the state and reported back to McGovern that his declaration for the Presidency would make his Senate reelection campaign more difficult —although not impossible. Still, McGovern never said no. He kept the door ajar. Later Kennedy would tell friends that if McGovern had been the rebel's candidate instead of McCarthy, he never would have entered the race himself. And on Robert Kennedy's funeral train, McGovern would tell Lowenstein, "If only I had run when you asked me, none of this would have happened."

California Congressman Don Edwards also informed Lowenstein that he would offer himself as an anti-Johnson symbol, if he could not get a Senator to run in New Hampshire. But then Lowenstein visited Eugene McCarthy, who unlike McGovern, was not up for reelection in 1968. McCarthy said he would prefer it if Robert Kennedy made the fight, but that he would be willing if all others quit the battlefield.

So in the third week in October, Lowenstein went back to Robert Kennedy. The appointment was a secret, and kept off Kennedy's official calendar. It took place in Kennedy's New York office on East 45th Street.

Unlike their August and September meetings, this time Lowenstein directly asked Kennedy to become the official candidate of the dump Johnson movement.

"Everything is falling into place," Lowenstein said. "We have local organizations in New Hampshire and Wisconsin, and the California Democratic Council is already committed to running an anti-Johnson candidate in the California primary. I've been across the country thirty times and I can tell we're going to win. Imagine what we could do *with you,* if we're going to win *without you!* You have to get into it! McCarthy and McGovern are both interested. We are not the West Side reform Democrats. We are grass-roots America. Johnson is finished."

But Robert Kennedy, spending his time in Washington and New York, was insulated almost as much as Johnson from the tides of ferment at the base of the society. Kennedy talked to other Senators, or older Washington journalists, or his 1960 campaign friends like Pat Lucey in Wisconsin and William Dunfey in New Hampshire. And they told him the dump Johnson movement was a collection of amateurs, fringe liberals, and long-haired students. Robert Kennedy just couldn't believe what amateur politicians like Lowenstein and Walinsky told him. They were great for thinking about issues, and mobilizing the alienated, but how could they know more than the team of 1960? How could they know more than all the professional pollsters? How could they dump the President without the ADA, and a single Senator, or *The New York Times* behind them at the start?

Robert Kennedy, remember, was not the personification of the new politics. He was only in transit from the old politics. He represented only one part of the new politics, the black slums, the white, brown, and red poor, and the B students. Just as Eugene McCarthy represented, and understood, only the other half of the new politics, the New Class in the suburbs, the intellectual elite, and the A students.

So Robert Kennedy, wanting to run, despising the war and the President, nevertheless informed Lowenstein, with great guilt and uncertainty, that no, he could not do this thing. Robert Kennedy, the imperfect politician, had misread the temper of his time.

Listening to the Voices
of the Old Politics

Up to the beginning of October, 1967, the Democratic Party's liberal factions and its satellite pressure groups did not view Lowenstein's organizing efforts as part of the real world. At its national board meeting, late in September, the ADA had voted ninety-eight to twelve against adopting an anti-Johnson resolution. The ADA also voted by a three to one margin against encouraging local chapters to cooperate with the anti-Johnson rebels, and against a motion asking the ADA to consider alternative candidates for President in 1968. Other old liberal institutions like the UAW and the NAACP followed the ADA lead. The same is true of almost all those university and journalistic liberals who had had personal experience with the office of the Presidency. The mythology of the office inhibited them from moving against it.

Only a few random rebels existed to show that insurrection was possible. The Young Democrats of Minnesota disaffiliated themselves from the national Young Democrats because of the latter's fealty to Johnson and the war. The Village Independent Democrats, one of the biggest of Manhattan's reform clubs, voted overwhelmingly to oppose the President's renomination. Zoltan Ferency, Michigan state chairman, joined the rebels, as did California Congressman Don Edwards. The *New Republic* published a rare front-cover editorial calling for the President's removal in 1968. Donald Peterson, the Democratic Party chairman in Wisconsin's 10th district and George McGovern's 1962 Senate campaign manager, became chairman of the Concerned Wisconsin Democrats.

Given the distribution of real power in America between the military-space complex, unions, senior Congressmen, television networks, universities, corporations, churches, and banks, these protest activities, as yet without a national candidate, seemed meaningless.

Lowenstein, myself, and Harold Ickes, the son of the New Deal curmudgeon, whose wild thatch of hair makes him look like John C. Calhoun, drove to Philadelphia on Wednesday night, October 11, to be guests on Jack McKinney's midnight to 2 A.M. radio talk program where we were to explain to those listeners who called asking questions the still unreal and invisible dump Johnson movement.

McKinney, a former boxer, is part of the media renaissance of proletarian Irish radicals that includes Jimmy Breslin, Pete Hamill, and Joe Flaherty. And he had invited us onto his show as a favor.

There was a uniform tone to most of the questions we received: I don't like the war, I don't like Johnson, but you guys can't be real because you don't have a candidate. Toward the end of the program I noticed Lowenstein absently doodling something while answering a question. He had jotted down a newspaper headline that read:

McCarthy Wins Wisc. Primary;
Beats LBJ With 60% of Vote

As Ickes drove back to New York, along the misty Jersey Turnpike, Lowenstein explained to us that the donish junior Senator from Minnesota appeared willing to do battle against the President. I was elated, and thought that Gene McCarthy did have the serene look of the one person on a crowded subway car to challenge a bunch of wild kids who were terrorizing the passengers.

Robert Kennedy and Eugene McCarthy were both Irish Catholics. Both antiwar Democrats. Both members of the United State Senate. But they were as different as fire and ice. Kennedy thought McCarthy was pompous, petty, and venal. McCarthy thought Kennedy was a spoiled, unintelligent demagogue. Each suspected the other, in the end, would make a separate peace with Lyndon Johnson.

When I first told Kennedy, a few days after the Philadelphia radio program, that McCarthy would probably enter the primaries, Kennedy responded, "I don't believe it. He is not that sort of fellow. And if he does run, it will only be to up his lecture fees."

Eugene McCarthy's decision to run in the primaries now completed the traps around Robert Kennedy. Kennedy did not wish to run himself. He did not wish to support President Johnson. He did not wish to endorse Senator McCarthy. He did not wish to remain silent and neutral.

Kennedy's mood during November and December of 1967 was one of misery and frustration. His stasis and caution continued to conflict with his own character. And with the desires of his young, antiwar constituency.

A few days after McCarthy actually declared his candidacy, I saw Kennedy in New York, and he spoke very candidly about his feelings toward McCarthy. McCarthy, he said, was "not moral" because he "votes one way in the Finance Committee to help his special interests, and then he votes the other way on the floor when the press is watching." Kennedy went on to complain about McCarthy's support for Lyndon Johnson rather than his brother in 1960:

"Gene McCarthy felt he should have been the first Catholic President just because he knew more St. Thomas Aquinas than my brother. . . . He made that Los Angeles speech for Stevenson just to help Johnson. . . . In 1965 he wouldn't vote for the anti-poll tax amendment just because Teddy was sponsoring it. He didn't care about the Negroes. He just wanted to give it to the Kennedys because he is so petty. He even told Joe Rauh that he wouldn't vote for the amendment because it was Teddy's."*

But in the same conversation, Kennedy also exposed how ambiguous his emotions about McCarthy really were. He recited, step by step, everything McCarthy should do to win the New Hampshire primary. "Make Johnson the issue, not the war. . . . Hire Fred Dutton and Bill Dunfey. . . . Talk about taxes outside the factory gates. . . ." It was clear to me then just how many times Kennedy had played a New Hampshire campaign in his own mind, and how tempted he was to run himself.

"Gene just isn't a nice person. In 1964 he was pulling all sorts of

* In January of 1969, McCarthy voted for conservative Russell Long of Louisiana, rather than Ted Kennedy, when Kennedy defeated Long for majority whip in the Senate Democratic caucus.

strings trying to get the Vice-Presidential nomination. Hubert Humphrey had been his friend for twenty years, and he was still trying to screw Hubert. At the same time, Bob McNamara twice turned down the Vice Presidency because he felt I should get it. This is the difference between loyalty and egotism."

This conversation took place in a car driving through Times Square. On that day an antiwar protest by students had spilled into the midtown area, and at one point an angry, bearded demonstrator stuck his head into the car, which was stopped at a red light. He shouted at a surprised Kennedy, "Senator, you're not giving us the help we need. Why don't you say something about this imperialist war?"

As the car pulled away Kennedy regained his composure, and smiling, poked his head out the window, and shouted back at the student, "Why don't you go help Gene McCarthy?"

Between October and the end of the year, Kennedy was much closer to running than either the public or the press imagined. He talked individually and collectively to dozens of friends and advisers about "my problem." At this early point they almost all counseled against combat with the President in the primaries: Mayor Daley, Secretary McNamara, Senator Clark, Governor Curtis, Bill Moyers. But Kennedy remained paralyzed between his intuition and his judgment.

The Kennedy circle of counselors held two formal meetings during this interval to discuss his political future. The first meeting was held in late October, in a suite rented by Pierre Salinger in the Regency Hotel in Manhattan. Salinger drew up the invitation list.

None of the people around Kennedy who thought that he should run was invited. This included Lowenstein, Walinsky, and Galbraith. Also excluded from the meeting were Kennedy Senate staff members who were open to the idea of an anti-Johnson race in 1968: Mankiewicz, Dolan, and Edelman.

The invitees were largely Salinger's colleagues from John Kennedy's Administration: Ted Kennedy, Steve Smith, Ted Sorensen, Pat Lucey, Fred Dutton, White House aide Chuck Daley, Richard Goodwin, and Ivan Nestingen, the former Mayor of Madison, Wisconsin, and former Under Secretary for the Department of Health, Education, and Welfare. Although it was agreed in advance that Robert Kennedy would not attend the meeting, at the last minute he anxiously phoned and said he wanted to come. His brother, however, convinced him that his presence would inhibit debate, and might alert the press.

Without Lowenstein or Walinsky there to make the case for boldness, Nestingen was the only proponent for a Presidential bid in 1968. And Nestingen, an outsider in this in-group, was merely brought along by Lucey and was not close to Kennedy.

Sorensen, Salinger, and Ted Kennedy were most opposed to a 1968 campaign. They argued that Kennedy couldn't win or even change the Vietnam policy by running. That he would help elect Nixon. He would be charged with ruthless ambition and splitting the party. He would damage his chances for 1972. He would damage his own influence, and the Kennedy family name, if he did poorly in the primaries. Even if he won every primary he entered, he probably still could not win the nomination.

Goodwin didn't agree, but felt it was not his prerogative to push Kennedy into the race against such heavy odds.

Arthur Schlesinger, who was out of the city at the time, was the first of the 1960 generation of advisers to suggest to Kennedy that he might wisely challenge the President in 1968. In a private memorandum, dated November 3, 1967, Schlesinger wrote to Kennedy:

> Until recently I have argued against the idea of your trying anything in '68. My main ground has been that, while you might conceivably get the nomination (I think Johnson is as vulnerable as Truman was in '48, and Truman probably could have been beaten then in the Democratic convention if his opponents had had a plausible candidate), the fight would shatter the party, render the Democratic nomination worthless and encourage the Republicans to nominate (I believe), if they think any Republican can win: i.e., Nixon. In other words, I have feared that your candidacy would result in making Nixon President.
>
> I am now having second thoughts about this argument. I think the country is feeling increasingly that the escalation policy has had a full and fair trial, that it just hasn't worked, that Johnson is not going to come up with anything new or different and that we must therefore have a new President. I think that events are moving faster than one could have supposed three months ago, and that the situation may be highly fluid indeed in another three months. I think that you could beat LBJ in the primaries and that you have unexpected reserves of strength in the non-primary states. And, if all this should lead the Republicans to nominate Nixon, so much the better. He is the one Republican candidate who would reunite even a divided and embittered Democratic party. I am sure he would be the easiest Republican for you, or any Democratic candidate, to beat.

All this is speculative. I have not had time to do the arithmetic, and, it is, of course, imperative that the arithmetic be done. Perhaps it has been. The only point of this letter is to urge you to take a fresh look at the situation.

On Sunday, December 10, the Kennedy advisers met in two sections. A brunch meeting of the inner circle of 1960 veterans and a rather pointless afternoon gathering of less intimate staff people and friends.

The crucial morning meeting took place in William vanden Heuvel's Manhattan apartment. Present were Robert and Ted Kennedy, Steve Smith, Kenneth O'Donnell, Fred Dutton, Pierre Salinger, Arthur Schlesinger, Theodore Sorensen, Joe Dolan, Richard Goodwin, and William vanden Heuvel.

Only Schlesinger and Goodwin said directly that Kennedy should defy history and enter the primaries. The others, led by Sorensen, were all against the race, although O'Donnell was beginning to feel ambivalent about it. Vanden Heuvel proposed that Kennedy try to maneuver his way onto the ticket with Johnson, but Kennedy dismissed that as "foolish."

According to one participant, "Robert and Arthur Schlesinger were the only guys in the room with any class. Arthur went out on a limb and said that Bob owed it to the kids to run, even if he lost. Bob was more focused on the war than anyone else besides Arthur. The rest of us talked in abstract generalities."

"The real mistake we made," Dutton recalled in July of 1968, "was that the subject on the agenda was Robert Kennedy's career. It wasn't Vietnam or the fate of the country. It was all just too political and professional. The talk was all about practical pluses and minuses, and this created a built-in atmosphere and bias against running. I know I was inhibited by the structure of the discussion, and didn't express all my doubts. . . . It was also a bad mistake not inviting Adam, Peter, and Frank to the meeting. They at least would have balanced the two Teds."

Schlesinger's recollection of the December 10 meeting is similar. "I felt very much at a disadvantage in the meeting, since so much of the talk was so narrowly political. I felt like an amateur and the impractical liberal again. . . . I got the feeling, though, that Bob would have been much happier if we all had asked him to go. It was all a little bit like the Bay of Pigs meetings, when the vocabulary and the context of the discussions undercut the liberals at a moment when the President needed reinforcement from the liberals. . . . I remember Bob saying with some emotion, 'I don't give a damn about '72. I care about Vietnam.' "

So Kennedy listened to the voices of the old politics: Sorensen, Vanden Heuvel, Salinger, and his brother Ted. These were the men close to the power of the Presidency with John Kennedy, and who were now awed by the mystique of that institution. These were the men who had directed the 1960 campaign, and still thought the only way to win a national nomination was by converting the professional party leaders like William Green, John Bailey, Richard Daley, and Charles Buckley. These were the men whose loyalty was not to issues or ideas, but to the Kennedy family, or to the Democratic Party. And these were the men who had no feel for the new politics. They did not understand that television had become the new vessel of values, replacing the political party, the family, the union leader, and the publisher. They did not understand what 10,000 student canvassers could do. They did not understand the new class of college-educated voters in the suburbs, and how much they hated the war in Vietnam. They did not feel the hunger in the country for a new moral leadership, because they did not visit campuses and slums. They did not have a reason for wanting to regain the White House, except nostalgia for past glory. They did not begin to comprehend the anguish and intensity of America's alienated. They did not understand that the late autumn of 1967 was Robert Kennedy's time, and, if he did not act then, the delicate balance of personalities, timing, and events could never be created again.

Among the people who pressed Kennedy hardest to run at that point were his wife and his sisters, Pat and Jean; Walinsky and Lowenstein; myself and Pete Hamill. We were among the least pragmatic and least conventionally political people Robert Kennedy knew.

I wrote in the December 28, 1967, issue of *The Village Voice*:

If Kennedy does not run in 1968, the best side of his character will die. He will kill it every time he butchers his conscience and makes a speech for Johnson next autumn. It will die every time a kid asks him, if he is so much against the Vietnam war, how come he is putting party above principle? It will die every time a stranger quotes his own words back to him on the value of courage as a human quality.

Kennedy's best quality is his ability to be himself, to be authentic in the existential sense. This is the quality the best young identify with so instinctively in Kennedy. And it is this quality Kennedy will lose if he doesn't make his stand now against Johnson. He will become a robot mouthing dishonest rhetoric like all the other politicians.

The next time I saw Kennedy I was expecting an argument—or at least a defense—from him. Instead, he began the conversation by saying, "My wife cut out your attack on me. She shows it to everybody."

When I asked him how he felt about it, Kennedy replied:

"I understand it. It was discerning. On some days I even agree with it. I just have to decide now whether my running can accomplish anything. I don't want to run only as a gesture. I don't want it to drive Johnson into doing something really crazy. I don't want it to hurt the doves in the Senate who are up for reelection. I don't want it to be interpreted in the press as just part of a personal vendetta or feud with Johnson. It's all so complicated. I just don't know what to do."

As conflict slowly built up within Robert Kennedy, a chain of events, beyond his influence, began to unfold and generate their own pressures on him.

The first of these was Eugene McCarthy's announcement on November 30 that he would contest the Presidential Democratic primaries. This is what dynamited the logjam, and made all the subsequent events possible. The rebels had been effectively discredited with the slogan "You can't beat somebody with nobody." But McCarthy's entry into the race gave them a credibility and unity they otherwise would have never achieved.

McCarthy's decision also would have the effect of creating the necessary concrete test at the polls of the President's vague unpopularity. It would soften Kennedy's obsessive fear that, if he did run, the press would characterize him as being motivated by envy, power, lust, and arrogance. It would heighten Kennedy's guilt feelings over not running himself. It would provide a transition for Kennedy, so that the other charge, that his candidacy would split the party, became less valid with the party already divided by McCarthy. It would force Kennedy to modify his public position, from support of Johnson to a fuzzy neutrality between McCarthy and Johnson. McCarthy's candidacy would puncture the psychology of inevitability that was the President's most potent political asset.

Kennedy was hardly aware of all these ramifications, since, like most people, he did not really expect McCarthy's campaign to strike a responsive chord in the country.

A week later, Robert Kennedy's last, best friend within the Johnson government was dismissed; or at least Kennedy regarded the exit of Robert McNamara more as a bloodless bureaucratic coup, than as a considered resignation.

According to Kennedy, he received a phone call at 5 P.M. on December 3 from *New York Times* columnist James Reston, who told him there was a reliable rumor in financial and diplomatic circles that Robert McNamara was about to be appointed president of the World Bank. Kennedy discounted the rumor, but said he would call McNamara to check it out. He did, and McNamara said he didn't know anything about it, but would call the White House, and then call Kennedy back. At about 5:30 P.M. McNamara called Kennedy and told him he was indeed going to the World Bank.

"I felt this was a very important development and I wanted to talk to Bob more about it. So I went right over to the Pentagon, where some reporters saw me go in. This was my big mistake, because it gave Johnson the opening to put the whole thing back onto me, and get it off the fact that McNamara had actually been eased out. . . ."

I then asked Kennedy why he took the chance of going to McNamara's office instead of just talking to him by telephone.

"Because I was always afraid my Senate phone was bugged," Kennedy answered, "and I wanted to talk to Bob about some delicate matters."

Jolted by this revelation, I asked Kennedy if he was saying that he felt the President was tapping his phone, and whether I could publish it.

"You certainly can't write it now. It would create too many problems. But when you're just starting to type the last page of your book, remind me about it, and maybe I'll say something more for the record that might make your book a best seller."

A few days after McNamara's "resignation" was announced, Ted Kennedy stated on the Senate floor that McNamara's exit was involuntary, and added later to reporters that McNamara had authorized him to say that he was not embarrassed by Ted's remarks.

Johnson, on December 4, leveled one of his few public attacks against the Kennedys. When asked about McNamara's departure from the Cabinet at an informal news conference in his office, he said: "I know

that some kids have been calling around some of your [news] bureaus.
. . . These same boys from time to time set up straw men and then
proceed to knock them down. They get about a two- or three-day run on
some of these things. Most of them are not as close to the situation as
they might like to be, or might desire to be. I would doubt that they
would have any information from the Cabinet that the President doesn't
have. . . ."

The episode again illustrated Kennedy's total mistrust of the President. He also interpreted his friend's fall from power as an omen of
intensified fighting in Vietnam, and as a personal defeat, since Mc-
Namara had been his best source of information about the course of the
war. Kennedy felt that a major reason McNamara had been dismissed
was his own close social relationship with the Secretary of Defense. The
episode also served to remind Kennedy that his differences with Mc-
Carthy were inconsequential when measured against his differences,
especially politically, with the President.

This feeling was reinforced a few weeks later when Johnson, on a
national television program, answered a question about Eugene Mc-
Carthy's candidacy, with a reference to the "Kennedy-McCarthy movement," and the innuendo that the two Senators were secretly united in a
conspiracy against him. Inserting Kennedy's name into his answer, the
President said, "I don't know what the effect of the Kennedy-McCarthy
movement is having in the country. I haven't followed it. . . . I just
observe they have had some meetings. . . . I do know of the interest of
both of them in the Presidency, and the ambition of both of them. I see
that reflected from time to time."

As 1968 began there were more events pulling Kennedy ineluctably
toward a struggle for the Presidency. His friend John Nolan, a Washington lawyer and a part of his old team in the Justice Department,
visited Vietnam, and returned to advise Kennedy that the American
government was lying to the public about casualty figures, and that the
pacification and refugee programs were failures. Ted Kennedy also
returned from Vietnam ten days later with the same conviction that
American policy there was more tragic and vicious than even the
harshest Senate critic imagined.

At the same time, McCarthy's public taunting of Kennedy for his
caution started to stimulate an anti-Kennedy backlash on the campuses.
For the first time in years Kennedy found himself being booed and

heckled by college students. "HAWK, DOVE OR CHICKEN?" asked a placard at Brooklyn College. These experiences hurt Kennedy, but he kept on returning to campuses, often visiting three in one week, as if he wanted the abuse to goad him into the race.

Also, more of his staff and friends drifted toward the position that he should enter the primaries. Frank Mankiewicz was one, and Joe Dolan was another who now felt he could no longer avoid the race. Dolan began working every day out of Dutton's law office, calling around the country, compiling lists of delegates, testing the political currents in the key states. He was so anxious to keep his probing a secret that he ordered a new telephone installed in Dutton's office, so that when phone calls had to be returned, the caller wouldn't recognize Dutton's number.

Kennedy's old team of unsentimental professionals from the Justice Department also began to think the race should be made: Burke Marshall, John Seigenthaler, and John Douglas. And Peter Edelman, less given to certitude than Walinsky, finally told Kennedy that he was now in favor of the confrontation with Johnson.

"My problem," Kennedy said to Edelman, "is that I don't have anyone to be for me what I was for my brother."

By mid-January, Kennedy also had two important politicians urging him to go: California Assembly Speaker Jesse Unruh, and somewhat less aggressively, Iowa Governor (now Senator) Harold Hughes.

Still flatly against it, however, were all the state chairmen, Senators, mayors, the people in the party he would need to win delegates and to win the primaries, and, with the exception of Arthur Schlesinger, the influential group of men who had served his brother in the White House. As a man with fierce loyalties to anyone who had helped his brother, the opposition of his brother's most intimate aides weighed heavily on Robert Kennedy. His plight was best symbolized on a day in early January when he received long memos from his brother's two biographers, Theodore Sorensen and Arthur Schlesinger. One warned him that his career was finished if he ran, and the other warned him his career was jeopardized if he did not run.

On January 19, Ronnie Eldridge and I spent the entire day with Kennedy, making a routine political tour through Westchester County, trying to convince him between stops to run the race.

I had by then become disillusioned by the McCarthy campaign, and believed that only Kennedy could mount the professional, exhausting effort required to dislodge Johnson. I felt that McCarthy's psychic distance from the Negroes and blue-collar workers and his mystic, moody style of campaigning could not crack the closed system of the nominating convention. So that, despite the fact that time was running short, Kennedy had to take the risk of entering the primaries.

On January 19 Kennedy seemed ready to run. His long stretch of morose introspection had been replaced by a playful exuberance. On this day, according to my notes, "RFK is acting high, liberated, like he's on some drug."

We met him at his UN Plaza apartment at about 9 A.M. and started driving up the East Side Drive. We began indirectly by informing Kennedy that the McCarthy campaign was starting to strike fire among the liberals and suburban professionals in New York, and that if he waited any longer, it would not be easy to displace McCarthy as the leader of this group. Kennedy, however, was still skeptical of this assessment. He still underestimated both the scope and intensity of the antiwar and anti-Johnson feelings among ordinary, middle-class voters. I also told him of the bitterness with which students viewed his passive role in the conflict. But here, too, he misjudged McCarthy's hold on his followers.

Kennedy's first stop in snow-blanketed Westchester was an auto parts factory, and when we arrived about eight hundred employees were lined up in two neat rows to welcome him. He walked down the lines, with that shy droop of his head, shaking each extended hand. John Parsons, an excellent ABC-TV local reporter, watched Kennedy move down the line, and said to me, "God damn, this guy is going to run! He's campaigning already!"

After a bantering visit with a group of senior citizens, a stop at a factory where he made a campaign speech, and a luncheon where he gave a talk on crime, Kennedy arrived at the new Grasslands Hospital for disturbed and mentally retarded children. As soon as we walked into the courtyard, his face changed; he was obviously moved and depressed. It was the old victim thing. Kennedy felt close to anyone who hurt, because he hurt. Walking into a noisy ward, a child of about eight or nine called out, "Look, there's President Kennedy." Robert Kennedy winced ever so slightly, and then cradled the child in his arms, caressing his neck and hands.

Suddenly, on a wild impulse, Kennedy announced to the room of nine children that he would come back in a few minutes, and take them all for a ride, but first he had to talk to the staff. The kids, of course, didn't believe him, and neither did I. But ten minutes later he returned, helped the patients dress, and to the astonishment of the doctors and his own aides, he piled nine excited children into his car and drove off with his driver, Frank Belotti.

About a half hour later, Robert Kennedy and nine shouting children returned. Each one had an ice cream or a piece of candy. Kennedy had driven them to a store a mile away from the hospital, and let each one pick out "one thing." As we drove away, Kennedy, nearly as elated as the children, remarked, "You know, when those kids tell their parents that Bobby Kennedy took them for a ride and bought them ice cream, they'll never get out of that place."

The last stop on Kennedy's Westchester schedule was a cocktail party sponsored by the county Democratic organization, whose chairman, William Luddy, was one of those warm, old Irish pols who had helped John Kennedy in 1960. At the reception, a local reporter came up to Kennedy and told him that Clark Clifford had just been appointed Secretary of Defense, and did he have a comment. Kennedy said no, but a few minutes later said to me, "Well, I think we're in luck. At least Johnson didn't appoint Attila the Hun."

We began the drive back to the city at about 6 P.M., and through a mix-up, a local party worker, Mrs. Lois Zenkel, ended up in the car with us. While Mrs. Eldridge and myself debated whether to reopen the conversation about running for President in front of a stranger, Kennedy turned to the woman, whom he did not know, and asked, "Tell me, do you think I should run against Lyndon Johnson?"

Mrs. Zenkel, hardly suspecting this was on Kennedy's mind, looked at him as if he was crazy.

"I'm asking your opinion," Kennedy said with his Katzenjammer look. "If you say so, I'll do it."

After a long silence, Mrs. Zenkel answered, "It will cost a lot of money, and cause a lot of confusion in the party."

"But what's your opinion. Should I run?"

"If it makes you happy."

Kennedy laughed uproariously, and then polled the rest of the car.

"Just vote yes or no, no ducking the issue," he commanded in his best mock-ruthless style.

"Yes," said Mrs. Eldridge.

"Yes," I said.

"I'll write you a memo," said Earl Graves, a New York staff assistant, who seemed stunned by the frankness and the whimsy of the conversation.

Kennedy then suddenly took his shoe off, and passed it around the car, pointing out an Adlai Stevenson-like hole in the bottom, saying, "This is a bad omen for my campaign."

Back in Manhattan, Kennedy stopped in on a cocktail party at El Morocco, in honor of reform State Senator Manfred Ohrenstein. There he was accosted by the Greek actress Melina Mercouri, who harangued him for ten solid minutes on the moral imperative of his running in the primaries against Johnson. When we got back in the car, Kennedy exclaimed:

"Isn't she just marvelous? What spirit! And she's so perceptive. Do you know what she said to me? She said did I want to go down in history as the Senator who waited for a safer day?"

The car began to head for Le Pavillon, where Kennedy was to have dinner, and we had only five more minutes to press our case.

"You can't *be* President just because you *want to be* President," Mrs. Eldridge said. "You have to be President for a reason. Because you stand for something."

I added, "The polls and the politicians are all wrong. This is a crazy moment in history. The anger and alienation are all just below the surface. You can feel it, but you can't measure it in a poll. The politicians are blind. They can't understand that everybody is against Johnson except them. The problem is Johnson's character, not just his policies, and that is why he is finished. He can't change."

The car was parked in front of the restaurant now, and Kennedy began to answer us, intense, his finger drumming on his front teeth.

"I can't run if there is no chance. My feeling now is that if one more politician, on the level of Unruh, asks me to run, I'll do it. . . . I don't care about 1972, or helping Nixon. That doesn't stop me. What bothers me is that I'll be at the mercy of events Johnson can manipulate to his advantage. . . . None of the doves in the Senate wants me to do it either, and that plays a role. They all say that, if I run, that will make their reelection campaigns much more difficult. It will split the Democratic Party in Oregon and Idaho, for example. So, all I'm doing is hurting them, while I'm not winning myself, or changing the policy. . . . It's much simpler for you two, or Adam and my wife to tell me to run because of how you feel about the war. But it's more complicated because of who I am. The politicians, who know something about it, they say it can't be put together. My brother Teddy knows something about the Rocky Mountain states because he worked there in 1960. Now he tells me there's no support out there for me. Steve Smith has canvassed all the Governors, and all the state chairmen, and the only one in favor of my doing this, in the whole country, is Harold Hughes. . . . Anyway, I'd rather run than not run. And, if one more politician says yes, I'll do it."

That night at dinner with Steve and Jean Smith, and Pat Lawford, Kennedy said he thought he would run, and told his sisters, "This is going to cost you a lot of money."

The same night I had dinner with three close friends: Paul Gorman, Harold Ickes, and Geoff Cowan. I told them about my day with Kennedy, and my sense that he was now at the edge of running. They all said they would go to work for him if he ran. But later all three would go to work for Eugene McCarthy, and refuse to defect to Kennedy when he finally did enter the race two months later.

The next day I checked with Mankiewicz and Edelman, and they also thought that Kennedy was now very close to running.

But inexplicably, pushed for the third time since October, he failed to challenge Johnson. No one seems to know why he pulled back from his apparent January decision to enter the race. The seizure by North Korea of the *Pueblo* and its crew on January 23 probably reminded him again just how much his candidacy would be at the mercy of events beyond his influence—but not fully beyond the President's influence. He also thought the *Pueblo* seizure would generate a patriotic surge of sympathy for Johnson.

Nevertheless, by the end of January, there was no excuse for Robert Kennedy not joining the race. The moral imperative was clear, and the evidence was all there. He simply miscalculated. As a Kennedy, his fear of defeat paralyzed him. And so, as if acting out a tragic drama by his great favorite Aeschylus, Robert Kennedy again violated his best self, and chose caution rather than courage.

January 30 was the worst of days for Robert Kennedy. That morning, at a long-scheduled, off-the-record background breakfast with a group of about fifteen Washington columnists and national correspondents, he authorized for attribution a single spare sentence:

"I have told friends and supporters who are urging me to run that I would not oppose Lyndon Johnson under any foreseeable circumstances."

This seemed the death blow to the Kennedy partisans around the nation. Their leader would not march. And so, many of them finally went over to Eugene McCarthy's army, trying to learn how to love Eugene on the rebound.

The statement surprised and angered Kennedy's Senate staff. They all felt it was a horrible mistake. Walinsky, who loved Robert Kennedy, nevertheless told him that he wanted to quit and work independently for Johnson's defeat. Dolan was also upset, and he silently resolved to continue working out of Dutton's law office, on the fragile hope that Kennedy might still change his mind. That afternoon Lowenstein slipped into Kennedy's office and told him, "You could have won if you just tried." As Lowenstein left, Kennedy, at the brink of tears, asked him three times, "Do *you* understand?" Lowenstein, near tears himself, recalled, "I sniffled, nodded yes, and walked out, watching him stand in the doorway in real pain."

By the time Kennedy arrived home that night, the Vietcong's Tet blitz was under way. What Allard Lowenstein began, General Vo Nguyen Giap was completing. Suddenly, the whole cancer of America's Vietnam policy was exposed. Downtown Saigon was not even secure from the supposedly depleted guerrillas. The American Embassy was under fire. The pacification program, despite all the official optimism, was now ruined. The war itself was a failure. America could not win. All the official pronouncements and all the predictions had been wrong.

Kennedy saw the magnitude of his own blunder, and slid into a pit of gloom. He simply didn't function the first few days after the Tet offensive began. He did not attend committee meetings. He didn't return his phone calls or read his mail. He spent hours moping and pacing alone in his office. He could almost visibly see millions of people, overnight, change their opinions about Vietnam, recoiling away from the President and his policy. And they were rallying not to him, but to Eugene McCarthy. He had removed himself as an alternative twelve hours too early. Kennedy felt rejected, guilty, helpless, and angry all at the same time. He had made one wrong decision, and he would pay ransom for that error with bits of his popularity the remaining four months of his life.

But, in fact, there was something he could do. If he would not run, then at least he could speak, to pacify his own conscience, and to reassure his disappointed followers that he would not lapse into silence. So with the stunning details of the Vietcong's coordinated attacks on thirty cities still crystallizing in news bulletins, Kennedy told Walinsky on February 4 that he wanted to make his previously scheduled book luncheon speech in Chicago on February 8 about "the meaning of Tet. . . . Johnson can't get away with saying it is really a victory for us."

Walinsky, still deeply wounded by Kennedy's decision not to run, wrote a cathartic and superb draft in a day, and then flew up to Cambridge, where he and Richard Goodwin polished it. It was Kennedy's first Vietnam text that was not defensive, apologetic, and understated.

> Our enemy, savagely striking at will across all of South Vietnam, has finally shattered the mask of official illusion with which we have concealed our true cirucumstances even from ourselves. . . . The time has come to take a new look at the war . . . to seek out the austere and painful reality of Vietnam, freed from wishful thinking, false hopes and sentimental dreams . . .
>
> We must, first of all, rid ourselves of the illusion that the events of the past two weeks represent some sort of victory. That is not so . . . The Viet Cong . . . have demonstrated despite all our reports of progress . . . that half a million American soldiers with 700,000 Vietnamese allies, with total command of the air [and] sea, backed by huge resources and the most modern weapons, are unable to secure even a single city from the attacks of an enemy whose total strength is about 250,000. It is as if James Madison [had claimed] victory in 1812 because the British only burned Washington instead of annexing it to the British Empire . . .
>
> We have misconceived the nature of the war . . . We have sought to resolve by military might a conflict whose issue depends upon the will and conviction of the South Vietnamese people. It is like sending a lion to halt an epidemic of jungle rot. This misconception rests on a second illusion—the illusion that we can win a war which the South Vietnamese cannot win for themselves . . . Government corruption [in Saigon] is the source of the enemy's strength . . . We have an ally in name only. We support a government without supporters . . .
>
> The third illusion is that the unswerving pursuit of military victory, whatever its cost, is in the interest of either ourselves or the people

of Vietnam . . . Their tiny land has been devastated by a weight of bombs and shells greater than Nazi Germany knew . . . More than 2 million South Vietnamese are now homeless refugees . . . Whatever the outcome of these battles, it is the people we seek to defend who are the great losers . . .

The fourth illusion is that the American national interest is identical with—or should be subordinated to—the selfish interest of an incompetent military regime . . . We can and we should offer reasonable assistance to Asia; but we cannot build a Great Society there if we cannot build one in our own country. We cannot speak extravagantly of a struggle for 250 million Asians when a struggle for 15 million in one Asian country so strains our forces that another Asian country, a fourth-rate power . . . dares to seize an American ship and hold and humiliate her crew . . .

The fifth illusion is that this war can be settled in our own way and in our own time on our own terms. Such a settlement is a privilege of the triumphant . . . We can no longer harden our terms every time Hanoi indicates it may be prepared to negotiate; and we must be willing to foresee a settlement which will give the Viet Cong a chance to participate in the political life of the country . . .

The events of last week [should be] not simply a tragedy but a lesson . . . which carries with it some basic truths. First, that a total military victory is not within sight or around the corner; that, in fact, it is probably beyond our grasp; and that the effort to win such a victory will only result in the further slaughter of thousands of innocent and helpless people . . .

The central battle in this war cannot be measured by body counts or bomb damage but by the extent to which the people of South Vietnam act on a sense of common purpose and hope with those who govern them . . . The current regime in Saigon is unwilling or incapable of being an effective ally in the war against the Communists . . .

Our nation must be told the truth about this war, in all its terrible reality, both because it is right—and because only in this way can any Administration rally the public confidence and unity for the shadowed days which lie ahead . . . Reality is grim and painful. But it is only a remote echo of the anguish toward which a policy founded on illusion is surely taking us.

Flying back to Washington from Chicago, Kennedy's melancholy began to fade. He had felt natural attacking the war, attacking Johnson, engaging in political battle. He was beginning to realize just how much against the grain of his character it had been to remain passive, cautious, even cowardly. In this new mood of liberation, Kennedy began to leaf through a thick folder of unread mail and memos that had accumulated in the past week. At the top of the pile, intentionally placed there by Mankiewicz, was an emotional letter from Kennedy's friend Pete Hamill, who was in Ireland finishing his novel, *A Killing for Christ*. It was a letter written in that narrow crevice between Kennedy's withdrawal and the start of the Tet offensive, and made the case for running in retrospect.

Kennedy was dazed by the letter. In the following days he carried it around in his attaché case, rereading it many times. He showed it to Salinger, Sorensen, and the other doubters. And later he would tell me, and others, that, reading it in his post-speech mood, marked the turning point in his thinking about whether to seek the Presidency in 1968. For that reason I quote Hamill's letter now nearly in full:

DEAR BOB:

I had wanted to write you a long letter explaining my reasons why I thought you should make a run for the Presidency this year. But that's too late. I read in the *Irish Times* this A.M. that you made a hard announcement, and that small hope is gone, along with others that have vanished in the last four years.

I suspect that all nations have their historical moment, some moment when it all seems to have been put together as an idea: our moment was 1960–1963. I don't think it's nostalgia working or romanticism. I think most Americans feel that way now.

The moment is gone now, and we have grown accustomed to living in a country where nobody would protest very much if Jack Valenti replaced John Gardner.

I wanted to say that the fight you might make would be the fight of honor . . . I wanted to say that you should run because if you won, the country might be saved . . . If we have LBJ for another four years, there won't be much of a country left. I've heard the arguments about the practical politics which are involved. You will destroy the Democratic Party, you will destroy yourself. I say that if you don't run, you might destroy the Democratic Party; it will end up nationally, the way it has in New York, a party filled with decrepit old bastards like Abe Beame, and young hustlers, with blue hair, trying to get their hands on highway contracts. It will be a party that says to millions and millions of people that they don't count, that the decision of 2,000 hack pols does. They will say that idealism is a cynical joke; that hard-headed pragmatism is the rule, even if the pragmatists rule in the style of Bonnie and Clyde.

I wanted to remind you that in Watts I didn't see pictures of Malcolm X or Ron Karenga on the walls. I saw pictures of JFK. That is your capital in the most cynical sense; it is your obligation in another, the obligation of staying true to whatever it was that put those pictures on those walls. I don't think we can afford five summers of blood. I do know this: if a 15-year-old kid is given a choice between Rap Brown and RFK, he *might* choose the way of sanity. It's only a possibility, but at least there is that chance. Give that same kid a choice between Rap Brown and LBJ, and he'll probably reach for his revolver.

Again, forgive the tone of this letter, Bob. But it's not about five cent cigars and chickens in every pot. It's about the country. I don't want to sound like someone telling someone that he should mount the white horse; or that he should destroy his career. I also realize that if you had decided to run, you would face some filthy politics, and that there are plenty of people in the country who resent or dislike you.

With all of that, I still think the move would have been worth making, and I'm sorry you decided not to make it.

The Decision to Run

In the book, *No More Vietnams,* Professor Hans Morgenthau suggests that the Vietcong's Tet offensive was the third great historical event of this century between Asia and the West: comparable to the Russo-Japanese War of 1905, and to Japan's defeat of the French, Dutch, and English during World War II. Tet's traumatic impact on America's internal politics in early 1968 almost justifies this sweeping judgment.

Day after day in early February, television newsreel footage and excruciating color photographs in the news magazines documented the disastrous and bloody drama of Tet even as Administration officials described the events in Vietnam as "a victory."

General Westmoreland said, during the first week of the offensive, "We have turned the tables on the Vietcong," and claimed that the Vietcong lost 31,000 men in a week—a figure almost no one believed. An anonymous State Department official was quoted by *Newsweek* as commenting, "This is the Vietcong's Bay of Pigs." President Johnson dismissed the offensive as "a failure." But the one Orwellian quote that characterizes America's involvement in the war was that of an American Army major looking at the destroyed village of Ben Tre: "It became necessary to destroy the town to save it."

Within two weeks of Tet, the campuses and the moneyed Jewish community in New York reacted by throwing themselves into Eugene McCarthy's campaign. In New Hampshire, McCarthy began his slow, remarkable conversion from idea to reality. The polls across the country indicated a rapid shift of opinion away from the war and President Johnson.

The informal group of men advising Robert Kennedy now became a microcosm of the changes going on in the country. Tet shifted, for the first time, the center of gravity within Kennedy's informal cabinet. Richard Goodwin, who was already for Kennedy's entrance into battle, drove up to New Hampshire to work for Eugene McCarthy. Arthur Schlesinger and Burke Marshall were reinforced in their belief Kennedy should run. Fred Dutton and Kenneth O'Donnell were nudged toward the thin dividing line, and they soon would favor the race. Steve Smith and Pierre Salinger became ambivalent, with Smith feeling, "It's in his blood, so maybe he should do it." Ted Kennedy's opposition became less certain. Of the inner circle, only Ted Sorensen and William vanden Heuvel remained firmly negative.

The Chicago speech had reconnected Kennedy with his instincts. His Washington office received more than 1,000 telegrams cheering the blunt speech. A dozen important newspapers, including *The New York Times, St. Louis Post Dispatch,* and *Boston Globe,* printed editorials praising the speech. By the end of February, Kennedy again seemed ready to run. Every few days he would talk to Goodwin or Lowenstein, who were in New Hampshire, and would hear a new, higher estimate of McCarthy's vote total there. His friend, Bill Dunfey, also told him that McCarthy was closing fast.

If Tet was the catalyst, Kennedy still needed a few more rationalizations for changing his mind. By March 1 he had them. George Romney had withdrawn, making the vulnerable and familiar Richard Nixon the likely Republican candidate. The President ignored the release of the Kerner Commission Report, which urged massive new Federal and private spending to heal the wounds caused by "White Racism." And Kennedy found out that General Westmoreland had formally requested 206,000 more combat troops for Vietnam.

The weekend of March 2 and 3 was an almost continuous meeting of Kennedy's informal cabinet at his home in Virginia. There were long-distance phone calls, and rotating participants, with Ted Kennedy, Kenneth O'Donnell, and Fred Dutton the pivots. Jesse Unruh told them that a new California poll showed Kennedy with 42 percent, Johnson with 32 percent, and McCarthy with 18 percent. The reports from New Hampshire now indicated that McCarthy might poll as much as 40 percent of the vote. Goodwin advised Kennedy by phone, "Declare now." It was during this hectic weekend that Kennedy, in his own mind, finally began to think of himself as a candidate for President. By this point Kennedy finally understood that running and losing would be less painful than not running and contributing to Johnson's renomination. His fear of being called ruthless for running was, at last, overcome by his fear of being called a coward for not running.

Dutton and O'Donnell, both tough, political men who disguised their liberal values and their emotions, eased him over his final doubts. The fact they were now for it made it appear less hopeless to Kennedy, more within the realm of possible politics. Dutton had been Pat Brown's campaign manager in 1966, and O'Donnell had run for Governor of Massachusetts that year. And as professional politicians they did not have to prove their pragmatism the way some of the intellectuals around Kennedy felt the need to do.

On Sunday night, March 3, Mankiewicz, unaware of these meetings, phoned Kennedy to remind him to watch a program segment I had done for the Public Broadcasting Laboratory on Kennedy's Bedford-Stuyvesant project.

"I don't think I can," Kennedy said. "We're having one of those conversations again about my future."

"Do I have a vote?" asked the press secretary.

"Sure."

"Put me down as a hawk. Go into everything after Wisconsin."

The last, enduring misconception about Robert Kennedy was that he decided to jump into the race for President only after Eugene McCarthy's strong showing in New Hampshire exposed Lyndon Johnson's vulnerability. But, in fact, Kennedy decided, in his own mind, to enter the race on Tuesday, March 5, a week before the New Hampshire primary.

On Monday, March 4, after the long weekend of soul-searching at Hickory Hill, Kennedy asked Fred Dutton to feel out his brother and see if he still objected to the race. Dutton saw Ted Kennedy on Tuesday morning, and, to his surprise, found Ted resigned to the idea, rather than hostile to it. "I think Bob is going to run," the youngest brother told Dutton, "and it's up to us to make some sense out of it."

At about noon that day, March 5, Dutton and Ted Kennedy walked over to Robert Kennedy's office on the third floor of the New Senate Office Building, to join Kennedy and Kenneth O'Donnell for the first hard talk about how to run, rather than whether to run.

For three hours, over lunch in Kennedy's office, surrounded by memorabilia of the New Frontier, the four close friends began to explore the monumental mechanics of a campaign for the Presidency. What support within the party could they count on? What tactics to use and what issues to make? What were the realistic chances of success? How and when to announce? According to Dutton:

"I left the meeting feeling that a decision had been made that Bob would run for President. . . . And I think all four of us felt that Bob probably could not win, but that he now had to try, because of the war and Johnson."*

So long repressed, Kennedy's first impulse was to announce his candidacy quickly that Sunday, March 10, in California, where he was scheduled to speak at a farm workers' rally for Cesar Chavez. But on second thought, he concluded that would appear to be ruthless—undercutting McCarthy on the eve of the vote in New Hampshire, as well as exploiting his special relationship with Chavez. Also, Sunday was considered too soon. There wouldn't be enough time to inform friends and allies across the country before word leaked out. And there wouldn't be enough time to begin the most rudimentary campaign chores, like renting a headquarters, or organizing a press conference.

On Thursday, March 7, Robert Kennedy asked his brother, Ted, to inform McCarthy that he was "probably going to enter the primaries after Wisconsin." But Ted, on his own, decided not to communicate the message, fearing McCarthy would use it somehow politically against the Kennedys. On Sunday, the tenth, when Kennedy phoned his wife from California and discovered that his brother had not yet relayed the message to McCarthy, he asked his wife to call Schlesinger, Goodwin, or Galbraith and have one of them perform the touchy task. By Monday morning, several people, including Ted Kennedy, had called Goodwin in New Hampshire, requesting him to be the messenger. On the evening before the voting in New Hampshire, Goodwin advised McCarthy that Kennedy was "thinking of running." The five-day delay in the transmission of Kennedy's vague message to McCarthy almost certainly contrib-

* Steve Smith also says, "The basic decision to go was made a week before New Hampshire."

uted to the subsequent mistrust and bitterness between the two antiwar candidates and their followers.

The botched message, however, was just a symptom; no modern Presidential campaign was probably born amidst more chaos and confusion than Robert Kennedy's.

The first formal meeting in John Kennedy's 1960 campaign was held on October 28, 1959, at Hyannis Port. At that time, sixteen people assembled in one place and carefully began to divide responsibility for different sections of the country; to build a staff, raise funds, and keep track of delegates; to commission polls; organize campaign committees; and orchestrate a coherent, overall strategy. Of that seminal group, in March of 1968, John Kennedy was dead. Larry O'Brien, John Bailey, and even Sargent Shriver worked for Lyndon Johnson. And Theodore Sorensen was still against making the race. The 1959 meeting took place more than two months before John Kennedy publicly declared his candidacy, and more than five months before the first primary test.

Ten days before he announced his candidacy, Robert Kennedy had already missed the filing deadlines for the first two primaries; many of his closest and oldest advisers had careers and families in cities scattered across the nation; he was challenging an incumbent President of his own party; and he now had to prepare for six primaries within three months.

On Friday, March 8, with Sorensen and Vanden Heuvel still arguing against the race, the first improvised stirrings of Robert Kennedy's Presidential campaign were beginning. In the Washington Senate office, Walinsky, Edelman, and Greenfield began researching Lyndon Johnson's record and public speeches. In Manhattan, Steve Smith, John English, and Ronnie Eldridge began the difficult job of securing Kennedy's fragmented home base delegation. In California, Speaker Unruh, and Kennedy's former Justice Department assistant, John Nolan, began lining up a slate of 172 delegates for the winner-take-all primary on June 4; an equally difficult task, since the Johnson and McCarthy slates had already claimed many of the state party's powers and personalities. On the same day, Kennedy spent ninety minutes with one of his favorite reporters, Haynes Johnson, of the *Washington Star*. After Johnson left Kennedy's office, he jotted down in his memo pad, "March 8, 1968— Spent 1½ hours with RFK. Certain he will run."

On Saturday night, March 9, Kennedy, en route to California, stopped off at Des Moines, Iowa, to speak to 4,000 people at a fund-raising dinner for Governor Harold Hughes, who was preparing to run for the Senate seat vacated by Bourke Hickenlooper. Kennedy's speech was a familiar one, patched together with bits and pieces of old texts. But it added up to an indictment of the President, and a platform from which to run against his record. Afterward, Kennedy met privately with four Midwestern Governors—Hughes; Robert Docking of Kansas; William Guy of North Dakota; and Warren Hearnes of Missouri—and listened to them pick Johnson apart and express doubts that Johnson could carry their states in November.

The next day, traveling with Edelman, John Seigenthaler, and Ed Guthman, Kennedy flew into Delano, the headquarters for the grape strike movement, in the Central Valley of California. Kennedy went there, at this crucial time for himself, because of his respect for Cesar Chavez; and despite the fact identification with the strikers would probably hurt him in the California primary, since few migrants are registered, and the growers often contribute large sums of money to political candidates.

The purpose of the rally, an ecumenical Mass, was to symbolize the end of a twenty-five-day hunger strike Chavez undertook to persuade his followers to keep faith in nonviolence. In the course of his hunger strike, Chavez' health failed so badly that his doctors had called Kennedy and asked him to persuade Chavez to give it up.

More than 4,000 Mexican farm workers filled Delano's sweltering Community Park as Chavez, clinging to the shoulders of two aides, and Kennedy arrived, marching in a colorful procession behind a large wooden crucifix, and a portrait of Our Lady of Guadalupe, the patroness of the Mexican revolution.

Chavez, who lost thirty-five pounds in twenty-five days, was too weak to speak, and his statement was read for him, first in Spanish, then in English, from an altar built on a flatbed truck. Chavez pleaded for continued allegiance to nonviolence, calling it "the ultimate act of manliness."

Chavez then broke his fast, nibbling from a home-baked loaf of bread given to him by a priest as part of the Mass. Then Kennedy ate from the same loaf, and walked to the altar, and told the emotional crowd:

> I am here out of respect for one of the heroic figures of our time—Cesar Chavez. I congratulate all of you who are locked with Cesar in the struggle for justice for the farm worker, and in the struggle for justice

for Spanish-speaking Americans . . . There are those of you who question the principle of everything you have done so far—the principle of nonviolence. Let me say to you that violence is no answer. . . .

Before flying back to Washington, Kennedy did speak to Unruh by phone, but he did not see a single California politician on this personal pilgrimage for a friend.

Monday, March 11. Eugene McCarthy continued to gain in the final hours in New Hampshire. His experimental new politics pastiche of party amateurs and student activists, united by a great moral issue, was cracking the hollow state party machine led by Governor John King and Senator Thomas McIntyre. The professionals had done everything wrong, and squandered their huge early lead. Their red-baiting campaign had boomeranged, and, at the end, they had few volunteers. The amateurs, meanwhile, with an unorthodox candidate, made few mistakes, ignored the long odds against them, and profited from the President's personal unpopularity.

Every half hour, on every radio station in the state on this day, one thirty-second spot announcement was repeated again and again:

"Think now how you would feel to wake up Wednesday morning to find out that Gene McCarthy had won the New Hampshire primary—to find that New Hampshire had changed the course of American politics."

This brilliant ad was created by Richard Goodwin, who understood that, in hawkish New Hampshire, the winning issue was an inchoate desire for change, and a desire to participate as individuals in the act of change.

Kennedy returned to Washington from California near dawn, and did not arrive at his office till almost noon. There he watched Dean Rusk testify on television before the Senate Foreign Relations Committee. Rusk talked as if Tet had never happened, and gave no sign future Vietnam policy would take that shattering event into account.

In midafternoon Arthur Schlesinger phoned Kennedy to suggest that he endorse McCarthy before the polls opened in New Hampshire, so that he might both diminish Johnson's vote, and gain some credit for McCarthy's. But Kennedy declined, saying such an endorsement would only further complicate his own entry into the race. Behind Kennedy's refusal, however, was pride, and his own belief that McCarthy would not, in fact, make a very good President. Kennedy felt that to endorse McCarthy would be hypocritical.

Later in the afternoon Kennedy, Dolan, and Mankiewicz speculated about what percentage of the New Hampshire vote for McCarthy would be most advantageous to Kennedy; they all agreed between 32 and 35 percent. But the astute Joe Dolan predicted that McCarthy would actually poll 42 percent.

It was also on Monday that Kennedy began to play out a Byzantine and mysterious subplot in the drama that removed the last possible barrier to his running. No one except Robert Kennedy knew all the pieces of this subplot, and it is reconstructed here based on interviews with secondary characters; an informative account of it in Jules Witcover's book, *85 Days: The Last Campaign of Robert Kennedy;* and a few casual conversations I had with Kennedy.

Anyway, Sorensen, who maintained independent lines of communication with the White House, was invited to see the President during the afternoon of March 11. Before going to the White House, Sorensen stopped by to see Kennedy in his office. The two men again debated whether Kennedy should run, with Sorensen still strongly against it, and Kennedy explaining he now had to run because of Vietnam, but confessing that he did not expect to win. Sorensen then told Kennedy he planned to suggest to the President that he appoint a top-level commission to review the entire policy in Vietnam, and perhaps use the commission's report as a rationale for a reversal in policy. A similar idea had been proposed to Kennedy during a private meeting with Mayor Daley, after his February 8 antiwar speech in Chicago. Kennedy's version is that he "didn't react one way or another" to either Daley's or Sorensen's suggestion.

Sorensen then went directly from Kennedy's office to the White House, where, in the course of a two-hour meeting with the President, he raised the idea of the commission. Kennedy later insisted that "When Ted proposed the commission, it was not in any way linked either to my running, or not running." The President told Sorensen that Mayor Daley had a parallel notion, and that he "welcomed" the idea, and asked Sorensen to suggest some possible members of the commission.

Sorensen reported his conversation with Johnson back to Kennedy, and on Monday night and Tuesday morning, Kennedy discussed the idea with his most intimate counselors: Ted Kennedy, Smith, Dutton, and O'Donnell. He talked to Daley, and Daley talked to the President. Daley's attitude at this point was apparently political support for Johnson's reelection, but a pragmatic dislike of the war, and a personal fondness for Kennedy, all of which led him to feel that the proposed commission might end the war, abort Kennedy's candidacy, and save Johnson's career. These were probably also Sorensen's objectives, and it was these two intermediaries who took the commission idea much more seriously than either of the principals—Kennedy and Johnson.

There were more secret conversations in the next seventy-two hours: between Sorensen and Johnson; between Kennedy and Daley; between Ted Kennedy and Clark Clifford; between Clifford and Johnson. Finally, at 5 P.M. on Thursday, Clifford informed Kennedy by phone that the President had flatly rejected the commission for two reasons: Kennedy's desire to be a member of the commission, and the fact President Kennedy had not appointed a similar commission following the Bay of Pigs. Kennedy told Clifford that he did not insist on being a member of the commission himself, and that his brother had, in fact, appointed a special study commission in the wake of the Bay of Pigs failure.

There were more phone calls between Clifford, Sorensen, Kennedy, and the White House Thursday night, at which time I was present at Kennedy's home for dinner. At about 11 P.M., Kennedy received his fourth phone call within an hour. As he was summoned to the phone, he quipped, "This may be your friend, the President, Jack. Do you want to speak to him?"

It turned out to be Sorensen with word of the final rejection of the commission by Johnson, with different reasons cited than those Kennedy had punctured a few hours earlier.

My own theory is that the commission idea was never taken seriously by Kennedy. He did not expect it to work, and he viewed it essentially as an experience whose primary value would be to demonstrate to Sorensen the President's rigidity, and the necessity for his own entry into the race. Schlesinger believes that Kennedy regarded the dance over the Vietnam commission "as something to be gone through, although not very important." Dutton says, "The whole thing was incongruous. It didn't fit with everything else Kennedy was thinking and feeling at the time . . . I never understood it." Kennedy's own view was, "I felt I had to go the last mile, to prove I was not running out of ambition, or some petty feelings about Johnson . . . I was not anxious to run if the war could be ended without my running. So the commission idea was something I felt compelled to explore, although I never thought it would happen. And it has subsequently been blown up out of all proportion."

. . .

Tuesday, March 12. A miracle. Six months after the national leadership of ADA had overwhelmingly rejected an anti-Johnson resolution, the Democrats of rural, conservative New Hampshire voted to dump Lyndon Johnson. Ten thousand college students beat the President of the United States and the Democratic Party of New Hampshire. Gene McCarthy, who was a joke in January, became a myth in March. He won twenty of twenty-four convention delegates; 42.2 percent of the Democratic vote, and half of the total vote when Republican write-ins were tabulated. Suddenly, Lyndon Johnson's renomination was in doubt.

Kennedy received the New Hampshire returns with Arthur Schlesinger and William vanden Heuvel at a Manhattan supper club. According to Schlesinger, "He was surprised McCarthy did so well. His mood was grim, rather than happy. He knew he now had a great problem about how to get into the race."

About midnight Kennedy returned to his apartment and called New Hampshire. He spoke first to Goodwin, who was excited, and told Kennedy, "All us amateurs were right from the start. You should never have trusted the traditional politicians." Then Kennedy congratulated the buoyant McCarthy in a brief, painful conversation. At about 2 A.M. Kennedy went to bed, still nursing the unrealistic hope that McCarthy might yet withdraw in his favor. But the terrible division within American liberalism was now destined to be played out to its tragic end. For the next three months, the two halves of the new politics would behave like two scorpions locked in a bottle.

Wednesday, March 13. For six months Robert Kennedy had unnaturally inhibited his instincts, and now liberated, they exploded abruptly, clumsily, humanly. Instead of playing the good, tidy politician, Kennedy blurted out his desires. At noon, upon getting off the Eastern Airlines shuttle at the Washington airport, several reporters encircled Kennedy and asked for a comment on the New Hampshire results.

Instead of the cool "no comment," Kennedy said, "I am actively reassessing the possibility of whether I will run against President Johnson. . . ."

The last week of the secret discussions about how best to enter the race were suddenly obsolete. Kennedy did not explain that he had been tortured by ambivalence for six months, or that he had virtually decided to run eight days earlier. In a few careless seconds he resurrected the sleeping stereotype of himself as a ruthless opportunist. In the same few seconds he cemented Eugene McCarthy's hold on his new movement. His impulsive airport comment was a classic political blooper that he would never live down, or adequately explain away. And in saying it, Kennedy was being unfair to himself.

By the time he reached his office, Kennedy knew he had made a mistake. The press was beginning to camp in the corridor outside his office. The phones were ringing. Telegrams were beginning to pour in at a rate that would soon reach seventy-five an hour. He called a few friends to alert them to his airport comments, and to remind them there would be a final meeting of all his advisers at 4 P.M. in Steve Smith's office.

Late in the afternoon, Kennedy and his brother met with McCarthy in Ted's office, for about fifteen minutes. Kennedy later said of the meeting, "There wasn't very much communication. I told him I was probably going to run, and that I hoped we might work together in some coordinated way. I offered to support him in Wisconsin. But he didn't respond. He just said I could do what I wanted, and he would do what he wanted. . . . I would say he was cold to us."

Just before this confrontation, Kennedy drove to the Washington CBS television studios to tape an interview with Walter Cronkite for use on the network news show that is aired in New York at 7 P.M. This time in a more calculated way, Kennedy took another step toward running. He began by praising McCarthy and his student activists in a futile attempt to blunt their fury at him for seeming to jump into the race after McCarthy had done all the work, and after he had earlier refused to take the risk of running. Kennedy then rehearsed his rationalizations for running. He cited Dean Rusk's Vietnam testimony on Monday, Johnson's failure to respond to the reform recommendations of the Kerner Report, and the likelihood of Richard Nixon's nomination as the "reasons I am taking another look at my own position, and what I should do in the future."

Meanwhile, the Kennedy advisers began to assemble gradually in Steve Smith's office at 200 Park Avenue. All those present at the earlier round of meetings were invited, as well as more remote figures like Barrett Prettyman, former Justice Department aide, and Jerry Bruno, Kennedy's virtuoso advance man. Not invited again for some unexplainable reason were the staff rebels, Walinsky, Edelman, and Greenfield.

The discussion, according to almost all those present, was unfocused, indecisive, and unsatisfactory. Some of the participants, led by Schlesinger, now felt that Kennedy should endorse McCarthy rather than announce his own candidacy. Schlesinger perceptively argued that Kennedy should permit McCarthy to enjoy his New Hampshire showing, and that a brutal entry now by Kennedy would only generate sympathy for McCarthy, and rekindle all the old liberal suspicions that Kennedy was only motivated by power. Sorensen and Vanden Heuvel, meanwhile, were still against Kennedy doing anything. Before 7 P.M. the entire group adjourned to Smith's apartment, at 1030 Fifth Avenue, to see Kennedy's taped interview on Walter Cronkite's program.

The floating cabinet of about twenty watched the interview, and immediately realized that their own deliberations were irrelevant; that Kennedy's televised remarks represented a tentative announcement of candidacy; that he would not endorse McCarthy, and that he could no longer remain passive and neutral.

"Bobby's therapy is going to cost the family four million dollars," quipped his brother Ted. Then all the participants sat down to a buffet of beef Stroganoff, ham, string beans, salad, and chocolate cake. The grave meeting to win the Presidency became a gay dinner party. There was more gossip and joking than hard political talk. Finally, Robert and Ethel Kennedy arrived at about 8 P.M. to cheers, laughter, and requests for his first campaign speech.

Thursday, March 14. The bitter backlash of the McCarthy movement hit Kennedy in the face. Dozens of activist students interviewed by reporters affirmed their loyalty to McCarthy, and asked where Kennedy was when they needed him. Mary McGrory wrote in the *Washington Star,* "Kennedy thinks that American youth belongs to him at the bequest of his brother. Seeing the romance flower between them and McCarthy, he moved with the ruthlessness of a Victorian father whose daughter has fallen in love with a dustman." Kennedy had no allies left in the press to explain that he had made his decision to run a week before New Hampshire. Some of the same editorial writers who were justly describing his entrance into the campaign as brutal and graceless were nevertheless still urging Nelson Rockefeller to enter the Republican race.

Almost a quarter of the seventy-five-per-hour telegrams coming into his Washington office urged him to endorse McCarthy; significantly, none of them expressed support for Johnson. A few more of his advisers joined Schlesinger in proposing that he endorse McCarthy, permit McCarthy to run in all the primaries, then engineer a draft for himself, and emerge as a compromise candidate at the convention. But Kennedy was too direct a man for such a strategy. He had to run. He had to earn it in the primaries. After ignoring his instincts for six months, Kennedy was now prepared to listen to them exclusively.

At 8 A.M. on Thursday, Kennedy returned to Washington on the Eastern shuttle, with Jimmy Breslin as his invited traveling companion. Breslin, like Kennedy, is Irish, tough, sensitive, blunt, intuitive. The two men were able to communicate in the Casey Stengel shorthand the Kennedys favored.

"Are you happy you're doing it?" Breslin asked.

"Yes."

"The guy did a helluva thing, didn't he?"

"Yes," with a firm nod.

"Could you have done this without him?"

"No."

Kennedy then began to read a piece in *The Wall Street Journal* that claimed he and McCarthy had already forced the President to shift his Vietnam policy.

"Do you agree with the story?" Breslin asked.

"You know, a few weeks ago I had a letter from Ethel's nephew, George Skakel. He was in the Army in Vietnam. He had six weeks left. He wanted to go to Japan when he was through. He had a great deal of interest in the Japanese, and he wanted to enroll in school and study Japanese philosophy. The Army insisted he had to fly home. He wrote to me about it. A girl in my office was looking into it. The boy was killed last week in Vietnam."

He and Breslin then sat in silence for a long while.

At 10:30 A.M. Kennedy met Sorensen in his office, and the two men drove together to the Pentagon for the meeting with Secretary Clifford on the Vietnam commission. Kennedy reported later that he emphasized to Clifford that the commission had to be "more than just a public relations gimmick," and that the commission's membership had to "signal a clear-cut willingness to seek a wider path to peace in Vietnam." Kennedy also said he made it clear to Clifford that "Ending the bloodshed in Vietnam is far more important to me than starting a Presidential campaign."

The rest of the meeting was taken up with discussion over possible membership of the commission, and ended with an agreement that the meeting would remain secret and confidential.

Kennedy, still accompanied by Sorensen, then went to lunch with antiwar Senators George McGovern and Lee Metcalf, and Congressmen Frank Thompson and Morris Udall. The four lawmakers all suggested to Kennedy that he not run immediately, but support McCarthy, at least through the primaries. They suggested an arrangement could be reached between the two men between the primaries and the convention, but that if Kennedy ran now, McCarthy would become impossible to negotiate with later on.

With a row of about twenty reporters sitting outside his office, Kennedy spent the afternoon shuttling between his office phone and the Senate floor, where he had to answer several quorum calls.

In the outer part of the office, Jeff Greenfield sat in a cubbyhole, reading through six volumes of Lyndon Johnson's public papers, Adam Walinsky leafed through a mound of telegrams, noting how many of the favorable ones came from Negro or Mexican districts. He saw one telegram that read: "I am the McCarthy coordinator at Harvard. What should I do?" The activist Walinsky called the sender in Cambridge and told him to go to work for Kennedy. He saw another telegram that read: "The hopes of our generation rest on your candidacy. Please run. (Signed) Four Stanford University students." Walinsky plucked that one out of the pile and showed it to Kennedy, who was then feeling the full brunt of the pro-McCarthy backlash.

Late in the afternoon Frank Mankiewicz told me that I was invited to Kennedy's house in Virginia for dinner. By previous arrangement, twenty-five middle-age, small-town, New York State weekly newspaper editors, in Washington for a convention, had been invited to the Kennedy home for dinner, and now the commitment had to be honored, regardless of what turmoil and pressures existed inside Robert Kennedy's head. Also invited—probably to entertain the editors—were Senator Fred Harris of Oklahoma; Mrs. Rene Carpenter, the nonconformist wife of astronaut Scott Carpenter, and a close friend of Ethel's; television reporter Roger Mudd; and Sylvia Wright of *Life* magazine.

By dinnertime Kennedy, who had been solemn and preoccupied all day, was again acting whimsical and liberated. His 5 P.M. meeting with Clifford was over, and it was now definite that he would run. When one of the guests pointed to the New York State flag in a corner of the living room, and asked what it was, Kennedy replied, "Oh, that's the Presidential flag. I have a small announcement to make to the group." And Ethel, at the close of saying grace before dinner, tacked on the phrase, ". . . And may the best man win."

Also, during dinner, Kennedy, who was seated at another table, overheard Mrs. Carpenter and me arguing noisily with several of his horrified guests, in favor of the legalization of marijuana. He made a face, and then passed me a note, which said, "Can't you talk about something else? You're going to cost me the election before it starts." He signed it Timothy Leary.

Mrs. Wright and myself were the last guests to leave. It was after midnight and very cold. Kennedy walked us out onto his porch; he was shivering, and his hands were jammed into his suit pockets in a pose reminiscent of John Kennedy.

"You think I have a right to run, don't you? Tell me if you think I am being unfair," he began.

We said no, and he continued his monologue, looking like a parody of all the ruthless cartoons of himself.

"I've thought about it. I want to do the right thing. I want to do what will help end the war, and what will be best for the country. If others can run, why can't I run, too?"

It was a remarkable tableau: Kennedy silhouetted by the house lights, the wind blowing his hair, his teeth chattering, his face a mask of pleading, begging to be reassured.

I reminded Kennedy that I had favored his running since last September and that I still preferred him to McCarthy. He nodded, and, without responding, went back to his house.

Friday, March 15. At 6:30 A.M. Frank Mankiewicz called me at my hotel to say that Kennedy was taking the 8 A.M. shuttle to New York, and I was welcome to join him. It was only at the airplane ramp that Kennedy told Mankiewicz that he wanted to announce the next morning in Washington, and, rather than accompany him to New York, Mankiewicz had better stay in Washington to arrange for the press conference. Also at the airport was Haynes Johnson, who had been called by

Kennedy's private secretary, Angie Novello, and invited to fly to New York with Kennedy.

The three of us boarded the second section of the shuttle, with Kennedy drawing stares from the passengers, most of whom seemed surprised to see him on a commercial flight. Kennedy took the window seat and began his nervous habit of tapping his front teeth with his thumbnail.

"How does it stand?" asked Johnson, after the plane had taken off.

Kennedy looked into Johnson's face, a rich, sensitive face that Kennedy was often drawn to. "I'm going to announce tomorrow morning," Kennedy said without any special emphasis.

Then Kennedy launched into a monologue of such candor that it made both of us feel a little uncomfortable.

"This hasn't been an easy decision for me to make," Kennedy started. "A lot of people who have been my friends will be distressed. It is going to make things very difficult for a lot of people. . . . I'm not going to push anybody to come out for me. I understand how it is for Mc-Namara, or Church, or O'Brien. . . . I feel sorry to make them have to choose. . . . I know I won't have much support. I understand I'm going in alone."

He recalled some of the crises he shared with his brother, the Bay of Pigs, Berlin, the Cuban missile crisis, the Nuclear Test Ban Treaty. Then he touched the core of his ordeal.

"My own brother suggested Lyndon Johnson to be the Vice President of the United States. All that is involved inside me. To break with the party that made my brother the President isn't a simple thing for me to do. . . . I keep thinking that I represent something more than just myself, or my own ambition."

He explained how his wife and sisters had wanted him to run from the start, and then added:

"It is a much more natural thing for me to run than not run. When you start acting unnaturally, you're in trouble. At least now I can start reacting normally to events and issues. . . . I have to face myself. I couldn't be a hypocrite. Not to run and pretend to be for McCarthy, while trying to screw him behind his back, that's what would really be ruthless. Making speeches for him, while I'm secretly trying to get delegates for myself—that's ruthless. . . . I'm trusting my instincts now and I feel freer. I know my brother thinks I'm a little nutty for doing this, but we all have to march to the beat of our own drummer. . . ."

He paused for a minute, looking down on the repetitive landscape of New Jersey, and then resumed his soliloquy, his face still sad and vulnerable.

"I was thinking that if I had asked twelve people whether I should have given my first speech against the war, they all would have been against it. If I asked the same twelve people about my running now, they would mostly be against it. . . . But I have to do what feels natural to me. I can't be a hypocrite anymore. I just don't believe Gene McCarthy would be a good President. If it had been George McGovern who had run in New Hampshire, I wouldn't have gotten into it. But what has McCarthy ever done for the ghettos or the poor? . . . I'm not asking for a free ride. I'm willing to let the American people judge me. I'm willing to work for it."

Then we were on the ground in New York. Tom Johnston met us and we drove to Steve Smith's apartment. The weather in New York was crisp, sunny, and windy, and the bright sun quickly lifted Kennedy's spirits; he seemed to draw in his energy from nature—sun, wind, water, mountains.

He dictated two telegrams that he wanted Johnston to send. The first was to Pete Hamill, whose letter had made such an impact on him. It said: "Have taken your advice. Am in trouble. Please come home." Hamill did—the next day. The other was to the editorial board of the *Harvard Crimson,* which had endorsed Kennedy the night before. This one just said, "Are we alone?"

At Smith's apartment, surrounded by pictures of John Kennedy, and trophies of his years in the Presidency, Robert Kennedy began to make the first of the endless number of phone calls. Pierre Salinger, who didn't know the race was on. James Wechsler, who remained loyal to McCarthy. Ronnie Eldridge, to whom he said, "Do you love in March as much as you did in December?" To Allard Lowenstein, now for McCarthy, whom he invited to dinner that night in Virginia, explaining, "You can keep me off your calendar," which was the way he used to see Lowenstein in the first, furtive weeks of the dump Johnson movement. He also called John Nolan, who was in California, organizing the Kennedy slate for the June 4 primary.

Jacket off, sleeves rolled up, tie loose, Kennedy was already trying to be both candidate and manager. For a few minutes he left the phone and disappeared into the bedroom for a conversation with Brooklyn county leader Stanley Steingut. It was curious; Robert Kennedy, seated next to a photo of his brother, pleading with a shabby local politician to support him for President. Steingut, who cared more about patronage and his own career than Vietnam or riots, sounded sympathetic, but gave no commitment. Then Kennedy was off for a busy and boring day of previously arranged touring in Nassau County.

As reporters canvassed political power brokers and kingmakers for their reactions, it quickly became apparent just how alone Robert Kennedy was at the start of his journey. Mayor Daley of Chicago, and Governor Richard Hughes of New Jersey, two backers of John Kennedy in 1960, again affirmed their loyalty to Lyndon Johnson. The state chairmen of Pennsylvania and Ohio, two states Kennedy needed, predicted that Johnson would control all their states' delegates at the convention. Two of the Senate's earliest critics of the Vietnam war— Joseph Clark of Pennsylvania and Wayne Morse of Oregon—declined to endorse Kennedy. David Dubinsky, the retired president of the International Ladies Garment Workers Union, told reporters he was "for Johnson." New York City Council President Frank O'Connor said Kennedy's candidacy "might well be endangering the future of the country." National chairman John Bailey, a charter ally of John Kennedy, said, "There is only one peace candidate this year, and his name is Lyndon Johnson." Meanwhile, the liberals were staying with McCarthy —Lowenstein, Rauh, Galbraith, Representative Edwards, Don Peterson. Kennedy was starting on the head of a pin, too late for the liberals, and too liberal for the rest of the party.

Friday evening, at the Kennedy home in McLean, was a bewildering mixture of gravity and gaiety. In the living room there was a previously scheduled dinner party for Ethel Kennedy's friends—Jim Whitiker, Kay Evans, the George Stevenses, Susie Markham, and the David Hacketts. In the living room, several of the Kennedy children and two large dogs romped and wrestled to the stereo accompaniment of the Jefferson Airplane. In the midst of this casual communal circus Robert Kennedy and his advisers tried to draft a statement and shape up a strategy for his campaign for the Presidency of the United States. It wasn't neat. It wasn't planned. And it wasn't the way John Kennedy would have done it. There was still no agreement about what attitude to take toward Eugene McCarthy's candidacy. Fred Dutton was for a hard line. Allard Lowenstein, who was publicly supporting McCarthy, was there, urging conciliation, and an offer for a united antiwar slate of delegates in the California primary. Arthur Schlesinger was still proposing, even on the eve of his announcement, that Kennedy delay, and back McCarthy. Kennedy's response to this was, "How can I retain any self-respect if I said Gene McCarthy should be President of the United States?"

At another juncture in the disjointed discussion, Kennedy asked Lowenstein, "Should I put into my statement that I told Gene I was going to run before New Hampshire?"

Lowenstein, who did not know this, exclaimed, "Yes, great! That will save you from looking like a vulture and an opportunist."

But then there was the explanation of the convoluted way in which McCarthy was told, the delay, the vague nature of the message, and the fear McCarthy might deny it to the press, which would inaugurate Kennedy's campaign with a conflict with McCarthy rather than Johnson. So the idea was dropped, partly as a result of the escalating mistrust between the two antiwar candidates.

All the differences within the group at the Kennedy home were focused on the announcement statement. Walinsky, Schlesinger, and Sorensen had each written a draft, and fought aggressively for their own special style, cadence, and politics. Walinsky wanted to stress the horror of the war, while Sorensen wanted to soften the breach with Johnson.

At one point Schlesinger remarked to Sorensen, "It's great to see Walinsky and Greenfield look at you, the way you and Goodwin looked at me and Galbraith in 1960."

At another point Kennedy read a sentence from Sorensen's draft, and said, "Ted, that doesn't make any sense. But then, this whole thing doesn't make much sense either."

After midnight, with the quarreling becoming sharper, and time running out, Kennedy asked Schlesinger to "reconcile" all the drafts. But at about 2 A.M. Schlesinger went to sleep, and in the morning it was Sorensen who got to write the announcement statement. And he began it with the exact same sentence that he began John Kennedy's statement in 1960—a sign of where his thoughts and perceptions really were.

Meanwhile, another drama was being enacted. Ted Kennedy, along with McCarthy's temporary aide, Dick Goodwin, and Blair Clark, flew to Green Bay, Wisconsin, for a 2 A.M. meeting with McCarthy. Ted Kennedy made the flight, he said later, to see if McCarthy was in a mood of cooperation. But he found McCarthy, with his wife, Abigail, "cold and noncommunicative. I didn't want to fly all the way out there just for the ride, but that's the way it turned out. He invited us, and then he hinted to the press that we 'woke him up.' "

At about 5:30 A.M., an exhausted Ted Kennedy returned to his brother's house, woke up Schlesinger, and told him, "Abigail turned us down. They won't cooperate."

Saturday, March 16. Embattled and isolated, Robert Kennedy announced for President in the same Senate caucus room his brother announced in eight years ago.

The statement, read before live network television cameras, was dominated by his defensive obsession about being accused of running only to settle his personal vendetta with the President.

"I do not run for the Presidency," he said in his second sentence, "merely to oppose any man, but to propose new policies." A few moments later he added, "I cannot stand aside from the contest that will decide our nation's future, and our children's future. The remarkable New Hampshire campaign of Senator Eugene McCarthy has proven how deep are the present divisions within our party and country. Until that was publicly clear, my presence in the race would have been seen as a clash of personalities rather than issues. . . ."

Kennedy went on to signal McCarthy a new peace feeler: "I made it clear to Senator McCarthy, through my brother, that my candidacy would not be in opposition to his, but in harmony. My aim is to both support and expand his valiant campaign. . . . My desire is not to divide the strength of those forces seeking a change, but to increase it. . . . "

Then the questions began to be shouted out, anonymously, from the small room choked with several hundred journalists.

"There have been speculations that this is opportunism on your part; that McCarthy had the courage to go into New Hampshire while you hesitated. Will you address yourself to that?"

Kennedy, the slightest look of hurt in his eyes, began:

"I don't believe that . . . As I said, I have spoken on these issues, and these questions for a number of years. . . . I think it was generally accepted that if I had gone into the primary in New Hampshire . . . it would have been felt at that time that this was a personal struggle. It would have been written in the press that this was a personal struggle.

"Every time I have spoken on Vietnam, every time I have spoken on what needs to be done as far as the cities are concerned, it has been put in the context of a personal struggle between myself and President Johnson. . . ."

Then, Robert Kennedy, lamed and late, was off and running the race. His staff and organization were in such disarray that he had to hurry to the airport to make a regular American Airlines commercial flight to New York; there had been no time to charter a plane, or even make reservations. He marched in the St. Patrick's Day Parade, where he was heckled by the Irish proletariat as a traitor, and as a friend of Hanoi; and he had a kiss blown to him from an open window by Jacqueline Kennedy. In the afternoon there were meetings and phone calls, and at 7:30 P.M. he flew back to the capital, again on a commercial flight, much to the surprise of the passengers beguiled by the myth of the "well-oiled Kennedy machine."

At 8:45 P.M., Robert Kennedy, a slouched, rumpled figure, began walking through the oddly deserted new American Airlines terminal. He was alone, and carried under his arm a copy of Shakespeare's *Love Sonnets,* which he had read fitfully on the flight back from New York.

He looked around, and could not see his driver, and said to a few stray reporters, as if trying to dictate their morning leads for them, "The hero returns, and a huge throng turned out to greet him. It took the police to hold them back."

Kennedy stood there alone for a few more moments, until a uniformed airlines employee rushed up to him to explain that his office had failed to locate his driver.

"Even my driver has deserted." Kennedy grinned. "It's nice to be so popular."

Kennedy, still looking lost, walked through the automatic doors, where a stewardess directed him to a limousine the airline had secured for him.

"How many with your party?" the stewardess asked with professional warmth.

"Just me. I'm alone," Kennedy answered, getting into the limousine, and beginning to rub the tiredness out of his eyes with his red, stumpy fingers.

Running Against LBJ

For fifteen days, across fifteen states, in every quadrant of the nation, until his voice gave out, Kennedy exposed himself to crowds in an orgy of emotion. His name was his slogan and his face was his platform. He was playing High Noon politics to win the streets and to generate energy; the delegates, he felt, would come later. At the start he was trying to blitz the party from below, from outside the structure. Without the unions, the business community, the regular party leaders, or the South, he had to show the delegates that he had the people. So in those first two weeks, before Johnson's withdrawal, Kennedy went to segregationist Alabama, to Republican Kansas, to angry, bruised Watts, and to college campuses where Eugene McCarthy was hailed as the new King.

"Our strategy," said Adam Walinsky the first day, "is to change the rules of nominating a President. We're going to do it a new way. In the street."

Robert Kennedy's campaign began on St. Patrick's Day night, at the New York airport named for his brother, where he, his staff, and forty reporters took off for Kansas on a commercial flight.

Kennedy was to speak at Kansas and Kansas State universities the next day, and he was apprehensive about how the students would greet him. He had just read a newspaper story that said a nationwide survey taken by The Associated Press showed that McCarthy was now twice as popular as he was on the campuses. And he had read Mary McGrory's column that knighted McCarthy as "the new hero of the college generation." And Kennedy was afraid it was all true. Although he bitterly resented the older liberals for jilting him for McCarthy, he was hurt that the students left him, and this obsessed him the entire campaign. He envied McCarthy's students and he even admired their loyalty for sticking with McCarthy.

At 8:30 P.M. on Sunday night, March 17, Robert Kennedy got off the commercial flight in Kansas City to walk 100 yards to Governor Robert Docking's private plane that would carry him to Topeka. To his astonishment, in heartland, Republican Kansas, 2,500 people were waiting at the municipal airport just to watch him change planes. They had been waiting for two hours, mostly high-school students and young married couples with children.

When Kennedy came down out of the plane, part of the crowd broke the police barricade and charged onto the runway as if it were the start of the land rush in Kansas one hundred years before. They engulfed him, jostled him, pinned him against the plane, pulled at his clothes, screamed his name, and shouted for a speech.

There was no microphone and no bullhorn, since there was no airport rally scheduled. Kennedy shouted a few remarks that only those closest to him could hear.

"I'm very appreciative of this," he said. "I'm grateful to be here in the Midwest, since I come from a great farm state myself—Massachussets. In the next five months I will need your help. But if you work hard in Kansas and Missouri, we will win. . . ."

After a few minutes of this, he stopped, and said, "That was my very first campaign speech. Now let's all clap." He clapped, and then the crowd that could not hear his words clapped, and then everyone laughed.

The night was mild and springlike, and Kennedy went to the wire fence, and began moving down the line, smiling timidly, shaking, actually touching hands, and nodding to the shouted words of support. The crowd pushed and shoved and nearly knocked Kennedy and his wife over. This was the subterranean longing for change that had been growing in the middle of America for two years, which Kennedy saw in 1966, and then forgot he knew. It was people who had never been to New York, and who disliked hippies, mobbing Robert Kennedy because he was finally running against Lyndon Johnson, running against the present.

At 9 A.M. the next morning, Kennedy arrived at Kansas State University at Manhattan, Kansas. This is not a campus where there have been student protests. The students are mostly from rural Kansas. The girls wear short hair, little makeup, and skirts below the knees. The boys had ties and crew cuts. There were 14,000 of them packed into Ahearn Fieldhouse. They sat in stairwells, on the basketball scoreboard, and they stood behind the platform. Many of them waved signs. Maybe thirty for McCarthy, and fifteen for Rockefeller. There were a few ecumenical "Kennedy and McCarthy" signs, and a few prowar banners: "RFK Prolongs the War," and "Father Ho Loves Bobby." And then there were dozens of Kennedy placards. "Sock it to 'em, Bobby." "Bobby is Groovy." "Kiss me, Bobby." "Go, Bobby, Go." They were adolescent, and they treated "Bobby" more as an equal than a leader. When Kennedy came in they cheered warmly, but short of hero-worship.

Kennedy, nervous, still uncertain of his hold on the generation, began with a joke about the proposed Vietnam study commission.

> The problem [he said] was that the President and I couldn't agree who should be on the commission. I wanted Senator Mansfield, Senator Fulbright, and Senator Morse appointed to the commission. And the President, in his own inimitable style, wanted to appoint General Westmoreland, John Wayne, and Martha Raye.

The crowd broke up; they didn't expect to hear that kind of irreverent humor from a candidate for President.

Kennedy opened his speech, written by Walinsky, with a quote from William Allen White, the old editor of the *Emporia* (Kansas) *Gazette:*

> If our colleges and universities do not breed men who riot, who rebel, who attack life with all the youthful vision and vigor, then there is something wrong with our colleges. The more riots that come on college campuses, the better the world for tomorrow.

And the wholesome, corn-fed, prairie faces let out a happy roar.

Kennedy began reading his text nervously. He stammered at a few places, and, behind the lectern, his right leg shook. His voice was flat.

After ten minutes, he began to speak of Vietnam, and the crowd began to cheer and clap, and he began to feel their emotion, and be nourished by it, and build on its playback.

> I am concerned [he said] that at the end of it all, there will only be more Americans killed; more of our treasure spilled out . . . so that

they may say, as Tacitus said of Rome: "They made a desert, and called it peace." I don't think that is satisfactory for the United States of America.

The cheering grew louder now. Emotion began to infuse Kennedy's voice, as he again frankly confessed error for his role in shaping the early Vietnam policy.

> . . . I am willing to bear my share of the responsibility, before history and before my fellow citizens. But past error is no excuse for its own perpetuation. Tragedy is a tool for the living to gain wisdom, not a guide by which to live. Now as ever, we do ourselves best justice when we measure ourselves against ancient tests, as in the *Antigone* of Sophocles: "All men make mistakes, but a good man yields when he knows his course is wrong, and repairs the evil. The only sin is pride."
>
> If the South Vietnamese troops will not carry the fight for their own cities, we cannot ourselves destroy them. That kind of salvation is not an act we can presume to perform for them. For we must ask our government, and we must ask ourselves: where does such logic end? If it becomes necessary to destroy all of South Vietnam to save it, will we do that too? And if we care so little about South Vietnam, that we are willing to see its land destroyed, and its people dead, then why are we there in the first place?

Now his hair was flopping over his forehead. He was jabbing the air with his small clenched fist in that haunting gesture. And pouring all his pent-up feeling into his finish:

> So I come here today, to this great university, to ask your help; not for me, but for your country, and for the people of Vietnam. . . . I urge you to learn the harsh facts that lurk behind the mask of official illusion with which we have concealed our true circumstances, even from ourselves. Our country is in danger: not just from foreign enemies, but, above all, from our own misguided policies—and what they can do to the nation that Thomas Jefferson once said was the last, best hope of man. There is a contest on, not for the rule of America, but for the heart of America. In these next eight months we are going to decide what this country will stand for—and what kind of men we are. So I ask for your help, in the cities and homes of this state, into the towns and farms, contributing your concern and action, warning of the danger of what we are doing, and the promise of what we can do in the future. . . .

Then Kennedy looked up from his text, raised up his right fist, and improvised the climax to his fifty-minute speech:

. . . not just in Southeast Asia, but here at home as well, so that
we might have a new birth for this country, a new light to guide us. And
I pledge to you, if you will give me your help, if you will give me your
hand, I will work for you, and we will have a new America.

Suddenly, the fieldhouse sounded as though it was inside Niagara
Falls; it was like a soundtrack gone haywire. The sound of screaming
filled the fieldhouse, and hundreds of students were running toward the
platform, overturning chairs, raising a haze of dust from the dirt floor.
They surrounded him, screamed his name, pulled his cuff links,
scratched his hands. One girl had a copy of John Kennedy's book,
Profiles in Courage, and thrust it out for the younger brother to autograph. For an instant, Robert Kennedy looked at the picture of his dead
brother's face on the cover of the book and froze inside the frenzy. Then
he signed the book, and squeezed the young girl's hand, holding it an
extra moment.

Stanley Tretick, the *Look* magazine photographer who was a special
favorite of all the Kennedys, looked at the hysteria and exclaimed, "This
is Kansas, fucking Kansas! He's going all the fucking way!"

The scene at the University of Kansas at Lawrence, eighty miles away
was, if possible, even wilder. At 1:30 P.M., the arena where Wilt
Chamberlain rewrote the college basketball record book was filled
beyond capacity; there were 16,000 students enrolled at KU, and
20,000 people were in Phog Allen Fieldhouse. They spilled out onto the
gleaming yellow basketball court on each side to the foul lines, leaving
only a small open space around the lectern at mid-court. A brass band
played and the students clapped in rhythmic unison as Kennedy appeared. Then the noise swelled to a crescendo as he slowly moved
through the crowd to the lectern; the students screamed, and clapped
until their hands hurt. And Kennedy waved, and mouthed the words
"thank you" with his lips.

Kennedy spoke extemporaneously here, weaving together paragraphs
from the Kansas State speech, with phrases from older speeches, but
beginning with the war, and calling for a bombing halt and negotiations
with the NLF. Then:

America is divided. . . . The poor are invisible . . . I say we can
do better . . . I think we need a change . . . We must end the dis-
grace of the other America of suffering. . . . We have made the war in

Vietnam an American war and that is unacceptable. . . . We have seen tanks patrolling American cities, and machine guns fired at American children. I don't think that is a satisfactory situation, and that is why I run for the Presidency of the United States.

Thunder from the stands. Two ears and the tail. It took Kennedy fifteen minutes to get back to his car. Later, Jim Tolan, Kennedy's favorite advance man, said, "It was the first time I was ever scared with him. Those kids were out of control. He could have got hurt they like him so much."

On the plane back to Washington, Jimmy Breslin asked Kennedy about the faces. "You could see them from where you were?" he asked.

"I saw them. I saw every face in the building," replied Robert Kennedy at the end of his first full day of running for President.

A Presidential nominating campaign is a little like a 15-round championship fight. One round is not necessarily like the next. Control ebbs and flows. Tactics change to meet new situations. The scoring is secret and no one is positive who is ahead. This was still the first experimental round for Robert Kennedy. A rhythm and a pattern were not yet established. It was not yet clear whether the passions of ordinary citizens outside the political process could be converted into convention delegates. Or whether the liberals would forgive Kennedy his sin of caution.

What was clear in those first few days was that the traditional party leaders, who controlled the big blocs of delegates, were holding firm for the President: Daley in Illinois; Bailey in Connecticut; Hughes in New Jersey; Mayors Barr of Pittsburgh and Tate of Philadelphia in Pennsylvania. But already, beneath the surface of the President's majority, there were omens of weakness. The latest Gallup Poll showed that only 36 percent of the country thought the President was "doing a good job." The last Harris Poll indicated that only 54 percent of the country now supported the war, a drop of 20 percent since the Tet offensive. And a variety of polls, public and private in Wisconsin, pointed to a victory for Eugene McCarthy over the President in the April 2 primary.

The liberals and suburban middle class, meanwhile, were staying with Eugene McCarthy. And this created a problem for Kennedy that he never found a solution for. He didn't respect McCarthy, but he coveted his movement. If he attacked McCarthy, he would alienate his movement, and appear to be "ruthless." If he did not attack McCarthy, he would feel frustrated, and fail to make visible McCarthy's votes against the anti-poll tax amendment, against increasing rent subsidies, in protection of the oil depletion allowance.

Kennedy, the rest of the first frenetic week, kept on playing the new politics—issue and student oriented, anti-Johnson, combative, risky.

On Thursday, March 21, he went to the University of Alabama at Tuscaloosa, where as Attorney General in 1963 he had forced integration over Governor George Wallace's defiance. Kennedy returned to the site of this bitter old confrontation to give a speech for "equality and reconciliation" to 8,500 white Southern students.

"When a man leaves his home to risk death 12,000 miles away," he told them, "while we live and study in comfort, I want him to find the door of opportunity open when he returns. And I think you want that, too. I want an America that understands that this is a matter of simple justice—an America that begins to do simple justice to all its people. . . ." The reaction was polite applause.

After his speech, during the question period, Kennedy was asked if he would accept "second place on a ticket with Lyndon Johnson." He quipped in response, "You don't understand. I said I was for a coalition government in Saigon, not here."

The same day, a few hours later, Kennedy appeared before 10,500 enthusiastic students at Vanderbilt University in Nashville, and told them in a fist-waving speech:

"Who is it that is truly dividing the country? It is not those who call for change. It is those who make the present policy, those who bear the responsibility for our present course, who have removed themselves from the American tradition, from the enduring and generous impulses that are the soul of this nation."

Then, after the roar swelled and ebbed, he ad-libbed, in a rasping, rising shout: "They are the ones, the President of the United States, President Johnson, they are the ones who divide us."

It was out in the open now. For three years Kennedy had obeyed the rituals of the old politics, praising Johnson, denying there was bad feeling between them, while all the time sucking on the sour juices of his private hate. Once Kennedy had told me:

"You know what Johnson [always it was Johnson, never the President, for his brother was the President] once said to me? He told me that when he used to campaign in Texas, that he used to throw his big hat into the crowd at the end of his speech, just to watch the poor Mexicans fight for it. He thought that was fun."

Friday, March 22, Kennedy spent catching his breath, and trying to think about organization, staff, and money for the first time. The legend of the "well-oiled Kennedy machine" was part of the inheritance of 1960, but it did not exist. A week into the 1968 campaign Kennedy still did not have a national campaign headquarters, a campaign plane, or a Robert Kennedy to be his manager. He didn't even have the new, unlisted phone number of Bronx Borough President Herman Badillo. The obsolete files from 1960 were not much help. In many places the campaign had to start from scratch. So the phone calls began to go out, and dozens of men agreed to abandon their families, and their jobs with law firms, newspapers, and universities, and go to Indiana, or Oregon, or California, to work for the Restoration.

Friday night Kennedy was to speak at a testimonial dinner for New York Democratic State Chairman John Burns in Binghamton. But fog and drizzle grounded all planes, and Kennedy and fifty other guests had to return to Manhattan by bus long after midnight. On the bus Kennedy saw Lowenstein and asked him if he was ready to switch from McCarthy. Lowenstein wanted to; McCarthy had cut him out of his campaign and had told ugly stories about him. But he told Kennedy that publicly he had to stay with McCarthy awhile longer. For a few minutes Kennedy brooded about this, about how he should have run earlier, and how Lowenstein understood loyalty. Then he scrawled a note to Lowenstein on a sheet of paper and passed it to him at the back of the bus, at 3 A.M., on the wet, foggy highway back to New York. It read:

> For Al, who knew the lesson of Emerson and taught it to the rest of us: "They did not yet see, and thousands of young men as hopeful, now crowding to the barriers of their careers, did not yet see if a single man plant himself on his convictions and then abide, the huge world will come round to him." From his friend, Bob Kennedy.

Saturday, March 23, 9 A.M. TWA Flight 59 for San Francisco was waiting for the thick fog to lift before departing. Taking up two-thirds of this regular flight was the heterogenous entourage that is Robert Kennedy's campaign party. The candidate and his two sisters, Pat and Jean.

His traveling staff of Mankiewicz, Dutton, Walinsky, Greenfield, Dick Tuck, the merry prankster, and Bill Barry, his security man, Assembly Speaker Unruh, and San Francisco antiwar Congressman Phil Burton, the only two major California politicians backing Kennedy. And forty reporters and fifteen still photographers and newsreel cameramen. This is to be Kennedy's first test with ordinary voters, rather than students. And in the state with the most important of all the Presidential primaries. Normally, Presidential candidates have time to perfect their style and tighten up their campaign in relative privacy during the early days of the New Hampshire primary, or even earlier. But Robert Kennedy was going on the road in a fishbowl, again doing his learning in public.

The flight took off an hour late, and Robert Kennedy, who only got two hours' sleep the night before, removed his jacket, dropped five pillows on the floor, pulled a blue blanket down on top of himself, and went to sleep until the plane reached the purple, cloud-crowned Rocky Mountains.

More than one thousand people were waiting for Kennedy when he got off the plane in San Francisco to change to a small charter plane for a day of city hopping in Northern California. Most of them were Kennedy fans, but more than a few were hecklers, some with print dresses and sports shirts shouting, "Where were you in New Hampshire?" and others, bearded, bereted members of the Peace and Freedom Party, screaming "Pig" and "Phony liberal."

The first stop was Stockton, in the Central Valley. It was hot and the small crowd in the town square was listless. "Dead crowd, dead town," summed up Richard Harwood, the cold-eyed pro from the *Washington Post*.

Stockton Mayor Joseph Doll introduced Kennedy, saying, "I know God is on your side."

"I hope I have some delegates to go with Him," Kennedy smiled. Then he began the speech he would give twice more that day:

> Decency is the heart of the matter. The death and maiming of young men in the swamps of Asia is indecent. . . . Here while the sun shines, men are dying on the other side of the earth. Which of them would have written a symphony? Which of them would have cured cancer? Which of them would have played in a World Series? These young men in the rice paddies of Asia are our most important natural resource.

We must bring them back to America. And that is why I run for President of the United States. . . .

Sacramento was next, and very different. It provided the first evidence of Kennedy's magic with crowds of white, high-school educated, working-class Americans. There was a rally on the mall of one of those new, plastic California shopping centers, and there were 15,000 people in the middle of a hot Saturday afternoon jammed into a place intended for 5,000. Some of the faces were Latin and Filipino, but a majority were white faces, young enough to remember John Kennedy.

They cheered his attack on the war, and when he finished they wouldn't let him leave. They tore at his buttons and hair, and then they tried to pull him out of his convertible as he left, so that Bill Barry, an ex-football player at Kent State, had to hang on to him with all his strength. When it was over, a television camera crew went back to look for some equipment lost in the crush, but found only five unpaired shoes.

At twilight, the sun setting in orange fire behind the mountains, a cooling breeze blowing, Robert Kennedy came to St. James Park in San Jose. At least 7,000 people, almost all under thirty, and almost all Mexican, filled the park. The roar went up as soon as Kennedy got out of his car, and it mounted in intensity as he slowly pushed behind a wedge of advance men toward the platform. Pete Hamill and I were standing at the steps of the platform, when Kennedy, tilted at a forty-five-degree angle, was being carried past us. He reached out to grab my shoulder for balance, and gasped, "You can write that I'm reassessing my position again." Kennedy spoke to them about the indecency of Vietnam, but he could have read them the Stockton phone book; they cheered and cheered, and again it took fifteen minutes for him to get back to his car, his shirttail hanging out, his cuff links gone.

On Sunday there was more. Before noon Kennedy's plane stopped at Monterey, a Republican bastion of the elderly and affluent, and there were 5,000 people at the airport for a rally announced two days before. A highway patrolman said, "The road from here to Salinas is one big parking lot. Five thousand more are still trying to get here. I've never seen anything like it."

Then, Los Angeles. There was almost a riot at the airport; the crowds were out of control, and there was a brief fistfight between a Kennedy enthusiast and a McCarthy heckler.

The motorcade left the airport without a police escort, and hundreds of cars, and dozens of motorcycles, joined it, following Kennedy, shouting to him, or shaking his hand. For a while I rode in Kennedy's open car and saw the joy, the happiness, in the faces that lined the curb to see him. I had not seen happiness in politics since the early days of the civil rights movement.

The faces made Kennedy high. A hippie trotted alongside of his car and gave Kennedy his draft card, and Kennedy autographed it, laughing. At another point, a housewife, in a red bathrobe and her hair in curlers, ran out of her house, hugged Kennedy and got his autograph. And Kennedy wrote on a piece of paper, "Bob Kennedy likes Walter Dombrow." Dombrow is a cheerful cameraman for CBC-TV, who was riding on the trunk of Kennedy's car.

Kennedy's first stop in Los Angeles was a rally of Mexicans at Olivera Street, but he had to get out of his car two blocks away, the crowd was so big and excited. From there he went to the Greek Theatre for a rally. Without a police escort, Kennedy was again snarled in a traffic jam. At one point a long-haired kid on a motorcycle, driving alongside Kennedy's open car at twenty-five miles per hour, took his hand off the steering wheel to snap a picture of Kennedy. Kennedy, fearing an accident, reached out, took the camera, and gave it to Jerry Bruno, who snapped the picture, and gave the camera back to the cyclist.

Abandoned cars started to clog the freeway a mile from the Greek Theatre. A half mile away, motorists were still walking up the steep hill. Five thousand people milled around outside, and 8,000 filled every inch of space inside.

The speech Kennedy gave at the Greek Theatre had been secretly written by Richard Goodwin, who was then still working for Senator McCarthy. It was blunt, and was later severely criticized by several influential journalists for being excessive and demagogic, particularly a passage that accused "the national leadership" of "calling upon the darker impulses of the American spirit, not, perhaps, deliberately, but through its action it sets an example where integrity, truth, honor, and all the rest, seem like words to fill out speeches, rather than guiding beliefs. . . ."

That night Kennedy, his face sunburned, and his hands scratched, said at dinner, "I'm still not sure I can make it, but those faces, those faces all day, they seemed starved. They want something. They show how much unhappiness there is in the country."

Later that night, Monday's *Los Angeles Times* hit the streets with the huge, eight-column, two-deck headline:

KENNEDY BESIEGED
Senator Gets Wild L.A. Welcome

The lead story, by Carl Greenberg, began:

> Senator Robert F. Kennedy was greeted here Sunday by one of the wildest demonstrations ever given a political figure in Los Angeles. . . . The reception Kennedy received here was uproarious, shrieking and frenzied. . . .

Monday Kennedy went to Watts, to speak in front of Budd Schulberg's Writers' Workship at the dingy corner of Graham Avenue and 103rd Street. He stood on a chair in the street, and spoke to about 2,000 people. He was protected by the grass-roots cadre of militants called Sons of Watts, because he insisted that no police accompany him into the ghetto that has become the universal symbol of black violence.

"I want to find jobs for all our people," Kennedy shouted into a bullhorn. "I want to find jobs for the black people of Watts, and the white people of Eastern Kentucky. I want a reconciliation of blacks and whites in the United States. . . ."

As Kennedy spoke, I asked one of the blacks guarding him why he liked Kennedy, expecting, perhaps, a uniquely black response. Instead he replied, "Because he is the only cat who can get this country's shit together."

And then, the cheering ringing in his ears, Robert Kennedy left the spent city, where he would be assassinated ten weeks later.

Kennedy maintained the same grueling pace the following week. Oregon and Washington on Tuesday, Idaho, Utah, and Colorado on Wednesday. Indiana on Thursday, to file in person for the May 7 primary. Then New Mexico and Arizona to visit several Indian reservations over the weekend. The receptions Kennedy received during this week were friendly except for Phoenix, but nothing like the California madness. In the course of the week, citizen participation joined the Vietnam war as his two most recurring campaign themes.

"I don't believe in the casual arithmetic of the party bosses," Kennedy cried in place after place. "I don't think a Presidential nominee should be chosen by a few thousand people talking to one another. I think it should be up to the people. I think the people should decide."

On Saturday, March 30, despite laryngitis and a cold, Kennedy went to Flagstaff, Arizona, to preside at a hearing of his Senate Subcommittee on Indian Education. The night before, when several members of his local campaign organization complained of his wasting time on the hearings when he could be out meeting voters, Kennedy snarled, "You sons of bitches! You don't really care about suffering!"

The leaders of sixteen tribes testified before Kennedy. They told him that the infant mortality rate among White Mountain Apaches was 99.2 per 1,000. Ronnie Lupe, an Apache, testified that unemployment among his tribe was 50 percent. When Kennedy heard that, he said that he had recently heard of an Apache mother feeling so hopeless that she had burned herself to death in front of her children.

Annie Wauneka, a leader of the Navajo tribe, informed Kennedy that the school administered by the Bureau of Indian Affairs in her community had just been closed, and now the children had to travel sixty miles each morning if they wanted to attend school. She added that it was impossible for Indians to remove incompetent school officials because of the Civil Service regulations that guide the Bureau of Indian Affairs.

"Indians are always beaten on the TV Westerns," she said, "and now we are beaten by the Civil Service. . . ."

"Annie, I'm on your side," Kennedy tried gently to explain.

That night, at a dinner, Kennedy delivered a slashing attack on the government's treatment of Indians, as white representatives of the Indian Affairs Bureau sat in uncomfortable silence in the front, while Indians standing in the back let out war whoops of joy.

The next day, March 31, with his voice still hoarse, and his cold persisting, Kennedy flew to New York for a planned day of rest and recuperation.

He had spoken to more than 250,000 people in two weeks. He had been seen and cheered by uncounted thousands more in motorcades. The scenes of hysteria in California had been witnessed by millions on television. He had released volcanic energies on the margins of the society. But it appeared that in that first burst of motion he had not moved any of the six or eight men who would control the Democratic convention in August. They were all still for the President.

At 9 P.M. that night, as the jet carrying Robert Kennedy was approaching Philadelphia, Lyndon Johnson went on national television to address the nation about the war in Vietnam. It was two days before the Wisconsin primary, and all the politicians were predicting the President would lose badly. The opinion polls pointed to an even more humiliating defeat in the climactic California primary in June. The latest national Gallup Poll showed that only 26 percent of the nation now approved of Johnson's handling of the Vietnam war, and only 36 percent approved of his overall performance as President. The President, whose desire was consensus and healing, had instead created polarization and hostility. He was tired and embittered, but no one thought he was ready to abdicate.

The speculation in Washington and in the press was that he would use the speech to announce a peace initiative in Vietnam to influence the voting forty-eight hours later in Wisconsin. And in the first thirty-five minutes of the speech, he did announce unilateral reduction of the bombing of North Vietnam, in an effort to begin peace talks.

But Johnson's mania for secrecy prevailed until the end. His statement of withdrawal from the race was not included in the text of his remarks distributed in advance to the networks and wire services. Not even his closest advisers, like Abe Fortas and Clark Clifford, or his staff, were certain that he would use the passages declaring his withdrawal. He had his staff prepare a similar valedictory for his State of the Union address in January, but at the last minute he decided not to read it. But on Sunday night, March 31, at the end of his televised speech, Johnson said:

> With American sons in the fields far away, with America's future under challenge right here at home, with our hopes and the world's hopes for peace in the balance every day, I do not believe that I should devote an hour, or a day, of my time to any personal partisan causes. Or to any duties other than the awesome duties of this office—the Presidency of your country.
>
> Accordingly, I shall not seek, and I will not accept, the nomination of my party for another term as your President.

A few minutes later, at about 9:50 P.M., American Airlines Flight 164 from Phoenix taxied to a halt at JFK International Airport, and

Dall Forsythe, twenty-four, the son of actor John Forsythe, and a member of Robert Kennedy's New York staff, pushed his way onto the plane, and half shouted to Kennedy, "The President withdrew, the President withdrew!" Democratic State Chairman John Burns, a half step behind Forsythe, his eyes wide, exclaimed, "The President isn't going to run!"

"You're kidding," Kennedy mumbled, half standing at his seat. Then, reading the joy etched in the faces of Forsythe and Burns, he slowly sat back down, trying to comprehend the new world.

Kennedy snaked through a cheering crowd of about two hundred at the airport terminal, and wouldn't talk to reporters. His driver, Frank Belotti, greeted him as "Mr. President," but Kennedy had disappeared inside himself. The only thing he said during the entire forty-minute ride to his Manhattan apartment was a tentative, "I wonder if he would have done it if I hadn't come in."

Kennedy's apartment at 870 UN Plaza was soon crowded. Ethel and Steve Smith were there. So were Sorensen, Schlesinger, Gwirtzman, Vanden Heuvel, Burns, Dutton, Walinsky, Mankiewicz, Greenfield, Carter Burden, and Kennedy's personal secretary, Angie Novello.

Kennedy, Smith, Dutton, and Sorensen went into the bedroom to start making long-distance phone calls, the first being to Teddy in Indianapolis. The others, trying to adjust, paced or speculated in the living room. Ethel Kennedy, always herself, brought out a bottle of Scotch, and said, "Well, he never deserved to be President anyway."

In the bedroom, the phone calls began to be made to the political leaders around the country, asking for support. One of the first calls went to Postmaster Larry O'Brien, who was with John Kennedy when he ran for the Senate in 1952; who had campaigned for Johnson the last week in Wisconsin; and who was now free to return to the Kennedys. He asked for a little time to think. Strangely, one of those who wasn't called in that first dazed hour was Mayor Richard Daley. "Nobody crowds Dick Daley," Dutton said later. After midnight, Kennedy himself suggested that he send a telegram to the President praising his decision, and requesting a meeting for "national unity." At 3 A.M. he went to sleep.

At first glance, Johnson's withdrawal appeared to benefit Kennedy. But in the long run it did not. The speech deprived Kennedy of his two great issues—the war and Johnson's record. It drained Kennedy of much of his driving desire; it made the campaign a campaign, rather than an emotional crusade. It made Johnson a figure of sympathy. It permitted the antiwar McCarthy staff and supporters the luxury of remaining with McCarthy, the fear of Johnson now gone. And, in a mysterious way, it made Robert Kennedy the magnet for much of the free-floating venom in the country that had previously been directed at the President. Kennedy had driven Johnson out of the race, only to become the new villain to many of the liberals who most hated Johnson. That night, Eugene McCarthy, with the Catholic's poet's sense of metaphor, remarked to his speech writer Paul Gorman, "Up to now Bobby was Jack running against Lyndon. Now Bobby has to run against Jack."

Without an issue, without a target, and without a purpose, Kennedy floundered awkwardly in the next few days, groping for a new beginning. On April 1, in Camden, New Jersey, he told an outdoor rally, "We take pride in President Johnson, who brought to final fulfillment the [party's] policies of thirty years." This just two weeks after he accused Johnson of "calling upon the darker impulses of the American spirit." The next night, in Philadelphia, at a Democratic fund-raising dinner, Kennedy described the city's hack machine mayor, James Tate, as "one of the greatest mayors in the United States." And on Wednesday, Kennedy spent a cordial ninety minutes meeting with Lyndon Johnson. This period was one of those gross lapses of behavior the contradictory Kennedy was always capable of. There would be others during the campaign, but he always managed to feel sufficiently ashamed to pull out of them. But the fact that he made them was further evidence of the grinding conflict continually going on inside him between the Good and Bad Bobbys. Yet, when the campaign was over, and Richard Nixon elected, Paul Gorman admitted: "Bobby, in retrospect, ran a more traditionally issue-oriented campaign, and a more programmatic campaign than McCarthy." But that in no way excuses Kennedy's lurch toward the old politics of blarney and accommodation in the confused days following Lyndon Johnson's abdication.

Martin Luther King had come to Memphis to put the prestige of his Nobel Peace Prize behind the strike of black garbagemen for union recognition from the city administration. He marched and preached, as he had all across the land since the Montgomery bus boycott of 1955–1956. On the night of April 3, in a sermon in a hot, crowded Baptist church, King told his followers that he had "been to the mountaintop," and that he wanted to be remembered as a "drum major for justice." The next evening, at 6:01 P.M., as he stood on the balcony outside his room at the Lorraine Motel, justice's drum major was assassinated by a sniper.

It was said that King was falling behind the times, that his faith in integration, God, and nonviolence made him irrelevant to the bottom layers of the black slums. But the ghettos responded to King's murder with a wail of grief, and then riots of rage. Medgar Evers had been assassinated, and then Malcolm X, and then James Meredith had narrowly escaped assassination, and the ghettos had remained quiet. But King had touched the poorer and younger blacks in ways so deep we couldn't see them.

When word of his death spread, the ghettos, sensing their loss, rose up in a way that had never been seen before in America. It began, naturally enough, in the South, in Greensboro, North Carolina and Nashville, Tennessee, the cradles of the old civil rights movement. And then it spread like a wayward, windblown spark, to the slums of Chicago, Baltimore, Detroit, and Washington, D.C., until bayoneted troops surrounded the Capitol, and the smoke of riot formed a bizarre shroud over the city. When the violent spasm of sorrow ended, 76 American cities had rioted; 70,000 troops and guardsmen were summoned to contain the riots; 46 were dead, all but five of them black; 2,500 were injured; 28,000 jailed; and property damage estimated at near $50 million.

Robert Kennedy first heard that King had been shot as his campaign plane left Muncie, Indiana, for Indianapolis. When he landed in Indianapolis, Kennedy was told that King was dead, shot in the head, a wound not unlike John Kennedy's. Robert Kennedy gasped, and then wept for his adversary turned comrade. Then he went directly to a previously arranged rally in a poor, Negro section of Indianapolis.

The crowd had not yet heard the news, and Kennedy, hunched against a cold wind in a black overcoat, told them, "I have bad news for you, for all of our fellow citizens, and people who love justice all over the world, and that is that Martin Luther King was shot and killed tonight."

The crowd of about 1,000 cried out in shock and pain, and then Kennedy, speaking extemporaneously, near tears himself, and inevitably thinking of Dallas, gave a talk that all his skilled speech writers working together could not have surpassed.

Martin Luther King dedicated his life to love and to justice for his fellow human beings, and he died because of that effort.

In this difficult day, in this difficult time for the United States, it is perhaps well to ask what kind of a nation we are and what direction we want to move in. For those of you who are black—considering the evidence there evidently is that there were white people who were responsible—you can be filled with bitterness, with hatred, and a desire for revenge. We can move in that direction as a country, in great polarization—black people amongst black, white people amongst white, filled with hatred toward one another.

Or we can make an effort, as Martin Luther King did, to understand and to comprehend, and to replace that violence, that stain of bloodshed that has spread across our land, with an effort to understand with compassion and love.

For those of you who are black and are tempted to be filled with hatred and distrust at the injustice of such an act, against all white people, I can only say that I feel in my own heart the same kind of feeling. I had a member of my family killed, but he was killed by a white man. But we have to make an effort in the United States, we have to make an effort to understand, to go beyond these rather difficult times.

My favorite poet was Aeschylus. He wrote: "In our sleep, pain which cannot forget falls drop by drop upon the heart until, in our own despair, against our will, comes wisdom through the awful grace of God."

What we need in the United States is not division; what we need in the United States is not hatred; what we need in the United States is not violence or lawlessness, but love and wisdom, and compassion toward one another, and a feeling of justice toward those who still suffer within our country, whether they be white or they be black.

So I shall ask you tonight to return home, to say a prayer for the family of Martin Luther King, that's true, but more importantly to say a prayer for our own country, which all of us love—a prayer for understanding and that compassion of which I spoke.

We can do well in this country. We will have difficult times. We've had difficult times in the past. We will have difficult times in the future. It is not the end of violence; it is not the end of lawlessness; it is not the end of disorder.

But the vast majority of white people and the vast majority of black people in this country want to live together, want to improve the quality of our life, and want justice for all human beings who abide in our land.

Let us dedicate ourselves to what the Greeks wrote so many years ago: to tame the savageness of man and to make gentle the life of this world.

Let us dedicate ourselves to that, and say a prayer for our country, and for our people.

Kennedy first canceled all his campaign appearances and withdrew into his hotel room. But after speaking to several Negro leaders by phone, he decided to speak once the next day against the retaliatory reflex of fire that was already beginning to flicker across the country. That night Walinsky and Greenfield, working in Indianapolis, and Sorensen, working in New York but transported by the tragedy back in time to Dallas, collaborated by phone on a speech that was probably the best written text of the campaign, and perhaps of Kennedy's public career. Greenfield, trying to finish it, fell asleep over his typewriter at about 3:30 A.M., and Kennedy had to go into his hotel room to shut off the light and put his assistant to bed. The next morning, Walinsky and Greenfield inserted Sorensen's moving contributions into the text, and finished it just in time to leave for Cleveland, where Kennedy would deliver it at a City Club luncheon. It was April 5, sixty days before Kennedy's own assassination, and the speech can now be read as his own epitaph:

This is a time of shame and sorrow. It is not a day for politics. I have saved this one opportunity to speak briefly to you about this mindless menace of violence in America which again stains our land and every one of our lives.

It is not the concern of any one race. The victims of the violence are black and white, rich and poor, young and old, famous and unknown. They are, most important of all, human beings whom other human beings loved and needed. No one—no matter where he lives or what he does—can be certain who will suffer from some senseless act of bloodshed. And yet it goes on and on.

Why? What has violence ever accomplished? What has it ever created? No martyr's cause has ever been stilled by his assassin's bullet. No wrongs have ever been righted by riots and civil disorders. A sniper is only a coward, not a hero, and an uncontrolled, uncontrollable mob is only the voice of madness, not the voice of the people.

Whenever any American's life is taken by another American unnecessarily—whether it is done in the name of the law or in the defiance of law, by one man or a gang, in cold blood or in passion, in an attack of violence or in response to violence—whenever we tear at the fabric of life which another man has painfully and clumsily woven for himself and his children, the whole nation is degraded.

"Among free men," said Abraham Lincoln, "there can be no successful appeal from the ballot to the bullet; and those who take such appeal are sure to lose their cause and pay the costs." Yet we seemingly tolerate a rising level of violence that ignores our common humanity and our claims to civilization alike. We calmly accept newspaper reports of civilian slaughter in far-off lands. We glorify killing on movie and television screens and call it entertainment. We make it easy for men of all shades of sanity to acquire whatever weapons and ammunition they desire.

Too often we honor swagger and bluster and the wielders of force; too often we excuse those who are willing to build their own lives on the shattered dreams of others. Some Americans who preach nonviolence abroad fail to practice it here at home. Some who accuse others of inciting riots have by their own conduct invited them. Some look for scapegoats, others look for conspiracies, but this much is clear; violence breeds violence, repression brings retaliation, and only a cleaning of our whole society can remove this sickness from our soul.

For there is another kind of violence, slower but just as deadly, destructive as the shot or the bomb in the night. This is the violence of institutions; indifference and inaction and slow decay. This is the violence that afflicts the poor, that poisons relations between men because their skin has different colors. This is a slow destruction of a child by hunger, and schools without books and homes without heat in the winter.

This is the breaking of a man's spirit by denying him the chance to stand as a father and as a man among other men. And this too afflicts us all. I have not come here to propose a set of specific remedies nor is there a single set. For a broad and adequate outline we know what must be done. When you teach a man to hate and fear his brother, when you teach that he is a lesser man because of his color or his beliefs or the policies he pursues, when you teach that those who differ from you threaten your freedom or your job or your family, then you also learn to confront others not as fellow citizens but as enemies—to be met not with cooperation but with conquest, to be subjugated and mastered.

We learn, at the last, to look at our brothers as aliens, men with whom we share a city, but not a community, men bound to us in common dwelling, but not in common effort. We learn to share only a common fear—only a common desire to retreat from each other—only a common impulse to meet disagreement with force. For all this there are no final answers. Yet we know what we must do. It is to achieve true justice among our fellow citizens. The question is whether we can find in our own midst and in our own hearts that leadership of human purpose that will recognize the terrible truths of our existence.

We must admit the vanity of our false distinctions among men and learn to find our own advancement in the search for the advancement of all. We must admit in ourselves that our own children's future cannot be built on the misfortunes of others. We must recognize that this short life can neither be ennobled or enriched by hatred or revenge. Our lives on this planet are too short and the work to be done too great to let this spirit flourish any longer in our land.

Of course we cannot vanquish it with a program, nor with a resolution. But we can perhaps remember—even if only for a time—that those who live with us are our brothers, that they share with us the same short movement of life, that they seek—as we do—nothing but the chance to live out their lives in purpose and happiness, winning what satisfaction and fulfillment they can. Surely this bond of common faith, this bond of common goal, can begin to teach us something. Surely we can learn, at least, to look at those around us as fellow men and surely we can begin to work a little harder to bind up the wounds among us and to become in our own hearts brothers and countrymen once again.

Martin Luther King's assassination was, I believe, a significant turning point not only in Robert Kennedy's campaign, but also in the way he thought about himself. It altered his own consciousness.

Kennedy sought the Presidency in 1968, he said, and believed, because of the war in Vietnam. But Dr. King's murder, preceded as it was by Johnson's abdication and the start of peace talks, enabled Kennedy to glimpse the deeper roots of America's internal disease, and to imagine himself as the possible healer of that disease.

Kennedy had for several years been tormented by the poverty and unhappiness of the other America. But it was only campaigning for the Presidency, feeling the love for him among the poor, seeing his huge vote margins from slum districts, that showed Kennedy that his passion for the poor was reciprocated.

This did not happen in one moment. It was perceived in action during the final weeks of Kennedy's life, as he spoke about poverty and racism, as he campaigned among the poor, and gradually came to comprehend how much he meant to them, and to understand that his career was no longer the private property of the Kennedy family, but that it also belonged to the dispossessed who cheered him with such hopes and voted for him in such numbers. And perhaps, it was only King's passing that crystallized this feeling in the ghettos, that Kennedy was now their last friend left. So it was only in those final weeks, in the midst of a furious passage through the primaries, that Robert Kennedy and the poor fully discovered each other, briefly and passionately.

The Primaries: Indiana

How to write about the Indiana primary? How to find the candidate beneath the meaningless mound of trivia, the pile of speech texts, the narcotic ritual of motels, rallies, motorcades, and airports? How to find the seeker behind the good speeches and the bad speeches, at the end of the good days and the bad days? How to find Robert Kennedy, running for President in public, and looking for himself in private?

A political campaign is a dehumanizing rite. Its only purpose is power, and tends to bring out the worst in men. Repetition, exhaustion, anxiety, and pressure must be endured cheerfully. Instincts have to be disguised. Sleep and privacy are elusive. Each day brings some new temptation to compromise a little. And for Robert Kennedy there was the added physical punishment from the crowds that grabbed at him all day long, so that he was scratched and swollen each night.

The central fact in the Indian primary was that behind the dazzling public ceremonies of sound and fury, at the center of the cheering crowds, Kennedy was brooding and lonely.

Kennedy had felt natural and right running against Johnson and the war. But in Indiana he was running against McCarthy, and favorite son, Governor Roger Branigin, neither of whom he felt it wise to criticize. And he was running indirectly now against Vice President Hubert Humphrey, whom he genuinely liked, and who had served his brother loyally and well. Kennedy was a man without an enemy. He was coming to accept his new burden as voice for America's voiceless, but he couldn't do it quite yet, not in conservative and provincial Indiana, in the middle of a primary campaign. He ached for the student activists to return to him, but instead they heckled him, and worked for Senator McCarthy. Kennedy often appeared depressed, and his campaign lacked the zest it had when Johnson was in the race. There were days in Indiana, it seemed, when only the shining eyes and outstretched hands of the poor kept Robert Kennedy going.

Indiana was singularly unpromising terrain for Robert Kennedy to make his first stand in 1968. Richard Nixon had carried the state against John Kennedy in 1960 by a margin of 225,000 votes. George Wallace had polled almost a third of the votes in the 1964 Democratic Presidential primary. The rural, southern quarter of the state, and the industrial slums of Lake County, were backlash bastions, and now on edge because of the riots following Dr. King's assassination. The two Indianapolis daily papers were not only editorially opposed to Kennedy, but also blatantly slanted their news columns against him. The regular Democratic Party organization, with 23,000 patronage jobs, was one of the richest and most efficient in the country, and was working hard against him.

Kennedy's assets in Indiana included money, his celebrity status, energy, the army of political technicians and organizers that poured into the state, and most of all, his mysterious chemistry with the lower classes. Not just the Negroes, but also the Slavs, Poles, Italians, and Irish, who earned $7,000 or $8,000 a year, and felt neglected.

Class, in the economic and sociological sense, was the key to understanding Kennedy's appeal in Indiana, in the country, and what he dreamed of doing if he ever became President. Late one night, near the end of the Indiana primary, Kennedy said to me, "You know, I've come to the conclusion that poverty is closer to the root of the problem than color. I think there has to be a new kind of coalition to keep the Democratic Party going, and to keep the country together. . . . We have to write off the unions and the South now, and replace them with Negroes, blue-collar whites, and the kids. If we can do that, we've got a chance to do something. We have to convince the Negroes and poor whites that they have common interests. If we can reconcile those two hostile groups, and then add the kids, you can really turn this country around."

Indiana's conservative anti-Negro, blue-collar groups felt that Kennedy was personally tough, meant what he said, and, not being a politician, was for the "little guy" and against "the Establishment." It was in his face, in his voice, in his small, tense frame. These personal qualities helped the lower classes to trust Kennedy, and feel comfortable with him. And it was this same constellation of characteristics that made the middle class mistrust Kennedy, and feel vaguely uncomfortable about him. What the poor saw as toughness, the middle class saw as ruthlessness. What the poor saw as emotional warmth, the middle class saw as emotional instability, or romanticism. What the poor saw as earthiness, the middle class saw as immaturity and lack of polish.

The same stylistic bias was true of McCarthy's base in Indiana. No matter what McCarthy said about recognizing mainland China, or in support of guaranteed annual income, because his manner seemed reasonable, mature, stable, and detached, even suburban Republicans were impressed enough to cross over and vote for him in the primary. Because the Indiana electorate was so little issue-oriented, the medium became the message.

It was, I think, partly Kennedy's rumpled, raunchy emotionalism that contributed to his unpopularity in the intellectual community. McCarthy looked, talked, and acted like an intellectual. It is interesting to note that of the handful of leftish writers who did prefer Kennedy to McCarthy how many had working-class backgrounds themselves: Norman Mailer, Daniel Moynihan, Willie Morris, Pete Hamill, Jimmy Breslin, and myself.

Kennedy received a lot of advice not to enter the May 7 Indiana primary. Most of the political leaders in the state told him that Governor Branigin could defeat Senator McCarthy in a two-man race and knock him out as a credible candidate. And many within the Kennedy campaign thought that Indiana was too conservative for Kennedy to run well in. A quick poll was commissioned, and it showed Kennedy three percentage points behind Governor Branigin, but comfortably ahead of McCarthy. In the end, the chancy decision to stand first in the unfamiliar quagmire of Indiana was Kennedy's own.

"I know it's a risk," Kennedy said shortly after he entered, "but the whole campaign is a risk. Life is a risk. If I'm serious, I have to run everyplace because I got in so late."

Later in the campaign, Fred Dutton said, "With the poll so close, I felt that Bob's campaigning hard in the state would be enough to turn it around. He always does better in person. Because Bob is so misunderstood, he has to show himself."

In mid-April, Robert Kennedy's Presidential campaign began its saturation effort in Indiana, ignoring the other primary states. The whole campaign was conceived as sort of an elaborate trapeze act: Kennedy had to swing safely from one primary to the next without falling, in order to build up momentum and drama.

By the time the blitz began in Indiana, the campaign had been joined by Larry O'Brien, who left the Johnson Cabinet, and Richard Goodwin, who defected from McCarthy's campaign. Goodwin, to the surprise and dismay of Kennedy's Senate staff, quickly aligned himself, within the campaign, with the faction that felt Kennedy, to win in Indiana, had to disguise his real politics, and stress the theme of law and order. The veterans of 1960—Goodwin, Sorensen, O'Brien, Salinger, and Ted Kennedy—had no trouble believing that the ends justified the means. McCarthy drew strength from a movement that was better than he, but Kennedy was weakened by a movement that was less than he.

In Kennedy's partial defense, however, it must be added, that he said the same things to white, black, and mixed audiences. And the extent to which he bowed to the provincial mores of Indiana was exaggerated by the press, which confused his long-held belief in citizen participation, local control, and mistrust of welfare and centralized bureaucracy with whoring after Hoosier votes.

Most of Kennedy's prepared speeches, and most of his newspaper and television ads, did go out of their way to emphasize his role as Attorney General ("the chief law enforcement officer in the country") and his opposition to riots, lawlessness, and violence. But on several occasions, Kennedy's deep feelings about race and poverty broke through spontaneously and by Election Day nearly everyone knew where he stood.

The most dramatic example of the Good Bobby routing the Bad Bobby on a public platform took place on April 26 at the Indiana University Medical Center. Kennedy came before about five hundred medical students and read some conventional remarks that were received with chilly indifference. At the end of Kennedy's formal speech, a Negro custodial employee shouted out from the balcony, "We want Kennedy." And dozens of white, middle-class medical students chanted back, "No we don't."

Then the questions began, each revealing a conservative point of view. Why should Social Security benefits to the elderly be increased anyway? Why shouldn't private insurance companies accept responsibility for higher medical costs, instead of the taxpayers? How can you say health services are inferior in the slums when everyone knows Negroes don't make use of the facilities that do exist? Finally, "Where are we going to get the money to pay for all these new programs you're proposing?"

"From you," Kennedy flared back. Kennedy's face was always a mirror of his mood, and now it was angry, yes, ruthless, looking out at the rows of satisfied WASP crew cuts. He walked forward and began to talk from deep inside himself, forgetting all the careful planning about campaign tactics in Indiana.

"Let me say something," he began, "about the tone of these questions. I look around this room and I don't see many black faces who will become doctors. . . . Part of civilized society is to let people go to medical school who come from ghettos. I don't see many people coming here from slums, or off the Indian reservations. You are the privileged ones here. It's easy for you to sit back and say it's the fault of the Federal Government. But it's our responsibility, too. It's our society, too, not just our government, that spends twice as much on pets as on the poverty program. It's the poor who carry the major burden of the struggle in Vietnam. You sit here as white medical students, while black people carry the burden of the fighting in Vietnam. . . ."

At this point some students in the crowd began to hiss and boo, and Kennedy glared back at them in contempt.

A few days later, Kennedy spoke at Valparaiso University, and was heckled both by conservatives and McCarthy partisans. During the question period he was asked again about Federal intervention in antipoverty efforts, and again reacted with an emotional lecture to an auditorium full of comfortable college students:

"Well, you tell me something now. How many of you spend time over the summer, or on vacations, working in a black ghetto, or in Eastern Kentucky, or on Indian reservations? Instead of asking what the Federal Government is doing about starving children, I say what is your responsibility, what are you going to do about it? I think you people should organize yourselves right here, and try to do something about it. . . . As Camus once said, 'Perhaps we cannot prevent this world from being a world in which children are tortured. But we can reduce the number of tortured children.' And if you don't help us, who else in the world can help us do this?"

It was during the Indiana primary that the national phenomenon of anti-Kennedy feeling reached its peak. Always misunderstood and mis-reported, always generating intense emotion, Kennedy was now in a bitter campaign for the Presidency, and all the poisons in the feverish country seemed to flow toward him. Especially with Johnson out of the picture. The wild attacks on Kennedy's personality reached such a pitch that James Reston devoted an entire column to them in *The New York Times* of April 24:

> There is a very large body of anti-Kennedy voters in this country these days [he wrote]. . . . You can't even ride with the Irish cabbies in Boston without hearing some vicious remark about Bobby's policies or his person. . . . The opposition to him is personal, almost chemical, and sometimes borders on the irrational.

Supporters of the war and the President had always, and understand-ably, been hostile to Kennedy. But in April, as he ran for President, even the McCarthy movement came to hate him more than they disliked Hubert Humphrey. A Gallup Poll released on April 28 showed that 41 percent of McCarthy's supporters would switch to Humphrey if their candidate withdrew, while only 31 percent would move to Kennedy. Conversely, the same survey revealed that a majority of Kennedy backers, supposedly less issue- and ideal-oriented, would switch to McCarthy rather than Humphrey if their man withdrew.

One night in Indiana I finally got Kennedy to talk about the wave of hostility breaking against him.

"Frankly," he began, "I don't understand it. I see people out there call me names, and say they want to actually hit me, and I just don't know what to say about it. The other day some fellow grabbed my hand in a motorcade and tried to squeeze it with all his might. . . . Another person showed up at a lot of different places holding up a sign that just said, 'You Punk.'

"I can understand how the student activists feel about it. They wanted me to run because of how they felt about the war. So when I didn't, it was natural they should turn to McCarthy. I feel now that I made a mistake in not going into New Hampshire, but that's past. I admire those students who go out and work for McCarthy very much, and I respect their loyalty to him. But what I can't respect are those lazy liberals in New York who say all those things about me now. They said them about President Kennedy in 1960, and they said them about me in 1964, and now they still say them. It's as if I had never made a speech about Vietnam, or poverty, or anything. I can't help it, but I resent it.

"I just feel that those New York liberals are sick. They're not doing any work. They spend their time worrying about not being invited to the important parties, or seeing psychiatrists, or they are bored with all their affluence. I personally prefer many of the poor white people I've met here in Indiana. They are tough, and honest, and if you help them, they remember it, like the people who live in the poorer sections of West Virginia. They're not fickle. Do you know there are people in New York who pleaded with me to come out against the war three years ago, and today they're for Hubert? I think I just like the Poles in Gary better than those New York reformers, who are so filled up with hate and envy."

At the outset, Kennedy's campaign in Indiana looked doomed. After Dr. King's funeral, Kennedy flew to rural southern Indiana, and small, indifferent crowds around Terre Haute. It is an area populated largely by people who had moved from Kentucky and Tennessee, and were more Southern than Midwestern. The papers were still computing the property damage from the riots. The next day, after a merely polite reception at a luncheon, Kennedy said to a few reporters, "So far in Indiana, they seem to want to see me as a member of the black race. I don't think I can win if that happens. If it keeps up, I'm lost. . . . These people never ask me, 'What are you going to do about the Negro problem, or what can we do for the Negro?' They always ask, 'What are you going to do about the violence?' "

On April 22, Kennedy came back to Indiana to start his blitz. Again the reflexes of the crowds were ominous. The children cheered, but the adults were passive. At places like Vincennes, Washington, and Logansport, Kennedy came, and spoke, and moved on, not knowing what the upturned faces, neither cheering nor booing him, actually thought: whether they saw him or his brother, whether they saw a celebrity or a politician, whether they were flattered or suspicious that a Kennedy had come to their little hamlet.

But, gradually, Fred Dutton's notion that Kennedy in the flesh was more appealing than Kennedy's image in type, or on television, was being confirmed. He began to go back again and again to places like Terre Haute, and each time the crowds were bigger and warmer. The magic with the ethnic, blue-collar whites in Gary and East Chicago was beginning to work. The campaign structure was starting to jell, with Larry O'Brien, Gerry Douherty, and Ted Kennedy the troika at the top. Arthur Schlesinger, Michael Harrington, and SNCC's John Lewis came out to speak at the pro-McCarthy universities and colleges. Manhattan Assemblymen Jerome Kretchmer and Al Blumenthal flew out to take charge of Lake County. And by the end of April it was all beginning to come together; the personal exposure, the punishing fifteen-hour days of campaigning, were washing away the myths of Robert Kennedy's reputation.

Thursday, May 2. From sunup till midnight, Kennedy toured northern Indiana in a marathon motorcade. And the scenes began to resemble that first weekend in California. Thick crowds, waving and shoving, lined the streets. Children ran for blocks alongside Kennedy's car. The brief speeches in the tree-shaded town squares were cheered, the whites cheering for law and order, and the blacks cheering for justice and equality. And everybody applauding the calls to end the war in Vietnam and to reconcile the races at home. In the town of Mishawaka, the crowd surged violently around Kennedy's open car and tried to pull him out; somehow Kennedy got his lip badly cut and his front tooth chipped. Later that night, feeling good, feeling optimistic for the first time since Johnson's withdrawal, Kennedy quipped to a small-town crowd, "Make like, not war. See how careful I am." But only a few reporters got the joke.

Saturday, May 4. Another good day of campaigning in Indianapolis. Kennedy's spirits were also lifted by reports of defections from the regular Democratic machine to his cause. Indiana's senior Senator Vance Hartke was now traveling with Kennedy as an invitation to his followers to vote for him. Saturday night Kennedy flew home to Virginia for ten hours of sleep.

Sunday, May 5. At noon in Washington Kennedy taped his final television appeal for votes in Indiana, and then campaigned for three relaxed hours among the Negroes of the District of Columbia, whose primary election was also on May 7; here Kennedy's opposition was a regular slate pledged to Hubert Humphrey. Then off to Louisville, and a twilight motorcade through the southern tip of Indiana, New Albany, and then to Evansville. Early in the campaign, a Kennedy rally in the 12,000-seat Evansville fieldhouse had attracted only 5,000 people. But tonight there were 2,000 at the airport, and John Herbers of *The New York Times* says, "A week ago I thought Branigin would win it. But now I think Kennedy will win."

Monday, May 6. The longest day of the first primary. The official schedule calls for Kennedy to leave the Evansville airport at 10:55 P.M., and end the day at a hotel reception in Indianapolis until after 1 A.M. on Tuesday.

The first stop is a rally at the courthouse in Fort Wayne, and there is a large crayoned sign in the crowd that reads, "Teenyboppers Luv You, Bobby." Kennedy's talk is mostly banter, and a teasing reminder to vote. At the edge of the crowd there is the familiar group of pro-McCarthy pickets, and I go over to talk to them. They are bright, friendly, antiwar college students. They don't hate Kennedy, and one of them admits to being upset by how many of the voters she has canvassed who admit they will vote for McCarthy because he isn't as identified with the revolutionary blacks as Kennedy. Behind where Kennedy is speaking, a new office building is under construction, and only the two Negro workers on the girders have stopped work to listen, and at the end, they wave their red helmets.

From Fort Wayne, Kennedy flies to South Bend, and the start of an incredible nine-hour motorcade through northern Indiana's cities and streets. In South Bend the trees and telegraph poles have signs stapled to them that read, "Robert Kennedy will pass through this way at 2 P.M. on Monday." At 3:30 P.M., when Kennedy does pass by, the streets are still lined four deep with people. It began in warm sunshine, and, at dusk, the motorcade reached Gary, with the temperature falling into the forties. At the Gary city line, two men climbed into Robert Kennedy's open car, and stood on either side of him, for the wild hour it took to navigate the clogged, happy streets. One was Tony Zale, the former middleweight boxing champion from Gary, who was a saint to the East Europeans who worked in the steel mills. The other was Richard Hatcher, the thirty-four-year-old Negro Mayor of Gary. Together, the three men, in a pose symbolizing the Kennedy alliance that might have been, clung to each other's waists, standing on the back seat of the convertible, waving to the cheering citizens of the city that so recently seemed at the edge of a race war.

At 1:30 that night, Kennedy invited a group of his friends to join him for a late dinner at Sam's Attic, the only restaurant open at that hour in Indianapolis. The pickup group included Loudon Wainright of *Life;* David Halberstam of *Harper's;* John Douglas, the son of the former Illinois Senator who had worked in Kennedy's Justice Department; Sue Markham, a friend of Ethel's; photographers Bert Glynn, Stanley Tretick; and myself.

As we entered the almost empty restaurant, we saw reporters Bill Chapman, David Murray, and Paul Hope at a front booth with a young girl, Alice Krakauer, who was a press aide to Senator McCarthy and a graduate school dropout.

"I know who you are," the girl said, her voice filled with challenge. Kennedy froze for a second, but she continued, looking not at him, but at me: "You're Jack Newfield. And I'm from Greenwich Village, too, and I'm for Gene McCarthy, not him," tossing a defiant look at the now-amused candidate. That was the entire encounter, but at least three times during the rest of the morning, Kennedy came back to it, commenting to me about the "spirit in the girl's eyes," her devotion to her candidate, and how too many of his own volunteers were motivated by "careerism" rather than "idealism."

Sitting at the center of two joined tables, Kennedy looked like a fighter at the end of fifteen savage rounds, waiting for the judges' decision. His stumpy fingers and knuckles were red and swollen and cut from the thousands of Hoosier hands. Exhaustion blotched his skin and slowed his speech and thickened his features. His eyes were dull, and pushed back into their sockets. But he was in an open, mellow mood, and with only a little prodding by Halberstam, began to ramble about his nostalgic feelings on the eve of the balloting.

"I like Indiana," he said. "The people here were fair to me. They gave me a chance. They listened to me. I could see this face, way back in the crowd, and he was listening, really listening to me. The people here are not so neurotic and hypocritical as in Washington or New York. They're more direct. I like rural people, who work hard with their hands. There is something healthy about them. I gave it everything I had here, and if I lose, then, well, I'm just out of tune with the rest of the country. . . . I loved the faces here in Indiana, on the farmers, on the steelworkers, on the black kids. . . ."

He stopped for a minute, and it looked as though he would fall asleep right here, at 3 A.M., in the restaurant. But then he started telling us about the study he had recently read, analyzing the drawings of Negro and white schoolchildren. "Did you know that when the black children drew a picture of a house, they almost never drew in the sun?"

At 11 A.M. the next morning, while Indiana began to vote, and most of the traveling press corps of 50 still slept, Robert Kennedy released his tension by playing touch football on the bright green lawn of the Holiday Inn.

At first I just watched the game of five per side, struck by how much Kennedy's style of play resembled the way he lived. Slow and small, he seemed not to have much natural skill, but compensated for it with determination and competitiveness. He automatically became the quarterback and called the plays for his team. On defense he took risks, often going for the interception instead of cautiously playing the receiver. He seemed to thrive on the jarring physical contact in the line, and the game soon became violent enough so that Halberstam, one of the biggest men on the field, had to retire with a bloody nose, and Bill Barry twisted an ankle.

After a while I joined the game on Kennedy's team, with the score tied one touchdown apiece. But soon Richard Harwood, an ex-Marine and as good an athlete as he was a reporter, beat Kennedy by two steps in the end zone, and was waiting for the ball to sail into his arms. Kennedy, then, in one of those ugly, but human lapses that remained within his nature, leaped at Harwood, jamming his palm into his face in a deliberate foul. But the much bigger Harwood still managed to make a circus catch for the winning touchdown. He then turned on Kennedy and told him, "You're a dirty player, and a lousy one, too."

But Kennedy, embarrassed by the play and hurt by the insult, nevertheless later invited Harwood to stay the night in his private suite, the only daily reporter given that special favor. And during the final month of the campaign, the two men grew closer and closer in mutual admiration of two professionals. Harwood had begun suspicious and hostile, but by the end he liked Kennedy so much that he asked to be assigned to cover someone else.

Election night, 7 P.M. The polls were just closing in Indiana and in the District of Columbia, and Kennedy was in the shower at the Holiday Inn. The suite of rooms on the fourth floor contained those restless staff members who had no responsibility to be at the drab Sheraton-Lincoln Hotel, downtown headquarters: Goodwin; Walinsky; Greenfield; Dutton; Gwirtzman; Ed Guthman; Hollywood director John Frankenheimer, who was working on advertising and media with Goodwin; Senator Hartke; Bill Barry; and Ethel.

At about 7:15 P.M. there was a phone call from Peter Edelman, who was in Washington, and could already see a Kennedy landslide emerging there.

Soon Larry O'Brien appeared with returns from the first weather vane precincts. They were all favorable. One poor, Polish precinct in South Bend gave Kennedy 241, McCarthy 86, and Branigin 62. An all-black district in Gary gave Branigin 16, McCarthy 52, and Kennedy 697. When Ethel heard that, she exclaimed with primitive honesty, "Don't you just wish that everyone was black?"

Kennedy, now dressed, paused in front of the television screen before leaving, just as his early vote total was switching from 54 percent to 48 percent. He made a child's face, said "eecch," and left for downtown.

By the time we arrived at the Sheraton-Lincoln, it was clear that Kennedy would win, and the evening settled down to trench warfare between Kennedy and the networks.

"Kennedy is not doing as well as expected," NBC's Frank McGee was saying.

"Not as well as *YOU* expected," Kennedy said to the television set. Dick Tuck was also angry, telling everyone that most of the press pool bets on Kennedy's percentage of the vote were between 38 and 44 percent, so how could 42 percent be interpreted as a defeat? Ed Guthman was also upset: "The problem is that press people are so intimidated by the charge of being taken in by the Kennedys that they have to bend over backward to prove their independence. If Kennedy had the relationship that McCarthy has with Shana Alexander and Mary McGrory, it would be a scandal. But Gene can get away with it because no one accuses him of buying off the press. So he gets a free ride. There is a double standard."

As the tone of the instant television analyses continued to be that the Indiana primary was really an inconclusive draw, Dutton complained to a network correspondent, "You guys are nuts! McCarthy got 42 percent of the vote in New Hampshire against one write-in opponent, and you call that an epic victory. Kennedy gets 42 percent here against two active candidates, one the Governor of the state, and you say it's really meaningless."

Then McCarthy came on the screen, and the room fell quiet. The

Senator said it didn't really matter much who came in first, second, or third. "That's not what my father told me," Kennedy said to the television. "I always thought it was better to win. I learned that when I was about two." Then he laughed.

By 9:15 P.M. the results were clear. Kennedy had won the Indiana primary with 42 percent of the vote, to 31 percent for Branigin, to 27 percent for McCarthy. In the District of Columbia, Kennedy had swamped Humphrey, 62.5 percent, to 37.5 percent. His mood was quietly satisfied, but hardly elated or excited, when he sat down beside Roger Mudd for an interview on CBS-TV.

But, suddenly, through a suggestion by David Schoumacher, who was with McCarthy, and the decision of a producer in the network studio, Kennedy was caught in a split-screen dialogue with McCarthy. Kennedy, already upset by the network interpretations, was now raging at what he regarded as a technological trick. So when Walter Cronkite asked him about the problem of campaign expenditures, Kennedy turned the question around into an attack on the television networks, saying they made enough profits to give all candidates free air time. And besides, the airwaves belonged to the people, not to private corporations.

By 10:30 P.M., Bill Haddad and his staff had a quick analysis of the raw vote for Kennedy. He had carried nine of the eleven Congressional districts, and all of the major cities except Bloomington and Evansville. He won seventeen of the twenty-five rural southern counties. He won more than 85 percent of the Negro vote. He carried the seven backlash counties that George Wallace had won in 1964. He only lost two counties in which he had campaigned personally the last two weeks.

By midnight Kennedy was ready to leave and eat some dinner, so he and his party drove out to the airport restaurant. Walking through the empty airport lobby, Kennedy saw his white whale again: two crestfallen McCarthy student volunteers, a boy with two McCarthy buttons in his jacket, and a pretty girl with red hair and a straw McCarthy campaign hat on her head. They were sitting on their luggage.

And Robert Kennedy, who wanted the delegates but needed the students, went to dinner with Taylor Branch of the University of North Carolina, and Pat Sylvester of the University of Massachusetts.

"You had such cruddy canvassers, and you still won," the girl said.

"Well, you can't blame all that on me."

"I felt we were much better."

"How does everybody feel about tonight?" Kennedy asked.

"We're going to stay with McCarthy," the girl said firmly.

"I don't know what happened," the boy said. "I canvassed Negro neighborhoods, and they wouldn't listen to me for five seconds."

"That's not your fault," Kennedy said. "Why wasn't McCarthy effective for you in those areas?"

"But you're a Kennedy," the girl came back. "It sounds like a newspaper rehash, but it's still right. You have the name."

"Look, I agree I have a tremendous advantage with my last name. But let me ask you, why can't McCarthy go into a ghetto? Why can't he go into a poor neighborhood? Can you tell me that he's been involved in those areas? Why did he vote against the minimum wage for farm workers? Why did he vote against a large proportion of people from the Minimum Wage Act?" Kennedy said all this quietly, puffing on a small cigar.

For a long while, the two students were silent. At the end, they were still for McCarthy, and Kennedy's white whale was still free to haunt him. It was after 2 A.M. and the winner told the losers, "You're dedicated to what you believe, and I think that's terrific." And then he told them he would drive them back into the city and find them a hotel room, so they wouldn't have to sit up all night in the airport, waiting for their early-morning flight.

The next morning, there was a victory breakfast of champagne and scrambled eggs on the campaign flight back to New York. But Kennedy's mood was blackened by *The New York Times*. Tom Wicker had written in a news analysis that the significance of the Indiana primary was that "Senator McCarthy, the man who first challenged President Johnson, had done the most to advance his own cause." And a *Times* editorial entitled "Kennedy's Inconclusive Victory" was largely an attack on Kennedy's conservative Indiana campaign.

"If I was really ruthless," Kennedy said, "I would figure out a way to get even with *The Times*."

When I asked him what he thought the underlying meaning of the Indiana vote really was, Kennedy answered, after thinking for a few moments, "That I really have a chance now, just a chance, to organize a new coalition of Negroes, and working-class white people, against the union and party Establishments."

The Last Thirty Days

Robert Kennedy after Dallas was always in a condition of change. This was especially true during the final month of his life, as he campaigned in the Nebraska, Oregon, South Dakota, and California Presidential primaries. He was increasingly becoming engaged, at newer and deeper levels, with the cause of the black and white poor. He was at last becoming emancipated from his brother's legend, quoting him less, invoking his name less, even imitating his gestures less. And he was finally becoming more at peace with his divided self, letting his private qualities show more in public, seeming less embattled and driven.

The Nebraska primary was one week after Indiana, and Kennedy worked the sparsely populated farm state by car and train. Much of the time he was still private and preoccupied, but he occasionally managed to get outside himself and reveal his witty, absurdist streak to crowds of adults.

At Bellvue, Nebraska, the local police arrested a man whose heckling had interrupted a Kennedy speech at the shopping center. Kennedy requested from the platform the police let the man go, but when they wouldn't, he said in a parody of a politician, "I promise that if I'm elected President of the United States, one of the first things I'm going to do is get you out of jail." It broke the polite crowd up, and won him a round of applause.

At the small hamlet of Wilber, Kennedy said to a crowd at the dedication of a low-income housing development for the elderly called "Czech Village." "None of my children are Czech. But if things keep going on

266

as they are now, one of them may be. I don't know precisely what that means, but it brings us closer together."

Kennedy ended his relaxed Nebraska swing with a speech in the Negro section of Omaha in a driving rainstorm. Despite the weather, about four hundred Negroes braved the downpour to listen to him. Suddenly, in the middle of his talk, Kennedy blurted out, "Shall I do you all a favor now and stop my speech? Of all the silly things to do, this is the silliest, for you to be out in this rain listening to a politician. And I must be out of my mind, too."

While Kennedy stumped the wheat-filled Nebraska prairies, and while his most effective political operatives like Steve Smith, John Seigenthaler, and Pat Lucey were tied down in other primary states, Hubert Humphrey began to consolidate his delegate strength in the non-primary states. It was an odd time. Humphrey, who seemed ruined as a political force six months before, was now, with the war eliminated as a political issue, and all the hate-Kennedy types rallying to him, making striking gains. Kennedy, meanwhile, suffered from all the disadvantages of appearing to be the front runner, while receiving none of the concrete benefits. Humphrey supporters and stand-ins were being repudiated by the voters in every primary, but Humphrey was winning the delegates in the party caucuses and state conventions where the professional politicians maintained tight control. Kennedy was finding out just how much the older, structured pols mistrusted him.

Humphrey, with the backing of Mayors Tate and Barr, and Steelworkers' President, I. W. Abel, nailed down most of Pennsylvania's 130 convention votes. With the support of the regular politicians, Humphrey also won commitments for most of the Maryland and Missouri delegations. Even in Northern industrial states like Ohio and Michigan, Humphrey was popular with the party organizations, contributors, and press, and Kennedy's agents had to wage a defensive holding action, asking only that no final commitments be made until after the California primary. The *Newsweek* delegate survey, taken just after the Nebraska vote, showed 1,279½ delegates solid or leaning to Humphrey, 713½ leaning to Kennedy, and 280 favoring McCarthy.

It was during the Nebraska primary that McCarthy's moody behavior began to baffle the press and irritate his own organization. Two days after the Indiana balloting, McCarthy accused Kennedy of "poisoning the well in Indiana," and added, "I think the direct confrontation that was denied us in Indiana will be given us in Nebraska." But two days later, McCarthy suddenly gave up in Nebraska, quit campaigning, downgraded the significance of the primary, and headed for Oregon and California. This left Kennedy alone in Nebraska the final days, running against the absent ghost of McCarthy, the write-in campaign for Humphrey, and a noncandidate President Johnson, whose name was still on the ballot.

When the votes were tabulated on the night of May 14, it was a solid victory for Kennedy; he won 51.5 percent of the total vote, to 31 percent for McCarthy, to 8.4 percent for the Humphrey write-in effort, to 5.6 percent for Johnson. Of equal significance was the fact that Kennedy's delicate alliance of slum Negroes and low-income whites had worked again; Kennedy received more than 80 percent of all the Negro votes, and almost 60 percent of the votes cast in low-income white areas. (Omaha, where Malcolm X was born, has a large black ghetto.)

Kennedy also carried every county that contained concentrations of East European ethnic stock. And in further confirmation of the Dutton theory, Kennedy swept twenty-four of the twenty-five counties in which he had personally campaigned.

When the campaign began, Kennedy had been apprehensive about the primaries in conservative states like Indiana and Nebraska. He was not worried about liberal, antiwar Oregon. He thought that McCarthy would be knocked out of the race by then, and Oregon would be easy. So in May the Kennedy organization deputized two of its utility men—lawyers Barrett Prettyman and William vanden Heuvel—to take responsibility for Oregon, while Smith and Seigenthaler went to California, and Lucey went to South Dakota. But liberal Oregon turned out to be Robert Kennedy's Dunkirk.

First, the population of the state did not contain any of Kennedy's natural constituencies; Oregon was only 1 percent Negro, and 10 percent Catholic. There were almost no Mexicans or East European blue-collar workers. It was mostly Protestant, surburban, well-educated and middle class. "I do my best with people who have problems," Kennedy often said. But there were few voters with problems in affluent, pretty, satisfied Oregon. When Kennedy said that America had to be "turned around," most of those living in Oregon didn't think so. When Kennedy ridiculed Humphrey's politics of joy and catalogued America's injustices, the Oregon voters were not moved. Oregon was the one state where McCarthy could boast that the well-educated voted for him, and the less-educated voted for his opponent, and not be hurt politically by such a crack.

Second, Oregon was the first primary state where the Kennedy campaign, to some degree, had the support of the existing, regular party structure. Congresswoman Edith Green, an old JFK loyalist, agreed to be Robert's Oregon manager. But her personal organization did not follow her into the Kennedy camp, and the parts that did failed to perform. Also her ancient feud with Wayne Morse kept Morse's followers out of the RFK campaign. The young McCarthy volunteers worked harder, longer, and more professionally than did Mrs. Green's professionals. Mrs. Green's party pros did things the old way; when a radical young organizer was dispatched to Oregon by Peter Edelman to challenge McCarthy on the campuses, he was sent home on the next plane because he wore a beard.

Third, the influential and well-financed labor unions in Oregon were monolithically anti-RFK because of his investigations in Teamster corruption in Portland during the 1950's. On May 9 the state AFL-CIO executive board, representing 50,000 members, endorsed Vice President Humphrey, and went all out for him the last three weeks.

Fourth, the most volatile issue in the state was gun control; and Robert Kennedy could not forget that Lee Oswald held a mail-order rifle that day in Dallas. So while McCarthy avoided the issue, Kennedy took it and ran with it right at the crowds of hunters.

The last weekend of the primary Kennedy came to Roseburg. Just before he got off the plane, Kennedy was handed a fact sheet on the city.

Population: 15,000
Principle Industry: Lumbering, mining, agriculture
Major Local Issues: Gun control, log exports, dams

In the middle of the mimeographed sheet, in bold, uppercase letters, it said:

LOCAL SHERIFF CAUTIONS THERE MAY BE AN AIRPORT DEMONSTRATION BY OPPONENTS OF GUN CONTROL LEGISLATION.

"That doesn't sound good," a reporter reading over Kennedy's shoulder said.

"I couldn't care less," Kennedy answered, and went off to confront the hostile faces and hostile signs: "PROTECT YOUR RIGHT TO KEEP AND BEAR ARMS."

Most politicians try to ingratiate themselves to hostile audiences, but Kennedy liked to challenge them. He debated with college students about their 2S deferments. He lectured businessmen about their responsibilities to society's untouchables. And in Roseburg, Oregon, to a crowd of lumber workers and hunters, in their plaid wool shirts, and weatherbeaten faces, he said:

> Nobody is going to take your guns away. All we're talking about is that a person who's insane, or seven years old, or is mentally defective, or has a criminal record, should be kept from purchasing a gun by money order. . . . So protect your right to keep and bear arms. This legislation doesn't stop you, unless you're a criminal.

And, finally, Kennedy committed a significant tactical error in ignoring McCarthy's frequent challenges to debate directly on television. Kennedy's rather transparent strategy in Oregon was to treat Humphrey as his real opponent, try to ignore McCarthy, and make the case that a vote for McCarthy was really a vote for Humphrey. But his refusal to debate backfired. It resurrected the old imagery of McCarthy as the courageous, serious man, who went into New Hampshire, while the cowardly, calculating Kennedy hung back.

Except for Mrs. Green and Fred Dutton, everyone on Kennedy's campaign staff with access to the candidate urged that he debate. Walinsky, whose political instincts were so often right, was so aggressive in pushing for the debate that he irritated Kennedy. But as mentioned before, Kennedy's personality was stronger than any one of his advisers, and probably stronger than all his advisers combined. He did not want to debate, and this costly mistake was his own.

Kennedy sensed he would lose in Oregon all through the last ten days of the campaign. His mood again became withdrawn and surly. The crowds were small and there was no playback to his emotions. The local scheduling and advance work were disorganized and even inept. The antiwar students continued to work for McCarthy and give him that issue in an antiwar state. In beautiful scenic settings, middle-class WASP's just didn't want to hear Robert Kennedy remind them of rat bites in Bedford-Stuyvesant or suicides on Indian reservations. By election eve, Kennedy appeared resigned to tasting the first defeat in his generation of Kennedys. His final talk to his campaign workers that night seemed more designed to cushion them against that defeat, than to inspire them for an all-out Election Day effort.

But Kennedy, raised to win, accepted defeat with more realism and more grace than McCarthy ever had. He did not try to rationalize or belittle the results. "I lost," he said. "I'm not one of those who think coming in second or third is winning." Kennedy also insisted on sending McCarthy a telegram of congratulations, although McCarthy had not. In interviews with reporters he blamed the defeat on himself, and not on his organization or the sociology of the state. When a reporter asked him if the defeat in Oregon hurt his chances to be nominated, Kennedy laughed, "It certainly wasn't one of the more helpful developments of the day." After the other reporters left to file their stories, Jules Witcover asked Kennedy how he managed to put up with so many foolish questions at a time like this. And Kennedy just put his arm around the familiar face, and said, "Because I like you."

A few moments later Kennedy came over to David Borden, his chief student organizer in Oregon, put his arm on his shoulder, and said, "I'm sorry I let you down."

Defeat in Oregon liberated Kennedy for California. All his life he had been schooled that nothing was worse than to finish second. But crushing fears are no longer so crushing once they are experienced. In Oregon, Kennedy discovered that he could taste defeat, and still go on. Emancipated from the pressures of winning, of winning every primary, of becoming President, he was a better man the last week in California. He was himself, talking about poverty, touching and being touched by the poor, attacking Humphrey, agreeing to debate McCarthy. Four days before the California primary he said to me, "I can accept the fact I may not be nominated now. If that happens, I will just go back to the Senate, and say what I believe, and not try again in '72. Somebody has to speak up for the Negroes, and Indians, and Mexicans, and poor whites. Maybe that's what I do best. Maybe my personality just isn't built for this. . . . The issues are more important than me now."

And ironically, defeat in Oregon seemed to help Kennedy in the delegate counts in the non-primary states. The last week he seemed actually to gain a few votes in Iowa, and Michigan, and Colorado. Once defeated, he looked less ruthless, more sympathetic, more human to the politicians and the press. Defeat peeled off another layer of myth, and permitted a few more people to see Robert Kennedy. So he went to California the morning after he lost in Oregon a free man, ready to be renewed by the alchemy between him and the other America.

California is a grotesque cartoon of America's future. It is a state of contrasts and portents. There are Disneyland and Watts. Aerospace technology and the grape strike. Forest Lawn and Haight-Ashbury. Orange County and San Francisco State. The clash of bored opulence and alienated poverty define the state. Nathanael West anticipated this a generation ago, when he wrote in *The Day of the Locust* of the violence lurking beneath The California Dream:

> All their lives they had slaved at some kind of dull heavy labor, behind desks and counters, in the fields, and at tedious machines of all sorts, saving their pennies, and dreaming of the leisure that would be theirs when they had enough. Finally that day came. . . . Where else should they go but California, the land of sunshine and oranges?
>
> Once there, they discover that sunshine isn't enough. . . . Nothing happens. They don't know what to do with their time. . . . Their boredom becomes more and more terrible. They realize they've been tricked and burn with resentment. . . . Nothing can ever be violent enough to make taut their slack minds and bodies.

California politically and culturally sets national trends. Berkeley had student protests in 1960 against HUAC and the execution of Caryl Chessman. The generational counter-culture of drugs, rock music, mysticism, and underground papers was spawned in California. The Hollywoodization of politics began in California with George Murphy and Ronald Reagan. Watts began one trend, and the Black Panthers another.

California in 1968 was the largest state in the union with 20 million residents. Its population was increasing at twice the rate of the rest of the country's. Thirty-five percent of the state's population was under eighteen. California had as many cars registered as the next two states—New York and Texas—combined. It stretched eight hundred miles down the Pacific coast, and it would send the second-largest delegation—174 votes—to the Democratic convention in August. It was the futuristic battleground of leisure, suburbs, new towns, shopping centers, television, and youth, where Robert Kennedy's bid for the Presidency would meet its last popular test. If he won, he would still have a chance to be nominated; if he lost, he would never again seek the Presidency.

The California Presidential primary had really begun in violent confusion a year before, when thousands of white, middle-class war protesters had picketed Lyndon Johnson at Los Angeles' Century City, and hundreds were beaten when police broke up the demonstration. In September of 1967, the California Democratic Council—the activist-liberal faction of the state party—met and vowed to run antiwar delegates in the 1968 primary against President Johnson, before they even knew Senator McCarthy would enter the race. In January of 1968, it was Jesse Unruh's polls and prodding that helped push Kennedy into combat. And on March 16—the day Kennedy announced—760 CDC delegates convened in Anaheim to endorse McCarthy and boo Congressman Philip Burton's appeal for Kennedy. By that time, a pro-Administration slate, headed by State Attorney General Thomas Lynch was also organized. At the last minute Kennedy had to throw together a slate of 172 delegates from scratch; it contained actress Shirley McLaine, Cesar Chavez, football star Gary Beban, and those local politicians loyal to Unruh, including only two of California's Congressmen—Burton and Tom Rees. (The Lynch slate contained seventeen Congressmen, former Representative James Roosevelt, former Governor Pat Brown, state chairman Charles Warren, and San Francisco Mayor Joseph Alioto.)

At first it seemed Kennedy would win in California easily. He was mobbed by wild, adoring crowds on his first visit to the state, the weekend after his announcement. The first polls showed him ahead of Johnson and McCarthy. And white liberal sentiment seemed moving reluctantly toward him. But then Johnson withdrew; the liberals latent mistrust of Kennedy hardened; and with the great fear of Johnson removed, they felt free to have their fling with the pure McCarthy. By mid-April, some private polls were showing McCarthy running 2 to 1 ahead of Kennedy in Jewish, liberal, middle-income districts.

At the same time, the Kennedy campaign in California was developing internal organizational problems. Unruh's people, liberal on economic issues, were still old-line machine types when it came to politics. They did not welcome volunteers. They took the Negroes and Mexicans for granted. They did not work very hard. They were politicians, and were not interested in foreign policy or participatory democracy. They were also very tough, and ignored the suggestions of Kennedy's two representatives from the East—businessman Charles Spaulding and lawyer Anthony Akers.

With a panic setting in, Kennedy abruptly altered his tactics in California during the first week of May. He sent his two most able managers—Steve Smith and John Seigenthaler—to California. Smith, aided by Frank Mankiewicz, took charge of Southern California, and Seigenthaler took command of the northern part of the state. They were placed at the top of the campaign structure, in positions to overrule and overshadow Unruh's lieutenants. One young Kennedy volunteer in San Francisco told me:

"The campaign changed the day Seigenthaler moved into the Fairmont Hotel. He told the Unruh people to go for a walk, or to just concentrate on getting out the vote. It was beautiful. Right away the campaign became more issue-oriented. More college kids began to get more involved, although never as many as McCarthy had. The minority groups stopped sulking. The campaign got back its early spirit and fire."

One of the first things the Smith-Seigenthaler axis did was begin to import a roster of influential speakers to tour the campuses and the liberal suburbs, in a bid to cut down McCarthy's strength there. Among those who flew out to California during May were Adam Yarmolinsky, Alexander Bickel, Daniel Moynihan, Harry Golden, George Plimpton, Roger Hilsman, Arthur Schlesinger, Michael Harrington, and Abba Schwartz.

Then, on May 11, McCarthy made a serious blooper in Sacramento; he told a morning news conference, "I see no objection to having some of the Humphrey people vote for me." He tried to explain this away later, but it contributed to the impression that he really disliked Kennedy more than he disliked Humphrey. This gave the Kennedy campaigners a wedge with the antiwar middle class, and it helped arrest Kennedy's decline in California.

On Wednesday, May 29, the morning after his defeat in Oregon, Robert Kennedy landed in Los Angeles and held a press conference at the airport. He began by confessing in a prepared statement that the Oregon results "represent a setback to my prospects for obtaining the Presidential nomination of my party—a setback, as I have previously stated, which I could ill afford."

He went on to make the point that the real significance of Oregon, and of all the primaries, was that 80 percent of the Democratic voters were opposed to the war in Vietnam, and wanted a change of national leadership. It was time, he said, "for the Vice President to confront the forces of progress and change within the Democratic Party." He went on:

"Vice President Humphrey is the leading contender for the Democratic nomination, even though he has been unwilling to present his views to the voters in a single state. . . . If the Vice President is nominated to oppose Richard Nixon, there will be no candidate who has opposed the course of escalation of the war in Vietnam. There will be no candidate committed to the kinds of programs which can remedy the conditions which are transforming our cities into armed camps.

"It is hard to believe," Kennedy continued, "after the recent months of hope that our political system will ultimately fail to offer the people a chance to move in a new and more hopeful direction."

He then offered to debate McCarthy, and implied that if he lost in California he would withdraw from the race. When a reporter asked him why he had changed his mind about debating McCarthy, Kennedy answered honestly, "I'm not the same candidate I was before Oregon, and I can't claim that I am."

How did he feel to be the first Kennedy to lose an election after twenty-seven straight victories?

"I feel like the man Abraham Lincoln described who was run out of town on a steel rail, and said, 'If it were not for the honor of the thing, I'd rather have walked.' "

And then Kennedy said to conclude the questioning, "I've got to go now because I have lots of fans waiting. I hope."

There were. It was possibly his most tumultuous welcome of the campaign. A sea of surging faces—black, brown, white—engulfed his open car, as a blizzard of confetti swirled down from the downtown business buildings of Los Angeles. Children were nearly trampled, and Kennedy was almost pulled out of his car by his fans. It was as if the people were consciously trying to make up for Oregon; a middle-aged blonde woman ran alongside Kennedy's car for a few blocks shouting, "Piss on Oregon, piss on Oregon."

The Kennedy motorcade inched through the narrow, impassable streets at about five miles an hour. Thousands lined the sidewalks, and other hundreds trotted alongside of the car, some trying to climb in and ride with the candidate. Every few blocks Kennedy would stop, ask the throngs to give him their hands and their votes on June 4, and then push on, his suit jacket off, his tie hanging loose, his shirt clinging to his back in gray swirls of sweat. By the time he reached the Beverly Hilton Hotel, his shirttail was hanging out, both his cuff links and his PT-109 tie clasp were gone, but his spirit was restored. At a luncheon at the Hilton Hotel he said: "If I died in Oregon, I hope Los Angeles is Resurrection City."

In Oregon, McCarthy, with his gift for clever insult, had scored heavily off Kennedy. But Kennedy had not counterattacked, fearing to antagonize McCarthy's followers, fearing to appear ruthless, and anxious to keep up the fiction that he was really only running against Humphrey.

In Oregon, McCarthy had mocked Kennedy for campaigning with his pet dog, Freckles, "when Mr. Kennedy didn't even want to run himself last March." McCarthy subtly tried to force Kennedy to run against his own brother in Oregon. "Mr. Kennedy's record until very recently," McCarthy said, "had been one of approving the involvement in Vietnam." If Kennedy were elected, McCarthy warned, "we might have future involvements like Vietnam." He was trying to make Kennedy appear to be less of an opponent of the war than he was.

Such distortions infuriated Kennedy, but he remained silent in Oregon, even though his May 6, 1965, statement about the war put him on record as a Vietnam critic before McCarthy. Why he didn't point this out in a strong antiwar state like Oregon is a mystery, but adds to my own view that Kennedy was an unsure politician.

In California, however, Kennedy, for the first time, felt free enough to swing back at McCarthy. On May 30, in a full-page ad in the *Los Angeles Times,* the McCarthy campaign had attacked Kennedy for participating "in the decisions that led us to intervene in the affairs of the Dominican Republic." The same advertisement claimed that, "Eugene McCarthy was the first man to cry out, 'Let the killing stop,' and he was the first man with the guts to add, 'Why are we there?' "

Kennedy, of course, was not in the Administration when the Dominican Republic was invaded, and, as a Senator, had spoken in opposition. And McCarthy had been far from the first Senator to oppose the Vietnam war, that honor going to Morse and Gruening. On May 31, in San Francisco, Kennedy said about the ad: "It completely distorts the facts in connection with the situation in Vietnam . . . [and] the facts in connection with the Dominican Republic. This great crusade that began for the future of the United States is now involved in a campaign to distort and stop me. . . ."

And during their nationally televised debate the next day, the two anti-Administration candidates had the following exchange over the ad:

MR. CLARK (moderator): Senator McCarthy, the McCarthy for President Committee, your McCarthy for President Committee has been running full-page ads in California papers in recents days saying that Senator Kennedy must bear part of the responsibility for the decision to intervene in Vietnam, and the implication seems to be that even though he has been a war critic for the past three years, he should be ruled out as President because of his participation in that decision in the Kennedy Administration.

Is that what you mean?

SENATOR MCCARTHY: I don't think we said it should be ruled out at all, Bob. He has said he would take some responsibility for it. The question is, how much responsibility?

I was talking more about the process. I said this is one of the things we ought to talk about, is the process by which decisions were made with reference to this war, because one of our problems has been to find out who decides and who is responsible, and on what kind of evidence did we have this kind of escalation?

SENATOR KENNEDY: It also said that I intervened in the Dominican Republic.

SENATOR MCCARTHY: That's right.

SENATOR KENNEDY: Now how did they get that?

SENATOR MCCARTHY: Well, I think what they did, I had—

SENATOR KENNEDY: I wasn't even in the government at the time.

SENATOR MCCARTHY: Well you weren't out very long.

SENATOR KENNEDY: But I—

SENATOR MCCARTHY: I don't want to fault you on that.

SENATOR KENNEDY: And then it ran again today.

SENATOR MCCARTHY: We stopped it—it may have run in two papers, but I don't think it ran twice.

SENATOR KENNEDY: I saw it again this morning. I wasn't involved in the Dominican Republic, I wasn't even in the government and I criticize this.

SENATOR MCCARTHY: What I said was that this was a process that was involved in our going into Cuba, involved in our going into the Dominican Republic, and also into Vietnam and that I wanted to talk about the process. In any case, I had not seen the ad. When I saw it I said, "Stop it," and they stopped it as soon as they could.

SENATOR KENNEDY: I appreciate that.

SENATOR MCCARTHY: Which is not quite what happened to the voting record of McCarthy which was distributed across the country and which is being mailed out in this state, right now.

MR. REYNOLDS: Would you like to respond to that?

SENATOR KENNEDY: I don't know to what he is referring.

SENATOR MCCARTHY: I have it in my pocket.

MR. CLARK: Senator Kennedy, you did get very upset about that ad in a speech—

SENATOR MCCARTHY: Well, I think he had some reasons. I got somewhat upset over what was said to be my voting record. But they were nice in that this guy, they took a picture of me when I was about forty years old. I looked young, it was a good comparison. I'm young in spirit, I'm about that young. . . .

MR. CLARK: But you [Mr. Kennedy] used these words on Friday. You said, "The great crusade that began for the United States is now involved in a campaign to distort me and to stop me."

Did you mean, or did you feel at that time, that Senator McCarthy was trying to distort you or stop you?

SENATOR KENNEDY: It was a distortion of the record which I think Senator McCarthy just agreed to.

During the last week in California, there was also a tactical dispute within Kennedy's campaign. McCarthy had been about fifteen percentage points behind Kennedy in the polls before Oregon, but now he was gaining fast. His campaign received additional financial backing from the East, the morale of his volunteers was high, and Kennedy's myth of invincibility was exposed.

The Unruh organization, that last week, wanted Kennedy to write off the middle-class liberals, and concentrate his limited time and energy on the more conservative, latently backlash suburbs. Kennedy's own people, especially Seigenthaler and Mankiewicz, felt he should still go after the liberal, educated vote, and, at the same time, continue to campaign among blacks and Mexicans.

As John Seigenthaler put it, "If the liberals could just listen to Kennedy, I felt they would still go for him. Also, it was a challenge for us to get them back. And if we couldn't get them now, we would be in trouble later on."

There were meetings and debates within the chaotic campaign structure, and in the end there was a compromise. Kennedy spent more time personally campaigning in more conservative areas, but the thrust of his speeches and statements was toward the middle-class liberals: antiwar, anti-Humphrey, pro-black.

On Memorial Day, a Thursday, Kennedy whistle-stopped along the Southern Pacific Railroad, through the lush, fertile San Joaquin Valley, from Fresno to Sacramento. At each stop during the hot, sunny day, he spoke from the rear of the train to responsive crowds ranging from 500 to 4,000. He joked with them—directing his humor mostly against himself, rather than others. At one point he saw a child, about nine or ten, racing alongside the train, and Kennedy said to him, "Don't ever run for President. It's very tiring." On Election Day, he would carry every county he stopped in that day, although he lost all the other counties in that valley.

On Thursday, Kennedy's campaign also released to the press the text of a telegram to Vice President Humphrey, challenging him to join the television debate on Saturday. It was, of course, a political ploy. Kennedy knew Humphrey would never risk the appearance. But he also was aware that McCarthy was attacking him more than Humphrey, and that some war critics were beginning to fear that McCarthy, in the end, might throw his support to the Vice President, instead of Kennedy. Kennedy was also aware that a strenuous effort, both in advertising and in union support, was being made for the pro-Humphrey Lynch slate in the primary. So he sent Humphrey a telegram, whose text was intended to be read by California's antiwar voters. It said in part:

> One great issue of contention within our party has been continued escalation of the war in Vietnam. In recent weeks, ever since President Johnson's speech of March 31, the intensification of the war has meant an increase in American deaths. In one recent week more American troops were killed in Vietnam than in all the years from 1961 to 1964.
>
> You have supported, and I have opposed the continued escalation of the war. There are also disagreements between us on the somber question of our national future—especially the racial injustices in our society, and the violence to which injustice has led. . . .

Kennedy then pointed out that he had supported the implementation of the reform recommendations of the Kerner Commission Report, adding:

> The Administration of which you are the second highest official has opposed this. My experience as Attorney General has convinced me of the urgent need for strong and compassionate action.
>
> I feel that our party and our country would be enlightened by discussion between us regarding the Commission report, and regarding your Administration's failure to fight poverty effectively, and to humanize our cities.

Saturday, June 1, was the day of the debate. Kennedy prepared for it all day: studying index cards, practicing answers to questions that might be asked during the debate, taking a nap and gearing himself mentally. McCarthy treated the debate more casually, refusing to cram, chatting with poet Robert Lowell, and singing old Irish ballads with a few friends.

The press—150 reporters following each candidate—spent the afternoon interviewing each other. Most of them expected that McCarthy would win the debate. As the McLuhanist candidate, he was ready-made for a cool medium like television. With his gray hair, handsome face, and firm jaw, he looked like a President. His manner—low-keyed and confident—seemed just the right antidote to five years of war, riots, violence, and emotionalism. Furthermore, he was supposed to be the more intellectual of the two, and Kennedy rarely performed well in the impersonal artificiality of a television studio; he needed faces and crowds for his sensual politics.

Outside the studios of KGO-TV on Golden Gate Avenue, about three hundred student supporters of McCarthy were assembled. They cheered and chanted, "We want Gene" as their candidate entered, and booed Kennedy, shouting taunts about New Hampshire and courage.

Kennedy's predebate strategy called for him to focus on three things: softening his reputation for ruthlessness; trying to be specific and to relate general questions directly to California, emphasizing his own record of experience.

All these things he did well. He was witty and relaxed. When McCarthy insisted on firing Secretary Rusk, General Hershey, and J. Edgar Hoover, Kennedy declined to deal in personalities.

"We cut $25 million from the Head Start Program," Kennedy said at one point, "which is going to mean that 1,000 students already in the

Head Start Program here in California will be excluded. . . ." A few moments later Kennedy said, "We have forty million Negroes (*sic*) who are in the ghettos at the present time. We have here in the state of California a million Mexican-Americans whose poverty is even greater than that of many of the black people. You say you are going to take 10,000 black people and move them into Orange County. . . . We can fight for freedom 12,500 miles away, but we must do something to deal with the quality of life here. The property taxes, for instance, here in the state of California, which are astronomically high, the problems of poverty . . ."

And repeatedly Kennedy referred to himself as "a former Attorney General . . . as a member of the Cabinet . . . as a member of the National Security Council . . . I have had, as I mentioned, the experience in the Executive Branch of the government. . . ."

The substance of the debate, however, was bland and disappointing. Its enormous buildup by the media had created expectations of grudges indulged, open anger, fundamental disagreements, and a final, decisive resolution. But instead, there were only differences of temperament and emphasis so small that most viewers did not follow them. McCarthy wanted to put a priority on integrating the suburbs, Kennedy on rebuilding the ghettos. McCarthy favored a coalition government in Saigon, Kennedy favored a coalition government in Saigon as a result of negotiations. McCarthy would fire Rusk, Hershey, and Hoover; Kennedy would not.

At the end, like high-school candidates for student council, each was asked to state his own qualifications for President. Here Kennedy seemed expressionless and halting, while McCarthy answered brilliantly, concluding:

> I think that in this year I sensed what this country needed; namely, it needed and wanted a challenge to the President of the United States on the policies of Vietnam and priorities for America, and I think there is something to be said for a President or a Presidential candidate who can somehow anticipate what the country wants, especially when what they want is on the side of good and justice, and to provide not real leadership in the sense of saying, "You have got to follow me," but at least to be prepared to move out ahead somewhat so that the people of the country can follow.
>
> And, thirdly, I think I sense what the young people of this country needed and where young students were dropping out and saying, "The Establishment is no good."

We have had a genuine reconciliation of old and young in this country, and the significance of that is, I think, that through the whole country now there is a new confidence in the future of America. It is a projection of this country in trust, which has always been the character of this country, and it is in that mood and in that spirit that I would act as President of the United States.

Later, when I asked Kennedy why he answered the final question so badly, he replied:

"You won't believe it, but I was daydreaming. I thought the program was over, and I was trying to decide in my mind where to take Ethel for dinner, when they asked that last question. I was lucky I didn't answer Joe DiMaggio's."

After the debate, I approached several of the three hundred newsmen who watched it on monitors in two special rooms at the KGO-TV studios and asked them what they made of it. Said Jimmy Breslin: "Kennedy won it, but the other guy had a helluva last round." Roland Evans replied, "Bobby. He was crisper and more factual." Hays Gorey of *Time* also thought Kennedy won, while Sol Stern of *Ramparts* insisted McCarthy had come off better. Most of the daily journalists, however, treated it as a tedious draw, although *The New York Times,* in an editorial, awarded the verdict to McCarthy.

Regardless of what the national working press thought, the voters of California felt Kennedy won. Soundings taken by professional politicians and volunteer canvassers, and telephone surveys taken by newspapers, all indicated that a heavy majority of voters thought that Kennedy had come off the best; a telephone poll conducted right after the debate by the *Los Angeles Times* gave the decision to Kennedy by 2½ to 1. Kennedy's own political technicians, Larry O'Brien and Fred Dutton, would later say that California was the first primary state where Kennedy received an even split of the late undecided vote. The tide had turned Saturday night. McCarthy's post-Oregon momentum was broken. Kennedy's slippage was stopped.

McCarthy had overused the debate issue. His goading and boasting had generated the expectation that he would visibly outclass his younger, less intellectual rival. Merely by holding his own, Kennedy won. Even McCarthy's own volunteers had expected a clear-cut outcome and were demoralized by the debate. And by debating, Kennedy took away from McCarthy the why-won't-Kennedy-debate? issue, which had been so effective in the closing days in Oregon.

Sunday, June 2. Kennedy began the day by flying from San Francisco to Concord, for a brief airport rally at Buchannan Field. It was an idyllic setting: cobalt, cloudless sky, rolling hills, azure mountains in the background. The temperature was in the seventies, and a cool breeze came in off the ocean. A Mexican band played "This Land Is Your Land"—which, rewritten, had become Kennedy's campaign theme song. The crowd was largely Mexican, and Kennedy spoke briefly about the "indecency" of the war and poverty, and the need for "reconciliation, compassion, and love."

Then it was off to Los Angeles, an hour's flight to the south. It was on this flight that I had my last conversation with Robert Kennedy. I was walking down the aisle with a Bloody Mary when Kennedy reached out and guided me down into the empty seat next to him.

His face looked like an old man's; there were lines I had never noticed before. The eyes were puffy and red and pushed back into their sockets. His hands shook, as they often did when he was speaking in public. He was so tired, I couldn't read his mood.

"I heard your song the other day," Kennedy began.

I looked at him quizzically until he explained: "Bobby Darin sang 'Blowin' in the Wind' for me. I really liked it. Especially that line, 'How many years can some people exist, before they're allowed to be free?' "

More than a year before I had given Kennedy a few albums by Bob Dylan. Kennedy had been fascinated by Dylan's reputation, but he didn't like the albums. He said he couldn't stand Dylan's whining voice, and felt most of the songs were "too depressing." But he remained curious about the jukebox bard with such a powerful influence on the styles and values of the young. When I had introduced Kennedy to folk singer Phil Ochs, he had quizzed Ochs intensely about Dylan. On another occasion he had told me he appreciated the title of the *cinema verité* film on Dylan—*Don't Look Back*.

"Is that his philosophy?" Kennedy said. "I think it's mine." Kennedy had also quoted Dylan in his last book. Now he had heard a more traditional singer sing Dylan's words, and it had registered on Kennedy's contemporary sensibility.

"Do you think you could introduce me to Dylan?" Kennedy asked.

I told him I doubted it, since Dylan had become almost a hermit, holed up in Woodstock, New York. I was thinking of proposing (half in jest) to Kennedy that he invite Dylan to sing at his Inaugural, when he asked another question:

"How is Lowenstein doing? Will he win? Tell him I'm with him."

Allard Lowenstein was running for Congress now in the New York primary, pledged to supporting McCarthy. "I think so," I replied. "He's getting help from a lot of kids who have become disillusioned with McCarthy."

My answer had returned the memory of the white whale to Kennedy's mind. The activist students. Why were they still against him? Didn't they understand they were only helping Humphrey now? What could he do to win them back?

Before I could answer, Kennedy's own interior life took over, and he turned his worn-out face away, to gaze out at the breathtaking California landscape below.

Kennedy's next stop on Sunday was a strawberry festival in Orange County, hard-core Reagan territory. He arrived at about 4 P.M. at Garden Grove City on Westminster Boulevard, where a friendly crowd of about 4,000 was waiting.

But Kennedy was exhausted. His voice had no feeling, and a few times he transposed words, or lost his train of thought. He began by saying, "What happens in California on Tuesday may determine who will be the next President of the United States."

A voice shouted out of the crowd, "You will, you will."

And as the endorsing cheer rose from the stands, Kennedy said almost to himself, "Well, if that happens, it won't be unanimous." Then he launched into a rambling attack on the Vice President and the continuing war in Vietnam. And he ended with a playful plea for votes:

"Will you all remember to vote for me on Tuesday? Promise? ["Yes, Yes."] Think of all my children. Think that if I lose, think of all the little tears that will come down all their cheeks."

After the Orange County rally, Kennedy, on impulse, decided to take six of his children to Disneyland on the way back to Los Angeles, and that was the end of his campaigning for the day.

That night, at about 11 P.M., Jeff Greenfield and I visited our friend Paul Gorman at McCarthy's headquarters at the Beverly Hilton Hotel. Our mission had a precise purpose—to see if Gorman was willing to defect to Kennedy if McCarthy lost on Tuesday.

We met Gorman in the McCarthy press room, where he was with four of McCarthy's young staff members. Greenfield and I quickly were drawn into a heated argument with one of them, Mary Davis. She was virulently anti-Kennedy and saw "no difference between him and Humphrey." She claimed that Kennedy had "bribed waitresses working in the bar of our Oregon campaign headquarters to eavesdrop on conversations between McCarthy staff people." When I said that at least indicated Kennedy no longer believed in wiretaps, she did not laugh, but moved on to attack Kennedy for "being too hostile to McCarthy," and "for taking a racist line in the debate with the crack about Orange County." The three other staff members seemed less personally antagonistic to Kennedy, but none seemed in a mood to give up, no matter how the vote went on Tuesday. There seemed to be a fanaticism at the core of McCarthy's campaign that was impervious to compromise or recognition of defeat.

Finally, Greenfield, Gorman, and myself adjourned to the hotel bar for a more fraternal and less partisan conversation. The two rival speech writers enjoyed a natural rapport, since they held analogous positions in the two campaigns: both to the left of the candidate, both under thirty, both somewhat disgusted by the small intrigues and conspiracies going on around them among the older professionals. Gorman particularly was upset that McCarthy had refused to deliver several of his drafts about race and poverty. Gorman also confessed to us a certain horror at the intense personal hatred of Kennedy at the center of the McCarthy campaign, and his particular unhappiness over the candidate's own contributions. "Some people think I'm a spy for Bobby because I don't hate him," Gorman said.

The three of us also agreed that both candidates, perhaps the two most progressive major party politicians in the country, had been compromised and brutalized by the pace and pressures of the campaign. We also agreed that the policy differences on substantive issues between them were marginal, and that there was a need to reinstate the Vietnam war and Vice President Humphrey as the real opposition after Tuesday. But when Greenfield and I pressed Gorman on whether he would come over to Kennedy if Kennedy won on Tuesday, his response was anguished and ambivalent. Much later, Gorman told me that his feeling at the time Kennedy was shot was "that I couldn't see myself working for McCarthy in New York, with all that sick, liberal hate-Bobby feeling there. But that I wouldn't defect to Bobby, and that I would probably just work for McCarthy in the sticks, where I wouldn't be hurting Bobby."

As we were getting ready to leave the bar, at about 2 A.M., Gorman asked me if I had thought about a title for my book on Kennedy. "If he loses on Tuesday," I said, "I think I'll call it *The Late Robert Kennedy*."

Monday, June 3, Robert Kennedy pushed his worn, tired body through one last excruciating day, until at the end his flesh rebelled and he nearly collapsed. In twelve hours, he traveled 1,200 miles, from Los Angeles, to San Francisco, to Long Beach, through Watts, and, finally, late at night, to San Diego, and back to Los Angeles.

Late in the morning Kennedy's motorcade pushed through the clogged, narrow streets of San Francisco's Chinatown. Suddenly, a fire cracker—maybe a cherry bomb—exploded, loud and close. Then five more on the same string went off, bang, bang, bang. The memory of Dallas flashed through the minds of the press. Was it happening again? Where was Kennedy? Could anyone see him? Ethel Kennedy, terrified, crouched down. But Robert Kennedy didn't flinch. He kept cool, refusing through will to show fear, shaking hands, waving to the people. When Kennedy saw his wife, trembling beside him, he asked a reporter trotting alongside the car to climb into the car and hold Ethel's hand, while he went on with the calm business of showing his face to the voters. He felt he had to ride in a convertible because his brother had been killed in a convertible. The whole incident took perhaps ten seconds, but the next day we would all remember it, remember how close to the surface of our consciousness Dallas had been all along, how we all had a secret fleeting premonition of how the last passionate passage of Robert Kennedy might end. We remembered how John Lindsay of *Newsweek* had warned us that first wild weekend in California, that "This country is going to kill another Kennedy. And then we won't have a country."

Kennedy's luncheon speech at Fisherman's Wharf was pedestrian. He was in a state well beyond fatigue, and it showed. But he came to life briefly for the final, romantic peroration:

> So on this last day of the campaign, I ask you not to support my poli-
> cies and programs, for that battle has been won.
>
> I ask you to recognize the hard and difficult road ahead to a better
> America—and I ask you tomorrow to vote for yourselves. The people
> must decide this election—and they must decide so that no leader in

America has any doubt of what they want. For your sake, and for the sake of your children, vote for yourselves tomorrow.

Then to Long Beach, where he again rambled almost incoherently to a crowd of about 6,000. When he got back to his open car, Dutton told him, "You had a little trouble with some words that time."

"I don't feel good," Kennedy confessed, something he would normally try to hide from his staff.

Then the grueling motorcade began, through flat, friendly Watts, and on to the Los Angeles suburb of Venice. There Kennedy told Dutton, "I've got an upset stomach. Can you get me some ginger ale?"

According to Dutton, "I got Bob three or four bottles of ginger ale, and he kept sipping it every few blocks. He didn't look too good, but the crowds were adrenalin for him, and he kept on going all afternoon, feeling sick, shaking hands, gulping the ginger ale."

Kennedy then flew to San Diego, for the final rally of the California campaign. The crowd at the El Cortez Hotel was so large and so rowdy that the rally had to be held in two sections. At the first rally the speech was rushed and disjointed, and ended abruptly. Kennedy walked offstage, the crowd cheering, and he sat down and buried his face in his hands, totally spent, like Roger Bannister at the end of history's first sub-four minute mile, collapsing at the tape, blood running out of his shoes.

Rafer Johnson and Bill Barry helped Kennedy to a men's room in back of the stage. And while Johnson stood guard at the door to keep away the press, Ethel and Dutton went in to see if Kennedy needed assistance. Said Dutton later, "Bob just needed some air and some rest. He did not vomit. He was just dizzy for a few minutes. He told me, 'I just ran out of gas.' "

Kennedy then returned to the platform and spoke to the second section of the rally, dazed, sick, but still lashing at the poverty, the war, and at Humphrey with his last reserves of stamina. That night Kennedy, his wife, and six of their children went to John Frankenheimer's secluded beach house at Malibu for sleep, and a day of reunion and rest on Election Day.

Something else happened on Monday that would have made headlines if the McCarthy press corps had been aware of it. David Garth quit McCarthy's campaign staff.

Garth, a Stevensonian liberal, was John Lindsay's television expert, and was one of a dozen members of the Lindsay Administration to volunteer for duty in McCarthy's campaign. Garth was in California the last week making a series of television ads—one of which was strongly anti-Humphrey—for saturation showing the last forty-eight hours of the campaign. But McCarthy refused to approve the one strong anti-Humphrey spot. Garth felt it was both principled and political to attack Humphrey, and he quit when the ad was killed. When I interviewed him much later, Garth explained:

"I was uneasy about all the hate-Bobby feeling around McCarthy. And when he refused to okay the anti-Humphrey spot, the contrast really got to me, and so I just flew back to New York that Monday night before the election. I had originally offered to help McCarthy because I had disliked Bobby ever since I worked for Stevenson in 1960. But by the end, I was sorry I had. I don't know whether McCarthy subconsciously didn't want to win, or whether he hated Bobby enough to want to make a deal with Humphrey. Either way, I didn't like it, so I quit."

The Day of the Locust

Tuesday, June 4 was a Los Angeles day: sunless, mild, a faint mixture of smog and haze in the air. I got up in my room at the Ambassador Hotel, and put on the radio, looking for some good music, finally catching Aretha Franklin on a station at the end of the dial geared toward Negroes. Suddenly a commercial to vote for McCarthy came on, claiming Martin Luther King had endorsed him. It angered me: a small, cheap trick of the old politics on this day for new politics. A few days before, Drew Pearson had written a syndicated column revealing that Kennedy, while Attorney General, had approved of phone taps on Dr. King. And the press was now speculating about whether this would discredit Kennedy with black voters.

Blacks and Mexicans are supposed to be lazy, indifferent voters, especially in primaries. But on this day, the blacks and Mexicans voted as they had never voted before in the history of California, and for a rich Irishman. In some Negro and Mexican districts, nine out of every ten registered Democrats came to the polls, a higher percentage than in many of the Jewish, middle-class districts where participation had been the pattern for years.

In Mexican sections people went door to door, spreading the simple message—"This is the day Cesar says to vote for Robert Kennedy." Kennedy had come to Delano in 1966 when no one else cared. And now, on this day, fourteen of every fifteen of California's Mexicans would vote for Robert Kennedy.

I spent the afternoon driving around Los Angeles with Adam and

Jane Walinsky, and Jeff and Harriet Greenfield, listening to rock music on the car radio, and soaking in the depersonalized character of the terminal, plastic city. Adam and Jeff finally purchased colorful hippie outfits for the victory celebration to be held that night at the jet set discothèque, The Factory.

Kennedy, who spent the day resting and swimming at Malibu, arrived in his fifth-floor suite at the Ambassador Hotel at about 7:15 P.M. He retired quickly to his room—511—while friends, reporters, family, and visiting celebrities began to gather in room 516, across the hall. The journalists Kennedy admired and liked were there: Harwood, Breslin, Hamill, Loudon Wainwright, Warren Rogers, Hays Gorey. Authors like Budd Schulberg, Theodore White, and George Plimpton. Photographer Stanley Tretick. Milton Berle and John Glenn. And the organizers of the poor—Charles Evers; Doris Huerta, the spirited aide to Cesar Chavez; and John Lewis, the former leader of the old SNCC, who had gone to jail forty times, and who still preached nonviolence.

At about 8 P.M. Kennedy, beaming puckishly, poked his head into room 516, and asked, "Do you want to hear about the Indians?" Then he announced that an Indian precinct in South Dakota had voted 878 for him, nine for a Humphrey-Johnson slate, and two for McCarthy. A few minutes later he spoke by phone to his South Dakota manager, Bill Dougherty, and learned that he would get 50 percent of the vote in Humphrey's native state.

Kennedy regarded the results in South Dakota as politically significant. They proved that he could win in a white, rural state, where Humphrey was born and had had time to campaign personally. The vote of the Indians added personal gratification.

By 8:30 the comic opera of the computers had begun; NBC was announcing McCarthy was winning, while CBS had Kennedy ahead. Kennedy, relying on reports fed to him by Salinger and O'Brien, knew he was doing well, although not quite so well as the CBS technological projections.

The atmosphere now was becoming more like a party in room 516. A bar was set up in the corner and we were all on our second or third drinks. The laughter was loud, the talk happy, and the corridor between the rooms of the suite began to fill up. Even Kennedy's own sanctuary began to grow so crowded that he would retreat into the bathroom occasionally for a few private moments with Smith, or Sorensen, or Walinsky.

At about 9 P.M. Kennedy, restless, prowled into the hallway and was besieged by a pack of radio, television, and print reporters. He was glowing now, the most inwardly serene I had seen him since before Johnson's abdication. He leaned back against the wall, folded his arms, smiling that toothy smile, trying to hear one question out of the noise. Someone said that McCarthy was beginning to sound less like an intellectual, and more like a politician.

"I like politicians," Kennedy said almost in a whisper, microphones sprouting under his nose. "I like politics. It's an honorable adventure."

A voice said that was a familiar phrase, an honorable adventure. "Do you know who made it up?" Kennedy asked. When no one knew the answer, he said very proudly, like a schoolboy, "That was Lord Tweedsmuir. Does anybody here know who he was?" Again the clot of twenty or thirty reporters fell silent. Kennedy, happy he had known something the press hadn't, explained he was John Buchan, the Scottish statesman and author who had written *The Thirty-nine Steps*. Then he withdrew back into his private room, to sit with Ethel, Dutton, Sorensen, Goodwin, Gwirtzman, and Breslin, and watch Eugene McCarthy interviewed on CBS.

McCarthy, as he had done in Indiana and Nebraska, tried to belittle the meaning of the primary, but this time it rang hollow, almost delusional.

CRONKITE: David Schoumacher is now standing by with Senator McCarthy at—in Los Angeles. Come in, David.

SCHOUMACHER: Right, Walter. Senator, what went wrong, I suppose is the easiest way to begin.

MCCARTHY: Well, I don't know as anything's gone wrong. This has gone about as we expected. We didn't have much time to campaign here. We've made our real test in Oregon, where there were no bloc votes, and we made the case as clear as we could there, neglecting California in order to run in Oregon, and expected it would go about like this. I don't know just what the margin may be, or the difference, but we're not surprised, though. I think we're showing, as far as I can read the returns now, that we can get the votes that no other Democrat can get, and that's what we've been demonstrating in most of the primaries across the country.

SCHOUMACHER: Senator, it's generally said that California, however, is a profile state; it's a little United States. Isn't it going to be very difficult for you now to make the argument that you can win where other candidates cannot?

MCCARTHY: I don't think so. I don't see any indications yet that Senator Kennedy could get any votes in the general election that I couldn't get, and I think the Northern California returns give you a profile of the country in that they're showing that I'm running better than he is, so that we're demonstrating what we said we're going to demonstrate across the country, that I could get votes that no other Democrat could get; and the contest, you know, within the Democratic Party for votes that anybody can get, if this was all the game was about, why we never would have started.

After the McCarthy interview I stopped to talk to Steve Smith in the crowded hallway between the two rooms. Smith, perhaps the most underrated figure in the Kennedy entourage, was standing against the wall, his long hair curling over the top of his collar, talking in his usual sentence fragments and shrugs. I asked him what was the strategy after California; what could they do now to win the nomination?

Smith answered with a series of clipped, staccato sentences; like Kennedy, it takes him time to warm up. It would be a hard, long struggle, he said. New York will be tough. But we have some tentative plans. A full-page ad in the Friday *Times* with close-up faces of Meany, Maddox, and financier Sidney Weinberger, and a little bit of type below asking if you wanted these three men to pick your next President. A ten-day trip to Europe—Rome to see the Pope, West Berlin, and then Poland. Then there was a chance to create a new primary by petition in Rhode Island in July, and dare Humphrey to enter. And then there will be exhaustive personal campaigning by Kennedy in all the non-primary states that he had to neglect because of the demands of the primaries.

At the time, listening to Smith, I didn't think it could be done. I didn't see how Kennedy could win in New York. But by the time I went to Chicago in August for the Democratic Convention, I was convinced Robert Kennedy would have been nominated for President. Humphrey's support in the large, industrial, non-primary states had crumbled in the interval. Humphrey did not wear well campaigning.

By August, Nixon was ahead of Humphrey in the public opinion polls. The country was getting impatient with the snail's pace of the peace talks in Paris, while those wooden boxes were still coming home from Vietnam. At Chicago, even Mayor Daley seemed to prefer the surviving Kennedy brother to Humphrey. Robert Kennedy, ten weeks buried, was the most alive candidate at the Democratic Convention. The memorial film about him touched the delegates more than any act or any speech by a live politician. After the convention, even the most loyal McCarthy supporters, like Murray Kempton, John Kenneth Galbraith, and Jeremy Larner, acknowledged that Robert Kennedy, had he lived, would have been nominated that bloody week in that armed city.

It was about 10:30 P.M. now, and the votes of the Negroes and Mexicans of Los Angeles were starting to come in, and confirm Kennedy's victory. His new majority of the poor and the young was adding up. Kennedy seemed—and it is the word I jotted down at the time—liberated. He was witty, relaxed, in control.

He went down first to the fourth floor to be interviewed by his old friend Sander Vanocur on NBC, and then back up to the fifth floor for an equal-time interview on CBS with another friend, Roger Mudd. The Mudd interview proved to be one of the most appealing and natural Kennedy ever gave on television. He was relaxed with Mudd. He was in a playful, mellow mood. And Mudd's jargon-phrased questions gave Kennedy a foil against which he could play an antiruthless role. What follows is the CBS transcript of Robert Kennedy's last interview.

MUDD: This is Stephen Smith's brother-in-law. How are you? I just heard you say, Senator, that without the cooperation of Senator McCarthy or his supporters—and/or his supporters—you thought Hubert Humphrey would get the nomination.

KENNEDY: Well, I just—I believe that I said that I thought it would be very, very difficult. I think it will be very difficult. I would hope we could come together. As I said from the beginning, I think that the primaries— Well, let me start, as the primaries I think have indicated quite clearly, that the Democratic Party wants a change. More than 70 percent of the electorate have voted against the Johnson-Humphrey policies of the last three years. We have an opportunity now to move the Democratic Party in a different direction, but if we are divided on our side, then I think that it's going to be much more difficult, and I would hope that with this California primary, the South Dakota in, and with the other primaries that have occurred, that perhaps we could unite now that the primaries are finished and completed—unite and try to accomplish what we all started out to accomplish, which was for a cause, for a purpose, not for an individual.

MUDD: Well, it appears though, doesn't it, that you're not going to be able to *shake* Eugene McCarthy?

KENNEDY: I think, really, it's up to him. I mean, he's going to have to make that decision himself. We've—this is a cross section of the country here in the State of California and if I'm successful here in the State of California, successful in South Dakota, successful in Nebraska, successful in Indiana, in the District of Columbia won against Hubert Humphrey's slate two to one, which is the regular Democratic organization, I think it's an indication that perhaps we can go on and accomplish something. But really, in the last analysis, it's up to him to decide, but I would hope people would now stop and think and make a judgment as to whether we really want to make this kind of a change or whether we're going to continue the policies of the past three years, in our cities, and in the war in Vietnam. That seems to me what's the major question.

MUDD: Senator, the other day when you arrived from Portland, at the Los Angeles press conference, you said on two occasions that you thought the country was heading—may be heading toward a Humphrey-Nixon contest in the general election—

KENNEDY: Yes, yes, and I said at that time that I'd abide by the results here in the State of California.

MUDD: And did that mean you'd drop out if you lost?

KENNEDY: Well, if—

MUDD: We all said it meant that.

KENNEDY: —I know that.

MUDD: I'd like to know what you—

KENNEDY: Well, let me say that it would appear that I had—that, according to what you say with your machine—that it's been successful, so I don't have to face that at the moment. But in any case, I said that I would abide by the results and I think that the words spoke for themselves. If we go into these primaries we go in on the basis that we have—we want to see if we have popular support. Hubert Humphrey dropped out after West Virginia when it was clear that he wasn't winning. And it seems to me that that—it's a lesson. If we're going to win, those of us who are opposed to the present policy, it's difficult enough as it is. If we're divided ourselves, after we've gone through the primaries, everybody's had an opportunity to judge us, judge our policies, judge what we want for the future, what we want to accomplish for the United States, what we want to have the United States stand for around the rest of the world. It seems to me, now that the primaries are finished, they are completed, that to try to come together would be terribly, terribly important.

MUDD: You have no way, now, between California and Chicago, to draw the Vice President into a *fight?*

KENNEDY: No, I—do I have to put it that way? (*Laughing.*)

MUDD: Well, I put it that way and—

KENNEDY: No, what I would like—I think there—I think it's unfortunate he didn't come into the primaries. He campaigned more in South Dakota than I did, but—and he wasn't successful there. I don't think that the policies that he espouses would be successful in the country, and I don't think they'd be successful with the Democratic Party and I think all the primaries have indicated that, but I think at least to have a discussion with me now in various parts of the country about the policies he espouses in Southeast Asia, in Vietnam, and what he intends to do in the cities and what I intend and what we're going to do about the rural areas and what we're going to do about the farmers—I think it would be very important for the Democratic Party and for the people prior to the time we go to the convention in Chicago. That's what I would like, and I would hope that he'd be willing to meet me.

MUDD: Well, are you saying, Senator, that if the Democratic Party nominates the Vice President, *it will be cutting its own throat in November?*

KENNEDY: Well, again you use those expressions. I think that the Democratic Party would be making a very bad mistake to ignore the wishes of the people and ignore these primaries. (*Wincing.*)

MUDD: And you would not be willing to join with Mr. Humphrey in order to help the Democratic Party win if it comes to that?

KENNEDY: In what way?

MUDD: As Vice President?

KENNEDY: In what order? (*Smiling.*)

MUDD: Well—

KENNEDY: Are you saying—

MUDD: Well, you would be second?

KENNEDY: No—well, no, I wouldn't. I'll be glad to help the Democratic Party—I believe in the Democratic Party—in what way I of course would have to work out. But I—particularly if Richard Nixon is the nominee of the Republican Party, which I think is unacceptable to the country, and I have strong disagreements, as I say, with Hubert Humphrey and the position that he espouses, and particularly what he said this week, that he would step aside if Lyndon Johnson then decides that he wants to run, that he would then step aside. That I don't understand.

MUDD: You felt that *was fairly shoddy politics,* I take it?

KENNEDY: (*Smiling*). Well, again, I—Roger, I—you know, I don't think —you're either in it, or you're not in it. And you don't say, "I'm in the middle of it and I want these delegates to support me, but if somebody else steps in, I'm going to step aside." That doesn't make any sense. At least, it doesn't seem to make sense to me.

What I would like to do is to—and what I think would be helpful to the Democratic Party, if we met and had a series of discussions and debates about what—where we're going and where we are at the present time, and where we're going as far as the future's concerned, so I think that what is most unfortunate is that he didn't come into any of the primaries—the Vice President didn't.

MUDD: You said a moment ago that you would support the nominee of the Democratic Party, even if he were Hubert Humphrey, in a way that would have to be worked out later. Are you saying that you haven't decided whether you would campaign for him?

KENNEDY: Well, let me put it this way, that I—I'm in it to win and try to talk about what I will do if I lose doesn't seem to me very profitable.

MUDD: No. Senator, as a result of this California—presumed California —victory, do you think now that there will be a further delay in the movement of the big city politicians?

KENNEDY: Well, I think we've had some success in that up to the present time, in Michigan and Ohio, which I think is very important, and so I would hope now that I'm free to go back and talk to some of them and also to talk to the people themselves in these various states and talk about really the—what is—what are the issues. I think that these primaries have indicated to the people in those states what the issues are, and they've clearly rejected the position that's been espoused by the Vice President—overwhelmingly—and I think the people in the other states will, and so that's why I think that the Democratic Party will make such a mistake if it doesn't recognize that.

MUDD: Are some of the delegates that are listed as leaning or even committed to the Vice President—*are they squeezable? Are they solid?*

KENNEDY: I don't like either of the expressions. (*Wincing.*)

MUDD: Well, that—you—isn't that the way you talk about it?

KENNEDY: No, I don't go that far, I don't, I don't. (*Smiling.*)

MUDD: Well, I—

KENNEDY: Probably somebody else does. (*Both laugh.*)

MUDD: Well, I mean, are they still *up for grabs* even though they're—

KENNEDY: I'm going to make an effort with them, although they are listed and I'm going to—and it's the first, really, opportunity that I've had at all, because I've been involved in these various primaries.

MUDD: Thank you. I'll work on my language for the next time, Senator.

KENNEDY: Thank you. (*Laughing.*)

CRONKITE: Roger, we all think back here you're eminently squeezable. (*Smiling.*)

Kennedy, still laughing and making little jokes about the Mudd interview, submitted to more dignified interrogations with Bob Clark on ABC-TV, and Dan Blackburn on Metromedia radio. Then he returned to his room—511. It was now about 11:30, and the happy crowd in the Embassy Ballroom downstairs was getting restless and a little rowdy. They chanted alternately, "We want Kennedy" and "We want Chavez," and they sang "This Land Is Your Land." They wanted the winner to come down and claim his victory before his workers in the traditional way. It was getting late, and it was very hot, and the computers were saying it was all decided. "We want Kennedy," the chant demanded.

Kennedy sat down on the floor, in a corner, to watch television and light up a small victory cigar. He seemed to savor every puff. Writer Budd Schulberg, intense and bearded, came in and began to talk to Kennedy, who wanted Schulberg's ideas for his victory statement.

"Well, of course, you know who won this election for you," Schulberg began.

"You're going to give me that speech about 85 or 90 percent black vote, and the Chicanos' practically 100 percent."

"Bob, you're the only white man in the country they trust."

"Is Cesar Chavez downstairs?" Kennedy asked. "I was hoping he would be on the platform with me." And then Kennedy began to talk to Schulberg about his projects—the Watts Writers' Workshop and the Douglas House Theatre. "I think you've touched a nerve. We need so many new ideas. I had one, about the private sector joining with the public to encourage business enterprise in the ghettos. . . . I have a feeling of what they need, and must have. But we need so many ideas. I've learned a lot since you and I first talked about civil rights. I think that workshop idea of yours is a kind of throwback to the Federal Theatre and Writers Project of the New Deal. We have to encourage not just mechanical skills and jobs in those areas, but creative talent. I saw it in Watts, at the Douglas House—so much talent to be channeled, strong self-expression. I'd like to see it on a national scale, with Federal help, I'll do everything I can. . . ."

At that point Speaker Unruh came over to tell Kennedy it was almost time to go down to the ballroom to claim his comeback triumph.

For a few minutes Kennedy disappeared into the bathroom with Ted

Sorensen for a private talk. When he came out it was almost the stroke of midnight. He looked down at Ethel who was stretched out, resting on the bed.

"Ready?" he asked softly, and Ethel bounced up.

"Do you think we should take Freckles down?" Kennedy asked puckishly. "You know McCarthy said I needed a dog and an astronaut to win."

Then they left the suite: the Kennedys, Unruh, Fred Dutton, Rafer Johnson, and Bill Barry, to take the honorable adventure's next step. I started to move toward the elevator with them, and asked Kennedy, "What are you going to do for an encore?"

"Try to talk sense to your sick liberal friends in Manhattan," he replied. There was a crush at the elevator, everyone pushing and shoving, and I fell back. "See you at The Factory," Kennedy waved, disappearing into the overcrowded elevator. With Robert Scheer of *Ramparts,* I went back to room 516 to watch Kennedy's victory statement in comfort, on television, and pour another victory drink.

There were about twenty of us, grouped in a happy semicircle around the television screen as Kennedy, looking out over a jungle of microphones, and flanked by his wife and brother-in-law, began his exuberant victory speech.

"I want to express my high regard to Don Drysdale, who pitched his sixth straight shutout tonight, and I hope that we have as good fortune in our campaign."

And then the list of thank-yous. Jesse Unruh. Steve Smith, "who was ruthless, but has been effective." And to his sisters, Jean and Pat, "and to my mother, and all those other Kennedys.

"I want to express my gratitude to my dog Freckles. . . . I'm not doing this in any order of importance, but I also want to thank my wife Ethel. Her patience during this whole effort was fantastic." The crowd was loving it, and the laughter and cheering mingled into the special sound of celebration. And Kennedy continued in a bantering way to thank people.

"All of the students who worked across the state [cheers]. I want to thank Cesar Chavez [great cheering] who was here a little earlier. And Bert Carona, who also worked with him, and all those Mexican-Americans who were supporters of mine. [More cheering] And Doris

Huerta, who is an old friend of mine, and has worked with the union. . . . I want to also thank my friends in the black community [cheers] who made such an effort in this campaign. With such a high percentage voting today, I think it really made a major difference for me. I want to express my appreciation to them.

"To my old friend, if I may, Rafer Johnson, who is here. And to Rosey Grier, who said that he'd take care of anybody who didn't vote for me [laughter]. In a kind way, because that's the way we are [laughter].

"And if I may take just a moment more of your time to express my appreciation to Paul Schrade, from the UAW, who worked so hard . . ."

At that point Carol Welch, Kennedy's campaign secretary, who used to work in the Johnson White House with Bill Moyers, came over to me and said, "Jack, the Senator is going to leave for The Factory right from his press conference in the Colonial Room. You ought to go down now, so that you don't miss him."

Robert Scheer and I took the elevator down, and pushed our way into the rear of the sweltering Embassy Ballroom as Kennedy was concluding his remarks.

"So I thank all of you who made all this possible. All of the effort that you made, and all of the people whose names I haven't mentioned, but who did all the work at the precinct level, who got out the vote. I was a campaign manager eight years ago. I know what a difference that kind of effort, and that kind of commitment made. I thank all of you.

"Mayor Yorty has just sent me a message that we've been here too long already. So my thanks to all of you, and on to Chicago, and let's win there." And he flashed a V-for-victory sign, and the students in the crowd signaled it right back to him. His hand flicked nervously at his hair, and he turned to leave. The crowd again began to chant, "We want Kennedy. We want Kennedy."

Scheer and I were about to walk over to the Colonial Room for the press conference when something seemed to be happening near the podium. There was an awful sound that rolled across the packed ballroom that was like a moan. Then a few people started running, and a girl in a red party dress, sobbing uncontrollably, came by me, screaming, "No, God, no. It's happened again." And the moan became a wail until the ballroom sounded like a hospital that has been bombed; the sound was somehow the sound of the twice wounded.

Other people were now running and crying, and one of them

screamed, "They've shot Steve Smith!" But somehow I knew it was Kennedy, and said it to Scheer. Numbed, I tried to find a television set, and wandered into another ballroom, where the victory celebration for Max Rafferty, who had won the Republican Senate primary, was going on. There were no panic and no tears here. Older people, all of them white, were blowing noisemakers, cheering and dancing. Steve Smith suddenly appeared on the television to ask very calmly for a doctor. Kennedy was clearly shot, but the Rafferty party went right on as if nothing had happened.

I ran back into the hysteria of the Embassy Ballroom. Girls in red and blue campaign ribbons, and RFK plastic boaters, were on their knees praying and weeping. A big Negro was pounding the wall in animal rage, shouting out of control, "Why, God, why? Why again? Why another Kennedy?" A college kid with an RFK peace button was screaming, "Fuck this country, fuck this country!" I found Scheer, and in silence we went back up to the Kennedy suite on the fifth floor.

Upstairs the victory party had turned into a vigil. I walked into Kennedy's bedroom, and Ted Sorensen was sitting on the bed, trying to comfort the wife of John Bartlow Martin. I thought how controlled Sorensen was, but perhaps it wasn't so terrible the second time.

In room 516, the people who had come to share the joy of winning with Robert Kennedy were united in sorrow around the television set, waiting for more details. There was something close to acceptance in many of the dazed faces, as if they all had a fatalistic premonition that he would end this way.

George Plimpton, who had helped capture the assassin, rushed in, his eyeballs the size of marbles, wanting the latest news. How bad was it? Was he still alive?

The television stations began to play and replay the tapes of Kennedy's zestful victory statement, and the longest night began to pass very slowly in the Kennedy suite. Stan Tretick sat on the couch in the corner, hugging his wife. John Lewis sat on the floor, shaking his head, and asking himself, "Why, why, why? Why him?" John Bartlow Martin, his gaunt face the color of chalk, said to no one in particular, "Bomb America. Make the Coca-Cola someplace else."

The phones began to ring, and Scheer and I, to keep our minds busy, began to help Carol Welch answer them. Did we need a surgeon? Could I give blood? One call came from London, another, barely coherent, from Edith Green in Oregon. A McCarthy worker, weeping, promised she would switch to Bobby "if he lives."

Slowly, the time passed. We finished all the liquor, but no one could get drunk. The television showed Frank Mankiewicz outside the Hospital of the Good Samaritan, saying the operation was still going on, longer than anyone thought. A bad omen. A woman moaned in another room, and I began to pace the hall. There were police everywhere now. I went into Kennedy's empty bedroom again, and a local television station was showing the tape of an old speech. Poverty was unacceptable. Starvation in Mississippi and suicides on Indian reservations were unacceptable. I began to cry for the first time. As I wept, two crew-cut employees of the Los Angeles telephone company came into the room and mechanically began to remove the special telephone lines that had been installed for the evening, direct lines to South Dakota and to the ballroom. They worked very professionally, pulling all the wires out of the wall and coiling them around the phones, while Kennedy's image preached, and I twitched to hold back the tears.

At about 5:30 A.M. somebody asked Scheer and me to take a campaign car and pick up Ed Guthman at the hospital. Outside the Ambassador Hotel, on the steps, sat Charles Evers alone, watching the gray sunless dawn come up. He embraced me, and croaked, "God, they kill our leaders and they kill our friends."

The streets were silent and empty until we got to the hospital. There a crowd of about five hundred, mostly press, milled gently behind a police barricade.

Out of the crowd in front of the hospital came a face I hadn't seen for three years, D. Gorton. D. was a poor white boy from Mississippi who had joined the old anarchist SNCC in 1963, and later worked with SDS in Chicago. He had two cameras with him, and it is his picture of Kennedy that appears on the cover of this book.

"I knew it was against my politics," D. said, "but I loved Bobby Kennedy. The way the Chicanos and blacks trusted him moved me so much that I supported him." I realized D. was talking about Kennedy in the past tense.

Guthman, his strong face a ruin, came out finally, and we began to drive back to the Ambassador in silence, through the now awakening city. After a long while Guthman said, "You know, there were a hundred people in that hotel who would have gladly taken that bullet for Bob."

I went back up to the fifth floor, and saw Fred Dutton sag into his room alone, shut the door, and soon his sobbing filled the hallway. I knew then that Kennedy would not live.

I went back to my room—it was now about 8 A.M.—and fell asleep in a chair with my clothes and the television both on. I woke up two hours later, Mayor Yorty's burlesque comic's face on the screen, saying something about Communists. "You helped kill him, you fuck," I thought, or maybe I said it out loud to myself.

I shaved and showered, and returned to the Embassy Ballroom. Scavengers were there, stealing banners, posters, and hats from the floor as souvenirs. I found Robert Scheer again, and, like drugged men, we went to the exact place in the serving pantry where Robert Kennedy had fallen. There was one red rose now on the dirty floor to mark the spot. On the wall above the rose was a neatly lettered cardboard sign that read "The Once and Future King." A kitchen employee explained to us that the sign had been up there for a few weeks.

Yorty, Disneyland, Nathanael West, Joe Pyne, Sirhan Sirhan. I had to flee Los Angeles. I left at 5 P.M., on a nearly empty TWA flight, with Kennedy still clawing to the edge of life.

The plane took off and quickly the stained city grew smaller, and vanished under a permanent shroud of haze. The flight, I thought, would retrace—West to East—America's geography of assassination. Los Angeles. Dallas. Memphis. New York. Kennedy. Kennedy. King. And Malcolm X. I imagined a bloody, crescent-shaped scar on the face of the land, linking the four killer cities.

I tried to read the Los Angeles papers, filled with sidebar stories about violence in America. Sociologists, politicians, and religious leaders blaming movies, comic strips, and television. No one seemed to think that Vietnam, or poverty, or lynchings, or our genocide against the Indians had anything to do with it. Just popular culture like *Bonnie and Clyde,* never political institutions, or our own tortured history.

I got home about 2 A.M. New York time, and put on the television to see a tape of President Johnson announcing a new commission to study the causes of violence in America. One of the members of the commission, he said, would be Roman Hruska, the Republican Senator from Nebraska who was the major Congressional spokesman for the National Rifle Association. I could imagine Bobby wincing as he heard the absurd news.

I unpacked, and then, with the lights out, I sat in a chair and tried to adjust to the reality of Robert Kennedy dying. Why did it happen? What did it mean? What did I think about violence? My thoughts were not clear: they were not strong enough to support my feelings. I finally wrote down just three words on a lined yellow pad. "He is irreplaceable." A little before 5 A.M. the phone rang, and it was Ronnie Eldridge. "He's gone," she said, her voice cracking. "They're bringing Bobby home tonight. Don't feel sad. Just think how privileged we were to have known him, even if it was so short."

Then I went to sleep, remembering he was only forty-two years old.

At 1 A.M. on Friday, June 7, 1,000 people already stood on line along East 51st Street, outside the great Gothic cathedral where Robert Kennedy's body lay. Some Kennedy would have recognized as "my people"—a few shaggy students, a Negro man in a wheelchair, several young Puerto Ricans. Police and television cameras, gawkers and mourners. All casting their shadows. At the fringes were the *Day of the Locust* people, the lost lonely souls whose daily lives are so empty they must associate themselves with a historical event in order to feel alive.

St. Patrick's would open at 5:30 that morning to the glare of television lights over the light mahogany coffin on its black steel frame. But now it was night and William Haddad was in the church with Ronnie Eldridge, improvising an honor vigil around the casket. Haddad beckoned to me and led me and my friends, Tom Hayden, Paul Gorman, and Geoff Cowan, a McCarthy worker in Connecticut, inside past heavy security.

As I waited my turn to stand vigil, I noticed Tom Hayden walk away from us and slump back in the shadows. Sitting alone in an empty pew, tears began to form in his eyes. Tom Hayden, a revolutionary, an apostate Catholic, a green cap from Havana sticking out of his pants pocket, weeping for Robert Kennedy.

I stood between actor Robert Vaughn and radio personality Barry Gray. In that moment I learned again just how much historical space Robert Kennedy occupied. Hayden, the personification of the New Left, was crying somewhere behind me, Barry Gray was holding back his tears and Irish Joe Crangle, the Democratic leader of Erie County, was off mourning alone. Paul Gorman, a McCarthy man, was weeping now too, lighting a candle for Bobby. And me. And the curious, bereft people waiting out on 51st Street all night long. And I thought again of the quotation from Pascal that Camus invokes at the start of *Resistance, Rebellion and Death:* "A man does not show his greatness by being at one extremity, but rather by touching both at once."

I stood there in tears while a priest intoned a prayer in Latin. I stood there where Robert Kennedy's raw hands should be, reaching out for black hands, making a pleading fist to 19,000 roaring students in Kansas, trembling behind a lectern while he says violence and hate are unacceptable.

Now I realized what makes our generation unique, what defines us apart from those who came before the hopeful winter of 1961, and those who came after the murderous spring of 1968. We are the first generation that learned from experience, in our innocent twenties, that things were not really getting better, that we shall *not* overcome. We felt, by the time we reached thirty, that we had already glimpsed the most compassionate leaders our nation could produce, and they had all been assassinated. And from this time forward, things would get worse: our best political leaders were part of memory now, not hope.

The stone was at the bottom of the hill and we were alone.

Index

Abel, I. W., 267
Abuse of Power, The (Draper), on Tet truce, 132
Adams, Francis, 154
Adventures of Augie March, The (Bellow), 128
Aeschylus, 48
AFL-CIO, and RK, 48, 80–81
Agronsky, Martin, 56
Aiden, G., 123, 136
Akers, Anthony, 274
Albano, Vincent, 151, 152
Alexander, Shana, 263
Alinsky, Saul, 83, 96
Alioto, Joseph, 273
Alsop, Joseph, 33, 122; advises RK against antibombing speech, 133; on RK, 174–175
American Civil Liberties Union, 45
Americans for Democratic Action (ADA), 29, 62, 55, 71, 73, 180, 187, 189, 218; RK on, 63; and RK, 64
Anderson, Patrick, 50
Anslinger, Henry, 67
Arab-Israeli war in 1948, RK on, 44
Ascoli, Dr. Max, reaction to RK's antibombing speech, 139
Astor Foundation, 97
Atlanta Chamber of Commerce, RK speech at World Trade Conference of, 98–99

Badillo, Herman, 237
Bailey, John, 195; backs LBJ, 213, 226, 235
Baldwin, James, 23, 88, 94

Ball, George, 112, 114, 119, 125
Barr, Joseph, Under Secretary of Treasury, 105
Barr, Joseph M., 235, 267
Barry, Bill, 238, 263, 287, 298
Bartlett, Charles, 113; quoted, 115, 119
Bay of Pigs, 29, 33, 62, 70, 78, 112, 118, 224; commission on, 217
Beame, Abe, 18, 148, 149, 157, 161, 207
Beban, Gary, 273
Bedford-Stuyvesant, Brooklyn, 29, 75; genesis of, 87–90; problems of, 92; RK and, 41, 87–109; riot in, 90–109
Bedford-Stuyvesant Renewal and Rehabilitation Corp., 97
Bedford-Stuyvesant Restoration Corp., 97, 101, 106
Belafonte, Harry, 94
Bellow, Saul, 128
Belmondo, J. P., 39
Belotti, Frank, 201; and RK, 244
Berle, Milton, 290
Bickel, Alexander, 274; on RK, 67–68
Bingham, Jonathan, 149
Black, Hugo, 28
Blackburn, Dan, and RK, 297
Blow-up, 46
Blumenthal, Albert, 145, 161, 183, 259
Bo, Mai Van, 130
Bobby Kennedy Nobody Knows, The (Thimmesch and Johnson), 38
Bogart, Humphrey, 39
Bosch, Mrs. Juan, 178
Boston Globe, on LBJ, 182; praises RK's speech, 210
Boston Post, 44

305

306

Bowles, Chester, 28, 112, 120, 133
Brammer, William, 38
Brandeis, Louis, 64
Brando, Marlon, 39
Branigin, Roger, 252, 254, 260, 263; loses in Indiana, 264
Bravo, Modesto, 101
Breslin, Jimmy, 190; and RK, 24, 45, 221, 235, 254, 290, 291; on RK-McCarthy TV debate, 282
Bronston, Jack, 146, 147
Brooke, Edward W., 136
Brooklyn Coordinating Council, 103
Brown, Malcolm, 112
Brown, Pat, 24, 62, 211, 273
Brown, Rap, 208
Bruno, Jerry, and RK, 219, 240
Buchan, John, Lord Tweedsmuir, 291
Buckley, Charles, 45, 144, 146, 149, 158, 159, 161, 195
Buckley, William F., Jr., 63, 150; on RK's Bedford-Stuyvesant plan, 98
Bundy, McGeorge, 50, 62, 118; and RK, 125-126; on Vietnam, 110
Burchett, Wilfred, 130; interview with Trinh, 129
Burden, Carter, 244; and RK, 100; on RK, 52; on Walinsky, 52
Burke, Arleigh, 78
Burns, James McGregor, 33
Burns, John, and RK, 24, 159, 237, 244
Burr, Aaron, 143
Burton, Philip, 238, 273
Byrd, Robert, 34

Califano, Joseph, 106
California Democratic Council (CDC), 179, 273
Camus, Albert, 18, 23, 51, 58-59, 256, 304
Capehart, Homer, 67
Caplin, Mortimer, 105
Carew, Colin, 74
Carey, Hugh, 24, 25, 169
Carmichael, Stokely, 63, 178
Carona, Bert, 298
Carpenter, Scott, 222
Carpenter, Mrs. Scott, 222, 223
Carroll, Joan, 153
Carson, Johnny, 59
Carson, Sonny, 103
Cavalier magazine, 24
CBS, "Face the Nation," 56
Central Brooklyn Coordinating Council, 91

Central Intelligence Agency (CIA), 28, 61, 62, 66, 70, 78, 115, 117; and NSA, 181; and RK, 78-79
Chamberlain, Wilt, 234
Chaney, James, 40
Chapman, Bill, 261
Chavez, Cesar, 44, 56, 63, 81, 273, 290, 297, 298; and RK, 212, 214, 289, 297
Chessman, Caryl, 62, 272
Children of Crisis (Coles), 49
Christian, George, 173
Church, Frank, 67, 120, 136, 224
Citizens Crusade Against Poverty (CCAP), 96
City (periodical), Walinsky quoted in, 99
City University of New York, college in Bedford-Stuyvesant, 108
Clark, Blair, 227
Clark, Bob, and RK, 297
Clark, Joseph, 81, 95, 192; refuses to back RK, 226
Clark, Kenneth, 107, 154
Cleague, Albert, quoted, 107
Cleveland, riots in, 60
Clifford, Clark, and LBJ, 243; named Secretary of Defense, 201; and RK, 217, 221, 223; and Ted Kennedy, 217
Coffin, William Sloan, 28
Cohelan, Jeffery, 169
Cohn, Roy, 28, 149; RK's hatred of, 142
Coles, Robert, 49
Commentary, on decentralization, 37
Concerned Wisconsin Democrats, 189
Conference of Concerned Democrats, 185
Congress of Racial Equality (CORE), 83, 96, 102; Brooklyn chapter, 103; Cleveland chapter, 106; 1968 National Convention of, 107; RK on, 74
Coniff, Frank, 112
Connally, John, 182
Conrad, Joseph, quoted, 38
Considine, Bob, 112
Conway, Jack, 47
Cooper, John Sherman, 136
Costello, Frank, 152
Costikyan, Edward, 150
Cousins, Norman, and RK, 134
Cowan, Geoff, 203, 303
Cowan, Paul, on RK, 83; on Wallace campaign, 83
Cox, Harold, 23

Cox, Mrs. Marjorie, 153
Crane, Hart, 25
Crangle, Joe, 159, 304
Crawford, Kenneth, 112; on RK, 36; reaction to RK's antibombing speech, 139
Cronkite, Walter, and JFK, 116; interviews Schoumacher, 291–292; taped interview with RK, 219, 220, 264
Crotty, Peter, 45, 144, 161
Cuba, and Cuban missile crisis, 18, 117, 224. *See also* Bay of Pigs
Culver, John, 24, 169
Curtis, Carl, 67
Curtis, Kenneth, 192
Curzan, Michael, 104, 106

D & S Corp., 97, 99
Daily News, 96
Daley, Chuck, White House aide, 192
Daley, Richard, 62, 192, 195, 244, 293; backs LBJ, 226, 235; and Vietnam review commission, 216–217
Darin, Bobby, 283
Davis, Mary, on RK, 285
Day of the Locust, The (West), 272, 303
Dean, John, cable leaked to *Newsweek,* 130; and RK, 129, 130
Death in Life (Lifton), quoted, 30
DeBadts, Jay, and RK, 82, 83
Decisions for a Decade (Ted Kennedy), 53
Deer Park, The (Mailer), 26
Democratic National Committee, on LBJ, 173
De Gaulle, Charles, 132
Democratic Party, 54, 61, 189; atrophy of, 180; in Indiana, 253; in New York State, 160; and RK, 66
De Sapio, Carmine, 142, 148, 162
Diem, Ngo Dinh, 78, 112, 114, 116, 117, 118
Dillon, Douglas, 95, 97, 98, 105, 122
DiMaggio, Joe (priest), 46
Dirksen, Everett, 175; and LBJ, 146
DiSalle, Michael, 161
Docking, Robert, and RK, 214, 231
Dolan, Joe, member of RK's staff, 48, 51, 54–55, 163, 192, 194, 199, 204, 216
Doll, Joseph, 238
Dombrow, Walter, and RK, 240
Dominican Republic, intervention in, 62, 77, 172, 276

Don't Look Back (film), 283
Dougherty, Bill, 290
Douglas, John, 50, 53, 199, 260
Douglas, Paul, 24, 62
Douglas House Theatre, 297
Douherty, Gerry, 259
Draper, Theodore, 110; on Tet truce, 132
Drysdale, Don, 298
Dubinsky, David, for LBJ, 226
Dulles, Allen, 78
Dunfey, William, 187, 191, 210
Dutton, Fred, as adviser and aide to RK, 50, 113, 134, 191, 192, 194, 199, 204, 210, 216, 227, 238, 244, 262, 270, 287, 291, 298, 302; on RK, 42, 81, 83; on RK in California primary, 282; on RK's decision to run, 210, 212; on RK in Indiana, 254–255; on RK in person, 259; on RK's personality, 259; 268; and RK's Presidential campaign, 211; and Ted Kennedy, 211
Dylan, Bob, 18, 39, 49, 283

Eastland, James, 23, 58
Economic Opportunity Act, 1966, 97
Edelman, Peter, as adviser and aide to RK, 47, 51–53, 54, 55, 72, 80, 137, 161, 162, 194, 199, 203, 213, 214, 219, 263, 269
Edwards, Don, 187, 189, 226
Egeth, Shanley, 162, 163
85 Days: The Last Campaign of Robert Kennedy (Witcover), 216
Eldridge, Mrs. Ronnie, 54, 145, 153, 162, 163, 199, 202, 213, 225, 303
Ellington, Duke, 89
Emerson, Ralph Waldo, 26
Encounter, periodical, 78
Enemy Within, The (RK), 66–68, 69
Englehardt, Charles, 66
English, John, 144, 156, 159, 160, 213
Erikson, Eric, 18
Evans, Kay, 226
Evans, Roland, 173, 282
Evers, Charles, 20, 178, 290, 301
Evers, Medgar, 20, 22, 40, 61, 70, 246

"Face the Nation," CBS, 56
Facing the Brink (Weintal and Bartlett), 113, 115; quoted, 119
Fall, Bernard, 110
Farley, James A., 133, 142

Farmer, James, 154
Fein, Arnold, 153
Feldman, Justin, 150, 152, 159
Ferency, Zoltan, 189
Fields, W. C., 39
Flaherty, Joe, 190
Fonda, Jane, 46
Ford, Henry, II, 98, 175
Ford Foundation, 97, 99, 106
Forrestal, Michael, 111, 114, 115
Forsythe, Dall, 244
Forsythe, John, 244
Fortas, Abe, 173; and LBJ, 243
Fortune, on RK, 99
Founding Father, The (Whalen), 47
Frankenheimer, John, 262–263, 287
Franklin, Aretha, 87, 289
Franklin, Benjamin, 63–64
Freedom Rides, 34
Frost, David, interview with RK, 59
Fulbright, J. W., 123, 124, 137, 138, 232

Galbraith, John Kenneth, 111, 136, 180, 192, 293; backs McCarthy, 226; and RK, 134; and RK's campaign, 212
Gallup Poll, on LBJ, 235
Galyen, Roy, 47
Gardner, John, 157, 207
Garth, David, quits E. McCarthy, 287
Gavin, James, 123, 184
Gay Place, The (Brammer), 38
General Motors, 29
Gerosa, Lawrence, 147
Giap, General Vo Nguyen, 204
Gide, André, 32
Gilligan, John, 23, 24, 169
Gilligan, Thomas, 90
Gilpatric, Roswell, 97
Ginsberg, Allen, 18, 26
Glenn, John, 46, 290
Goldberg, Arthur, 52, 62; and RK, 134
Golden, Harry, 274
Goldman, Eric, 173
Goldwater, Barry, 33, 67, 73, 144, 171; on RK's "treason," 121
Goodell, Charles, 107
Goodman, Andrew, 40
Goodwin, Richard, 36, 37, 50, 52, 69, 118, 137, 173, 192, 193, 194, 210, 227, 263, 291; advises Kennedy to run, 211; backs McCarthy, 210, 215, 227, 240; on Che Guevara, 79; on decentralization, 37; leaves McCarthy for RK, 255; and RK, 42,

133, 212, 218; as speech writer for LBJ, 172; writes Los Angeles speech for RK, 240; writes RK's Tet offensive speech, 205
Gorey, Hays, 290; on RK-McCarthy TV debate, 282
Gorman, Paul, 203, 303, 304; and Jack Newfield, 284–286; and McCarthy, 244, 245; on RK, 245
Gorton, D., and RK, 301
Graves, Earl, 202
Gray, Barry, 304
Great Society, 93
Green, Edith, 269, 270, 301
Green, William, 161, 195
Green Berets, 113
Greenberg, Carl, on RK campaign in Los Angeles, 241
Greenfield, Harriet, 290
Greenfield, Jeff, as adviser and aide to RK, 36, 51, 53–54, 219, 222, 227, 238, 244, 262, 284, 285, 290; on Bedford-Stuyvesant legislation, 104; prepares for RK's campaign, 213; writes RK's Cleveland speech on Martin Luther King, 248
Grier, Rosey, 299
Gruening, Ernest, 119, 120, 122, 136; opposes Vietnam war, 276
Guardian, periodical, 33
Guevara, Che, 39, 79, 113
Guthman, Edwin, as adviser to RK, 50, 214, 262, 263, 301
Guy, William, and RK, 214
Gwirtzman, Milton, 52, 161, 244, 262, 291

Hackett, David, 226
Haddad, William, 48, 264, 303
Haggerty, C. J., 80
Halberstam, David, 112, 114, 261; awarded Pulitzer Prize, 112; and RK, 261; on RK, 21
Halsey Street Block Association, 101
Hamill, Pete, 190, 195, 225, 254, 290; letter to RK quoted, 207–208
Harkins, Paul, 111, 117
Harlech, Lord, 122
Harper's Magazine, 21, 260
Harriman, Averell, 62, 111, 114, 115, 116, 128, 165; advises RK against antibombing speech, 133; and RK, 145
Harrington, Michael, 34, 83, 259, 274; on RK's Bedford-Stuyvesant plan, 98

Harris, Fred, 222
Harris, Mark, 38
Harris Poll, on LBJ, 235
Hartke, Vance, 259, 263; letter to LBJ on Vietnam bombing, 123
Harvard Crimson, endorses RK, 225
Harwood, Richard, and RK, 238, 262, 290
HARYOU, 96
Hatcher, Richard, 260
Hatfield, Mark, 136
Hayden, Tom, 18, 49, 63, 134–136, 303
Hearnes, Warren, and RK, 214
Heir Apparent, The (Shannon), 38
Hemenway, Russell, 153
Hentoff, Nat, 64, 65
Herbers, John, on RK, 260
Hershey, Lewis B., 280, 281
Hester, James, 148
Hickenlooper, Bourke, 214
Higgins, Marguerite, 112
Hilsman, Roger, 111, 112, 113, 114, 115, 116, 274; leaves State Department, 121; quoted, 115
Hoeh, David, 185
Hoffa, James, 43, 66; and RK, 67, 69, 73
Hogan, Frank, 145, 148
Holiday, Billie, 88
Hoover, Herbert, 67, 172
Hoover, J. Edgar, 67, 280, 281
Hope, Paul, 261
House Un-American Activities Committee, 176, 272
Housing and Urban Development Department, U.S., 105
Howe, Irving, 177
"Howl" (Ginsberg), 26
Hruska, Roman, 303
Huerta, Doris, 290, 298–299
Hughes, Harold, 199, 203, 214
Hughes, Richard, backs LBJ, 226, 235
Humphrey, Hubert, 20, 28, 62, 63, 77, 80, 124, 164, 178, 180, 181, 192, 257, 259, 267, 275, 284, 285, 287, 288, 292, 294, 295, 296; and California primary, 279, 290; in Oregon primary, 269; and RK, 252; and RK's formula for coalition government in Vietnam, 125

Ickes, Harold, 190, 203
I. F. Stone's Weekly, 132. *See also* Stone, I. F.
Impellitteri, Vincent, 154

Indiana primary, 164
International Business Machines (IBM), at Bedford-Stuyvesant, 98, 108
Irvin, Sam, 67
Ives, Charles, 67

Jack, Hulan, 160
Jackson, Henry, 138
Javits, Jacob, 95, 96, 97, 100, 103, 136, 139; and RK, 49; on RK, 82
Jefferson, Thomas, 37, 62, 143
Jefferson Airplane, 49
JFK & LBJ (Wicker), quoted, 118
Johnson, Haynes, and RK, 213, 223
Johnson, Lyndon B., President, 38, 46, 55, 62, 80, 118, 121, 147, 170, 171, 211, 214, 268, 295; "abdicates," 20, 32, 243, 245; announces commission to study violence, 302–303; attacks Kennedys, 197–198; Bailey backs, 226; and bombing of North Vietnam, 118; clashes with RK, 126, 131–132; decline in popularity, 171–181 *passim;* and Dirksen, 146; discrediting of RK, 105–106; escalates war in Vietnam, 118–141 *passim;* and Fulbright, 123; and ghetto rehabilitation, 106; and Hartke, 123; and JFK, 33, 173, 174; and Kerner Report, 219; and Mailer, 51; "the new," 27; and the "new politics," 169–188 *passim;* possible renomination of, 211; and RK, 39, 66, 72, 144, 224, 229, 245; reaction to RK's antibombing speech, 138; reelected President, 60, 91; renomination in doubt, 218; resumes "full-scale hostilities," 132; and Sorensen, 216; on Tet offensive, 209; as Vice President, 111, 182; as victim of "new politics," 175–188 *passim;* and Vietnam review commission, 216–217; war protesters picket, 273
Johnson, Rafer, 287, 298, 299
Johnson, William, 38
Johnston, Tom, as adviser and aide to RK, 51, 135, 225; on New York mayoralty election, 148; and RK's antipoverty program, 93, 95, 99
Jones, J. Raymond, 147, 151, 154, 155, 156, 160, 162
Jones, Thomas, 94, 97, 100, 102

Kahin, George McT., 134
Kaplan, J. M., 97

Kaplan Fund, 97
Karenga, Ron, 208
Katzenbach, Nicholas, 55, 70, 128, 131
Kazin, Alfred, 65
Keating, Kenneth, 51, 64, 100, 119, 145
Kempton, Murray, 65, 293; on RK, 38, 46, 134
Kennan, George, 65, 123
Kennedy, Edward (Ted), 30, 49, 51, 52, 122, 191, 192, 194, 195, 203, 210, 216, 217, 244, 255, 259; advises RK against antibombing speech, 133; and Eugene McCarthy, 227–228; eulogy for RK, 141; on McNamara's resignation, 197; opposed to RK's campaign, 193; on RK's Presidential aspirations, 211–212; in Vietnam, 198; on Vietnamese refugees, 121
Kennedy, Ethel (Mrs. Robert F.), 45, 54, 125, 195, 203, 212, 220, 222, 223, 226, 244, 261, 263, 282, 286, 287, 291, 298
Kennedy, Jacqueline, and RK, 229
Kennedy, John F., assassination of, 29, 50, 61, 74, 118, 182, 302; and Byron White, 55; on coalition government, 126; Inaugural Address quoted, 113; and LBJ, 173, 174; and McCarthyism, 47; Mailer and, 38; and Massachusetts politics, 156; mental qualities of, 46; myth of, 174; 1960 campaign, 213; and patronage, 173; as politician, 33; as President, 195, 208; Profiles in Courage, 224; and RK, 39, 78, 170, 183; Senate campaign against Lodge, 28; on Senate Rackets Committee, 67; Vietnam policies of, 54, 62, 110–118; White House staff of, 50; and William Luddy, 201
Kennedy, Joseph P., 67; and RK, 42
Kennedy, Robert F., and ADA, 63, 64; and AFL-CIO, 80–81; and Adam Walinsky (see Walinsky, Adam); aggressiveness and rudeness of, 28, 29; and Albert Camus, 59; and Allard Lowenstein, 178, 181, 184–187 passim; ambivalent relationship with LBJ, 224; antiwar speeches, 139–141; on Arab-Israeli war in 1948, 44; assassination of, 74, 299–302; and assassination of JFK, 29, 50, 182; attitude toward poverty, 34; as Attorney General, 23, 152, 154, 182; background and makeup of, 17–19, 41, 42; backs Bronston-Steingut alliance,

146; and Bedford-Stuyvesant, 75, 81, 91–109; body at St. Patrick's Cathedral, 303–304; and the CIA, 78–79; in California primary, 270–287; campaign for Beame, 149; campaign for Presidency, 230–251, 266; and Cesar Chavez, 81, 212; as chairman of Interdepartmental Committee in Charge of Central Intelligence, 78; challenges LBJ's Vietnam policy, 94; and change, 72; character of, 40–59; circle of advisers, 49–57; and civil rights, 23; and Clark Clifford, 217, 221; Cleveland speech on Martin Luther King, May, 1968, 248–250; and communications media, 34–38; and Communism, 70–71; and competition, 42–44; contemporaneity of, 48–49; on CORE, 74; on cowardice of LBJ, 77; decentralist policies of, 74–75; decision to run for Presidency, 210–229 passim; defeat in Oregon primary, 268–271; on democracy, 37; and Democratic Party, 66; and Democratic Party of New York State, 142–165 passim; early attitude to Vietnam, 111, 113–114, 116–117, 119–122, 124–125; effect of LBJ's "abdication" on, 245; elected new Senator from New York, 91; and Eugene McCarthy, 43, 190, 191–192, 198, 211, 212, 218, 219, 220, 222, 224, 225, 227, 228–229, 267–268, 270, 277, 280–282; fatalism of, 56, 58; feeling against, 257–258; on Floyd McKissick, 74; formally announces for Presidency, 228–229; formula for coalition government in Vietnam, 125; and Frank O'Connor, 23–25; Frost interview with, 59; at Grasslands Hospital, 200; hardening convictions on Vietnam war, 126–134; hatred of LBJ, 142; hatred of Roy Cohn, 142; and Herbert Wechsler, 152; and Hoffa, 67, 69, 72–73; identity crisis of, 30–31; indecision of, and "old politics," 191–213; in Indiana primaries, 252–265; and Indians, 242; on intervention in Dominican Republic, 77, 276; interviewed by Mudd, 293–297; introduces employment bill, 1967, 104; introduces Federal housing measure, 105; investigative work on Select

Committee on Improper Activities in the Labor or Management Field, 67; and Jacob Javits, 49; and JFK, 19, 20, 39, 43, 50, 182, 183; and John Glenn, 46; and John Lindsay, 154; and Joseph Kennedy, 42; and Joseph McCarthy, 28; and juvenile delinquency, 69; in Kansas City, and at Kansas State University and University of Kansas, 231–235; Kempton on, 46; lack of preparation for Presidential campaign, 213–214; and LBJ, 39, 66, 72, 119, 181–188, 190–191, 196, 229, 245; liberalism, 66, 72–83; on Martin Luther King, 57, 246–251; meeting with Hayden and Lynd, 154–136; meeting with Manac'h, 129; and migrant labor, 82–83; myth and the man, 21–39; on NAACP, 74; in Nebraska primary, 266–268; and Negro movements, 74–75; and Nelson Rockefeller, 83; as New York junior Senator, 143; opposes Arthur Klein as surrogate judge, 151–153; on opposition to Vietnam war, 77–78; on overthrow of Diem, 118; politics of, 19, 20, 60–83; and politics in New York, 142–165; popularity in 1966, 169–171; and primary election in California, 289–299; pro-Johnson speech at fund-raising dinner in 1967, 183; and pro-McCarthy backlash, 22; and problems of Indians, 81; Puritanism of, 45–46, 66; race and antipoverty speeches of, 92, 93; reaction to his antibombing speech, 138–139; reaction to his Chicago speech, 210; reaction to death of Martin Luther King, 246–251; reaction to LBJ's "abdication" speech, 244–245; reads antibombing speech, 137–138; and Red China, 77; and religion, 41–42, 44–46; response to the ghetto, 75; and Robert McNamara, 197; romanticism of, 47–48; runs for U.S. Senator from New York, 144; second education of, 70; sense of the absurd, 58; on South Vietnam elections, 139; on Southern Christian Leadership Conference (SCLC), 74; speeches: 92–93, 139–141, 183, 298–299; antibombing speech, 137–138; at Atlanta Trade Conference, 98–99; Cleveland speech, 248–250; at Des Moines, Iowa, 213–214; at Indiana University

Medical Center, 255–256; on politics of the spirit, 64; to students at Free University of West Berlin, 32; on Tet offensive, 205–206; at University of Alabama, 236; and at Valparaiso University, Indiana, 256–257; "survivor guilt," 30; taped interview with Cronkite, 219, 220; television interview with Mudd, 35; on ten-day tour of Europe, 129; on Urban League, 74; victory speech in California, 298–299; and Vietnam review commission, 216, 217; on Vietnam war, 18, 19, 29, 40, 44, 47, 56–57, 66, 70, 71–72, 77; visits Southeast Asia, 113–114; wins United States Senate race, 145

Kennedy (Sorensen), quoted on JFK and Vietnam war, 111
Kennedy Circle, The (Sidey), on RK, 29
Kerner Commission Report, 106, 210, 219, 280
Kheel, Theodore, 148
Killing for Christ, A (Hamill), 207
King, John, 215
King, Martin Luther, 22, 61, 74, 96, 176, 178, 179, 289, 302; assassination of, 30, 57, 245–246, 253; reaction to assassination of, 246–247
King, Mrs. Martin Luther, 17
Kinsolving, Charles, 163
Kirk, Claude, 95
Klein, Arthur, 151, 154; and Costello, 152
Kopkind, Andrew, on RK, 186
Kosygin, Aleksei, 138; meets with Harold Wilson, 132
Kraft, Joseph, 122, 173
Krakauer, Alice, 261
Kraslow, David, quoted, 129–130
Kretchmer, Jerome, 161, 183, 259; and RK, 145, 146; on RK, 49
Kristol, Irving, 77
Krock, Arthur, 42
Ky, General Nguyen Cao, 62, 124

Lacoutre, Jean, 110
Laing, Margaret, 37
Laird, Melvin, 63
Larner, Jeremy, 293
Lawford, Patricia, 45, 195, 203, 237, 298
Lehman, Herbert, 143, 148, 150, 165
Lehman, Mrs. Herbert, 145

Lehman, Orin, 159, 160
Lester, Julius, poem on RK quoted, 33
Levitt, Arthur, 157
Lewis, John, 134, 259, 290, 300
Liberal Party, New York State, 149, 151, 152, 153, 154, 158, 161
Life, 172, 261, on RK, 169
Lifton, Robert J., quoted, 30
Lilienthal, David, 97
Lindsay, John, 18, 22, 65, 66, 95, 96, 98, 100, 103, 148, 149, 171, 287; candidate for mayor, 149; elected mayor of New York City, 150; as mayor, 151; and RK, 154
Lindsay, John, *Newsweek* writer, 286
Linowitz, Sol, 157
Lippmann, Walter, quoted, 119
Lockwood, Lee, and RK, 49
Lodge, Henry Cabot, 117; as Ambassador to South Vietnam, 114; JFK's campaign against, 28
Loeb, James, 185
Long, Huey, 150
Long, Russell, 34, 63, 191
Loory, Stuart, quoted, 129-130
Los Angeles Times, attacks Kennedy, 276; on RK campaign, 241; on RK-McCarthy TV debate, 282
Lowell, Robert, and E. McCarthy, 280
Lowenstein, Allard, 188, 189, 190, 192, 195, 204, 210; backs McCarthy, 226, 227, 237; and dump Johnson movement, 177-188 *passim;* and RK, 134, 178, 181, 184-187 *passim,* 225, 227, 237; runs for Congress, 284
Lowery, Jim, 102
Lubell, Samuel, poll quoted, 34
Lucey, Pat, 187, 192, 193, 267, 268
Luddy, William, 201
Lupe, Ronnie, and RK, 242
Lynch, Thomas, 273, 279
Lynd, Staughton, and RK, 120, 134-136

Maas, Peter, 65, 161
McCarthy, Eugene, 17, 19, 22, 33, 43, 44, 58, 59, 65, 124, 125, 164, 171, 181, 186, 187, 188, 190, 198, 203, 204, 257, 260, 261, 263, 274, 280, 289, 294; in California primary, 273, 274, 276, 280-288 *passim,* 290; campaign for Presidency, 190-191, 200, 209-228 *passim,* 230-231, 232, 235, 274; declares candidacy, 191; Don Peterson backs, 226; endorses bombing halt, 136; enters Presidential

Democratic primaries, 196-197; Galbraith backs, 226; in Indiana primaries, 252-253, 254, 264, 265; Lowenstein backs, 226, 237; mistrust between RK and, 212-213; and New Hampshire primary, 215-216, 218; and Paul Gorman, 245-246; as progressive, 66; Rauh backs, 226; and RK, 198, 211, 219, 220, 222, 224, 225, 227, 264, 267-268, 270; RK on, 43, 190; and RK in TV debate in California, 277, 280-282; in TV interview on California primary day, 291-292; in Wisconsin primary, 190
McCarthy, Mrs. Eugene, 228
McCarthy, Joseph R., 24, 28, 33, 45, 63, 67
McCarthy, Mary, 110
McCarthyism, 33, 47
McClellan, John, 67
McClellan Committee, investigation into labor racketeering, 28, 66
McCone, John, 78, 111, 115
McDonough, Henry, 159
McGee, Frank, 263
McGivern, Owen, 151
McGovern, George, 63, 120, 121, 136, 137, 186, 189, 222, 225
McGrory, Mary, 133; on E. McCarthy, 230, 263; on RK's candidacy, 220
McIntyre, Thomas, 215
McKeon, William, 147
McKinney, Jack, 190
McKissick, Floyd, 74, 178
McLaine, Shirley, 273
McLuhan, Marshall, 18
McNamara, Robert, 48, 62, 65, 111, 115, 116, 122, 123, 192, 224; advises RK against antibombing speech, 133; leaves LBJ Administration, 197; and RK, 128, 139, 197
McPherson, Harry, 173
Maddox, Lester, 95
Mailer, Norman, 26, 110, 254; on JFK, 38; and LBJ, 51; quoted, 39; and RK, 164
Malcolm X, 61, 62, 208, 246, 268, 302
Malraux, André, 28
Man Who Would Be President, The (De Toledano), 38
Manac'h, Etienne, meeting with RK, 129
Manchester, William, 50; on JFK, 38
Mankiewicz, Frank, adviser and aide to RK, 51, 54-55, 58, 136, 137, 184,

192, 194, 199, 203, 207, 216, 222, 223, 238, 244, 301; and RK in California primary, 274, 278; and RK's Presidential campaign, 211; on RK, 56

Mansfield, Mike, 123, 137, 232

Mao Tse-tung, 113, 115, 132

Marcantonio, Vito, 33

Mark the Glove Boy (Harris), 38

Markham, Sue, 226, 260–261

Marshall, Burke, and RK, 18, 50, 134, 199; urges RK to run, 210

Martin, John Bartlow, 36, 300

Mazo, Earl, 38

Meany, George, 81, 175

Mercouri, Melina, and RK, 202

Meredith, James, 61, 70, 154, 178, 246

Metcalf, Lee, and RK, 222

Meyer, André, 95, 97

Minnesota Farmer Labor Party, 77

Mississippi, University of, and integration, 33, 40, 70

Mobilization for Youth project, Manhattan, 96

Monde, Le, on Tet truce, 132

Morgenthau, Hans, on Tet offensive, 209

Morgenthau, Robert, 18, 147, 156

Morris, Willie, 254

Morrissey, Francis, 154

Morse, Wayne, 120, 122, 124, 136, 232, 269; opposes Vietnam war, 276; refuses to back RK, 226

Moses, Bob Parris, 120

Motive magazine, 51

Moyers, Bill, 118, 173, 192, 299; and RK, 126, 134

Moynihan, Daniel, 63, 83, 95, 254, 274

Mudd, Roger, 222; and RK, 264; interviews RK, 35, 293–297

Mumford, Lewis, 37

Mundt, Karl, 67

Murphy, George, 272

Murray, David, 261; on RK, 57

Murray, Thomas, 147

Murrow, Edward R., 28

Muste, A. J., 52

Naked and the Dead, The (Mailer), 26

Nation, The, 65

National Association for the Advancement of Colored People (NAACP), 61, 189; RK on, 74

National Security Council, and Rusk, 115

National Student Association (NSA), 60, 78; Congress in College Park, Maryland, 181–182

Nelson, Gaylord, 120, 136

Nestingen, Ivan, 192, 193

Neville, Mike, 43

New Deal, the, 61, 62, 73

New Detroit Committee, 106

New Frontier, the, 28, 62, 93, 110

"New politics," the, 175–188 *passim*

New Republic, 65, 97; on LBJ, 189; on LBJ and RK, 105

New York Herald Tribune, 125; against RK's Senate race, 145

New York magazine, on assassination of RK, 74

New York Post, 91, 152; predicts RK's Vietnam speech, 136; on RK in New York politics, 150

New York Review of Books, The, 49

New York Times, The, 38, 45, 113, 187, 197, 260; against RK's Senate race, 144–145; on anti-Kennedy feeling, 257; on Klein, 151; on LBJ and RK, 105; on McCarthy in Indiana, 265; on Office of Economic Opportunity, 97; on RK, 17, 18, 36, 210; on RK in Indiana primary, 164; on RK-McCarthy TV debate, 282; on RK meeting with Dean in Paris, 131

New York Times Magazine, The, RK article on USSR in, 73

New York University School of Social Work, and Bedford-Stuyvesant, 88

New Yorker, The, on Guevara, 79; on LBJ, 173; on RK, 21, 22

Newark, rioting in, 76

Newark Community Union Project (NCUP), 96

Newfield, Jack, at Bedford-Stuyvesant riot, 91; and dump Johnson movement, 185, 188, 190; early estimate of RK, 22; first contact with RK, 22, 23; introduces Hayden and Lynd to RK, 134–136; last conversation with RK, 283–284; and Lowenstein oppose LBJ, 176–177; 178–179; off-the-record conversations with RK, 78–79; and Paul Gorman, 284–286; on political tour in Westchester with RK, 199–203; protests Vietnam war, 176–177; and RK, 223–224, 254, 261; at RK headquarters in Los Angeles on primary day, 290–301 *passim;* and RK's praise of LBJ, 184; on RK's candidacy, 195; RK to, on children, 49; RK to, on confrontation with LBJ, 131–132; RK to, on CORE and McKissick, 74; RK to, on ghetto upbringing, 90; RK to, on LBJ's cowardice, 77; RK to, on pessimism, 56; RK to, on Vietnam war, 127–129; with RK as reporter, 23–27

Newsweek, 46, 118, 132, 286; Dean cable leaked to, 130; delegate survey, 267; reaction to RK's antibombing speech, 139; on RK, 36, 169; on RK meeting with Dean in Paris, 131; on Tet offensive, 209

Next Kennedy, The (Laing), 37

Nhu, Ngo Dinh, 116, 117, 118

Nhu, Madame Ngo Dinh, 114

Nicholas, William. *See* Johnson, William; Thimmesch, Nick

Nickerson, Eugene, 160; and RK, 156, 158

Nixon, Richard, and Benno Schmidt, 100; on California politics, 55; and Cardinal Spellman, 46; defeat of, 43; election of, 245; and Hubert Humphrey, 275, 292, 294, 295; Mark Harris on, 38; "the new," 27; RK on, 202, 219; Schlesinger on, 193; strength in Indiana, 253

No More Vietnams (Hans Morgenthau), on Tet offensive, 209

Nolan, John, 50, 198, 225; prepares for RK's campaign, 213

Nolting, Frederick, 111, 114, 117

North Vietnam, bombing of, 62, 112, 118–121. *See also* Vietnam

Nostromo (Conrad), 38

"Not in memory of Robert Kennedy" (Lester), 33

Novak, Robert, 173

Novello, Angie, secretary to RK, 224, 244

Nuclear Test Ban Treaty, 224

Oates, James, 97

Oberdorfer, Lou, 50

O'Brien, Lawrence, 54, 224; and JFK, 50, 173, 244; joins RK, 255, 259, 263, 290; and LBJ, 213; on RK, 32; on RK in California primary, 282

Ochs, Phil, 49, 283

O'Connor, Frank, 157, 158, 159, 160; and RK, 23–25, 156, 160–161; on RK's candidacy, 226

O'Donnell, Kenneth, 173, 194, 210, 212, 216; and JFK, 50; and RK's Presidential campaign, 211; urges RK to run, 210

O'Dwyer, Paul, 148, 149

O'Dwyer, William, 148

Office of Economic Opportunity programs, 94

Ohrenstein, Manfred, 159, 202

O'Rourke, Maurice, and RK, 162

Ort, Dorothy, 92

Ortiz, Frank, 103

Oswald, Lee Harvey, 269

Other America, The (Harrington), 34

Other Side, The (Hayden and Lynd), 134

Paley, William, 95, 97, 100

Parker, William, 67

Parsons, John, on RK, 200

Peace Corps, 51, 55, 62

Peace and Freedom Party, 33

Pearson, Drew, on RK, 289

Pei, I. M., 108

Pell, Claiborne, 136

Percy, Charles, 97, 171; home ownership legislation, 106

Perkins, James, 157

Peterson, Donald, 185, 189; backs McCarthy, 226

Pfaff, William, on Vietnam, 62

Pike, Douglas, 134

Pike, Otis, and RK, 156

Plimpton, George, 274, 290, 300

Podell, Bert, 150

Potter, Paul, 120

Powell, Adam Clayton, 88, 144, 161

Powell, James, 90

Pratt Institute, survey of problems of Bedford-Stuyvesant, 91–92

Presidential campaign of 1960, 33; of 1968, 33

President's Men, The (Anderson), 50

Prettyman, Barrett, 219, 268

Price, Robert, 152

Procaccino, Mario, 159

Profiles in Courage (JFK), 234

Progressive, 65

Pueblo, seizure of, 203

Pursuit of Justice, The (RK), 69, 70, 72

Pynchon, Thomas, 52

Pyne, Joe, 302

Rafferty, Max, 300
Ramparts, 49, 282, 298; on RK's Bed-ford-Stuyvesant plan, 97–98
Rankin, John, 33
Rauh, Joseph, 180, 185; backs Mc-Carthy, 226
Ray, Manuel, 78
Raye, Martha, 232
Raymond, George, 92
Reagan, Ronald, 95, 170, 272
Rebellion in Newark (Hayden), 49
Rees, Tom, 273
Republican Party, 37, 171; in New York State, 149
Resistance, Rebellion and Death (Camus), 59, 304
Resnick, Joseph, 33
Reston, James, 197; on anti-Kennedy feeling, 257
Reuther, Walter, 77, 96
R.F.K. (Schaap), 37
Ribicoff, Abraham, 80
Ridgeway, James, 97
Riesman, David, 65
Robert Kennedy at 40 (Thimmesch and Johnson), 38
Roberts, Charles, 118
Robinson, Sugar Ray, 88
Roche, John, 62, 77
Rockefeller, David, 95
Rockefeller, Nelson, 22, 23, 106, 146, 147, 156, 160, 177, 220, 232; and RK, 83; wins the gubernatorial race, 161
Rogers, Warren, 290
Romney, George, 36, 37; withdraws from Presidential campaign, 210
Roncalio, Teno, 24, 169
Roosevelt, Eleanor, 148, 184
Roosevelt, Franklin D., 65, 66, 143, 171
Roosevelt, Franklin D., Jr., 156–157, 158, 161
Roosevelt, James, 273
Roosevelt, Theodore, 48, 181
Rose, Alex, 151, 152, 157
Rosenberg, Marvin, 159
Rossetti, Frank, 162, 163
Rostow, Walt, 111, 118, 131, 178
Rovere, Richard, on JFK circle, 50; on LBJ, 173
Rusk, Dean, 111, 112, 115, 121, 123, 124, 178, 215, 219, 280, 281; and Allard Lowenstein, 178; reaction to RK's antibombing speech, 138; and war protests, 176
Ryan, William F., 148, 149

St. Louis Post Dispatch, praises RK speech, 210
Salinger, Pierre, 43, 50, 51, 55, 192, 194, 207, 255, 290; opposed to RK's campaign, 193; and RK, 225; urges RK to run, 210
Samuels, Howard, 156, 159, 160
San Francisco, riots in, 60
Sartre, Jean-Paul, 40
Schaap, Dick, 37
Scheer, Robert, 298, 300; and RK, 49, 299; on RK's Bedford-Stuyvesant plan, 97–98
Schell, Jonathan, 49
Scheuer, James, 24, 149
Schlesinger, Arthur, 18, 50, 78, 115, 134, 136, 185, 218, 220, 227, 228, 244, 259, 274; advises RK to run, 193–194; backs McCarthy, 227; on CIA, 79; on coup of November 1st, 1963, 117; drafts RK candidacy an-nouncement, 227; on JFK and Viet-nam war, 111; and RK, 133, 199, 215; on RK, 21; and RK's Presiden-tial campaign, 212; urges RK to run, 210; and Vietnam review commis-sion, 217
Schmidt, Benno, 97; on RK and Bed-ford-Stuyvesant, 99–100
Schoemann, Peter T., 80–81
Schoenbrun, David, 110
Schoumacher, David, 264; Cronkite in-terviews, 291
Schrade, Paul, 299
Schulberg, Budd, 241, 290, 297
Schwartz, Abba, 274
Schwerner, Michael, 40
Screvane, Paul, 148, 149
Second Civil War, The (Willis), quoted, 107
Secret Search for Peace in Vietnam, The (Kraslow and Loory), quoted, 129–130
Sedgewick, Harry, 153
Sedita, Mayor Frank, 159
Seigenthaler, John, adviser to RK, 50, 199, 214, 267, 268; and RK in Cali-fornia, 274, 278
Select Committee on Improper Activ-ities in Labor or Management Field, 67

Semple, Robert, on LBJ and RK, 105
Senate Foreign Relations Committee, U.S., public hearings on Vietnam, 123
Shakespeare, William, 26
Shannon, William, 38, 146
Shaw, George Bernard, 57
Shea, William, 151
Sheehan, Neil, 112
Shepard, Dr. Martin, and RK, 179
Shriver, Eunice, 42
Shriver, Sargent, and LBJ, 213
Shull, Leon, 180
Sidey, Hugh, and LBJ, 172
Silverman, Samuel, 160, 161; opposes Arthur Klein, 152–155
Sinatra, Frank, 39
Sirhan, Sirhan, 302
Skakel, George, 221
Smith, Al, 143, 150
Smith, Jean, 195, 203, 237, 298
Smith, Steve, brother-in-law and adviser to RK, 49, 55, 143, 144, 150, 152, 154, 155, 161, 173, 192, 194, 203, 216, 219, 225, 244, 267, 268, 274, 291, 293, 298; and assassination, 300; backs Bronston-Steingut alliance, 146; and Jack Newfield, 292; prepares for RK's campaign, 213; on RK, 292; and RK in California, 274; urges RK to run, 210
Sorensen, Theodore, as adviser to RK, 48, 50, 51, 52, 54, 55, 192, 194, 195, 199, 207, 217, 220, 221, 222, 244, 255, 291, 298, 300; against RK's anti-bombing speech, 133; drafts RK candidacy announcement, 227; on JFK, 38, 111; and LBJ, 216; opposed to RK's campaign, 193, 210, 213, 216; suggests review commission for Vietnam, 216; and Vietnam review commission, 217; writes RK's Cleveland speech on Martin Luther King, 248
Southern Christian Leadership Conference (SCLC), RK on, 74
Spaulding, Charles, 274
Speck, Richard, 61, 64
Spellman, Francis Cardinal, 46
Spivak, Larry, and RK, 156
Spock, Benjamin, 176, 179
Stark, Abe, 147
Steinbeck, John, 161
Steingut, Stanley, 144, 146, 147, 157, 158, 159, 161, 226

Stern, Sol, on RK-McCarthy TV debate, 282
Stern Fund, 97
Stevens, George, 226
Stevenson, Adlai, 62, 63, 65, 112, 144, 191, 202, 288
Stevenson, Jim, on RK, 21, 22
Stokes, Carl, 61
Stone, I. F., 51, 64, 65, 120, 125, 133
Stratton, Sam, 144, 145, 156
Straus, R. Peter, 145
Student Nonviolent Coordinating Committee (SNCC), 96, 290, 301
Students for a Democratic Society (SDS), 120, 133, 179, 181
Subversive Activities Control Board, 71
"Superman Comes to the Supermarket" (Mailer), quoted, 39
Sutton, Percy, 163

Tacitus, 48
Taft, William Howard, 181
Tannenbaum, Martin, 157
Tate, James H. J., 245, 267; backs LBJ, 235
Taylor, Maxwell, 78, 111, 114, 115, 116, 117, 118, 122, 123; and RK, 128, 137, 139; on RK, 125
Teamsters Union, and RK, 67
Tennyson, Alfred, 47
Tet offensive, 204, 235
Thimmesch, Nick, 38
Thirty-nine Steps, The (Buchan), 291
Thomas, Frank, 100; on Bedford-Stuyvesant, 101–102
Thomas, Norman, 177, 184
Thompson, Frank, and RK, 222
Thompson, Sir Robert, 71, 113
Thoreau, H. D., 37, 48
Thousand Days, A (Schlesinger), 78; on CIA, 79; on JFK and Vietnam war, 11; on RK, 21
Time, 282; on RK, 131, 169
To Move a Nation (Hilsman), 112; quoted, 115, 117
To Seek a Newer World (RK), 52, 58; quoted, 37, 68–69, 73–78, 80
Tolan, John, 235
Toledano, Ralph De, 37, 38
Travia, Anthony, 146, 147, 156
Tretick, Stanley, 261, 290, 300; on RK's campaign, 234
Trinh, Nguyen Duy, 130; Burchett interview with, 129
Trujillo, Juan, 157

Truman, Harry, 62, 172, 193
Tuck, Dick, 238, 263
TWO. *See under* Woodlawn Organization, The

Udall, Morris, and RK, 222
"Ulysses" (Tennyson), 47–48
United Auto Workers, 189
U.S. Gypsum, and RK's Bedford-Stuyvesant plan, 98
United States in Vietnam, The (Kahin and Lewis), 134
Unruh, Jesse, and RK, 161, 199, 202, 210, 215, 238, 273, 274, 278, 297, 298; prepares for RK's campaign, 213
Urban Coalition, 106
Urban League, RK on, 74

Valenti, Jack, 207
vanden Heuvel, William, and RK, 50, 54, 152, 157, 194, 195, 218, 220, 233, 268; advises RK against antibombing speech, 133; against RK's running for President, 210, 213
Vann, Albert, 103
Vanocur, Sander, and RK, 293
Vaughn, Robert, 304
Vidal, Gore, 64, 65
Vietcong, 112. *See also* Vietnam war
Vietcong, The (Pike), 134
Vietnam war, issue of, 61; and liberalism, 62; RK's early attitude toward, 18, 40, 47; RK opposes, 22, 29, 33, 47, 51, 70, 77–78
Vietnam Summer Project, 179
Village of Ben Suc, The (Schell), 49
Village Independent Democrats, New York City, 189
Village Voice, The, 46, 49, 83; quoted on LBJ, 176–177; quoted on RK's candidacy, 195
Vivian, Wes, 180
Voznesensky, Andrei, 18, 24

Wagner, Mrs. Edith, 153
Wagner, Robert, Jr., 143, 144, 146, 147, 149, 154, 158, 165; declines to run for mayoralty, 148; and RK, 156
Wagner, Robert, Sr., 143
Wainright, Loudon, 261, 290
Walinsky, Adam, as adviser and speech writer to RK, 36, 37, 51–52, 53, 54, 55, 65, 72, 92, 95, 99, 132, 133, 184, 187, 192, 194, 195, 199, 203, 204,

205, 219, 222, 227, 230, 232, 238, 244, 262, 270, 289–290, 291; drafts RK's candidacy announcement, 227; influence on RK, 133, 134; prepares for RK's campaign, 213; prepares statement for RK on Vietnam war, 123; and RK's antipoverty program, 93, 94, 95; and RK's guerrilla warfare speech, 122; urges RK to run for President, 170–171; works on major Vietnam speech for RK, 132; works on RK book, 185; writes RK's Cleveland speech on Martin Luther King, 248; writes RK's Tet offensive speech, 205
Walinsky, Jane, 290
Wall Street Journal, The, on LBJ and RK, 105; and RK and McCarthy, 221; on RK's Vietnam policy, 127
Wallace, George, 55, 73, 81, 83, 236, 253, 264
Wallace, Henry, 62
Walsh, Joseph, 163
Warren, Charles, 273
Warren Report, published, 145
Washington Post, 56; quoted, 119
Washington Star, 213
Watson, Marvin, 131, 180; and LBJ, 173
Watson, Thomas, 95, 97, 148
Watts, riots in, 18, 60, 92
Watts Writers' Workshop, 297
Wauneka, Annie, and RK, 242
Wayne, John, 232
Weaver, Robert, 105
Weaver, Warren, on RK, 36
Wechsler, Herbert, 152
Wechsler, James, 21, 33, 65; on Klein and Costello, 152; and RK, 225; on RK, 34; on RK in New York politics, 150
Weinberger, Sidney, 292
Weinstein, Jack, 159, 160
Weintal, Edward, 113; quoted, 115, 119
Weisel, Edward, 159
Welch, Carol, 299, 301
West, Nathanael, 302; quoted, 272
Westmoreland, William, 232; reaction to RK's antibombing speech, 138; requests more troops for Vietnam, 210; on Tet offensive, 209
White, Byron, 48, 55
White, Theodore, 290
White, William Allen, quoted, 232
White, William S., 173

Whitiker, Jim, 226
Whitman, Charles, 61, 64
Whitney Company, J. H., 99
Why Are We in Vietnam? (Mailer),
    110
Wicker, Tom, 118; on McCarthy in
    Indiana, 265; and RK, 56
Wilkins, Roy, 154, 175
Williams, G. Mennen, 62
Willis, Garry, 107
Wilson, Harold, Prime Minister, meets
    Kosygin, 132
Wilson, Woodrow, 62
Winnick, Lou, quoted in *City,* 99
Wiretapping, 33
Witcover, Jules, 216
Woodlawn Organization, The (TWO),
    96
Wright, Marian, 56
Wright, Sylvia, 222, 223

Xerox, and RK's Bedford-Stuyvesant
    plan, 98

Yarmolinsky, Adam, 274
Yeats, William Butler, 25
Yevtushenko, Yevgeny, 25, 161
Yorty, Sam, 170, 299, 302
Young, Stephen, 120
Young, Whitney, 106
Young Democrats, 189; of Minnesota,
    189
Youth-in-Action (YIA), 92, 103

Zale, Tony, and RK, 260
Zaretzki, Joseph, 146, 147, 163
Zenkel, Mrs. Lois, and RK, 201
Ziegler, Steve, 106
Zinn, Howard, 110